Color, Line, Light

EDITORS
Margaret Morgan Grasselli
Andrew Robison

INTRODUCTION
Richard R. Brettell

ESSAYS
Victor Carlson
Elizabeth Easton
Marina Ferretti Bocquillon
Margaret Morgan Grasselli

NATIONAL GALLERY OF ART, WASHINGTON

DELMONICO BOOKS • PRESTEL
MUNICH LONDON NEW YORK

Color, Line, Light

FRENCH DRAWINGS, WATERCOLORS, AND PASTELS FROM DELACROIX TO SIGNAC

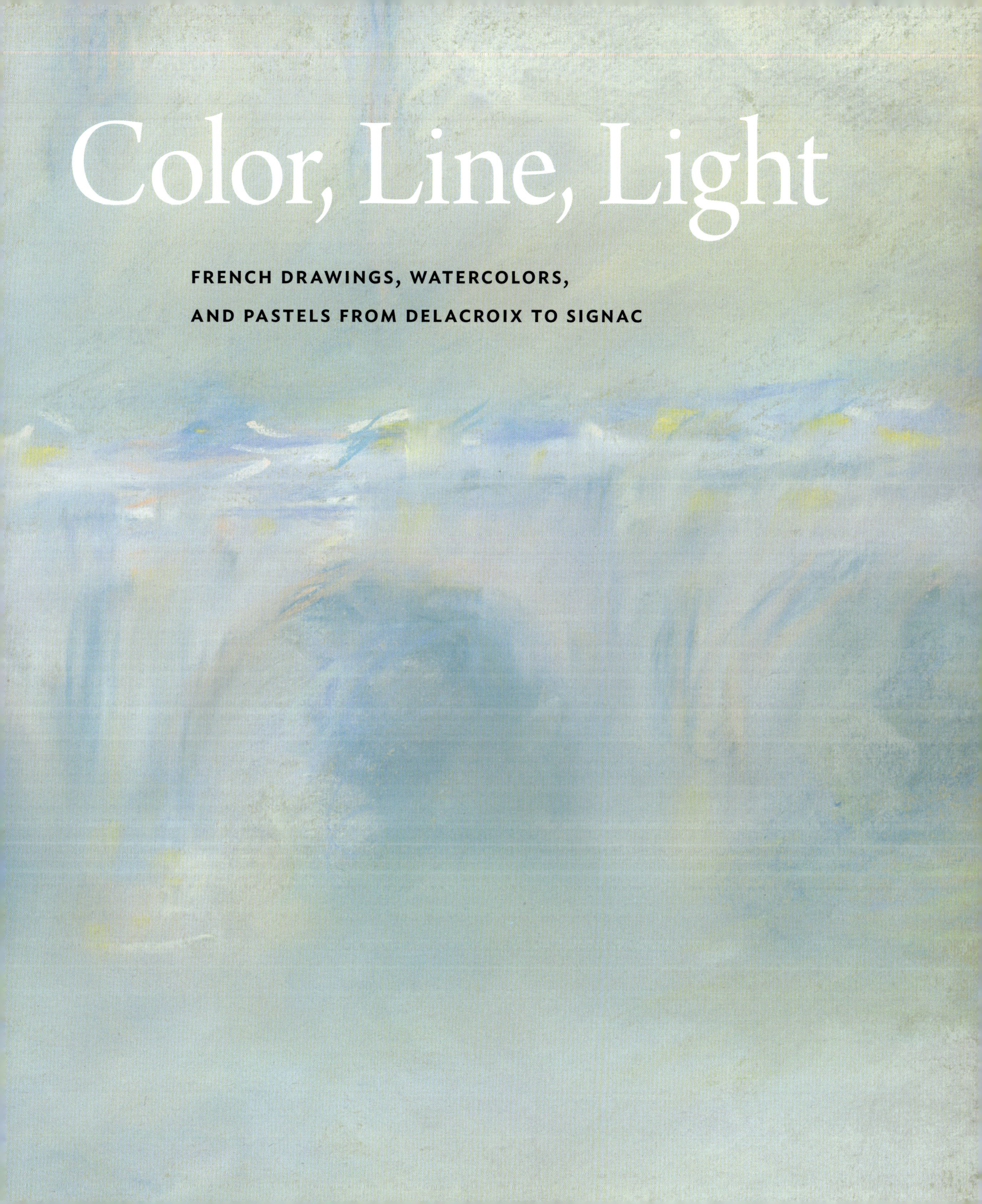

The exhibition is organized by the National Gallery of Art, Washington, in association with the Musée des impressionnismes Giverny

EXHIBITION DATES

Musée des impressionnismes Giverny
July 27–October 31, 2012

National Gallery of Art Washington
January 27–May 26, 2013

10 9 8 7 6 5 4 3 2 1

Produced by the Publishing Office, National Gallery of Art, Washington

Judy Metro, editor in chief

Designed by Chris Vogel, deputy publisher and production manager; edited by Tam Curry Bryfogle, senior editor

Sara Sanders-Buell, photography rights coordinator; John Long, assistant production manager; and Mariah Shay, production assistant

Essays by Marina Ferretti Bocquillon translated by Judith Terry, Montreal, Quebec

Typeset in Arno Pro and Ideal Sans by National Gallery of Art Printed on 150 gsm Profimatt by Die Keure, Bruges, Belgium

Published by the National Gallery of Art (www.nga.gov), and DelMonico Books (www.prestel.com), an imprint of Prestel Publishing, a member of Verlagsgruppe Random House GmbH.

Prestel Verlag
Neumarkter Strasse 28
81673 Munich
Germany
tel 49 89 4136 0
fax 49 89 4136 2335
www.prestel.de

Prestel Publishing Ltd.
4 Bloomsbury Place
London WC1A 2QA
United Kingdom
Tel: 44 20 7323 5004
Fax: 44 20 7636 8004

Prestel Publishing
900 Broadway, Suite 603
New York, NY 10003
Tel: 212 995 2720
Fax: 212 995 2733
E-mail: *sales@prestel-usa.com*
www.prestel.com

LIBRARY OF CONGRESS CATALOGING-IN-PUBLICATION DATA

Color, line, light : French drawings, watercolors, and pastels from Delacroix to Signac / Margaret Morgan Grasselli and Andrew Robison, volume editors; introduction by Richard R. Brettell; essays by Marina Ferretti Bocquillon, Victor Carlson, Elizabeth Easton, Margaret Morgan Grasselli. — 1st edition.

pages cm

The exhibition is organized by the National Gallery of Art, Washington, in association with the Musée des impressionnismes Giverny.

Includes bibliographical references and index.

ISBN 978-3-7913-5228-2 (alk. paper)

1. Drawing, French — Exhibitions. 2. Watercolor painting, French — Exhibitions. 3. Dyke, James T. — Art collections — Exhibitions. 4. Drawing — Private collections — Arkansas — Little Rock — Exhibitions. 5. Watercolor painting — Private collections — Arkansas — Little Rock — Exhibitions. I. Grasselli, Margaret Morgan, 1951– editor of compilation. II. Robison, Andrew, editor of compilation. III. National Gallery of Art (U.S.) IV. Musée des impressionnismes (Giverny, France)

NC246.C59 2012
741.944'074753 — DC23
2012009408

French edition
ISBN 979-10-91400-8

Vanessa Lecomte, editorial supervision, with the collaboration of Anne Chapoutot

French translations of texts by Richard R. Brettell, Victor Carlson, Elizabeth Easton, Margaret Morgan Grasselli, and Andrew Robison by Jeanne Bouniort and Danielle Chaput

NOTE TO THE READER

Dimensions are given in millimeters, height before width.

For provenance information and full descriptions of works of art in the exhibition, please consult the checklist (pages 158–162).

For birth and death dates of artists whose works are included in the exhibition, please refer to the alphabetical listing at the back of the book (page 163).

SECTION OPENINGS

pp. ii–iii: Claude Monet, *Waterloo Bridge* (detail pl. 51)

p. vi: Paul Cézanne, *A Stand of Trees along a River Bank* (detail pl. 50)

p. viii: Paul Signac, *The Fountain in the Rue Grande in Saint-Paul de Vence* (detail pl. 94)

pp. xiv–1: Hippolyte Petitjean, *A Broad Valley at Sunset* (detail pl. 84)

p. 16: Paul Huet, *A Meadow at Sunset* (detail pl. 8)

p. 46: Charles-Émile Jacque, *The Shepherdess* (detail pl. 27)

p. 72: Edgar Degas, *Two Women Ironing* (detail pl. 45)

p. 94: Odilon Redon, *A Vision of a Saint with a Poppy* (detail pl. 69)

p. 126: Georges Seurat, *Strolling Woman with a Muff* (detail pl. 76)

pp. 154–155: Henri-Joseph Harpignies, *Sun behind the Clouds at Saint-Privé* (detail pl. 35)

Contents

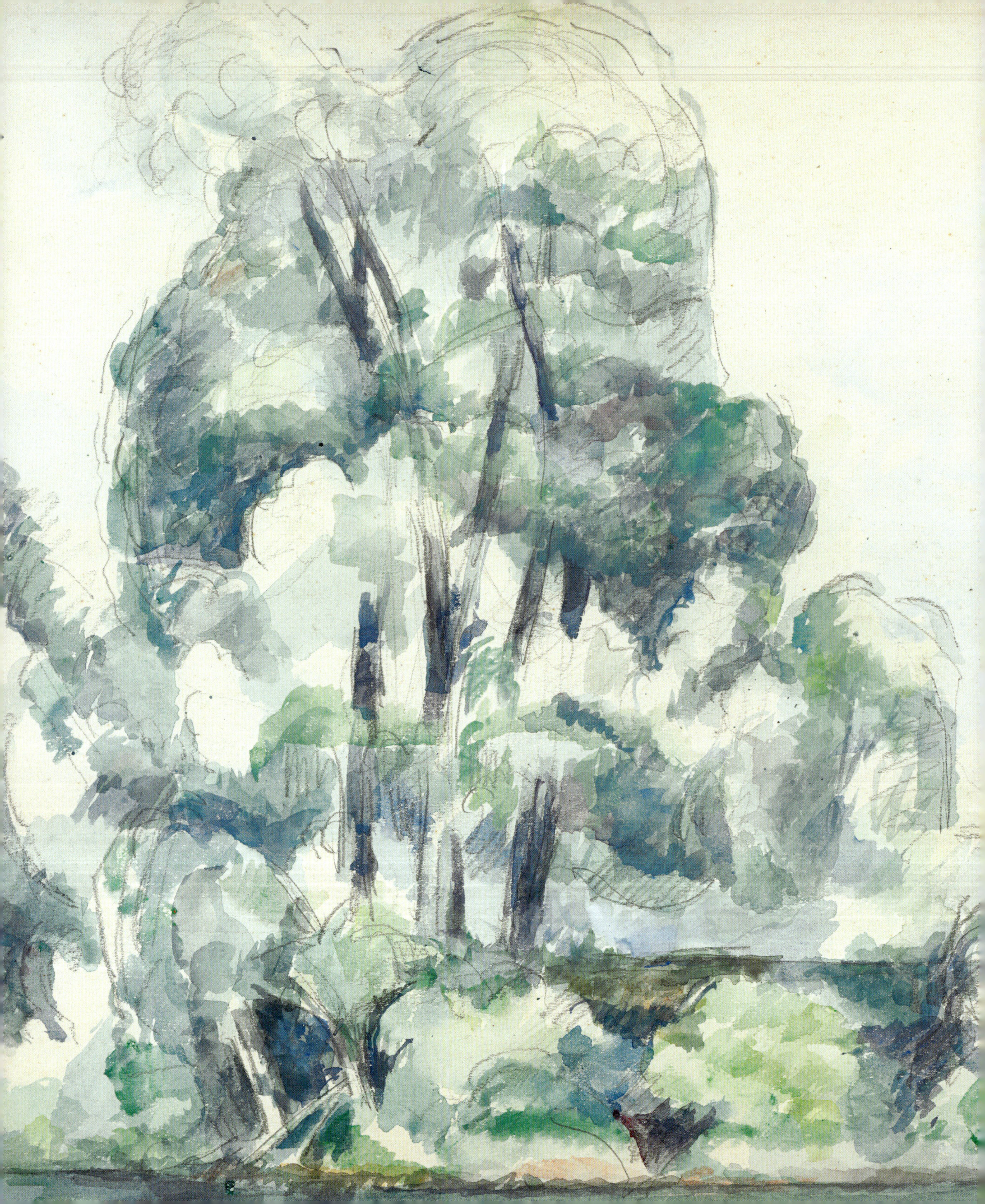

Directors' Foreword

WHILE THE NATIONAL GALLERY OF ART in Washington, since its founding in 1941, has regularly paid homage to French art of the nineteenth century through its acquisitions and exhibitions, the young Musée des impressionnismes Giverny has taken as its focus a specific period that is particularly rich in artistic innovations. Thus it is a great pleasure to present this important private collection of French drawings, watercolors, and pastels from the period, assembled by James T. Dyke. Jim is an astute collector who has built not only one but three insightful personal collections. From 1984 through 2000 he put together an outstanding group of 133 beautiful watercolors and drawings by Paul Signac. These works were catalogued and exhibited at the Musée Marmottan Monet in Paris and the Arkansas Art Center in Little Rock. Then in 1999 and 2001 Jim generously donated the entire group of drawings and watercolors to the museum in Little Rock, making his native city a world locus for the study of Signac's graphic art. Since 2000 Jim has been acquiring a wide range of international contemporary drawings, watercolors, and pastels, with emphasis on the varieties of American realism. A special exhibition at Florida's Naples Museum of Art and at the Arkansas Art Center in 2007–2008 featured 118 of these works. And for a much longer period, beginning in 1970 and continuing to the present day, Jim has pursued works on paper by classic nineteenth-century and modern artists, especially French. This third collection has grown almost spontaneously, work by work, achieving the impressive breadth and quality we admire in this exhibition.

Jim Dyke and his wife, Helen L. Porter, collect only art that they like. They live with their drawings every day, and we are deeply indebted to them for allowing us to borrow so many of their cherished works in order to share them with the public. Their gifts and loans are among many generous ways they have supported art institutions, both in the United States and in Europe, including contributions toward the purchase of works of art and the presentation of activities they recognize as vital to the mission of art museums.

We thank Margaret Morgan Grasselli and Andrew Robison for conceiving and organizing this exhibition and catalogue. We are also grateful to the international group of scholars who wrote essays to elucidate the subject, both broadly and specifically: Marina Ferretti Bocquillon, Richard R. Brettell, Victor Carlson, and Elizabeth Easton. We greatly appreciate the effort and expertise of friends and colleagues who have brought this project to successful realization.

Earl A. Powell III
National Gallery of Art
Washington

Diego Candil
Musée des impressionnismes
Giverny

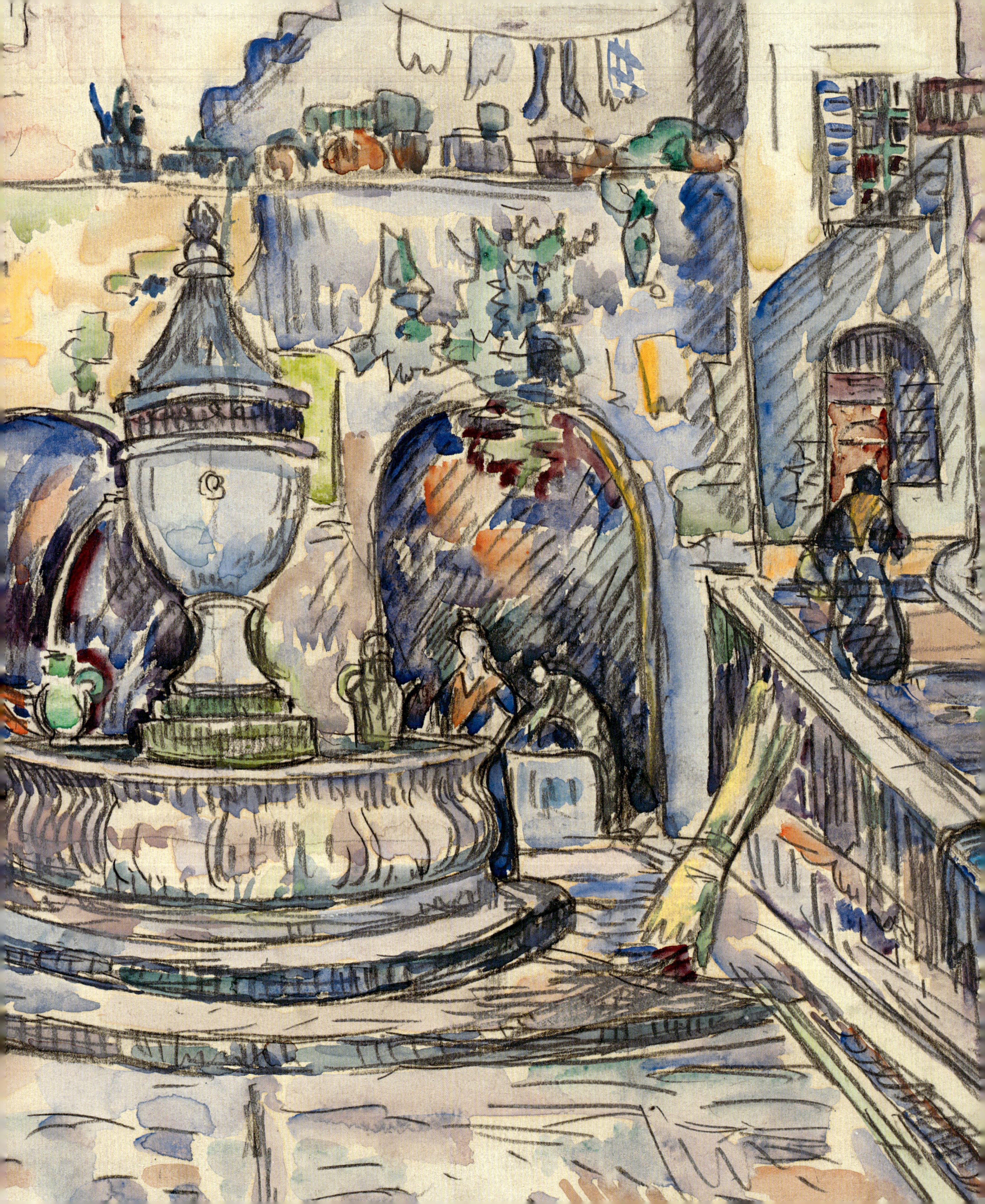

Collector's Statement

MY WIFE AND I HAD BEEN ACQUIRING nineteenth-century French drawings, watercolors, and pastels for many years, but the particular concept for this collection was developed in the spring of 2001.

Shortly after the exhibition of our collection of Signac drawings and watercolors at the Musée Marmottan Monet in Paris, I wondered aloud to a French dealer friend what direction my collecting might take now. She reached for a notepad, jotted down the titles of two major French art reference books, handed me the paper, and said, "Go across the street to the bookstore; buy these and see where they take you."

Both books — Lydia Harambourg's *Dictionnaire des peintres paysagistes français au 19ème siècle* (Neuchâtel, 1985) and Gérald Schurr and Pierre Cabanne's *Dictionnaire des petits maîtres de la peinture, 1820–1920,* 2 vols. (Paris, 2003) — made fascinating reading, and a wealth of possibilities emerged. Two themes in particular intrigued me. First, many "minor" artists produced one or more exceptional works. Second, academic categorization of artists does not seem to acknowledge the stylistic flexibility that even well-known artists sometimes expressed. For example, no one would suggest that Delacroix was, strictly speaking, an impressionist; but take a close look at *The Normandy Cliffs* (pl. 15).

So the focus of this collection evolved into a search for exceptional works by artists both major and minor, with the objective of demonstrating that good work is simply that, regardless of the current fame or obscurity of the artist.

James T. Dyke

Prologue

THE NINETEENTH CENTURY IS A BIG CENTURY — big in every way. Among the most obvious features are the extraordinary scientific discoveries circulated widely through publication; the economic and social relationships that changed radically through industrialization; the increasing ease of transportation and communication throughout the world; and the resulting complexity of national and international politics, or at least awareness of them through globalized diplomacy and journalism. Correspondingly, encyclopedic scholarly publications and growing knowledge of vast numbers of artists and their works reveal the richness of nineteenth-century literature, music, and fine arts. Even within the culture of one country, France, the plethora of visual artists and associated friends, schools, and influences makes a dazzling kaleidoscope of paintings, drawings, prints, sculpture, architecture, and other works of art.

In an effort to make French nineteenth-century art more intelligible, historians have organized artists into movements or "schools" — such as neoclassicism or romanticism, Barbizon or impressionism — and then portrayed these as dominant during a certain time period, one succeeded by another. Such distinctions are helpful for initial comprehension, but further study shows they must be considerably relaxed to account for intermediate stages or styles and exceptions to general rules. This becomes obvious when one steps back to ask the comprehensive question, for example about drawings, as Richard R. Brettell does brilliantly in his introductory essay, "The Paper Century": "What drawings actually were produced in nineteenth-century France?" The answer is voluminous in type as well as number.

Another way of beginning with actual drawings rather than intellectual constructs is that of a passionate collector who searches without preconditions through auctions and dealers' stocks and may look at thousands of works in a year. Such a collector is James T. Dyke, who studies each individual work in its concrete character and chooses just those that hold visual appeal for him. He is not filling pigeon holes in a pre-existing scheme, even in his main area of interest. Thus he does not include works even by such major French draftsmen as Théodore Gericault, Honoré Daumier, Jean-Baptiste-Camille Corot, or Auguste Renoir unless he sees a drawing, watercolor, or pastel for sale that piques his desire. Nevertheless, over time, his empirical gathering of delightful and great drawings by obscure as well as well-known artists has resulted in the rich variety presented in this exhibition. Further, the Dyke collection of French drawings does include works before as well as after the chronological period presented here (for example, see fig. 1).

The specific contents and the range of art in the Dyke collection of French drawings from Delacroix to Signac also reflect Jim's longstanding relationship with the National Gallery of

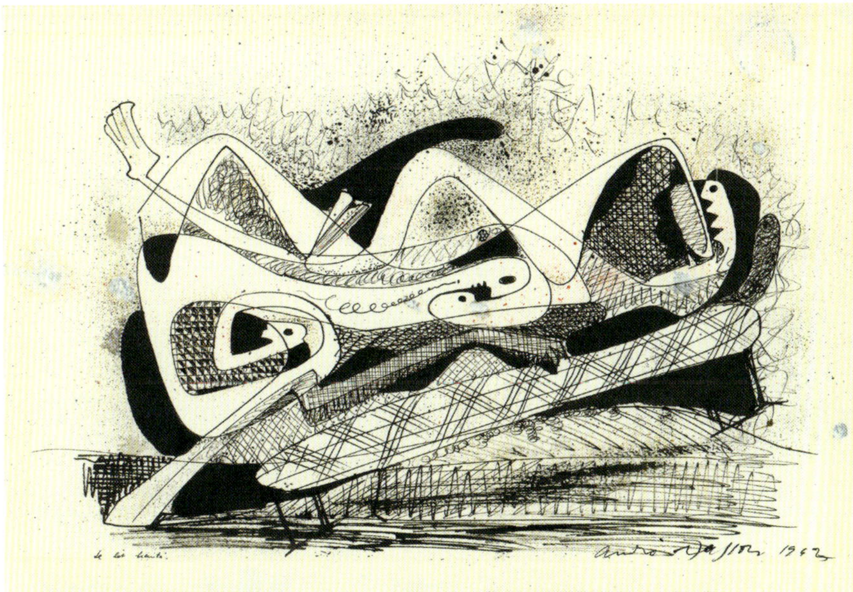

1 André Masson, *Le Lit Hanté*, 1942, watercolor, pen, brush and india ink, Helen Porter and James T. Dyke, Promised Gift to the National Gallery of Art, Washington

Art. For a quarter century we have looked at drawings together and have studied and discussed them, seeking to learn, enjoy, and strengthen both his collection and the Gallery's. Jim has given numerous drawings to the Gallery and has generously supported the acquisition of others (not always within his primary focus of interest). Thus many works in this exhibition already carry the Gallery's credit line, as gifts from Jim and his wife, Helen Porter. Jim also knows that the Gallery's collection provides a broad basis against which one may view his own collection, with the portrayal of nineteenth-century French drawing supplemented by types of less direct personal appeal to him. Two general areas spring to mind. Neoclassicism began in the eighteenth century, but it also inaugurates the nineteenth century. The neoclassicists' preference for antique subjects or style often finds expression in crisp forms and sharp, linear outlines — beautifully shown, for example, in works by Jacques-Louis David (fig. 2), Jean-Auguste-Dominique Ingres (fig. 3), and Pierre Paul Prud'hon. A second major area not included in the Dyke collection is mid-century academic drawing, which was basically a continuation of the Renaissance use of drawing to study individual figures or variations on a composition in preparation for creating paintings. Frequently these works manifest a similar linear style to that of the neoclassicists, as seen in works by Jean Léon Gérôme (fig. 4) or Thomas Couture (fig. 5).

With these few exceptions, the Dyke collection does give a comprehensive overview of nineteenth-century French drawings, watercolors, and pastels. To highlight this, Margaret Morgan Grasselli and I have organized the ninety-five works in this exhibition and catalogue into five sections, with objects related by style, author, and period. We have used standard art historical terms to identify these divisions, but we have broadened their range. That is, we feature not "romanticism" but "the romantic impulse." The former term might normally be limited to a time period from about 1790 to 1840, yet its dominant practitioners continued to work much longer — Eugène Delacroix into the early 1860s. In addition, even later works, like the monumental 1870 drawings here by Gustave Doré and Maxime Lalanne are eminently romantic in subject as well as in stylistic treatment. Likewise, "impressionism" might refer to the period of the eight impressionist exhibitions, 1874–1886. But its major and undisputed practitioners were working much earlier — Manet from the early 1860s — or much later, including Renoir and Monet well into the twentieth century. Thus we stretch the standard terms here to indicate not so much chronological periods as, we hope, coherences of style and artist.

Speaking also for my curatorial colleagues Meg Grasselli and Judith Brodie, we always find working with Jim Dyke a delight of visual pleasure and intellectual exploration. We share the thrill of acquisition as well as pride in the national collection as it grows and is enjoyed by our visitors and scholars. The *Color, Line, Light* exhibition and catalogue provide an exciting opportunity to celebrate the expansive, intriguing, illuminating collections that Jim has formed and has helped the National Gallery to strengthen, and we are extremely grateful to him and Helen for their exceptionally generous gifts and loans.

Meg Grasselli and I also greatly appreciate the willingness of our curatorial and scholarly colleagues to write enlightening essays on various facets of nineteenth-century French drawing: Marina Ferretti Bocquillon, Richard R. Brettell, Victor Carlson, and Elizabeth Easton. Marina also serves as the scientific director and curator for the Musée des impressionnismes Giverny, the opening venue for this exhibition, and it has been a great pleasure to work with her and with director Diego Candil as well as associate curator Vanessa Lecomte. Many National Gallery colleagues have also contributed to the project. The works of art received expert treatment in the paper conservation department led by Kimberly Schenck, with particular attention from conservators Marian Dirda and Linda Owen and from matter-framers Shan Linde and Caroline Danforth. The logistics of packing and shipping the works were overseen by associate registrar for exhibitions Melissa Stegeman in close collaboration with loans and exhibitions conservator Beth-ann Heinbaugh. Administrative issues were effectively handled by exhibition officer Ann Bigley

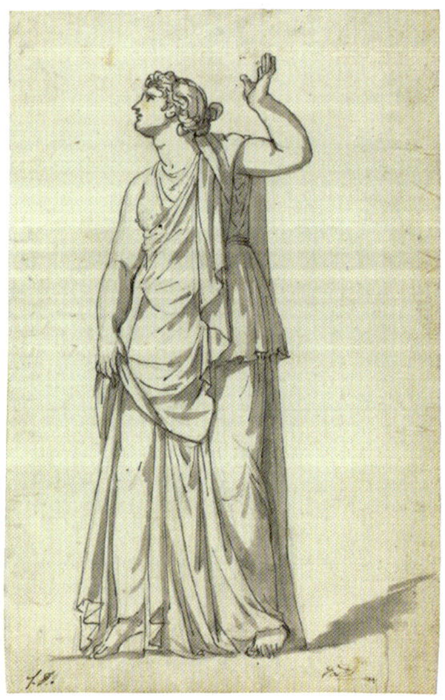

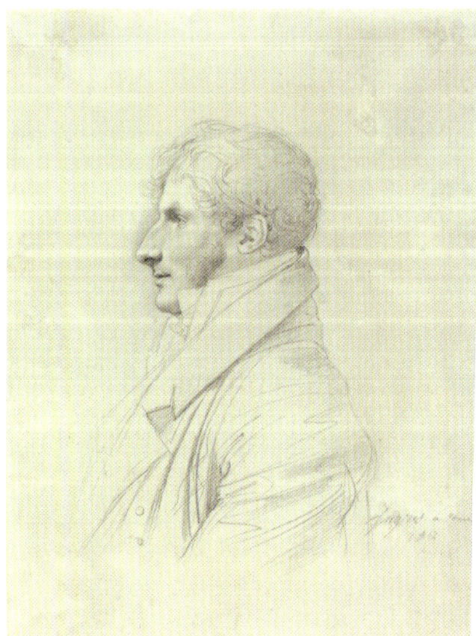

2 Jacques-Louis David, *Antique Roman Statue of a Muse*, 1775/1780, pen and black ink with gray wash, National Gallery of Art, Washington, Ailsa Mellon Bruce Fund, 1980

3 Jean-Auguste-Dominique Ingres, *Philippe Mengin de Bionval*, 1812, graphite, National Gallery of Art, Washington, Woodner Collection, 1991

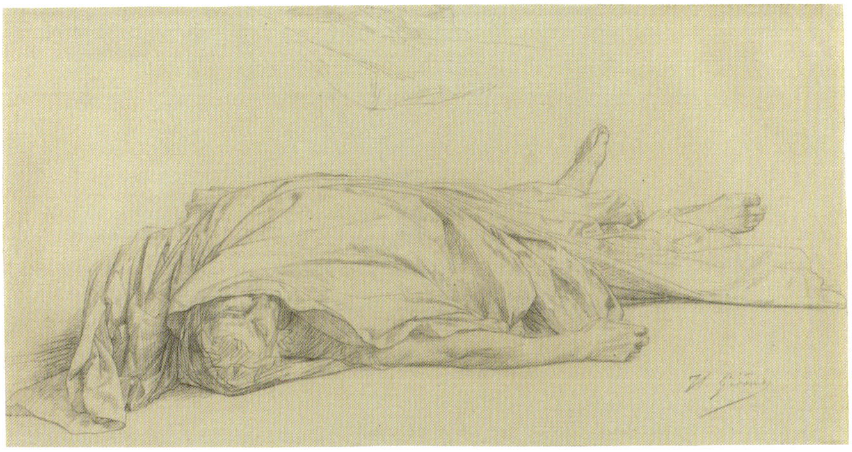

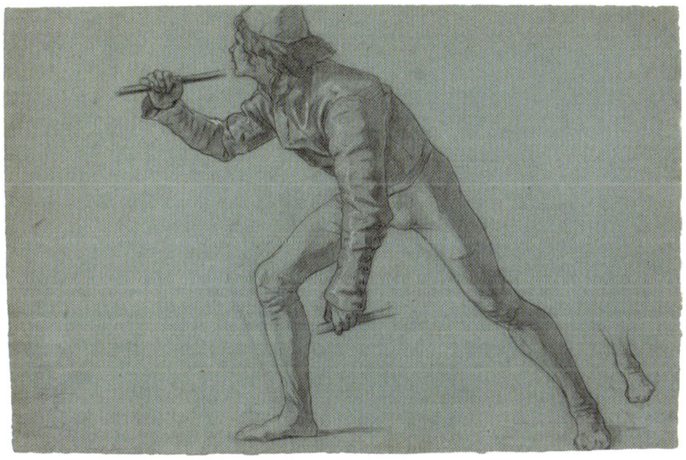

4 Jean-Léon Gérôme, *The Dead Caesar*, c. 1859, graphite, National Gallery of Art, Washington, Ailsa Mellon Bruce Fund, 1991

5 Thomas Couture, *A Boy in Florentine Costume*, c. 1863, black chalk heightened with white chalk on blue paper, National Gallery of Art, Washington, Ailsa Mellon Bruce Fund, 1998

Robertson. The task of producing high-quality images for the plates was accomplished by Lorene Emerson and especially photographer Ric Blanc, while Ira Bartfield and Kate Mayo secured images and permission for comparative illustrations. Under the supervision of editor in chief Judy Metro, the catalogue was thoughtfully edited by Tam Curry Bryfogle and beautifully designed by deputy publisher Chris Vogel, while Sara Sanders-Buell organized photographic material for the plates, Mariah Shay assembled comparative illustrations, and John Long coordinated production activity with the copublisher and our French colleagues in addition to typesetting the French edition of the catalogue. For the elegant installation at the National Gallery of Art we are grateful to chief of design Mark Leithauser and his staff, especially his deputy and chief lighting designer Gordon Anson as well as architect and designer Jamé Anderson. We hope that visitors to the exhibition and readers of the catalogue will find as much enjoyment in viewing and studying the works in the Dyke collection as we have in presenting them.

Andrew Robison

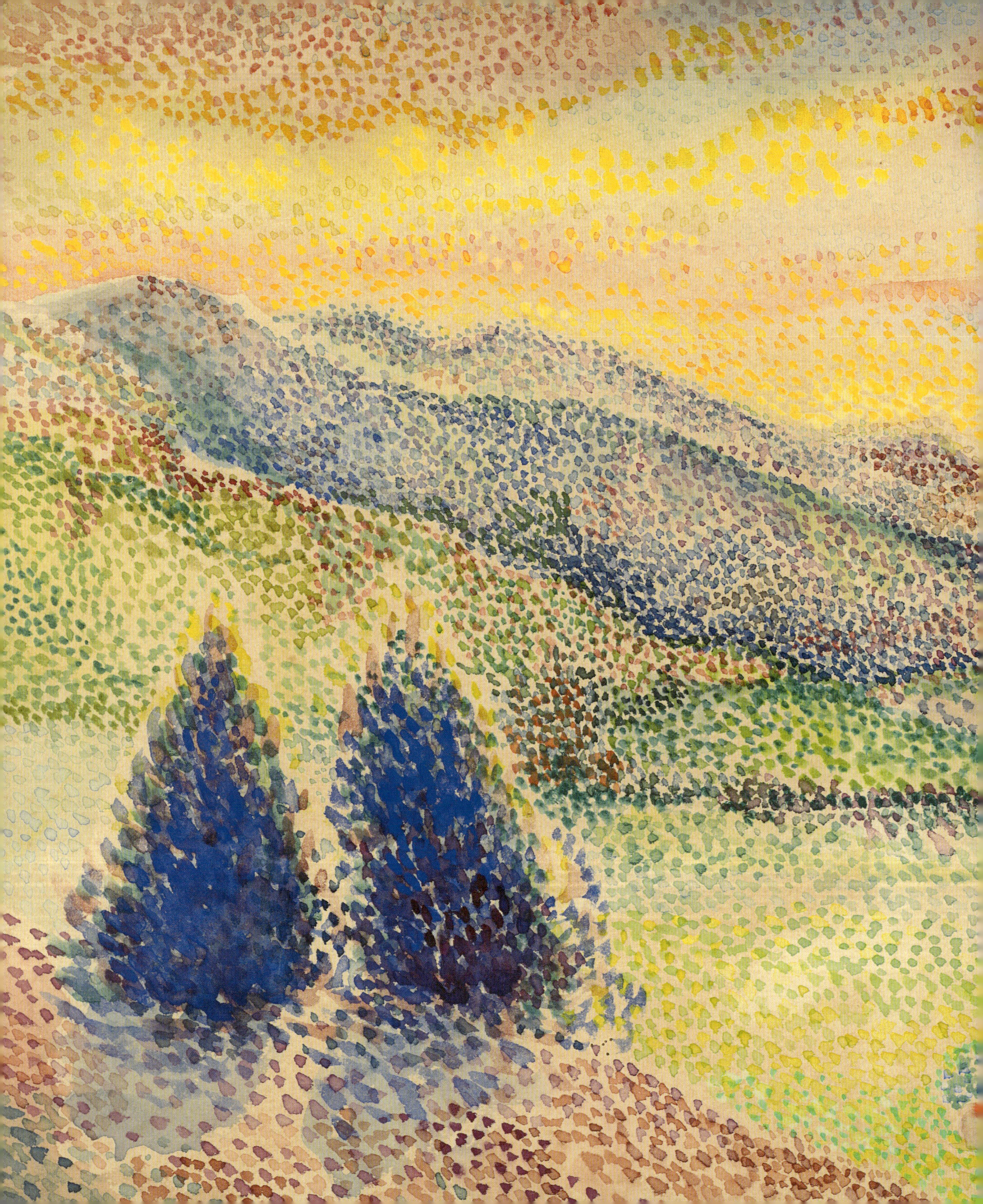

The Paper Century: French Drawing in the 1800s

RICHARD R. BRETTELL

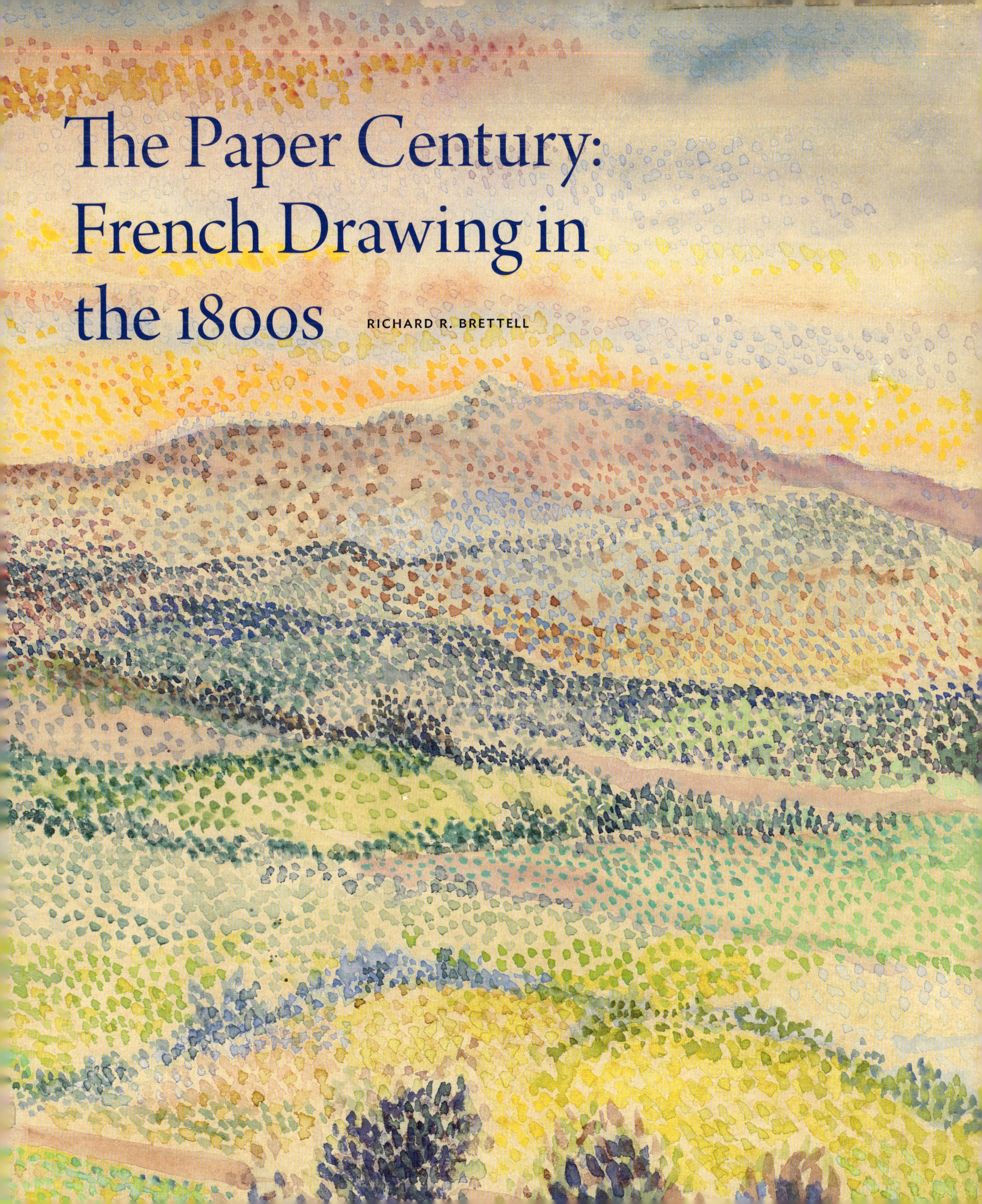

THE GRAPHIC IMPULSE — THE DESIRE TO DRAW — pervades art, both Western and non-Western, and there are no cultures or periods in the history of world art without drawings. Yet perhaps because of the very pervasiveness of drawing, there is a curious absence of writing about the graphic impulse in general and about its roles in the larger history of art. Books and articles about drawing tend toward the particular, telling us a good deal about individual collectors of drawings, about the drawings of this or that artist, and about the techniques of drawing for the future practitioner or curator. This has resulted in some ambiguity about what a drawing actually *is*. And this ambiguity persists even when we confine ourselves to the graphic arts in nineteenth-century France.

In the West today drawings are generally defined as representations made by hand on paper, and until the widespread availability of paper in the Renaissance, drawings were — and are — rare. Not only in the sixteenth century but especially by the seventeenth and eighteenth centuries, when paper became more widely produced and less expensive, drawings became more common; and by the nineteenth century, with mass-produced papers, drawings became so abundant as to flood the art world with works for art lovers, collectors, dealers, connoisseurs, and curators to describe, catalogue, and evaluate. For that reason drawings survive in ever increasing numbers as paper becomes less and less expensive and more and more available. Whereas an early fifteenth-century artist had to think carefully about even making a drawing, so expensive was paper, by the late nineteenth century prebound sketchbooks and sheets of cheap paper were so easily accessible that an artist like Édouard Vuillard could make literally thousands of drawings in a lifetime and could fill a sketchbook in a day without a care. If only Pisanello or Jan van Eyck had had such easy access to paper!

Drawings cabinets and graphic arts or prints and drawings departments are now common in Western art museums, and since the seventeenth and particularly the eighteenth centuries, dedicated collectors of drawings have existed to prime the market for works on paper, both from the past and from their contemporaries. Because drawings, unlike most prints, are unique, markets for collecting them have been more rarified and expensive, leading in turn to a specialized branch of art history in which drawings — the vast majority of which are unsigned — can be convincingly attributed to particular artists by connoisseurs. These men and, in a few cases, women have created a canon of great draftsmen (or, to be less sexist following the great historian of drawing Deanna Petherbridge, "drawers"), which has been refined and expanded as more connoisseurs, curators, dealers, and collectors have entered the field. This very act of refinement has thus sidelined through devaluation much of the actual history of drawing.

The National Gallery of Art in Washington has one of the most distinguished collections and curatorial departments in America devoted to drawings. In the past generation it has purchased or received as gifts literally thousands of Western drawings. Because the collections of paintings and sculpture in the National Gallery have strength in French nineteenth-century art, the drawings collection has been developed to share that strength — working in the case represented by this exhibition with a particularly enthusiastic private collector and patron to add substantially to this collection. The present publication celebrates the Dyke collection and is a physical embodiment of the collaboration between an institution and an individual collector that is in itself not only admirable but a model for other public collections. In this case the curators and the collector independently seek important and beautiful works and confer frequently. When either finds a suitable work, it can be purchased directly for the National Gallery or for the collector to enjoy at home and perhaps eventually give to the museum. In each case both the curators and collector have extensive knowledge of the public collection of drawings at the National Gallery, and the purchase is often made with the idea of strengthening that collection.

Virtually every French artist of the nineteenth century drew, and the literature devoted to their works is massive. From the studio of Jacques-Louis David, who himself produced many drawings, to the cubist drawings of Braque, Picasso, and their colleagues or imitators, drawings have played a role in the enterprise of modernist art history. Of French artists generally recognized as "major," only a handful have no monograph or extended study of their drawings, while for several (Ingres, Delacroix, Corot, Millet, Degas, Pissarro, Gauguin, Seurat, Van Gogh, Cézanne, and Redon) such publications make it impossible to imagine their oeuvres without drawings.

Yet there are two critical caveats that we must make here. First, despite the fact that drawing is considered central to the oeuvres of many of the greatest modern artists, drawing itself plays a peripheral and highly specialized role in the *written* history of modern art, a history so dominated by painting that the graphic arts are like a withered appendage or a gland of uncertain function in the body of modernist art history. So numbingly familiar are discussions of the flattening of pictorial space, the role of color, and the importance of facture in the history of modern painting that the graphic impulse, though central to all art, is even less discussed in the histories of modern art. The second caveat concerns our real knowledge of art — painting as well as graphic art and sculpture — in the last two long centuries. Art historians and connoisseurs inside and outside museums have all made valiant efforts to define the history of art as the history of "great art" or the history of art produced by "great artists." This has created a sort of history-as-executivesummary in which we know so much about the work of so few artists and, conversely, so little about the work of so many artists that a critic of art history would not be remiss in asking whether art historians actually have a proper basis for reaching their conclusions. Indeed, if canonical or "great" artists have received the lion's share of study, their combined oeuvre is a minuscule percentage of the actual production of all known artists. It is, for example, with considerable embarrassment that a working art historian today picks up a copy of any of the major compilations or lists of artists like those produced by Thieme-Becker or Bénézit. If any of us were asked to name even one work by ninety percent of those artists, we would fail, despite having spent decades studying the "history of art" in this or that period.

Because our knowledge of art history in the last two centuries is skewed toward painting and because we know a tiny percentage of the actual history of art, what can we say about modern *drawing*? Or to ask a related, but separate question: if modern art is defined as urban and cosmopolitan, if its undisputed capital in the nineteenth century was Paris, and if drawing plays a role in this larger history of modernism, how do we figure out what that role was? Before dealing with drawings themselves and their markets and exhibitions, let us look at what the two major encyclopedias created by the French in the modern age thought drawings were.

The first, of course, is the great secular Enlightenment *Encyclopédie* created by Denis Diderot and his many colleagues to describe the entire known world and the human mind, produced in many volumes throughout the third quarter of the eighteenth century. Most of the entries for the visual arts were written by a scientist named Louis de Jaucourt, but the entry crucial to us — on "drawing" (*dessein*, as it was then spelled) — was written by the amateur artist and printmaker Claude-Henri Watelet, who had deep knowledge of graphic practice in Europe. His entry on drawing is short, succinct, and telling. He began by linking drawing to the art of *painting* and then defining drawing as the production of a painter using the media of the pen (and ink) or the *crayon*, by which he meant chalk or charcoal. He then proceeded to the crux of his definition, that *dessein* (drawing) was in necessary opposition to *couleur* (color), and he spent most of his elegantly simple prose dealing with the philosophical and aesthetic opposition between line and color in art.

What is vital for us to recognize is that the support — paper — was not of importance to Watelet and was not discussed in his entry. For him, drawing was the analysis of form by either contour or shadow, neither of which was associated with color. Like many earlier writers about art, he made clear that *dessein* was the basis for all art and that it was to be practiced regularly throughout an artist's career, almost as a form of exercise. Watelet's formal definition is somewhat suspect in terms of actual usage in his day; and while his definition is clear and concise, it does not at all conform to the definition of drawing in today's museum, a definition that privileges paper — the support — to the medium. For Watelet, watercolors or pastels on paper (all of which are grouped with prints and drawings rather than paintings in the modern museum) were not *desseins*, because each was about color. And although he did not include the brush in the two media mentioned at the beginning of his definition, he would clearly not have had trouble calling an ink and wash on paper a *dessein*, because the ink is monochrome and hence not about color.

Let us fast-forward, as historians have done for centuries, to 1866, when the next great French encyclopedia began to appear. The *Grand dictionnaire universel du XIXe siècle* (Great universal dictionary of the nineteenth century) was published between 1866 and 1878 under the direction of Pierre Larousse, who defied the encyclopedists by not using their word in his title. Yet the lengthy entries (which appear following the definitions of each term) were produced by French scholars and experts in the Second Empire and Third Republic and were called *encyclopédies*. They are often longer and more complex than those of their eighteenth-century predecessors. So too for "drawing," or *dessin* (now spelled in the modern manner), which is defined in the 1870 volume devoted to *D* with a simplicity that Watelet would have admired: "the representation on a surface of the form and not the color of an object." This dialectical definition follows completely the restrictive lead of Watelet in the eighteenth century, down to the two most common types of drawing: listed as *dessins au traits* (line drawings that render only contours or the linear aspects of form without indication of shading) and *dessins ombrés* (shaded drawings that deal with light and shadow).

Yet when we get to the essay, the tidy world of the encyclopedists and the definers of words gives way to what was clearly the messy conceptual and practical reality of drawing. Indeed, the first long quotation in the entry is from the great colorist Eugène Delacroix, whose drawing practice defied everything in the definition that precedes the essay. The passage, from a Delacroix essay of 1850, actually agrees in large measure with Watelet by concluding that the *poésie* of color cannot be achieved without already having understood the form and perspective of nature through drawing. What is interesting, however, is that Delacroix sees the development of artistic *poésie* as part of the evolution of art, which was given huge impetus in the sixteenth and seventeenth centuries by artists like Titian and Rubens. Because earlier artists had progressed so far, the modern artist, in Delacroix's view, had an advantage over artists from the past, because the entire history of art had already progressed from form to color — albeit on a sort of scaffolding of form. Hence, the graphic schooling of the modern artist was, for Delacroix, highly compressed, and "the old days" of endless graphic study before color were over forever. In the dictionary sense of the word, drawing had a smaller and smaller role to play in art as time progressed — an odd thing to say in what we might call *the* century of drawing.

The essay that quoted Delacroix is perhaps the best ever written in French about drawing, and its considerable bibliography is a wonderful guide for students of drawing in the history of art and of the place of drawing in the education of the then-contemporary artist. Although unsigned, its author was most probably Jean-Marie (called Marius) Chaumelin, listed as a collaborator with Larousse for "history of painting." Like most of Larousse's collaborators, Chaumelin was a man of the left, of working-class and Provençal origins — far from the elegance, wealth, and privilege of Watelet. Because Larousse's entire enterprise was consciously post-revolutionary, many of its authors and authorities were either self-educated or part of a first-generation educational elite produced by revolutionary meritocracy. For this reason the essay on drawing has both a practicality (much of it concerns the role of drawing in manufacturing, architecture, and engineering) and a non-hierarchical quality missing in Watelet's learned speculations.

What had changed in the art world in the century between the writing of these two essays? To begin with, the sheer quantity of drawings — no matter how drawing is defined — had increased exponentially. In addition, there were many more venues for the exhibition and sale of drawings than at any previous time. But this alone is not sufficient as an explanation. Indeed, the entire art world played a much larger role in culture in general than it had in the eighteenth century, when the population of professional artists and knowledgeable collectors and dealers was more restricted. By the Second Empire, when Chaumelin began to write about art and art history, the visual arts were part of what we now call mass culture; and people with little money, social standing, or education were willing consumers of art, whether they passively attended mass cultural events like world's fair pavilions or actively sought out works of art to purchase. If we are truly to understand the role of drawing in nineteenth-century French art, and particularly in what we now call modern art, we must begin by assessing the ways in which ordinary people saw drawings and then the ways in which drawings were sold as part of the commodity culture essential to modern life.

There is no doubt that the major venue for public exposure to art in nineteenth-century Paris was the Salon exhibition, which went from a relatively modest biennial affair early in the century to a vast annual trade fair with literally thousands of exhibited "products" by its end. It is not surprising that drawing played an increasing role in the Paris Salon of the nineteenth century. Although artists had exhibited pastels and probably even watercolors in eighteenth-century Salon exhibitions, these were not listed as such in the Salon booklet (catalogue), meaning that they were listed, if at all, in the largest section of the catalogue, called *Tableaux* (paintings). This did not change until 1843, when a major new section of the Salon catalogue was created under the heading *Peinture* and designated for "miniatures, pastels, paintings on porcelain, etc." This section, though not as large as that devoted to oil painting, was more prominent than those for sculpture, engraving, or lithography (the last of which had achieved its own special section in the Salon catalogues in 1830).

By 1864 the number of artists who sent drawings to the Salon had increased to such an extent that a new category was created: the subheading for *Dessins* specifically mentioned "watercolors, pastels, miniatures, enamels, porcelain painting, and cartoons for stained-glass windows," and this section attained immense proportions in the final decades of the nineteenth century. The sheer fact of the creation of this section indicates that the market for works on paper—particularly for "finished" or signed works on paper—was large enough that artists worked hard to cater to its demands. This multimedia inclusivity also held true for the vanguard exhibitions organized by the group of artists now called impressionists from 1874 to 1886 (54 of the 165 listed works in the first exhibition were on paper, and 80 out of 244 in the last) as well as for the variously formal but non-governmental exhibitions like the Salon des Indépendants, the Salon d'Automne, and many others. Indeed, artists like Degas, Cassatt, Pissarro, Cézanne, Redon, and Seurat showed works on paper along with paintings when they sent works to the unjuried impressionist exhibitions, but it must be said that these were most often as highly finished as the artists' paintings. Drawings like those by Pissarro in the Dyke collection would most likely not have been exhibited in the artists' lifetimes but would have been kept in the studio for future use. Yet we must stress that it became essentially impossible to be an important artist in the last four decades of the nineteenth century without making and exhibiting works on paper, both drawn and printed, and this graphic preoccupation was reflected in the markets, exhibitions, and reviews. To some extent, this was motivated by the desire to reach new markets, which is why both dealers and artists participated in the paper revolution.

Since French academic art formally detached itself from modern art with the realists and the impressionists, the scholarly study of academic art has had its own specialist status among historians of modern art. With few exceptions, artists who continued to exhibit with the Salons have received significantly less scholarly study in the past than those who contributed to the "independent" history of modern art. And this discrepancy persists today; the role of drawing in the Salon enjoys considerably less attention than that given to painting and sculpture. What can we say about the role of drawing in "official" or academic art after 1864? Most notably, paintings submitted to and accepted by the Salon far outnumbered drawings. The Salon catalogue of 1864 has entries for 1,995 paintings and only 492 — or about a quarter as many — drawings.

For each artist who exhibited in both categories, that fact was noted in the catalogue entries in both sections. No one was allowed more than two works in one category, thus artists could effectively double the number of their works shown in the Salon if their drawings as well as paintings were accepted. Yet a minority of artists who submitted as painters also submitted a drawing, suggesting that, in spite of the advantages of the new category, artists continued to acknowledge the greater prestige of painting. In 1864, for example, only 335 artists exhibited drawings, and most PhD-trained historians of French nineteenth-century art could identify the names and the oeuvres of perhaps less than five percent of them. Not a single artist then working in France and now considered "great" submitted drawings to the 1864 Salon. It is frankly numbing to read the names; they are *so* unfamiliar, creating such an abundance of obscurity that we feel at once ignorant and fortunate to be so.

The next year, 1865, we find a lone drawing, now famous, by Degas (listed as "De Gas [edgard], Scene de guerre au moyen age, pastel, no. 2406") and nothing by any of Degas's friends or future colleagues (Monet, Manet, Renoir, Bazille, or Pissarro) or by the artists he admired (Ingres, Corot, Millet, or Rousseau). Indeed, well-trained students of French nineteenth-century drawing whose curatorial teeth were cut in the great public drawing collections of France, England, Germany, or the United States would be at a loss for words if they were asked to characterize the state of French drawing in 1865 based on the Salon catalogue alone. What, we must ask ourselves, happened to all these other drawings listed in that catalogue? Did they disappear? Are they now catalogued under different artists? Were they destroyed? Or, somewhat tantalizingly, do they await discovery in the immense public collections and the numerous "antiquaries" and auction houses of France? I suspect the latter. Some adventuresome curators have begun, and it is time now for more students of French graphic arts also, to search through these vast collections in addition to working and reworking the graphic oeuvres of the forty major artists and the two hundred or so minor ones we already know. The field is enormous, and we, as scholars, have allowed ourselves to narrow it too quickly and with too little knowledge of its extent to justify our exclusions.

By 1874, the year of the first impressionist exhibition, the situation for drawings at the Salon had not changed significantly, but we do find individual sheets by Édouard Manet and his student Eva Gonzalès as well as major drawings by Jean-Paul Flandrin, François-Louis Français, Paul Gavarni, Henri-Joseph Harpignies, Maxime Lalanne, Léon Augustin Lhermitte, Pierre Puvis de Chavannes, and Augustin Théodule Ribot (works by seven of whom are to be found in the Dyke collection) amid the hundreds of artists whose oeuvres are unknown today. The drawings tend to be chalk, pastel, or watercolor, with paintings on porcelain, faience, and metal in the minority. They were installed together, apart from the paintings, and played a clearly subsidiary role in the immense exhibitions. Yet they were present, and their numbers increased as the century progressed and as artists recognized that they could multiply their presence in the Salon by submitting in both categories.

When we begin to look at the submissions of successful academic artists to the Salons in the 1870s and 1880s, we see that many of these artists created highly finished works of art and submitted them either as paintings (if on canvas) or as drawings (if on paper), with certain artists submitting works to both sections of the Salon. Occasionally artists like Jean-Léon Gérôme and Gustave Doré also included sculpture and printmaking in their Salon repertoire. This was something quite new in French academic art, with the Salon encouraging artists to create and submit ambitious works on paper that would compete for attention in the drawing section, giving greater prominence to the artists who submitted works in more than one category, each of which had a numerical limit. This can be easily measured in the Salon catalogues when we look at the submissions of artists like Adolphe Appian as well as Français, Doré, Lhermitte, Lalanne (all in the Dyke collection), and others. This multiplying effect was important to artists, and some, like Lalanne, chose not to compete in the crowded domain of painting, attempting dominance in the graphic arts, both drawings and prints.

Little is known about this type of official or "exhibition" drawing in France. Institutional collections outside of France are weak in such drawings, largely because foreign and to some extent French collecting of French nineteenth-century art has intensely favored the avant-garde and neglected — even denigrated — their academic or Salon-based colleagues. Fortunately, the Dyke collection has done more than a little to correct that imbalance for the National Gallery of Art, and it is illuminating to consider the large-scale finished works on paper in the larger context of French Salon drawing. What can be said — and said strongly — is that the encyclopedia and dictionary definitions of drawing held dear in the eighteenth and nineteenth centuries had almost nothing to do with the exhibition drawings of the Salon or with many of the highly finished and complex works on paper by vanguard artists like Degas, Pissarro, Cassatt, Morisot, Gauguin, and others — the majority of which were dominated by color. Indeed, if color and drawing had been rigorously separated in art theory of the period, they were essentially married in art practice; and paper became a support for pastels and watercolor "paintings" as integrated as any *tableau* or oil on canvas.

Thus, as this exhibition and publication make abundantly clear, the nineteenth century is essentially the century of color-drawing, with artists across the aesthetic spectrum creating works on paper that privilege color over line or shading — in theory the two purviews of drawing at that time. There were many reasons for this: economic, practical, and aesthetic. The primary reason was the new exploration and popularization of watercolor. Although the medium had existed in art since medieval times, it did not attain widespread use (and specialized markets and societies) until the nineteenth century, when it was taken up by non-professional or "amateur" middle-class artists, particularly women, and non-art professionals like archaeologists, travelers, historians, geographers, botanists, and so on. For well-educated people to travel without material for drawing and watercolor in the nineteenth century was exceptional, and entire exhibitions could be mounted of highly competent, even beautiful works on paper — both drawings and watercolors — produced by nonartists. There were thus much better educated markets for works on paper than for painting and sculpture in the nineteenth century, because paper-support media had such widespread amateur use.

This was particularly true for watercolor, which, although practiced throughout the century in France, was considered an essentially English medium. Indeed, the Society of Painters in Water Colours (subsequently the Royal Watercolour Society) was founded in London in 1804, and its leadership consisted largely of amateur artists. As this group became increasingly professional in the course of the century, the New Water Colour Society was founded in 1832 to bring more artists and amateurs into association. The French Société des Aquarellistes was not founded until 1879 (even the Belgians preceded the French), by which time the medium had no need of such an organization, as watercolor supplies had been readily available in all major French cities through color merchants and the medium had been included in the Salon since the 1840s.

One aspect of watercolor manufacture and standardization that has been little studied in relation to the larger enterprise of color painting is the early date by which premade colors were produced, for professionals and amateurs alike. In 1781 William and Thomas Reeves were awarded a prize for standardizing the "moist watercolour paint cake," which could by then already be purchased in specialized boxes with full palettes of color. This was decades before the production of oil paint colors in tubes of reliably consistent color, often touted as a breakthrough in the pictorial arts in the 1850s and 1860s. Much more research needs to be done to uncover the links between the sequential regularization of color, first in watercolor and then in oil.

Watercolors in the Dyke collection run the entire spectrum of French production, being one of the most diverse single representations of French watercolor in any American collection. From famous artists like Delacroix, Cézanne, Signac, and Redon to those less well known like Jean-Achille Benouville, Théodore Chassériau, François-Auguste Ravier, Gabriel-Hippolyte Lebas, and Luigi Loir, the collection includes watercolors of every type and style, prompting a scholar of French art to realize that much remains to be done in both studying and writing the *real* history of color painting in France — with the most English of media playing an essential part. Indeed, there was an entire building constructed for the display of watercolors at the Paris World's Fair of 1900, and it would be fascinating to know what it contained. This is not the place to rehearse the acrimonious arguments between the watercolor purists who preferred only transparent water-based color marks and the eclectics who used gouache (with white lead to make the color opaque rather than translucent) and even tempera-based media either in preference to or in addition to watercolor itself. But the works in this exhibition make clear that French artists used these color media on paper with great elasticity and verve, only a few being purists. This collection offers a definitive survey of watercolor in French art from Delacroix to Signac, paralleling those done so often for British watercolors.

We now know that works on paper, whether color or not, were pervasive in French art practice in the nineteenth century and that their place within both public exhibitions and the various art markets was secure by mid-century. We find records of them at the Salon, in dealer exhibitions, and on the walls of small shops like stationers and art supply stores or color merchants. And because of their lightness and portability, they also came to spawn a whole species of street carts and quay stalls for the most important international industry in nineteenth-century Paris: tourism. Whether we look at contemporary *cartes postales* or the urban paintings by Pissarro,

Childe Hassam, Giovanni Boldini, and other less lofty artists who specialized in Paris street life, we see these stalls along the quays and in the parks and public squares frequented by tourists. Works on paper also began to fill boxes and folders arranged by subject or artist in shops that sold prints, old books, curios, and, increasingly, antiques. The *antiquaires* of France all sell a wide variety of material — from furniture and art to metals, porcelain, and glass. And there are virtually always small cabinets or wooden stands where works on paper are gathered for sale, sometimes even arranged by price. It is the sheer ubiquity of what we might call paper markets that makes them so maddeningly difficult to study. Where are the sale records? How do we know who bought what when? Where were they concentrated?

For these reasons, in France, with its institutional division of objects, it is actually the French national library rather than the great art museums that has the most comprehensive collections of the autograph "graphic traffic" from the nineteenth century. The vast number of works on paper would overwhelm the ability of any art museum's prints or drawings curator to make critical judgments about quality. But in the print cabinet of the Bibliothèque Nationale there are hundreds of thousands, perhaps millions of nineteenth-century drawings and photographs that have been collected not for their quality, but for their value as documents of landscapes, buildings, plants, regions, rocks, houses, and so on. Many were acquired by wealthy amateurs who hired others to organize the images by subject and paste them onto large sheets of paper that were in turn bound into volumes to be *used*. Take, for example, the Destailleur collection, formed by a major French architect from the last half of the nineteenth century who worked for the Rothschild family. Gabriel-Hippolyte Alexandre Destailleur based many of his designs on aspects of older French buildings and thus formed enormous collections of drawings, prints, and photographs that were categorized by place and are preserved today in their luxurious bindings *au goût Rothschild*. Within these volumes are works by amateurs and minor artists together with beautiful watercolors and drawings by artists whose names we wish we knew better and the occasional gem by a major artist, bought not for the name of the artist, but for its role as a document. Before condemning this approach, we must remember that many important artists themselves thought of their drawings as documents to be used in the creation of more complex works of art. From academic artists, studying patterns of drapery or poses of the human body or details of architecture for use in paintings, to avant-garde artists like Millet, Degas, Pissarro, Gauguin, Seurat, Vuillard, and Bonnard, the idea of drawing as being somehow more essentially *useful* than painting is integral to its nature.

Just as drawings in the nineteenth century ran the gamut in terms of function, from studies to highly finished works of art for exhibition, so too did their styles vary. The very idea that there is a generic "graphic style" in French nineteenth-century art is preposterous. The variety of function, style, material, scale, and support was intrinsic to drawing in that most complex of centuries for art. But a hierarchy of drawing does exist, which shifts as the century progresses. At the foundation was a type of drawing that, while as old as the graphic impulse itself, only became a dominant practice in the nineteenth century. It is what the French would call *croquis*, a term that is frustratingly difficult to translate into English with any precision. The croquis is a kind of quick sketch, a drawing made from life in a single sitting. Croquis are usually small, made in a sketchbook with a single, simple medium. Artists were often taught to move their drawing instrument across the surface without lifting it, so as not to lose their place while looking fixedly at the motif. The most common medium was graphite, and the most common support was a standard-sized sketchbook that could be easily put into the artist's pocket. The standard size and portability were critical to the croquis, because the better an artist knew the medium and support, the easier it was to capture the essential qualities of the motif without looking at the drawing itself. Thus croquis are the most instinctive and the least planned of drawings. They are also a form of graphic exercise that was not necessarily intended to create a drawing for exhibition.

Countless croquis were made throughout the lifetimes of hundreds of thousands of artists working in the European world during the nineteenth century. Precisely because they are so common and were not always successful as works of art, their survival rate is low. There are no croquis in the Dyke collection, though the wonderfully fresh Delacroix view of cliffs and the cityscape by Johan Barthold Jongkind may have started out as graphite sketches, which were then "completed" as watercolors, possibly on site. Even the seemingly rapidly executed drawings by Manet and Degas are the product of complex working methods with at least two and perhaps more discrete work sessions. Yet it was the croquis that replaced the careful practice of studio drawing as the basis for art making by the mid-nineteenth century, and this change reflects an aesthetic sea change that has been much better studied in painting than in the graphic arts.

Perhaps next in the hierarchy of drawings are what we would call life drawings from posed figures. These are among the oldest types of drawing in Western art and are at the root of the classical or academic tradition. Interestingly, the Dyke collection has drawings of this type only by vanguard artists: Delacroix, Degas, Pissarro, Gauguin, and Laugé. The two great academic figure drawings in the collection — by François Bonvin and by Lhermitte —

were each carefully contrived large drawings made for exhibition and sale. They are emphatically not figure studies for use in preparing multifigure painted compositions like those of the vanguard artists. None of the drawings of human figures in the Dyke collection are of posed nude models. Although virtually every nineteenth-century artist, whether vanguard or academic, made such drawings, particularly at the beginnings of their careers, nude studies were not actively collected or exhibited in the nineteenth century except in the pedagogical context of art schools or academies.

Nor does the Dyke collection contain many study drawings such as those that artists made of pictorial elements (trees, rocks, foliage, drapery, hands, heads, clouds, buildings, architectural elements, figures from other works of art) when preparing more complex compositions. This type of drawing — whether of contours, shading, or both — is so common in the history of art that most surviving drawings can be categorized in the end as studies made either for specific use or as part of the graphic exercise of the artist. They were not the type of drawings that had a ready market in the nineteenth century unless they were made by old master artists (Dürer, Rembrandt, Veronese, Guercino, Watteau, Fragonard, Goya, David) and had attained the patina of rarity and art historical importance. Within an artist's lifetime these drawings were kept in the studio or given to a fellow artist or family member rather than sold.

Another major type of drawing in the history of art — the compositional study — had been all but subsumed in the nineteenth century by the oil study on paper. As a result, few such drawings survive from the period. More typical at this time were drawings made to record in miniature already completed paintings so that they could be translated into print media, either photomechanically or by hand. These drawings are relatively common in the oeuvres of artists like Manet who wanted control over the reproduction of their works. Yet the Manet drawing in the Dyke collection is not based on a painting; instead, the etching based on it seems meant to replicate the drawing itself. Although many compositional studies have come down to us because they reproduce important paintings, they are notably absent from the Dyke collection — with one possible exception: a small-scale oil sketch on paper by Théodore Rousseau was made either as a study in light and dark for the now-famous painting of the same composition in the Louvre (there is another version in the Wallace Collection) or as a black-and-white "translation" of that painting after its completion. Given its scale and its complete fidelity to the famous painting, I would assume the latter.

By far the most significant contribution of the Dyke collection to a renewed understanding of the role of drawing in nineteenth-century French art is its large number of spectacular exhibition drawings — works that would not have been considered drawings by the authors of the dictionary definitions but that began to dominate the Salon and other exhibitions in the nineteenth century. Because the National Gallery of Art has numerous finished works on paper by major impressionists and post-impressionists, the addition of this serious group of academic exhibition watercolors puts those better-known achievements into a real historical and aesthetic context. It also teaches us — whether scholars or knowledgeable members of the public who often attend exhibitions — that we have much to learn about the history of modern art from drawings and that many of our cherished ideas will need to be revised the more we learn and the more we open ourselves up to this immense and barely charted subject.

When I learned the history of nineteenth-century drawings from college courses and museum collections in the late 1960s and early 1970s, I studied drawings from David and Ingres through Delacroix and Chassériau, through the great realists Millet, Courbet, Rousseau, and Corot, through impressionism (principally Degas with a little of the stylistically elusive Manet), and finally through the masters of post-impressionism, all of whom had important graphic oeuvres: Cézanne, Seurat, Gauguin, Van Gogh, Redon, Vuillard, and Bonnard. So when I came upon a group of more than 250 drawings by Camille Pissarro as a graduate student, I was completely unprepared for them, because shockingly I had been taught that, aside from Degas, impressionists did not draw (or make drawings worth studying). Since then we have learned a great deal, and thanks to the more adventuresome museum and private gatherings like the Dyke collection, we have gained a glimpse of how much more there is to explore.

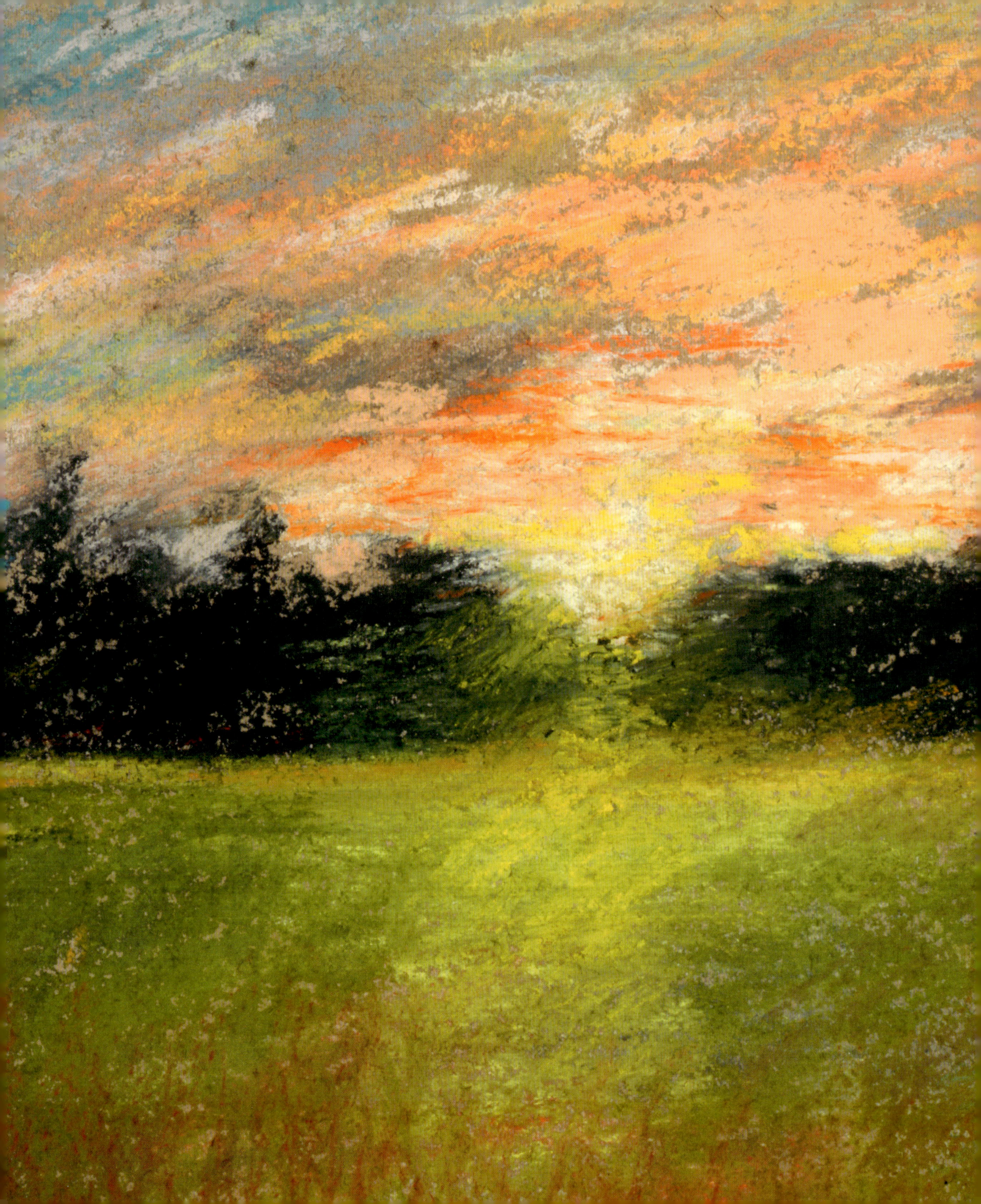

The Romantic Impulse

VICTOR CARLSON

THE EARLIEST EXAMPLES of French drawing in the James Dyke collection are by so-called romantic artists, whose formation took place between 1815 and 1850 — a time of profound change in literature, the visual arts, and music that decisively challenged the standards and practice of these arts. The term "romanticism," however, has been defined so broadly over the years as to preclude any agreed-upon meaning. Indeed, the romantic movement had no single, commanding voice to define its goals, no style shared among its artists, no program of commonly held ideas. If the disparate personalities in the movement did agree on one point, it was the overriding importance of the individual's voice and his or her right to be heard despite opposition from entrenched defenders of tradition.[1]

The first sustained attempt to discuss romanticism in terms of specific themes or issues was Madame de Staël's lengthy book *De l'Allemagne* (On Germany), first published in London in 1813 because Napoleon Bonaparte's censors heard that it contained unflattering criticism of the French nation.[2] No friend of Napoleon, Madame de Staël had been exiled from Paris on October 15, 1803, and immediately set out for Germany, where in the course of her travels she met many of that country's leading intellectuals. German writers and artists were redefining their approaches to literature, philosophy, and aesthetics, among other concerns. Their aim was the creation of a "fusion of all areas of human knowledge and experience, which eighteenth-century rationalism had segregated. At a stroke the artist's sphere of influence was vastly increased; from being a mere craftsman or technician, he was immediately promoted to the role of philosopher, scientist, priest, and social legislator, all in one."[3] Madame de Staël summarized her definition of romanticism in a chapter titled "On Classical Poetry and Romantic Poetry."[4] Although her terms are somewhat opaque at times, her overarching intention was to encourage innovation over blind adherence to outmoded practice, which she saw as no more than a support for unexceptional abilities.

Ten years later Stendhal [Marie-Henri Beyle] wrote the pamphlet "Racine et Shakespeare" (1823), taking on a basic issue for the romantics: the power of the individual's statement versus the weight of tradition. He wrote a spirited defense of Shakespeare, whose characters derive much of their dramatic intensity from their irrational, even brutal, actions and speech. By contrast, the seventeenth-century dramatist Jean-Baptiste Racine was constrained to develop the characters of his plays within plots that unfold in one place during the course of one day (unity of time and place) and dialogue spoken within the metric requirements of a specific verse form. In short, and to paraphrase Stendhal, romanticism will give the most pleasure to present-day audiences, while classicism gave the most pleasure to their great-grandparents.

At first romanticism was seen primarily as a literary movement, but when Charles Baudelaire wrote his review of the 1846 Salon, the term had been understood for some time to include the visual arts. In his critique of the exhibition the poet noted: "Romanticism is precisely situated neither in choice of subject nor in exact truth, but in a way of feeling." He was more specific a few lines later: "To say the word Romanticism is to say modern art — that is intimacy, spirituality, colour, aspiration towards the infinite, expressed by every means available to the arts."[5]

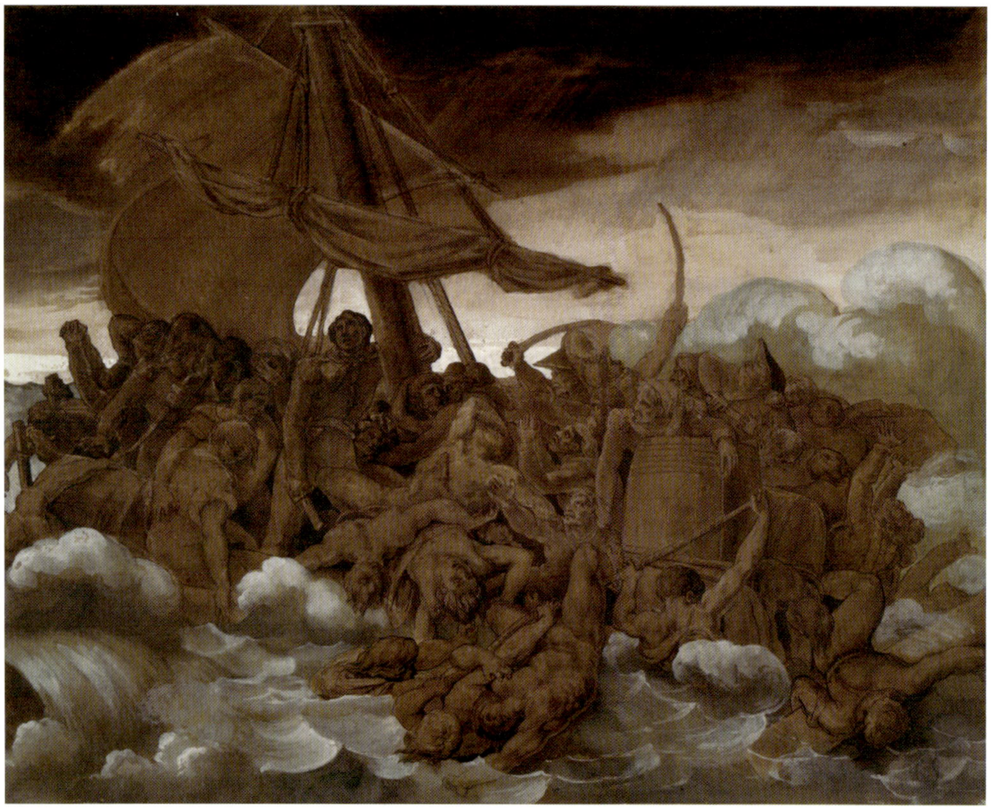

1 Théodore Géricault, *The Mutiny on the Raft of the Medusa*, 1818, black chalk, black crayon, white chalk, and watercolor with white gouache on brown paper, Harvard Art Museum, Fogg Museum, Bequest of Grenville L. Winthrop, 1943

Théodore Géricault was "head of this new school that has as its goal the faithful representation of forceful and stirring emotions," as noted by Arnold Scheffer in his anonymously published review of the 1827 Salon.[6] No doubt he had in mind the brief career of the artist who had been made famous by *The Raft of the Medusa* (Musée du Louvre, Paris), exhibited at the 1819 Salon (for a preparatory drawing, see fig. 1). The huge canvas had created a sensation because its subject was based on a naval disaster that sparked a scandal for the government of King Louis XVIII. Those who survived the experience of being abandoned on a raft with no provisions later told horrific stories of suicide and cannibalism. Géricault read illustrated accounts of the tragedy and was reportedly able to borrow cadavers and body parts from a local morgue or hospital that he kept in his studio to use as models for his paintings and drawings.[7] Shortly after exhibiting *The Raft of the Medusa*, he painted a group of heads of insane patients treated by his friend Dr. Étienne-Jean Georget, a young practitioner interested in mental illness.

Subjects such as cannibalism or insanity would have shocked those who believed these were boundaries that art should not trespass. But Géricault's disregard for these proprieties must have made the painter a sympathetic figure to Victor Hugo, himself a romantic artist (fig. 2), who wrote: "Besides, everything is subject-matter, everything comes within the sphere of art; everything has the right of citizenship in poetry."[8] It was in part due to Hugo and his writings that the spirit of romanticism stretched beyond the terminus of 1850 nominally covered in this essay — hence the inclusion here of drawings from as late as 1870, such as Maxime Lalanne's *Alpine Castle above a Wooded Lake* and Gustave Doré's *Shades of French Soldiers from the Past Exhort the Army to Victory* (pls. 19 and 20).

The exhibition of Eugène Delacroix's *Massacre at Chios* and Jean-Auguste-Dominique Ingres's *Vow of Louis XIII* (both Musée du Louvre, Paris) at the Salon of 1824 polarized the critics. For artists, however, the impact of the exhibition was their exposure to the work of British painters such as John Constable (see fig. 3), who sent two paintings, *The*

Hay Wain (The National Gallery, London) and *View on the Stour near Dedham* (The Huntington Library, Art Collections and Botanical Gardens, Pasadena, CA).[9] After seeing Constable's landscapes, Paul Huet wrote: "It was the first time perhaps that one felt the freshness, that one saw a luxuriant, verdant nature, without blackness, crudity, or mannerisms. A cottage half hidden in the shade of beautiful and fresh trees, a limpid brook traversed at a ford by a wagon, the countryside of London humid with English atmosphere."[10] British artists exhibited some fifty works at the Salon, about three-quarters of which were watercolors. This reflects the esteem the medium had there, as signaled too by the Society of Painters in Water Colours, founded in London in 1804. The key to understanding the British appreciation of these works is the word "painters," which implied that the artist's goal was to use these water-based pigments to approximate the effects of an oil on canvas — requiring less time and expense.

The watercolor society would surely have approved of Eugène Isabey's *Fishing Boats Tossed before a Storm* (pl. 13), where fishermen struggle to wrest control from the heaving sea swells. This work was executed with all the attention the artist gave to his oils and on a scale that approximates a typical easel painting. *Sunset in an Oriental Landscape* (pl. 11) by Gabriel-Hippolyte Lebas is another watercolor executed with a finish comparable to what an artist would have given an oil painting. The wonderful freshness of this sheet indicates that it has not received much exposure to light, which might suggest that it was once part of an album. At this time many collectors bought or commissioned such drawings and watercolors to fill the blank pages of their books, usually organized around a theme (perhaps exotic travel in this case).

In the nineteenth century it was possible for non-French artists to exhibit at the Salons.[11] One romantic artist in the Dyke collection who benefited from this inclusive gesture was the Swiss-born Alexandre Calame, who now could expand the audience, and thus the market, for his landscapes, whether painted or drawn. Highly finished drawings such as his *Ancient Pine Forest with a Mountain Stream* (pl. 12) very likely appealed to contemporary collectors who could not afford oil paintings. In addition, travel across the Channel became easier following the collapse of Napoleon's First Empire in 1814, benefiting both British and French artists. For instance, the young Richard Parkes Bonington followed his family to Calais, then to Paris, where in 1819 he entered the studio of Antoine-Jean Gros and would have met Eugène Isabey and Paul Huet.

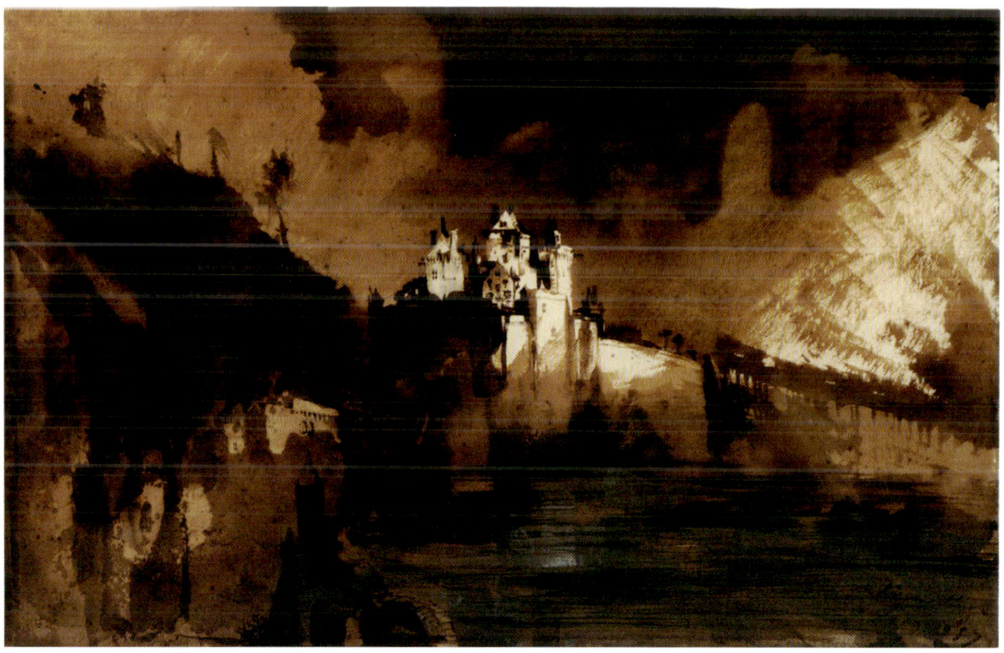

2 Victor Hugo, *Landscape with a Castle on a Cliff*, 1857, brush and brown wash, with stenciling and touches of white gouache, British Museum, London

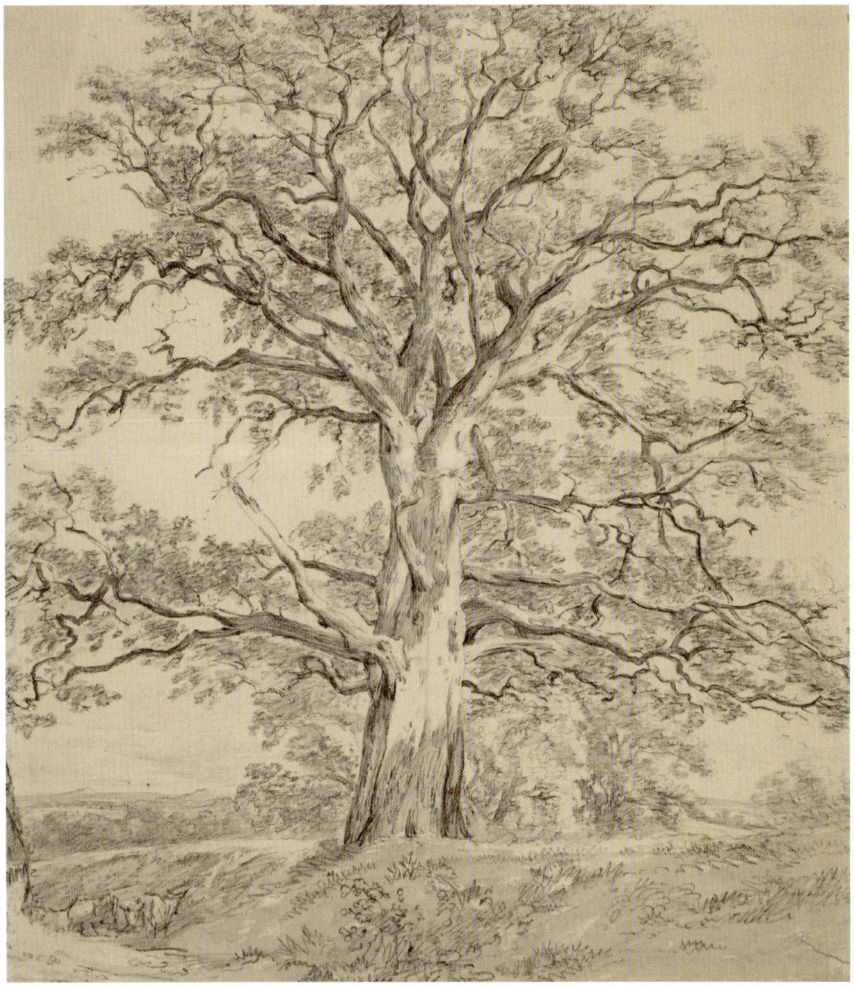

3 John Constable, *A Great Oak Tree*, c. 1801, black chalk with gray wash, National Gallery of Art, Washington, Gift of Paul Mellon, 1985

During the summer of 1825 Bonington also met Delacroix in London, and the two artists are known to have toured the coastal towns around Calais with Isabey that August; now back in France, Delacroix invited Bonington to share his studio in Paris, which the latter did for several months.

During the romantic period, manufacturers of artists' supplies expanded their offerings, introducing innovative versions of familiar products (watercolor pigments, pastels, pencils, and charcoal) together with papers made especially for these media. Artists ignored such specificities as often as not, but because available materials have always had their role in creating the final image, it is worth considering some of the drawing materials favored by the romantics.[12]

As Richard Brettell notes in his introduction to the present catalogue, draftsmanship in nineteenth-century France was, as never before, about drawing with color. And the Dyke collection has an important group of watercolors, demonstrating various approaches to the medium. In addition to the finished "painting in watercolor" sheets by Isabey and Lebas mentioned above, three Delacroix watercolors show the artist's use of the medium to achieve quite different results. The earliest is the highly finished *English Cavalier* (pl. 1), probably based on a scene from Sir Walter Scott's book *Woodstock, or The Cavalier*, which had appeared in 1826.[13] This was a time when Delacroix was involved in creating illustrations for works by Goethe and Shakespeare, among others. In this watercolor the artist paid great attention to the descriptive detail needed to situate a scene from Scott's work in time and place: likely the event in chapter 19 where Colonel Albert Lee (probably the dashingly attired cavalier) came through a window to enter Woodstock Castle, a royal lodge guarded by his father, Henry.[14] In so doing, he knocked over a chair that is seen here under the open window. The artist indicated the textures and pattern of the figure's costume with carefully applied layers of watercolor, using an area of blank white paper to define the cavalier's white collar, with its meticulously drawn lace border. Washes of ink describe the dimly lit room, while the evanescent landscape shimmering through the window may have been created by carefully removing some pigment while it was still damp with something like a rag.

Delacroix's *English Cavalier* is a bravura demonstration of the artist's command of every aspect of "painting in watercolor." His *Moroccan Courier* (pl. 2), on the other hand, hastily defines the figure with little more than a few strokes of watercolor to capture the man's sullen expression, languid pose, and loose-fitting garment. In preparing for a voyage to North Africa from late January to July 1832, the artist packed quantities of drawing materials, including seven sketchbooks, four of which survive intact. Together with several hundred separate sheets, they record an experience that he later recalled as a decisive event for his future development. As Arlette Sérullaz has written, "More than the discovery of a country and a race, it is the revelation of light and its multiple effects on form and colour which constitutes the key to Delacroix's voyage."[15]

The third watercolor by Delacroix in the Dyke collection is a rapid notation of cliffs and some rocks that the artist saw during one of his trips to the Atlantic coast (pl. 15). He boldly sketched the essentials of his composition in pencil and used watercolor to add only the minimal details necessary to define the scene — but sufficient to evoke the pleasures of a summer day at the seashore. Each of Delacroix's watercolors is a fully realized example of romantic draftsmanship, yet on occasion the artist was wary of his being associated with the movement, perhaps because he was suspicious of the oversimplifications labels can impose. All the same, it is impossible to discuss romanticism without referring to such masterpieces as his paintings *Massacre at Chios* from 1824, *Death of Sardanapalus* from 1827, or *Liberty Leading the People* from 1831 (all Musée du Louvre, Paris), which are among the defining images of this epoch.

Delacroix remained in touch with some of the artists he met during his formative years, among them Paul Huet. Huet's pastel *Abbey by a Wooded Lake at Twilight* (pl. 5) is a remarkably early version of romantic fascination with the mysterious mood of shadowed and barely visible forms. In the Salon of 1831 the oil of this subject was accompanied by a short poem by Victor Hugo, a friend of Huet. In it the poet searches for a place "hidden deep in silence and shadow," a quiet refuge conducive to reverie.[16] In a different mode, Huet's crystalline watercolor of *Rock Cliffs along the Romanche* (pl. 17), a river in the Alpine region of France, is a study of these rugged formations, where over time the rocks have sheared away, leaving a pattern of jagged surfaces that evidently fascinated the artist. A much smaller, boldly drawn watercolor of exactly this site is known, perhaps a page from a sketchbook, with an inscription identifying the location as the "Route d'Oisans," as is also noted on the Dyke collection sheet.[17] It remains unclear why Huet executed the larger, more complex composition, perhaps simply to study the rock formations in greater detail or perhaps with the hope of finding a purchaser for this imposing study.

Huet's art went largely unnoticed by state officials; he never received a public commission, thus he had to rely on private sales, always a precarious situation. Delacroix noted in his journal that he visited Huet in his studio on the afternoon of April 13, 1858, and his remarks are a candid assessment of Huet's art: "I was greatly impressed with his pictures. They are uncommonly vigorous. There are still some vague passages, but that is characteristic of his talent. One cannot admire anything without also finding something to regret. Altogether great progress in his good qualities. And that is enough with pictures that stick in the memory, as his do in mine. All this evening I have been thinking about them with pleasure."[18]

A contemporary of Huet, Jean-Achille Benouville was best known in his time as a painter of historical landscapes (*paysages historiques*) — that is, landscapes composed from idealized natural features to serve as the setting for a mythological or historic event. He made numerous studies directly from nature, however, including *Sunset from a Rocky Coastline* (pl. 7), an early work that displays the artist's immediate response to the beauty of the modest site, seen with the typically romantic focus on sunrise and sunset. Bénouville's subtle palette is expanded by the pale blue paper he chose, which defines the sky and also contributes to the dull blue-green foreground, where the paper's hue is visible under the transparent, very pale yellow watercolor covering most of this area (a small strip of blue paper partly covered by watercolor is visible in the lower left corner revealing the interaction of the two materials).

Watercolor is a medium affected by such issues as the fluidity of the pigments, the absorbency of the paper, and the responsiveness of the artist's brush. Some romantic artists deliberately exploited these variables, as is brilliantly demonstrated by the two watercolors by François-Auguste Ravier in the Dyke collection (pls. 9 and 10), each showing a bit of featureless countryside at sunset. The very absence of a subject enabled the artist to concentrate all his attention on light and color as they appeared at certain times of day, reflected in the ever-changing surfaces of the ponds and marshes. Ravier brushed one color over another, allowing the layers of watercolor to bleed into each other or not. When his watercolors had dried, he might add streaks of pigments with a dry brush (as in *Sunset over a Pond*), or he might scrape away the surface to create fine lines that indicate the grasses at the edge of a marsh. The artist preferred to live in the area around Lyon, deliberately choosing small country towns where he could lead a fairly isolated existence. The sense of melancholy that imbues some of Ravier's landscapes recalls lines of poetry by Alphonse Lamartine such as: "Often at sunset I sit sadly below the mountain, in the shade of the old oak tree; I let my eyes wander at random over the plain whose changing vista spreads out at my feet."[19] Although largely self-taught, Ravier did know such contemporaries as Théodore Caruelle d'Aligny (pl. 4), who gave him a few lessons, and Jean-Baptiste-Camille Corot, who painted alongside him at Crémieu. Not surprisingly, he admired the watercolors of Joseph Mallord William Turner (see fig. 4), themselves stellar examples of an artist's willful transformation of conventional practice.[20]

One of the most basic drawing materials is a pencil, usually made of powdered graphite in com-

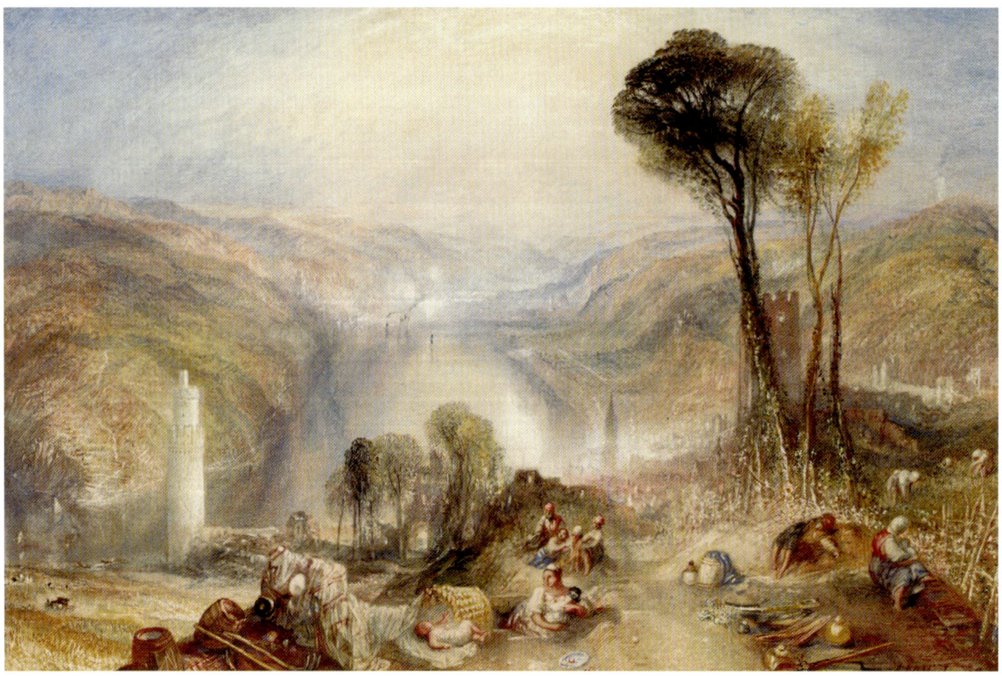

4 Joseph Mallord William Turner, *Oberwesel*, 1840, watercolor and gouache over graphite with scratching-out, National Gallery of Art, Washington, Paul Mellon Fund, 2007

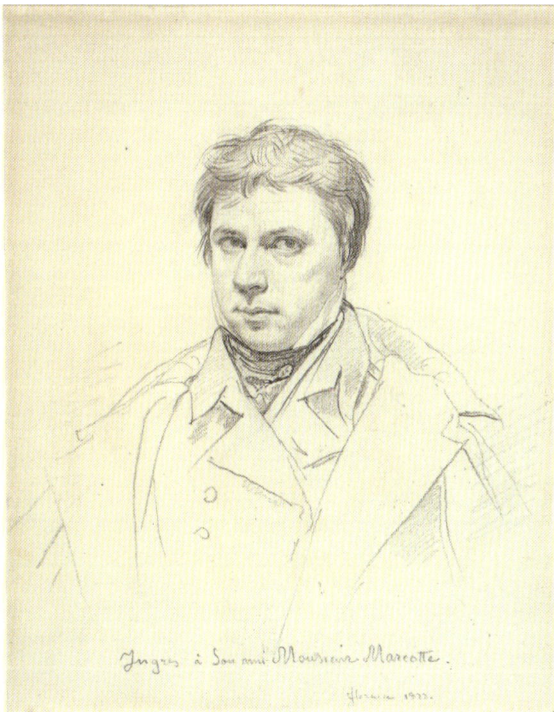

5 Jean-Auguste-Dominique Ingres, *Self-Portrait*, 1822, graphite, National Gallery of Art, Washington, Collection of Mr. and Mrs. Paul Mellon, 1995

bination with binders that create varying degrees of pliability. Théodore Chassériau's portrait of the sculptor Auguste-Louis-Marie Ottin (pl. 3) is an early work by an artist who by this time had begun to turn away from the example of his first mentor, Ingres, with whom he studied from 1830 until 1833.[21] For this drawing Chassériau chose pencil and paper with quite different qualities than the materials Ingres typically used. Ottin's portrait was drawn with a very soft graphite that formed dense lines to define the sitter's bold, craggy features, which were then further modeled by lightly spreading layers of graphite across the paper's rough surface. The soft pencil lines were caught only by the uppermost paper fibers, leaving the imprint of the horizontal wires of the mold used in manufacturing these sheets clearly visible along the left side of Ottin's face and jacket. The subtlety of tone reinforces the vigor of Chassériau's characterization — though Ingres might not agree, as he overwhelmingly preferred to draw portraits with a hard pencil on smooth paper, the better to register the clarity of each line (fig. 5).

Chassériau's *Drover with Oxen Pulling a Cart* (pl. 14) is related to the artist's series of murals decorating the staircase of the Palais d'Orsay, a commission he received in 1844. That work was destroyed or badly damaged during a fire on May 23, 1871, that ruined the building. A number of fragments of the oil-on-plaster wall paintings were rescued, which together with numerous preparatory drawings makes it possible to reconstruct much of what has been lost.[22] This vigorously executed study of a drover hurrying his oxen along relates to similar, although not identical, figures in the mural *Paix* (Peace). The watercolor owes much of its sense of raucous activity to the artist's decision to work with brush, the medium most responsive to the slightest change in direction or pressure from the draftsman's hand. Because Chassériau could not erase his corrections, his initial positions for the cattle's legs remain visible, and we are privileged onlookers as he tests one idea and then another.

Brush-and-ink washes are among the most frequently used materials for drawing, and Gustave Doré's nocturnal vision of the ghosts of French soldiers exhorting the army to victory during the 1870 Franco-Prussian War (pl. 20) is a powerful, otherworldly experience — realized in brush and brown ink, highlighted with white gouache, on brown paper. In thinking about a plan for this theme, Doré

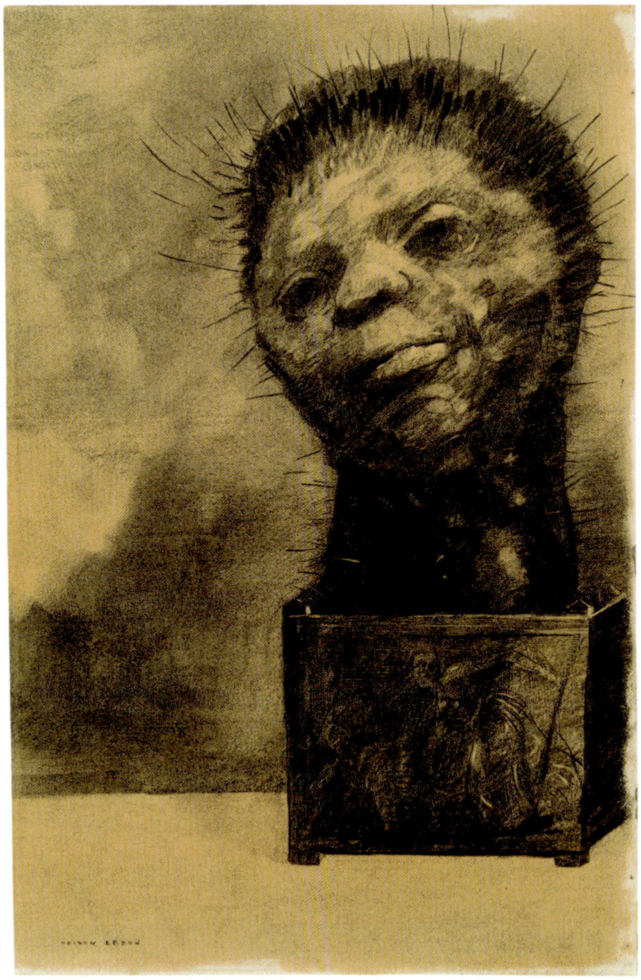

6 Odilon Redon, *Cactus Man*, 1881, various charcoals on light brown wove paper, Andrea Woodner, New York, Promised Gift to the National Gallery of Art, Washington

may have recalled a celebrated lithograph, Auguste Raffet's *Nocturnal Review* (1836), in which the specters of Napoleon and his troops were shown in a moonlit field, their weapons represented by simple diagonal lines, as in this drawing. The writer Théophile Gautier described the print as "drawn with a pointed ray of moonlight,"[23] which would be an effective description of Doré's romantic evocation of military heroism as well.

In the hands of romantic artists charcoal was used to achieve a range of tonalities and expressive vividness that accounts for the continuing attraction of draftsmen to the medium. By the middle of the century sticks of compressed charcoal became available, along with tins of charcoal powder that could be applied with a brush or a fingertip. The medium could be used with other materials such as white chalk and colored papers, as seen in Maxime Lalanne's *Alpine Castle above a Wooded Lake* (pl. 19), the apex of the period's fascination with creating tonal, even painterly charcoal drawings. Here the artist first covered the beige sheet with a translucent layer of charcoal to establish a tinted ground over which darker strokes could delineate the subject of the work, such as the blasted trees in the foreground and the lake and castle. The ground could also be lightened with erasures and scraping to evoke light playing over the water's surface and to define the rugged mountains as well as with white chalk to indicate highlights and the clouds encircling the distant mountain peaks. The valley depicted here was once a verdant, lushly wooded place, but it has been decimated by an unknown tragedy. Lalanne used procedures described in his book *Le fusain* (Charcoal), published in Paris in 1869, as well as other guides. These lessons were certainly read by

Redon, whose *noirs* (black drawings) reflect a knowledge of Lalanne's charcoals, which the younger artist must have seen in exhibitions in Bordeaux, where both men grew up. Redon later exhibited his own dramatic charcoal drawings in the Paris Salons (see fig. 6).[24] The importance of charcoal drawing continued into a new generation of artists, including Adolphe Appian and François Bonvin, who further explored the possibilities of this medium (see pls. 24 and 28).

Disagreements may remain concerning the meaning of romanticism and the roles of various artists and nations in shaping events. But no one is in doubt that a profound evolution occurred in the way we see our world. As Honoré de Balzac has written: "A man who has thought at his disposal is a sovereign. Kings command nations for a time, the artist commands whole centuries; he changes the face of things, he molds a revolution; he weighs on the globe, he fashions it."[25]

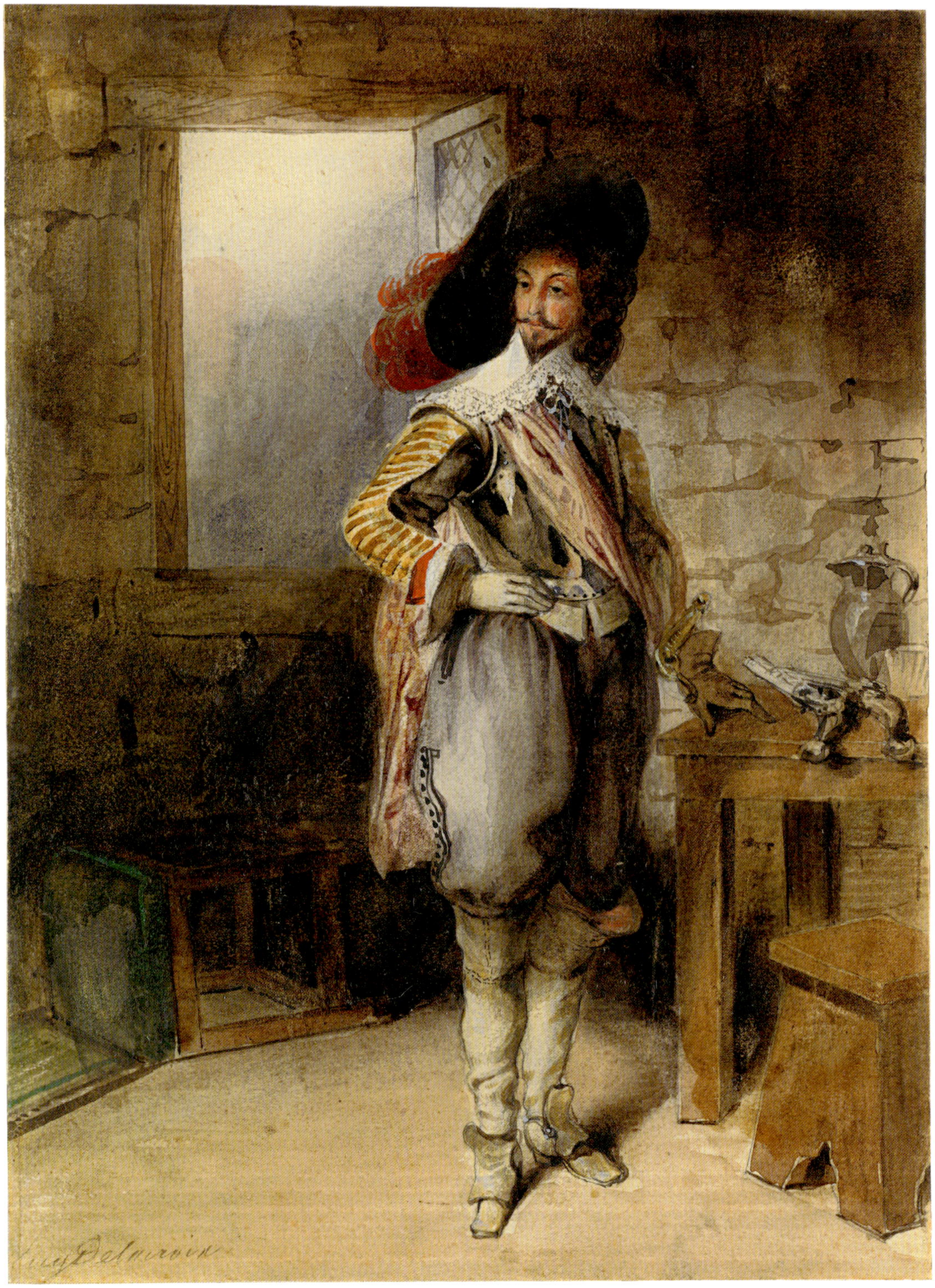

1 Eugène Delacroix, *An English Cavalier,* 1826/1830
watercolor, 210 × 150

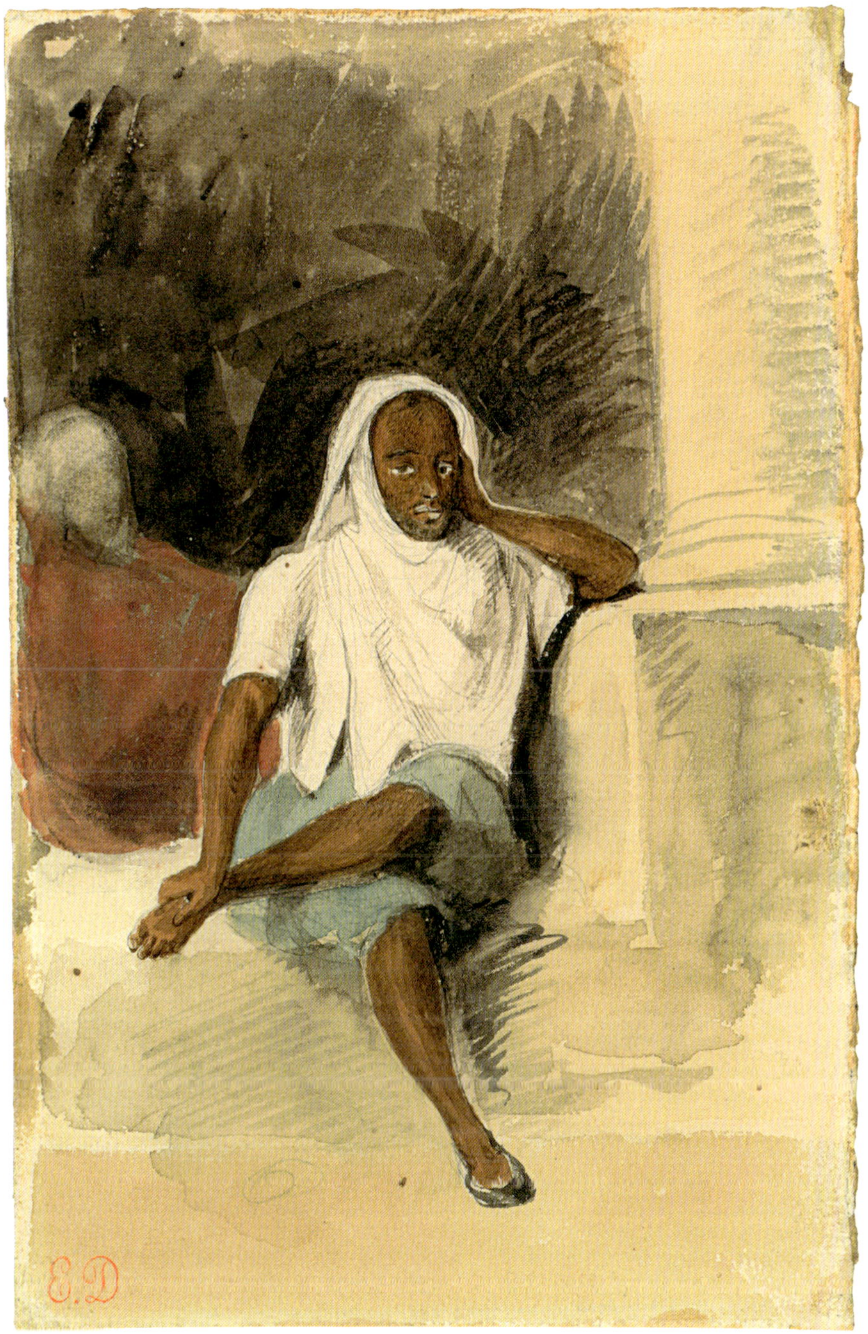

2 Eugène Delacroix, *The Moroccan Courier,* 1832
watercolor, 175 × 115

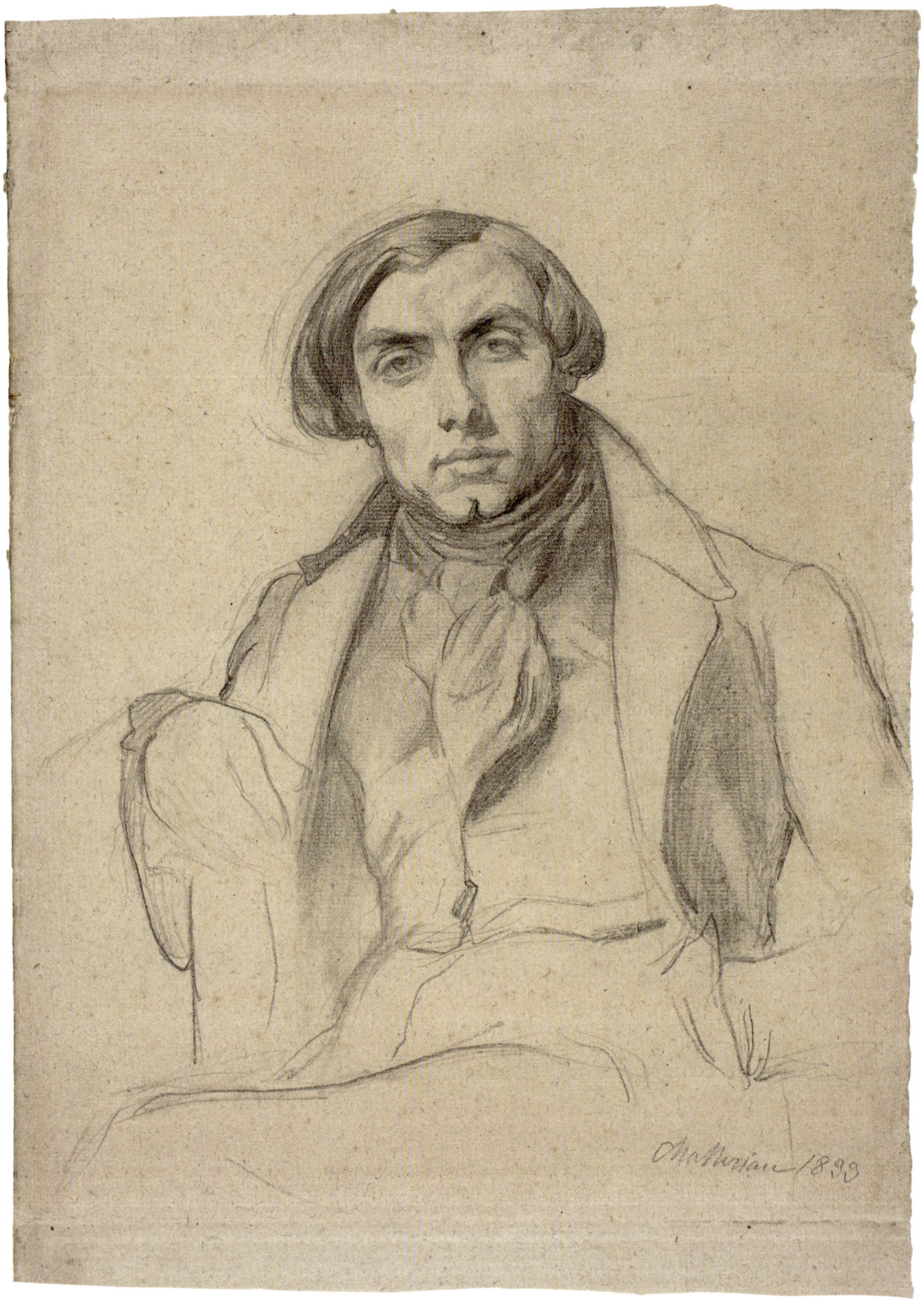

3 Théodore Chassériau, *Auguste Ottin,* 1833
graphite, 408 × 295

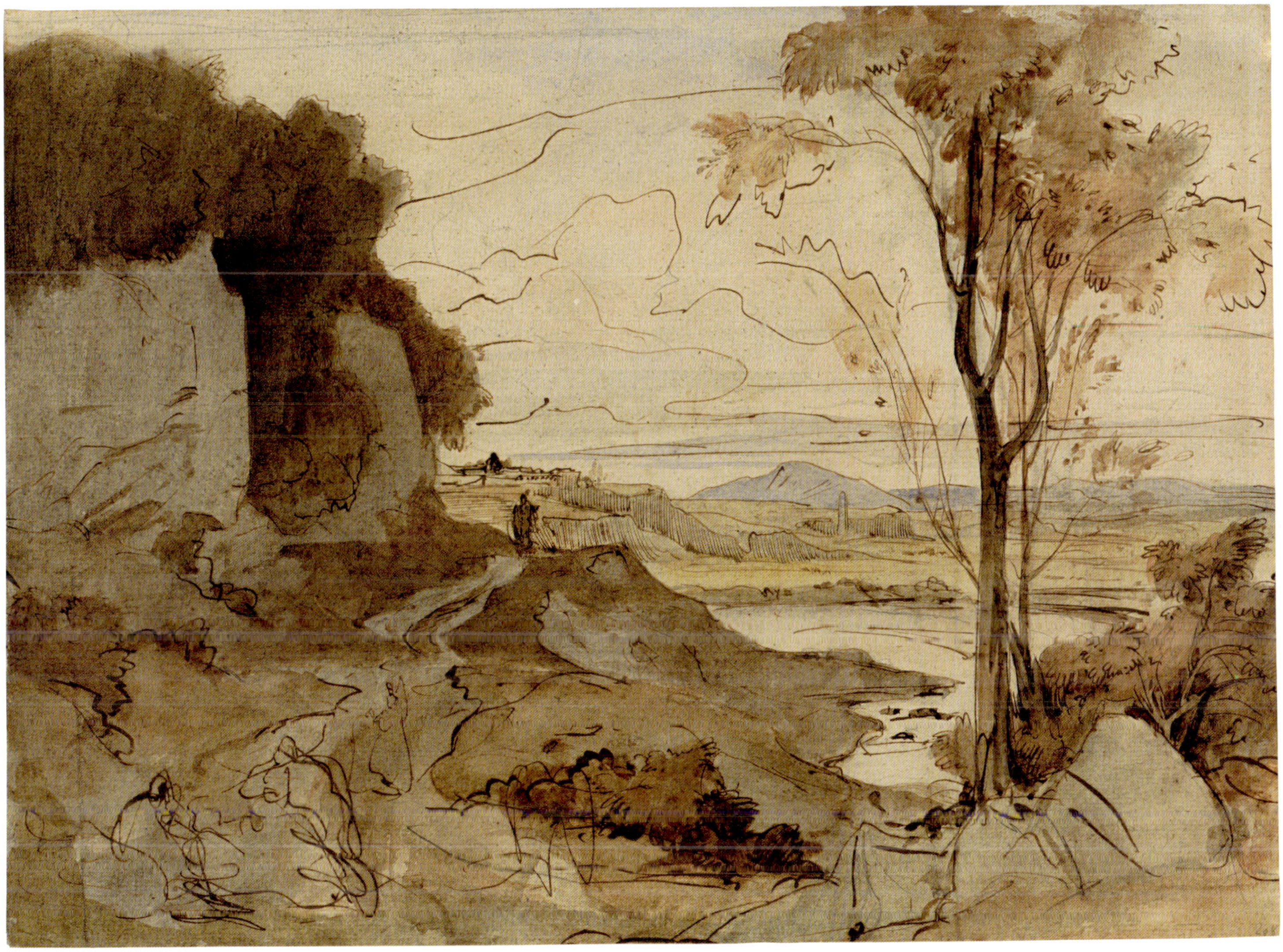

4 Théodore Caruelle d'Aligny, *Traveler in a Rocky Landscape,* c. 1830
pen and ink with wash and watercolor, 282 × 389

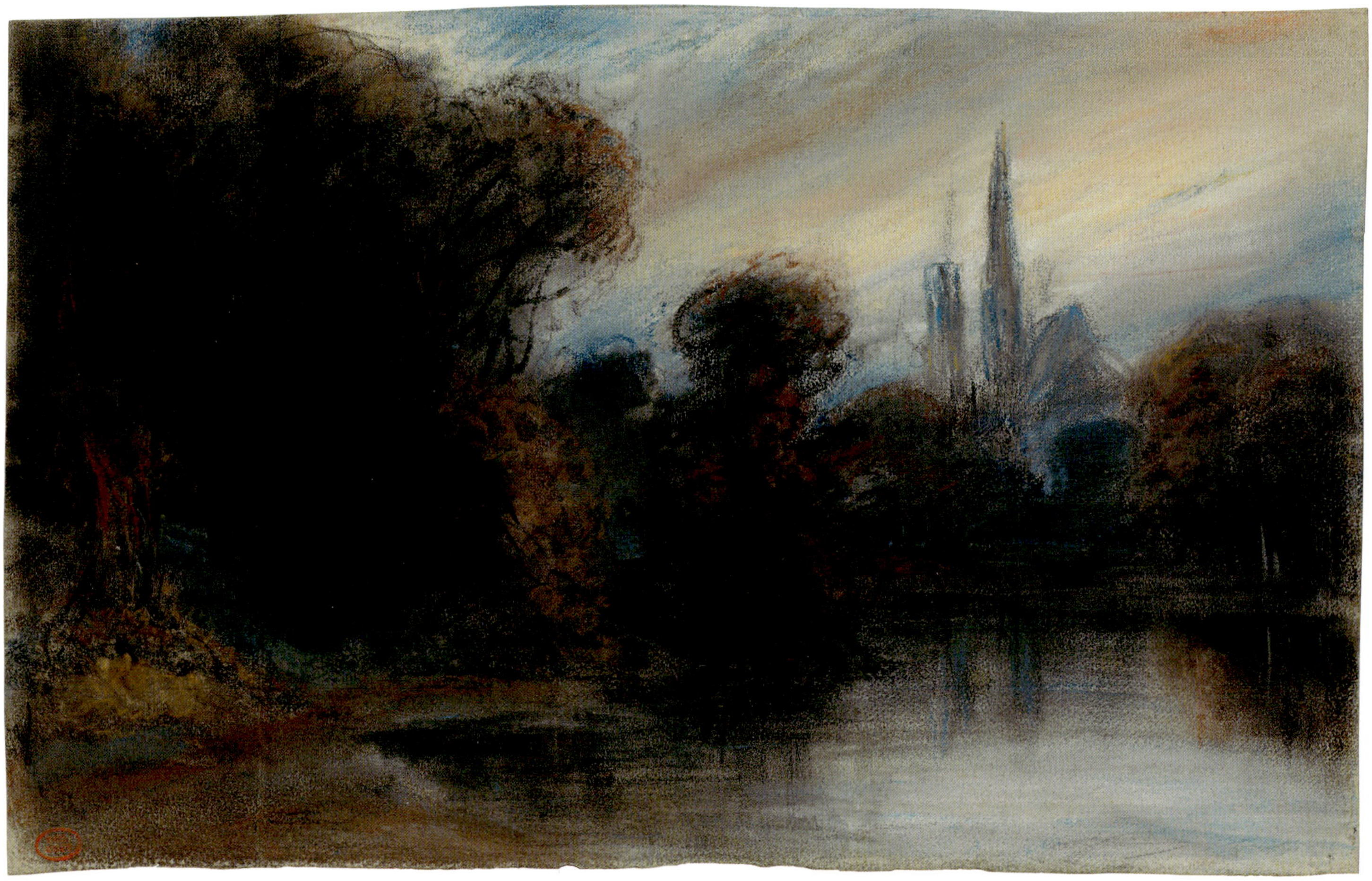

5 Paul Huet, *An Abbey by a Wooded Lake at Twilight*, c. 1831
pastel, 230 × 375

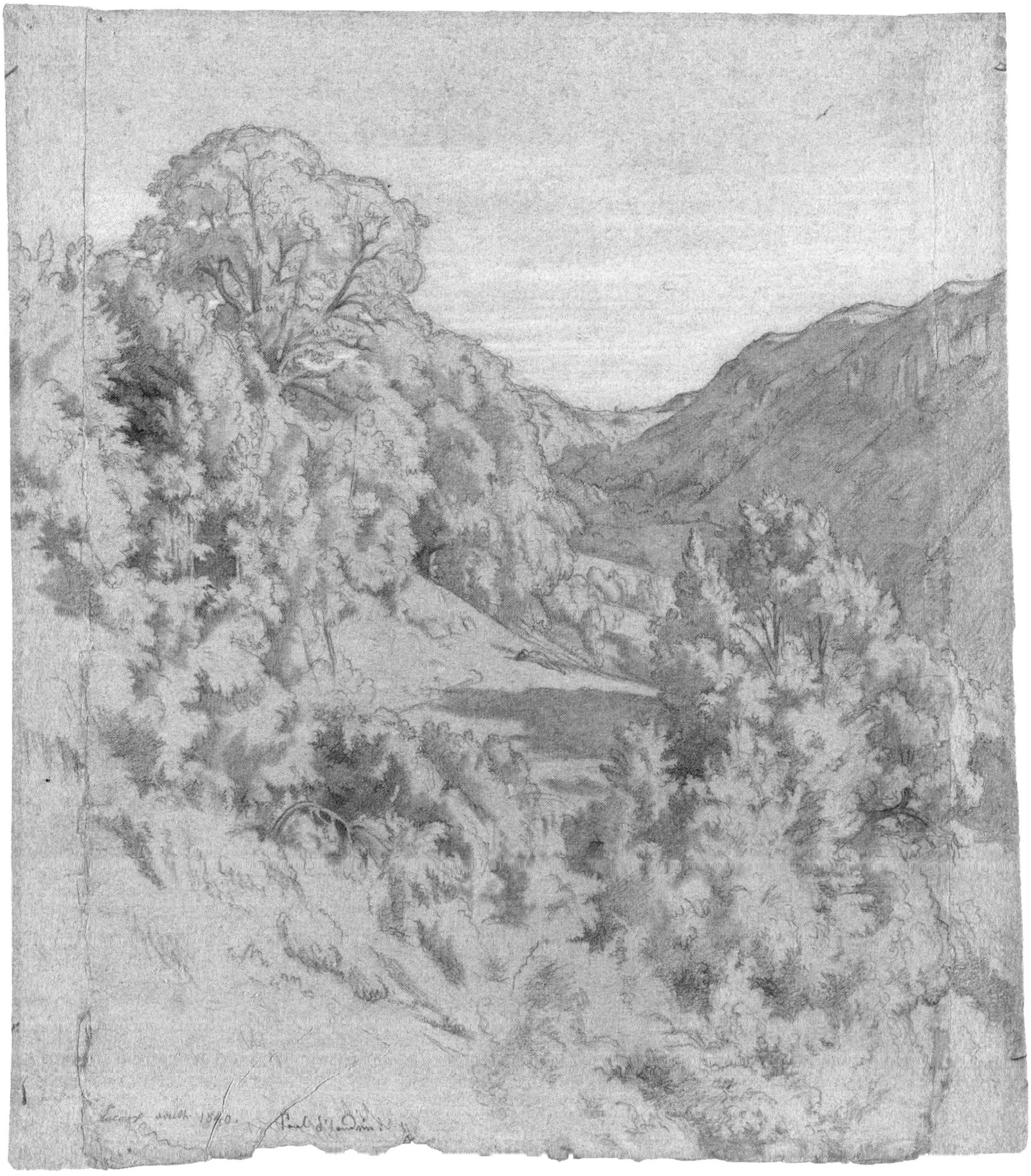

6 Jean-Paul Flandrin, *Sunlit Trees in a Valley near Lacoux,* 1840
black and white chalk, 289 × 267

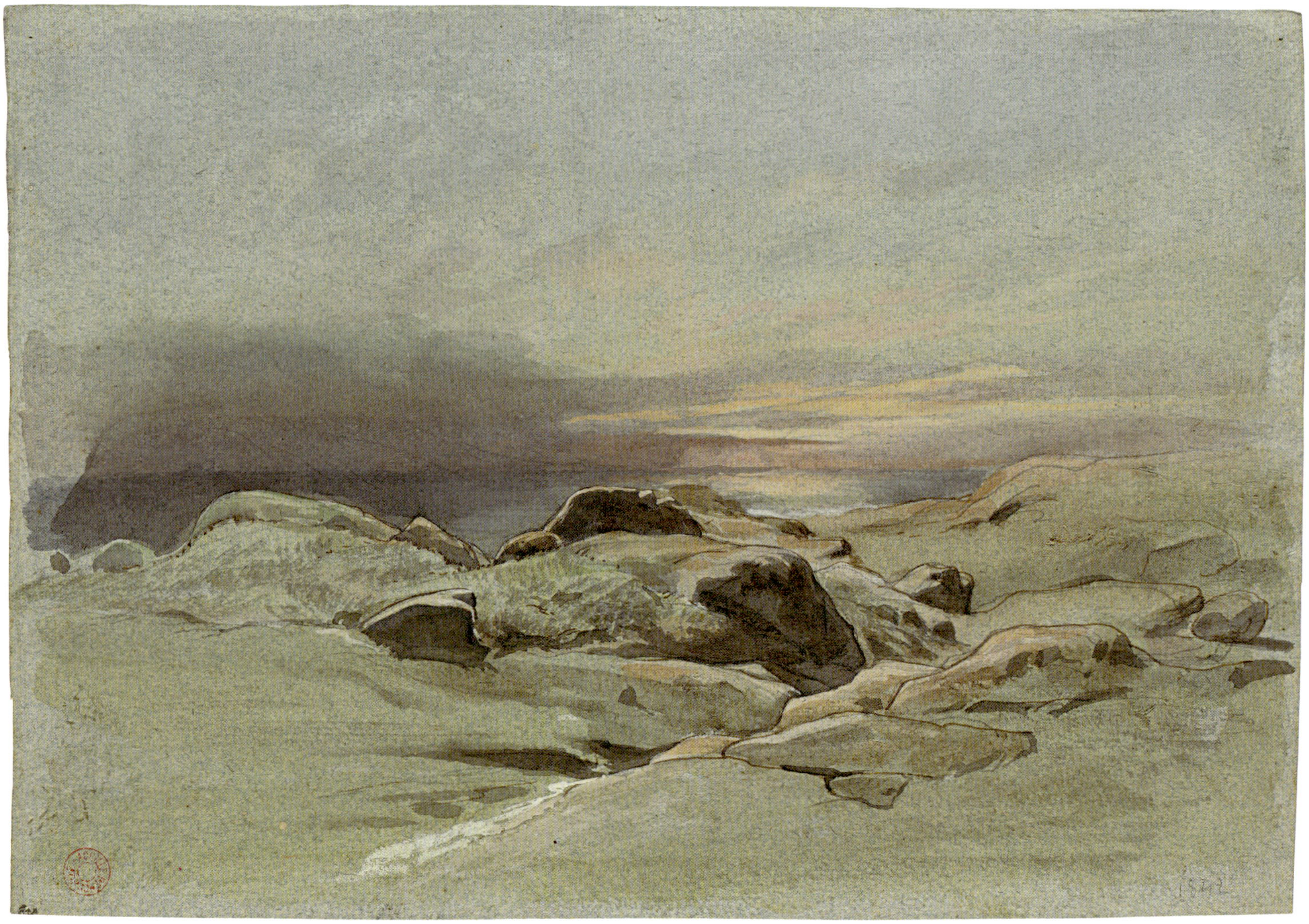

7 Jean-Achille Benouville, *Sunset from a Rocky Coastline,* 1842
watercolor and gouache with pen and ink, 201 × 289

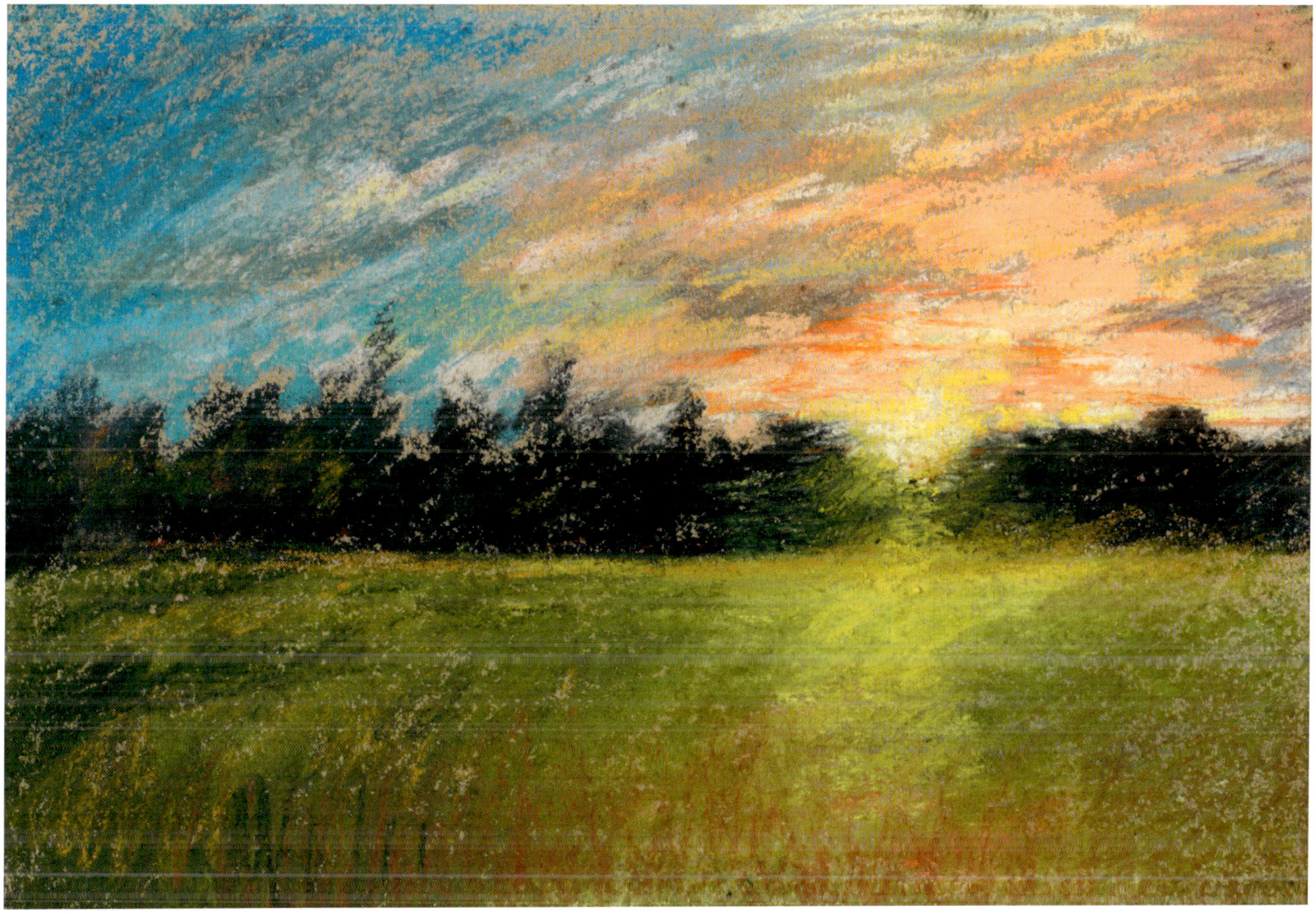

8 Paul Huet, *A Meadow at Sunset*
pastel, 135 × 195

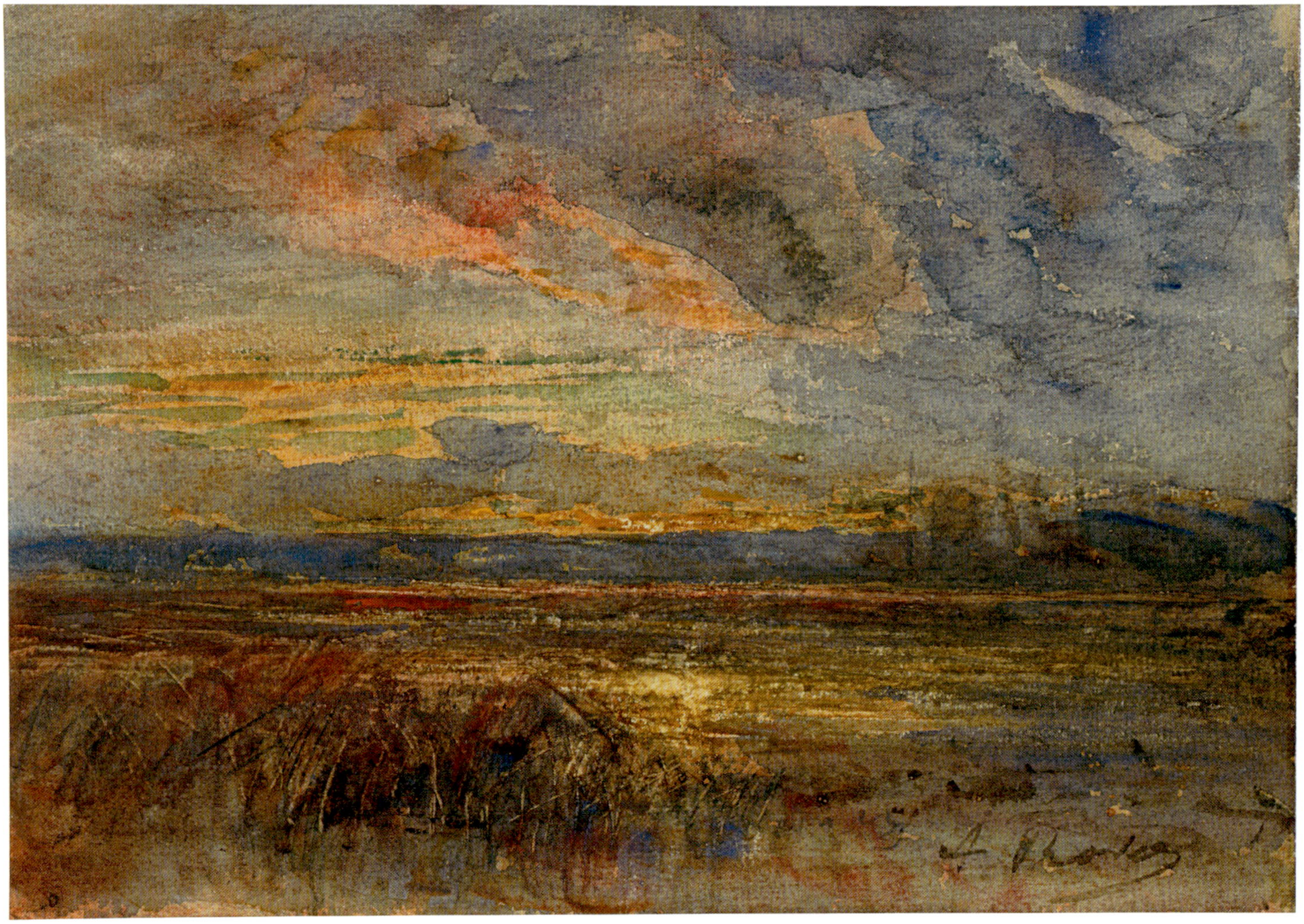

9 François-Auguste Ravier, *A Marsh at Sunset*
watercolor, 175 × 250

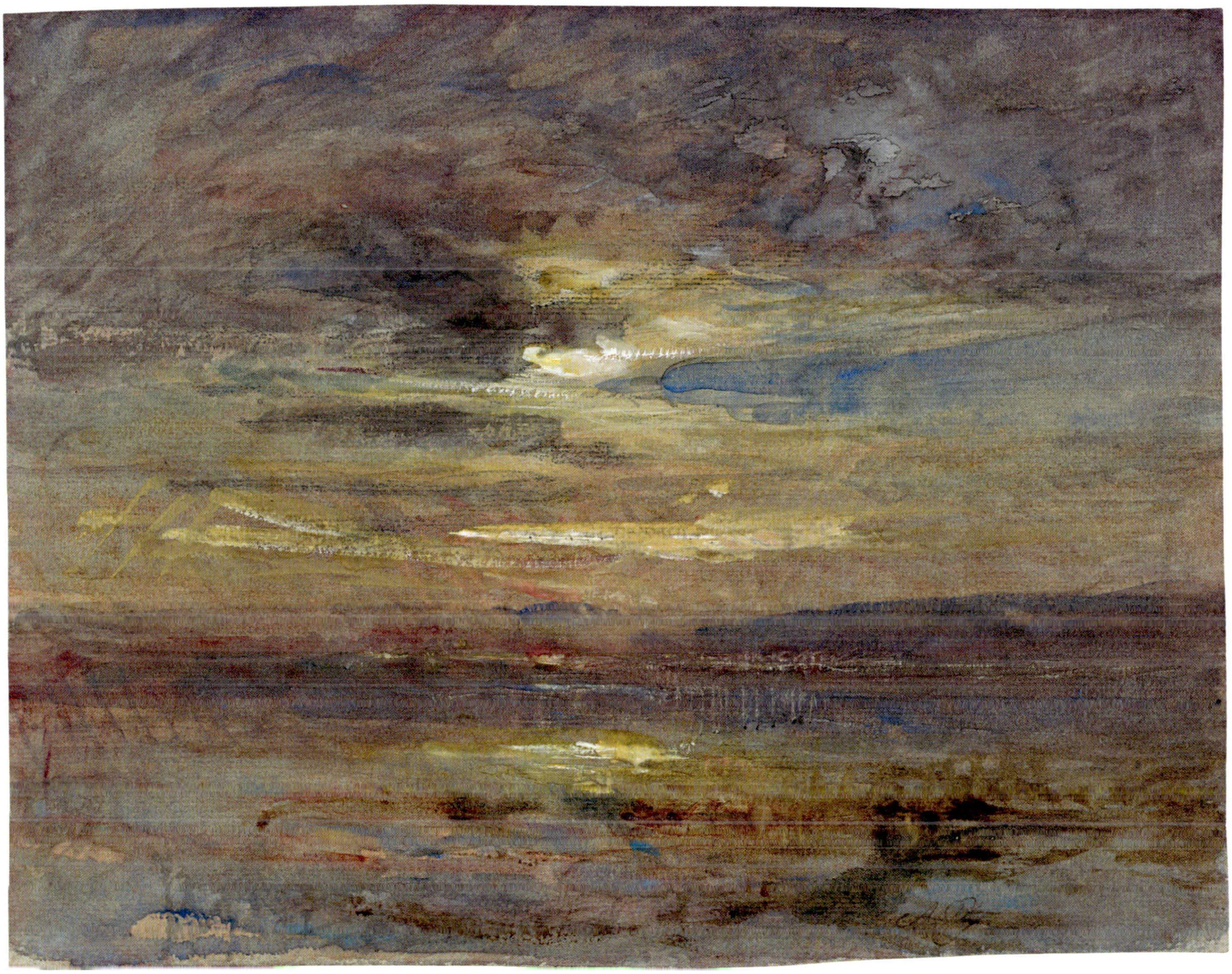

10 François-Auguste Ravier, *Sunset over a Pond*
watercolor with gouache, 200 × 230

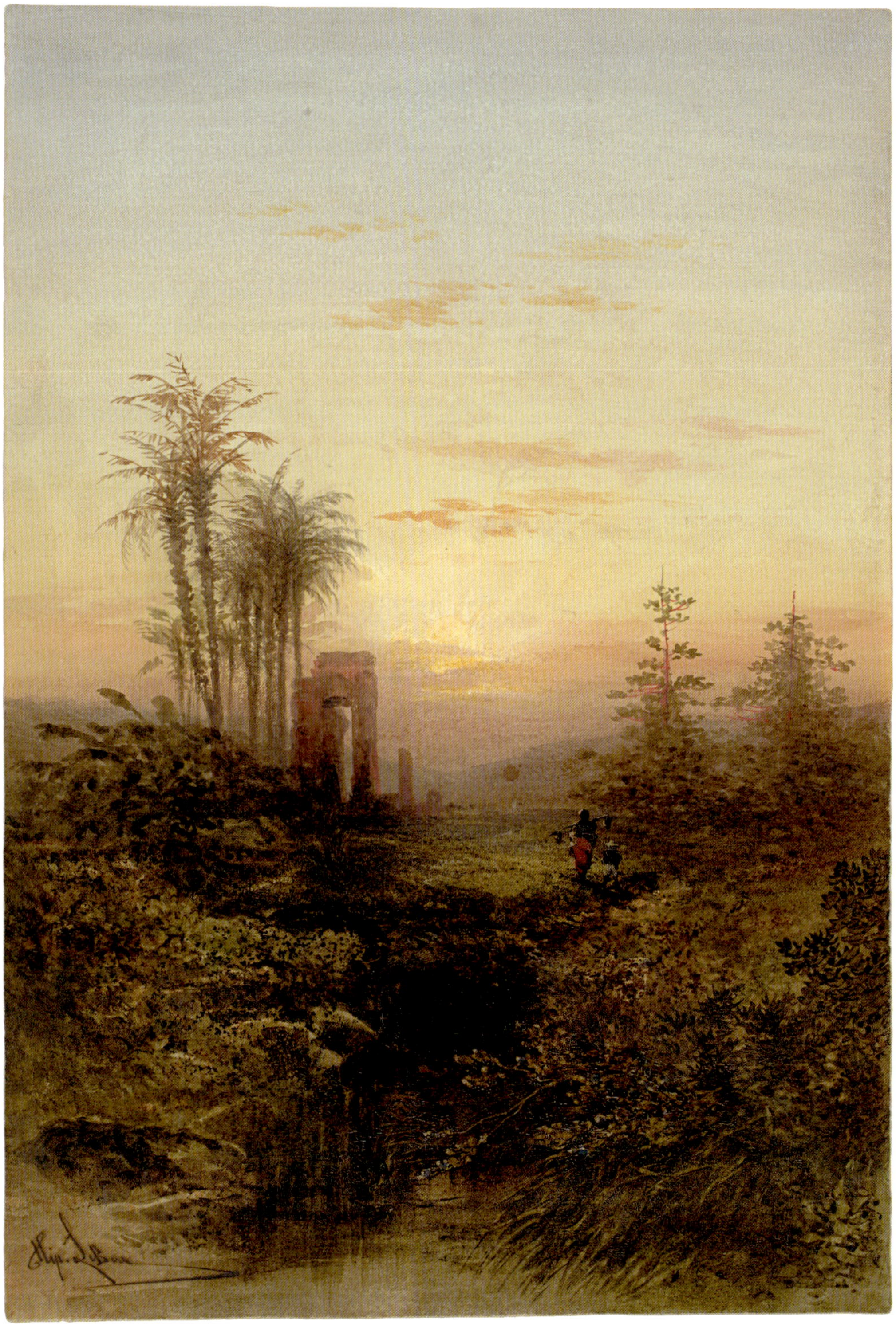

11 Gabriel-Hippolyte Lebas, *Sunset in an Oriental Landscape,* c. 1845
watercolor and gouache with gum arabic, 446 × 308

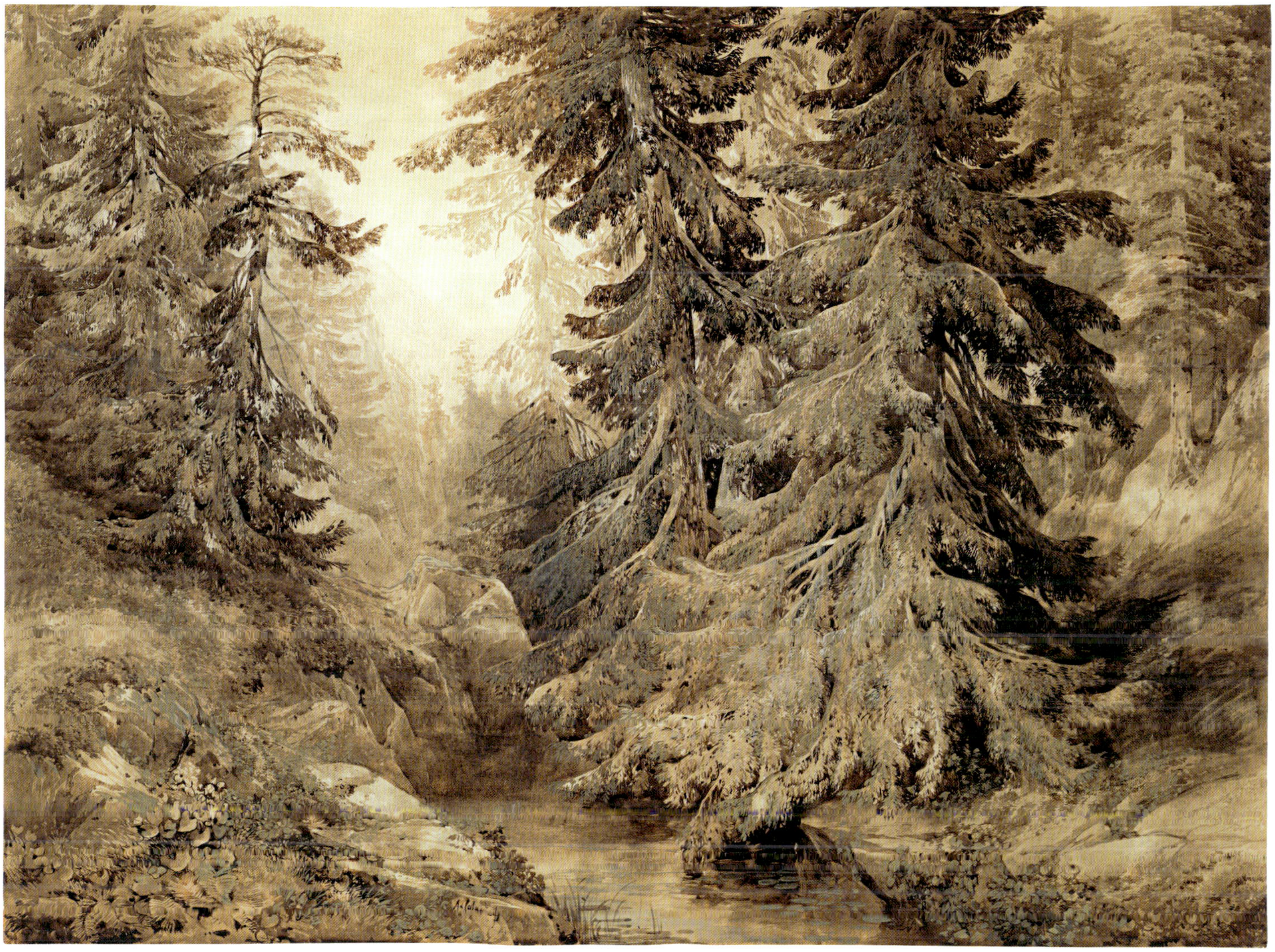

12 Alexandre Calame, *An Ancient Pine Forest with a Mountain Stream,* 1847
watercolor and gouache over charcoal, 612 × 842

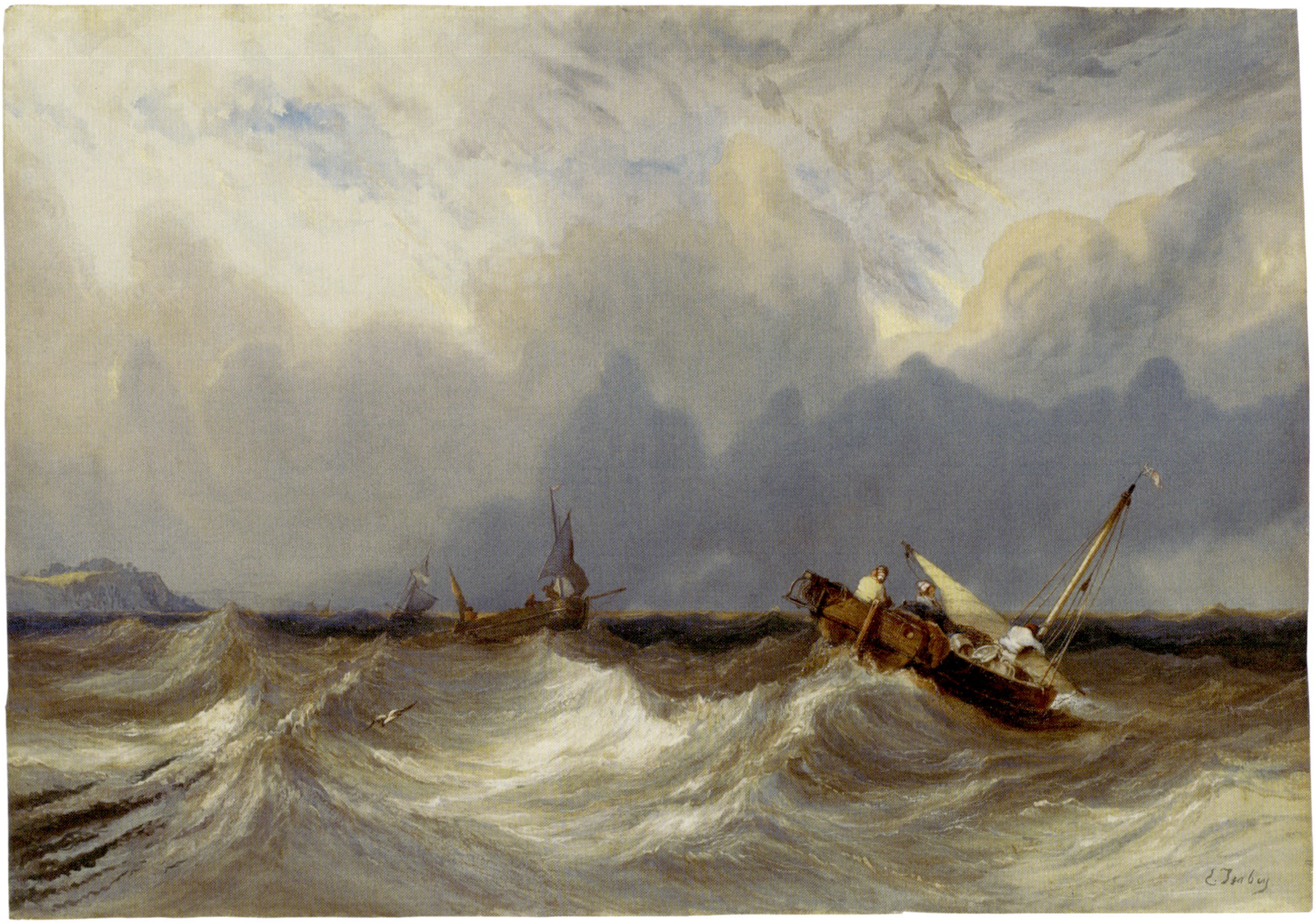

13 Eugène Isabey, *Fishing Boats Tossed before a Storm,* c. 1840
watercolor and gouache over black chalk, 639 × 933

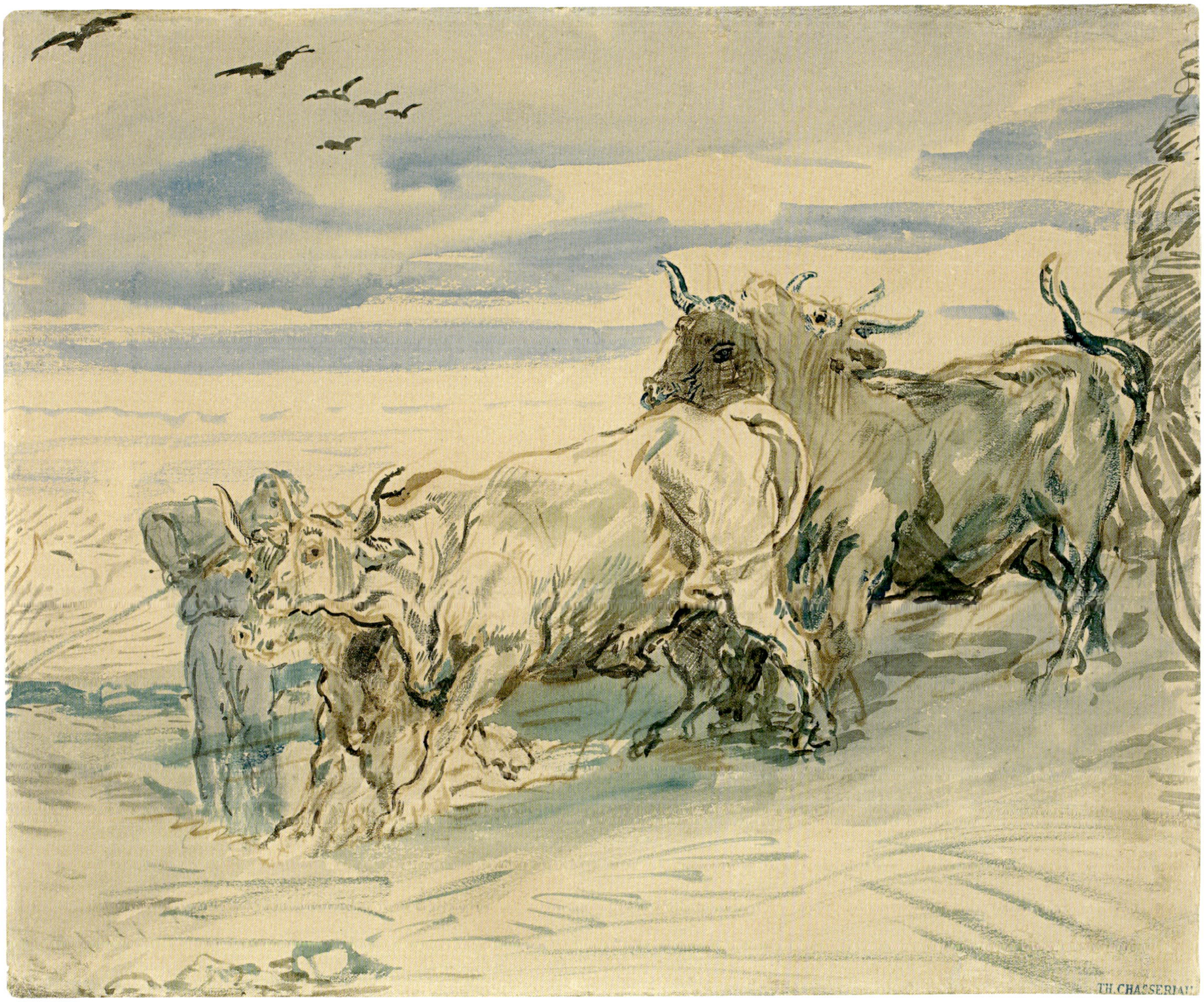

14 Théodore Chassériau, *Drover with Oxen Pulling a Cart,* 1840/1841
watercolor, 250 × 306

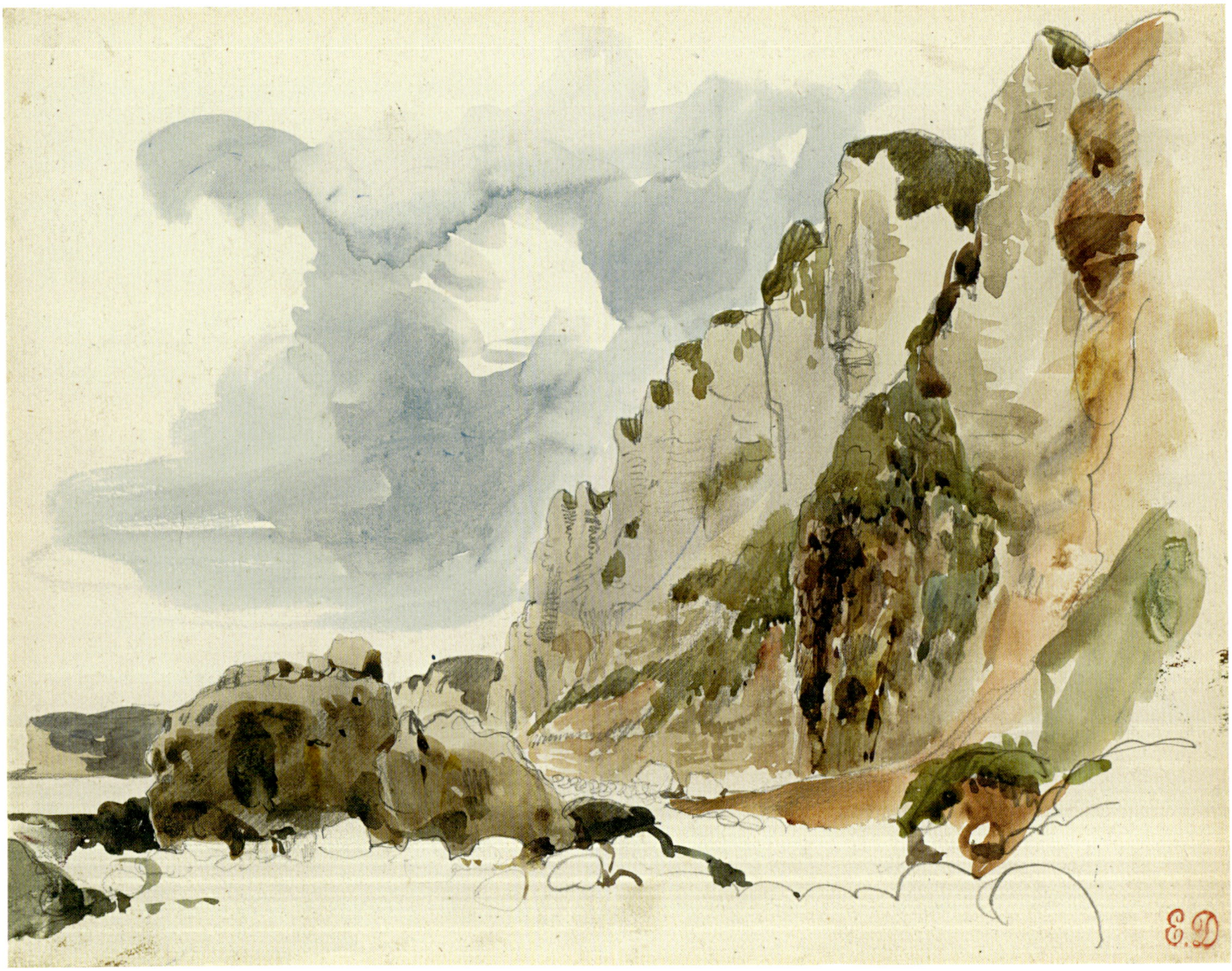

15 Eugène Delacroix, *The Normandy Cliffs,* 1849/1852
watercolor and graphite, 175 × 225

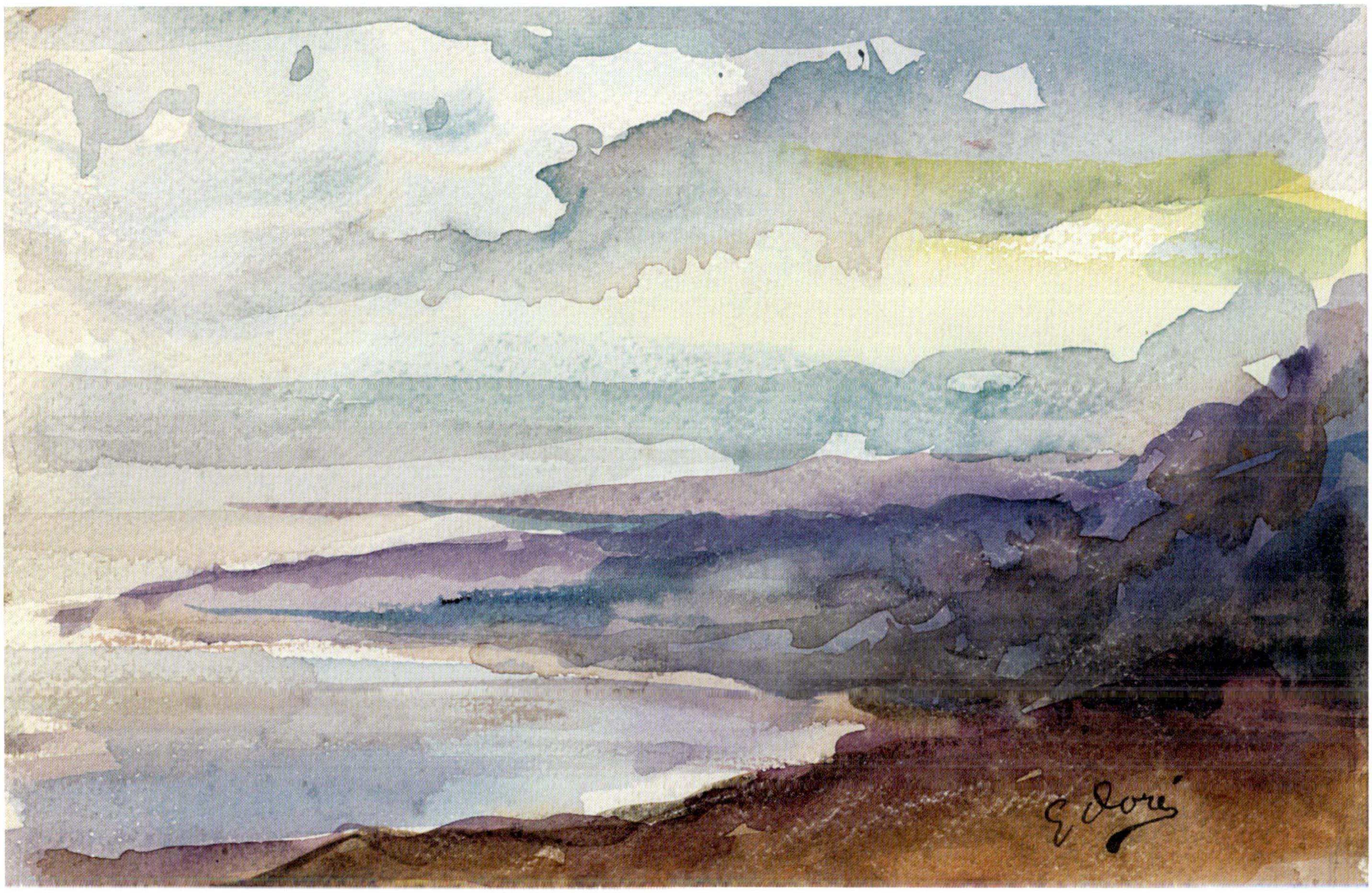

16 Gustave Doré, *Coastal Landscape*
watercolor, 130 × 205

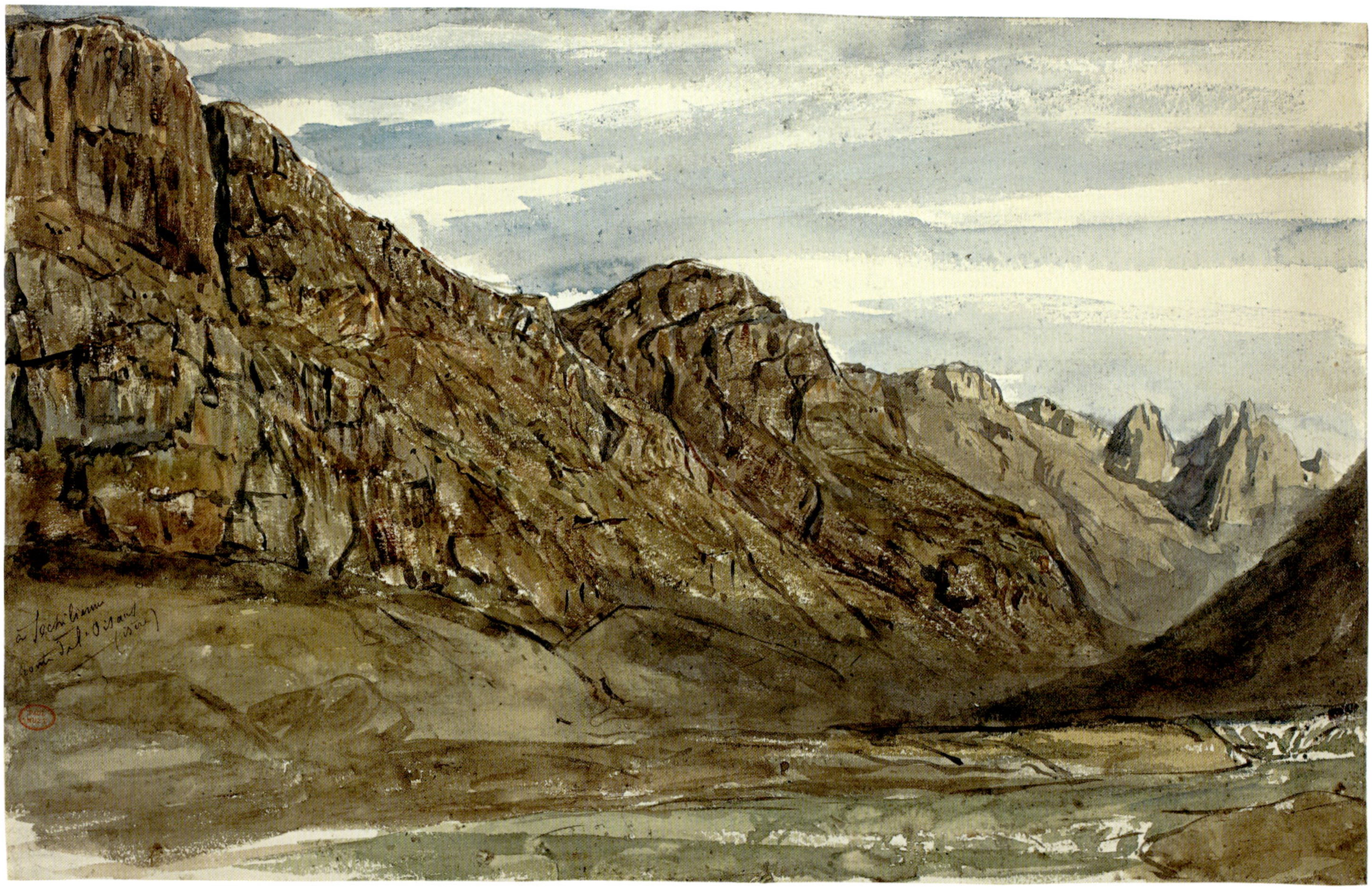

17 Paul Huet, *Rock Cliffs along the Romanche*, 1858
watercolor, 303 × 484

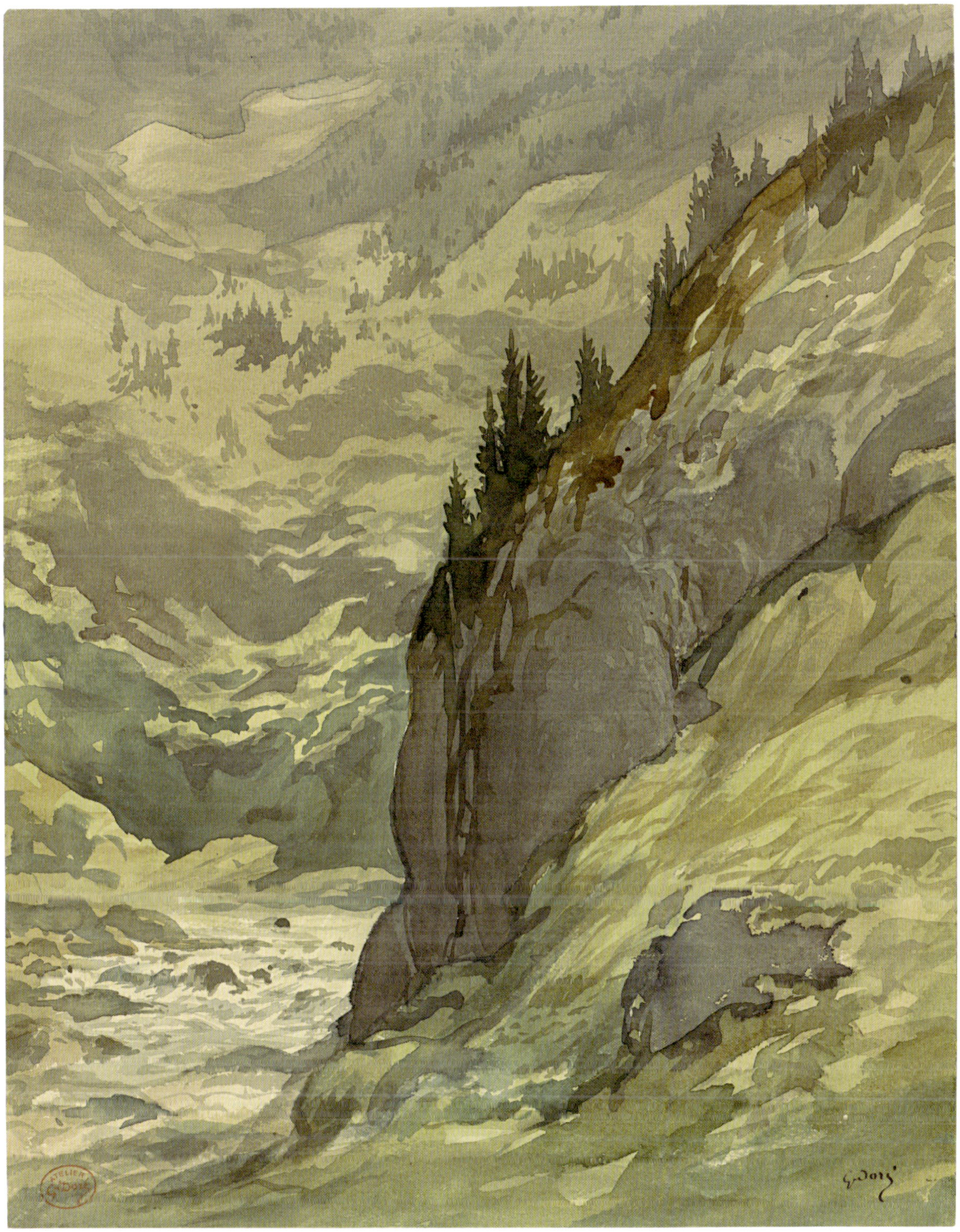

18 Gustave Doré, *A River Gorge in a Mountain Landscape*
watercolor, 387 × 305

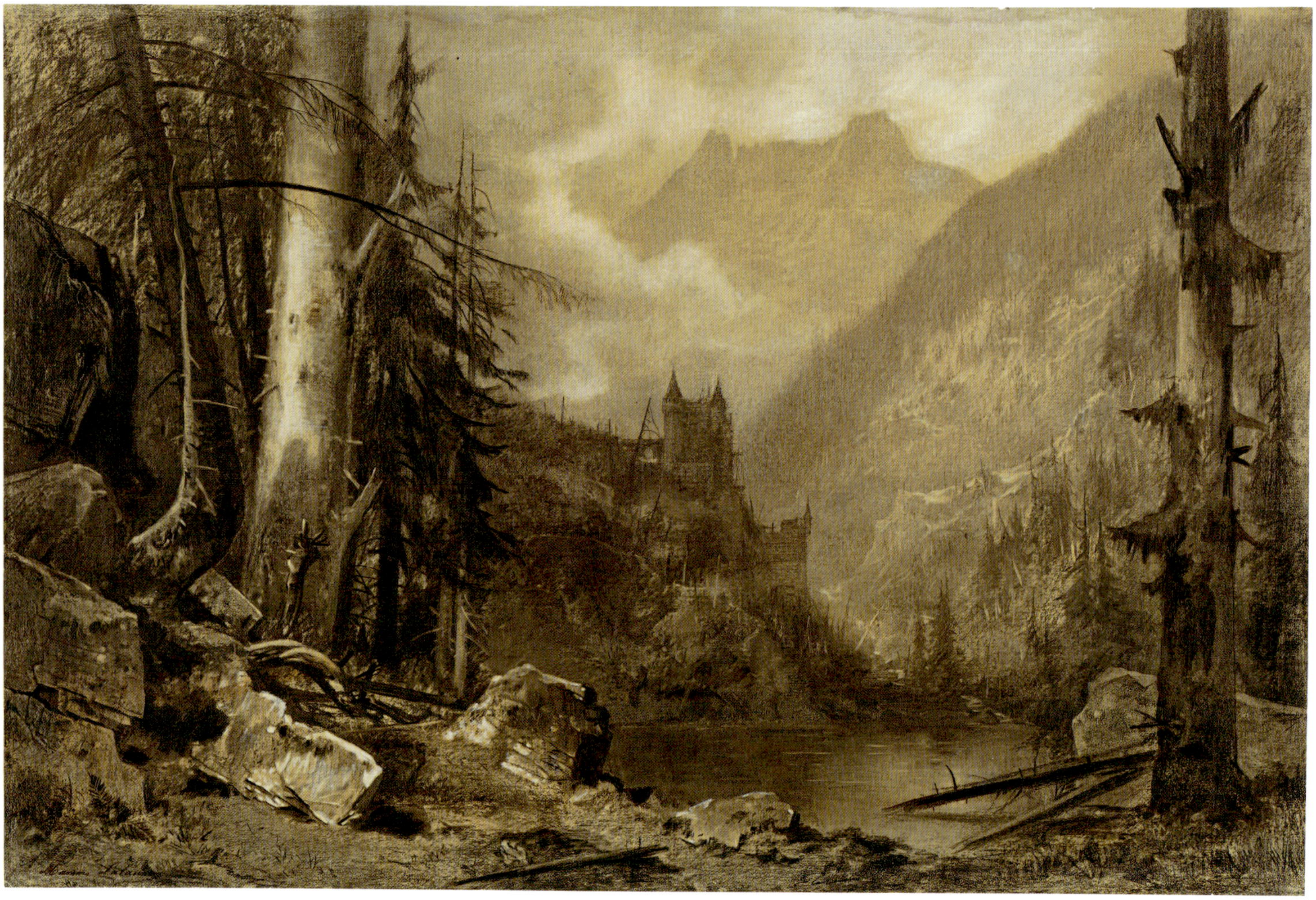

19 Maxime Lalanne, *Alpine Castle above a Wooded Lake,* c. 1870
charcoal and white chalk, 690 × 1030

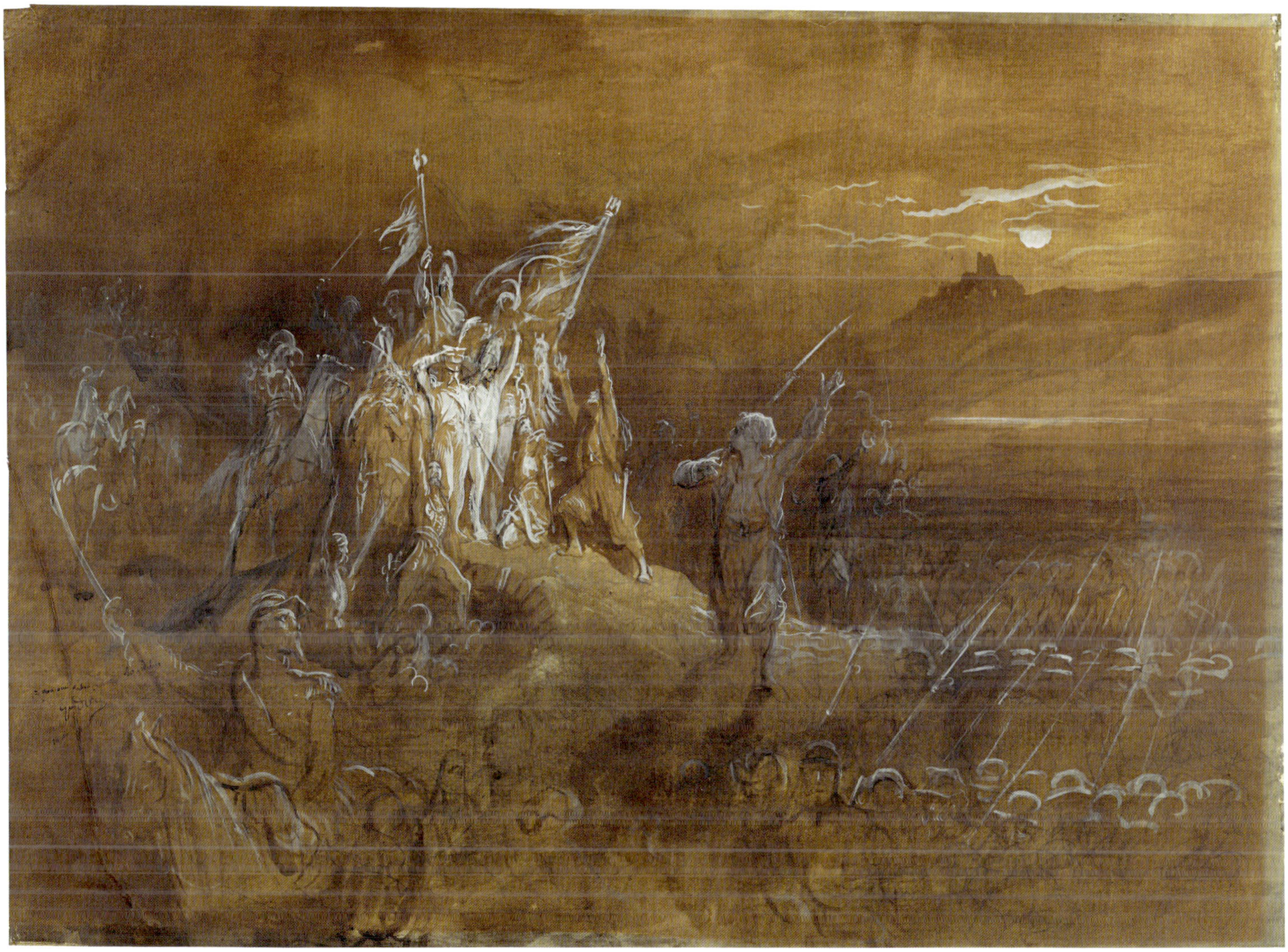

20 Gustave Doré, *The Shades of French Soldiers from the Past Exhort the Army to Victory,* 1870
brown wash and white gouache, 655 × 910

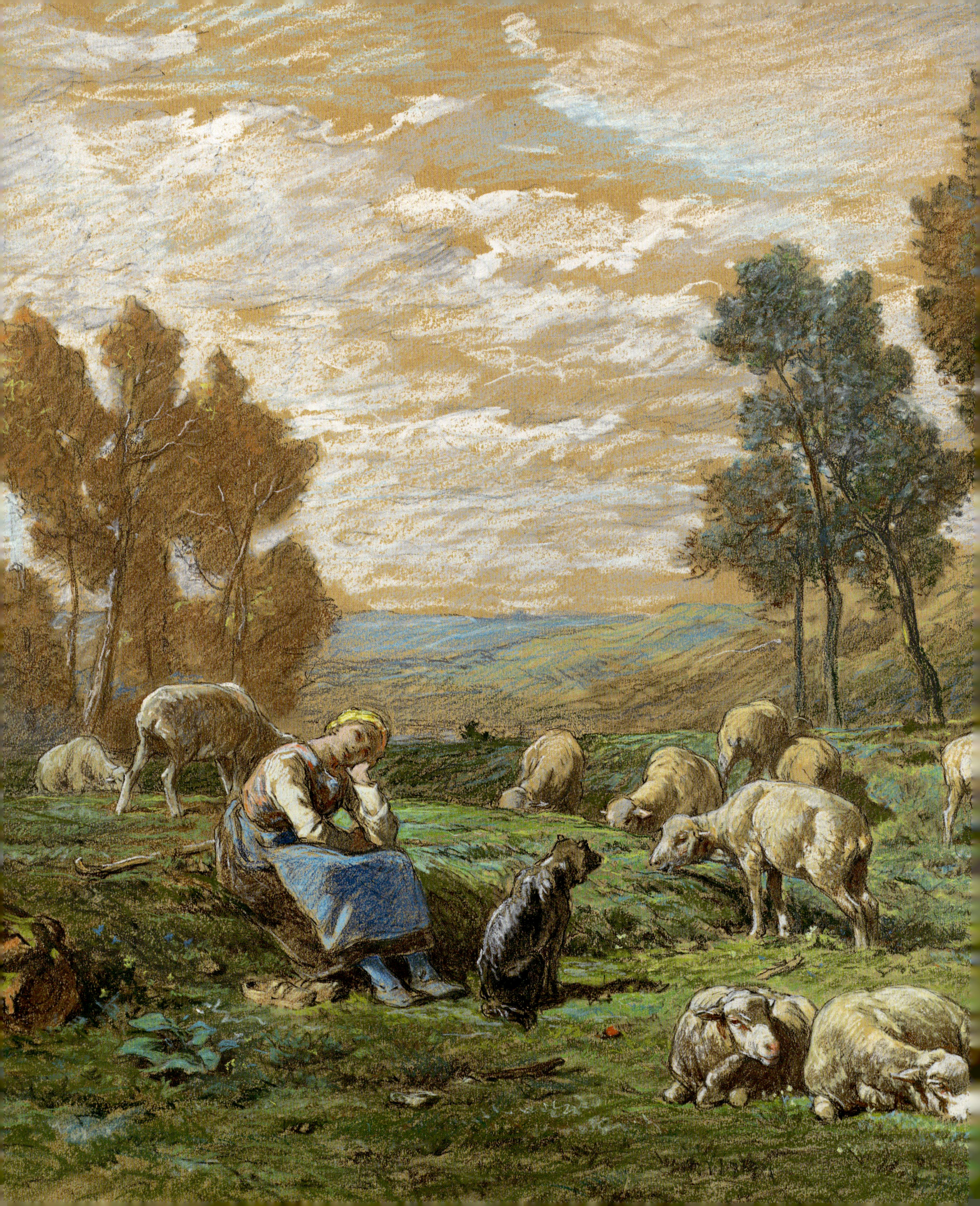

Rendering Reality: The Natural Landscape and Everyday Life

MARGARET MORGAN GRASSELLI

THE IDEA OF DRAWING the world as it truly appears was by no means an invention of the nineteenth century. Since the Renaissance, artists had been studying and drawing nature, with the goal of imitating it and learning from it. The difference in France in the 1800s — echoing the tendencies of seventeenth-century Holland — was the effort to draw people and places without idealizing them or imposing a personal artistic interpretation, rendering them as objectively and accurately as possible. While thus fixing their art in nature, artists also broadened their subject matter to include virtually every facet of the everyday world and contemporary life, no matter how humble or ordinary.

The French passion for drawing landscape and the elements of nature *sur le motif* is rooted in the examples of Nicolas Poussin (1594–1665) and Claude Lorrain (1604/1605–1682), the twin gods of French classical theory and style. Both made their careers in Italy, and both made a practice of roaming the Roman countryside to study and understand the vital structure of the landscape and its forms, the changing patterns of light, and the effects of weather. For them, such close study of the world was intended to enhance their ability to compose in the studio works that had the aura of authenticity yet featured an artfully idealized version of nature, better than it could appear in reality.

After a period in the 1700s when French landscape draftsmanship moved away from the classical ideals of Poussin and Claude, the neoclassical movement at the end of the eighteenth century placed new emphasis on the accurate rendering of nature as essential to the creation of authentic-looking paintings — even if those works, to our twenty-first century eyes, often seem profoundly stilted and *un*natural in their highly orchestrated presentation. Accuracy of observation and delineation was imperative, and artists were expected to treat nature with a new respect that allowed their imagination only the most limited scope.[1] That is not to say that the artist's role was reduced merely to the imitation of nature, or indeed that perfectly objective reproductions of what the artist saw were even possible. The draftsman necessarily had to bring selection and interpretation to what he or she saw, whether in the style, quality, and precision of the execution or in conscious or unconscious omissions or additions that might be made in depicting the motif. There was always an element of art or artfulness in every rendering, even as the goal was to approach as closely as possible the actual appearance of the landscape, figure, or object being observed.

Through the early years of the nineteenth century, most of the groundbreaking work in the creation of a French landscape style and theory took place in Italy, where the southern climate, strong sunlight, and generally cooperative weather allowed artists to work outdoors for prolonged periods. The best young prospects, all of them academically trained, were sent to Rome to study the great art of antiquity and the revered artists of the Renaissance and the baroque, but a key part of their education was the study of nature during rambles and sojourns in the Roman *campagna*. Jean-Baptiste-Camille Corot (1796–1875) was one of the most gifted of the new landscapists, who, while being immersed in the ideals of structure and restraint that were essential parts of the classical tradition, were also committed to the direct experience and faithful portrayal of nature. *A Clump of Trees at Civita Castellana* of 1826 (fig. 1), executed with both elegance and

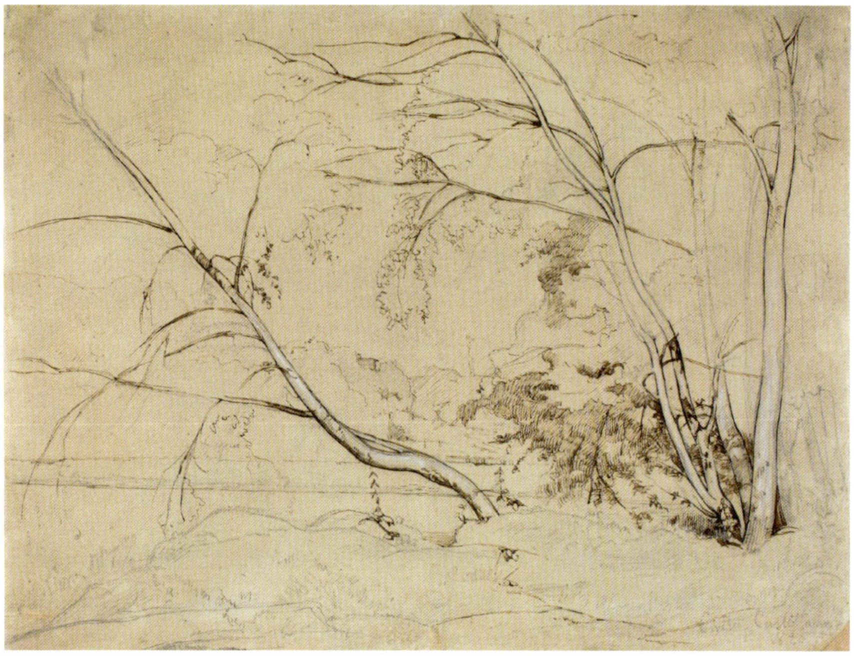

1 Jean-Baptiste-Camille Corot, *Clump of Trees at Civita Castellana*, 1826, pen and brown ink and graphite with white heightening, National Gallery of Art, Washington, Gift of Walter H. and Leonore Annenberg, in Honor of the 50th Anniversary of the National Gallery of Art, 1990

precision, shows the delicate balance Corot could achieve between these two forces in his early plein-air sketches.

Young artists like Corot who had studied the Italian landscape so assiduously, and with such enjoyment, not surprisingly wanted to continue to draw outdoors after their return to France. The French countryside around Paris, however, did not have the same appeal as Italy, and there were limited opportunities to draw a nature that remained essentially untamed. The wild environs of the forest of Fontainebleau, just thirty-five miles south of Paris, offered the perfect solution.[2] By the 1820s it had become a magnet for a host of painters and draftsmen who were attracted by its robust topography, primeval forest, towering rocks, and rugged vistas. The hamlet of Barbizon, situated at the western edge of the forest, eventually became the central gathering place for artists who wanted to experience and draw an unspoiled nature — especially those who had not been able to make the trip to Italy. "Barbizon" soon became synonymous with a new French school of landscape painting that eschewed classical reformation and focused instead on the representation of the world in as natural a way as possible.

One of the most innovative of the new landscapists was Théodore Rousseau, an exceptionally talented painter and draftsman who made frequent visits to the forest from the 1830s onward. In the absence of an Italian sojourn, Rousseau, like many of his contemporaries, turned instead to northern artists for his models, especially Jacob van Ruysdael (c. 1628–1682) and Meindert Hobbema (1638–1709), whose landscape visions had much in common with the character of the area around Barbizon. In both his drawings and his paintings, Rousseau sought to make "portraits" of trees,[3] objective studies that expressed their vital character and captured their individual qualities. He worked in a wide variety of media and was as adept with the brush as with pen and chalks, but while his drawings tend to present a relatively detailed reality, in his oils he studied more general effects of color, light, and shade, creating images that were both atmospheric and evocative. The nearly monochromatic *Sunset from the Forest of Fontainebleau* (pl. 22) is a particularly luminous example of his work in oil on paper, looking out through a dark framework of trees and foliage from the edge of the forest toward the sun setting beyond distant fields. Rousseau's intense study of nature is evident in every stroke, but at the same time, the sunset subject gives this scene a clear romantic twist. Indeed, Rousseau's works often teeter between realism and romanticism, for as much as his landscapes are rooted in his close scrutiny of nature, they are often imbued with a romantic moodiness or emotional aura that links them in spirit to many of the drawings discussed in the previous section of the present catalogue.[4]

Among the major Barbizon artists, the one who most influenced the course of French draftsmanship in the middle years of the nineteenth century was Jean-François Millet, whose choice of subject matter and unique vision set him apart from his fellows. Instead of the forest landscape, he painted the people who toiled nearby, the rustic laborers who worked the fields and the impoverished peasants who gathered wood and lived off what they could glean from the forest and harvested fields. For Millet, their daily struggle and their close association with nature and the soil brought them nearer to God, and in his depictions — both painted and drawn, especially in highly finished pastels — he endowed them with deep spirituality and a monumental dignity. Yet Millet's observation of nature and his attention to the authentic portrayal of his subjects were paramount, and his drawings played an essential role in rooting his art in life. Millet's early preoccupation with the human figure is evident in *Nude Reclining in a Landscape* (pl. 21), made a few years before he settled in Barbizon in 1849 and preceding a series of at least fifty studies he made of the posed nude around 1847.[5] More typical of Millet's considerable gifts as a draftsman are compositions like *Twilight* (fig. 2), dating from about 1859/1863 and executed in the Conté crayon Millet preferred, here combined with pastel and white chalk to add both light and subtle touches of color to the scene. Executed as a complete work of art in itself,[6] it is drawn almost entirely using tone and hardly a single contour, silhouetting the shadowy figures against the last light of the waning day and coaxing their forms out of the dusk-shrouded landscape. Such a drawing stands as the direct precursor to the neo-impressionist Conté crayon drawings of Georges Seurat (pl. 76) and Charles Angrand (pl. 81) from the 1880s.

Sharing Millet's interest in peasant subjects was another Barbizon artist, Charles-Émile Jacque, represented in the Dyke collection with an outstanding pastel, *The Shepherdess* (pl. 27). Jacque's particular skill in the rendering of sheep is much in evidence here, but so too is his talent as an observer of the

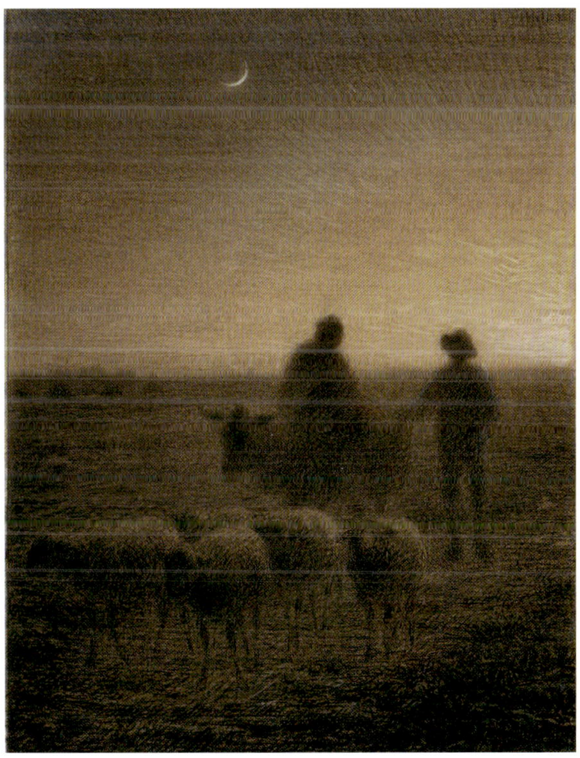

2 Jean-François Millet, *Twilight*, 1859/1863, Conté crayon with pastel, Museum of Fine Arts, Boston, Gift of Quincy Adams Shaw through Quincy A. Shaw, Jr., and Mrs. Marian Shaw Haughton, 1917

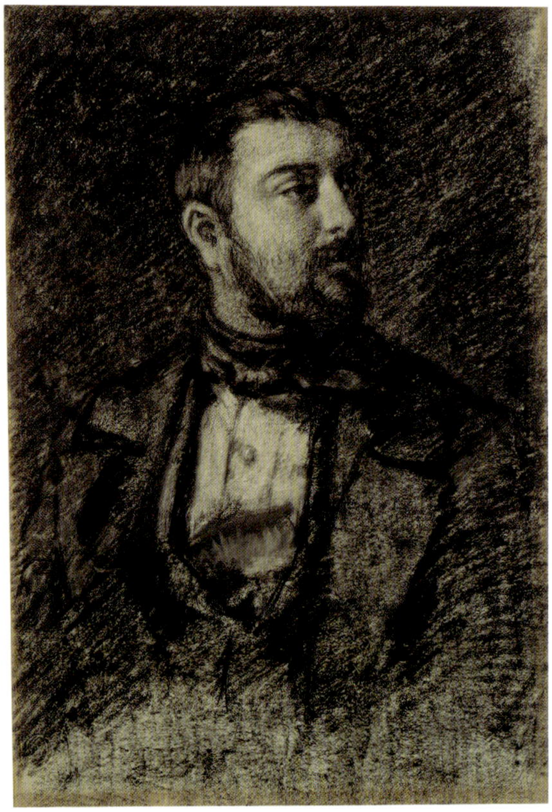

3 Gustave Courbet, *Portrait of a Man (Urbain Cuénot?)*, 1847/1848, black chalk and charcoal, Andrea Woodner, New York

natural landscape. For Jacque, as for Millet and other contemporaries, pastel offered a means through which the artist could approach even more closely the appearance of nature by replicating its colors as well as its forms. Pastel had risen to prominence in the eighteenth century, especially as a medium for portraiture, but had fallen out of favor by the early 1800s. For the Barbizon artists, however, the easily portable pastel sticks proved to be a useful tool in their efforts to reproduce as exactly as possible what they observed, as they could use them in direct confrontation with nature as well as in the studio.[7] The popularity of pastel grew rapidly in the second half of the nineteenth century, reaching new heights of innovation and expression in the hands of the impressionists, especially Edgar Degas, whose experimental approach to the medium stretched its possibilities well beyond traditional limits (pl. 42).

Rivaling Millet in his mastery of tonal drawings was Gustave Courbet (1819–1877), the artist whose name is nearly synonymous with realism in mid-century France. Radicalized by the social and political upheavals caused by the Revolution of 1848 — which had also precipitated Millet's move to Barbizon — Courbet quickly shook up the art world with paintings of unconventional images that were considered by contemporary art critics to be disturbingly iconoclastic. It is in fact to Courbet's paintings that the term "realism" was attached as early as 1851, and not at all in a complimentary way.[8] As explained by Francis Wey, writing in defense of his friend Courbet, the object of realism was "to reproduce objects such as chance has made them, without choice, without arrangement, and to insist absolutely on this maxim, 'Nothing is beautiful except the truth.'"[9] The ideas expressed by Wey conform quite closely to the goals of the Barbizon landscapists, but where Courbet shocked his audience was in his large-scale figure paintings and his selection of subjects that were regarded as inappropriate for exhibition at the Salon and other public venues. Courbet's realism was far more palatable in such drawings as his *Portrait of a Man* of about 1847/1848 (fig. 3), but that is in part because portraits by their very nature are expected to be accurate representations of the sitter. This drawing undoubtedly met that requirement, but in a world that was used to the refined and precisely drawn pencil portraits of Ingres (see p. xii, fig. 3; and p. 35, fig. 5) and his many emulators, Courbet's rugged handling of the chalks and the lack of a smoothly polished finish to the likeness would probably have startled his audience.

In a century when color played such a major role in raising the stature of drawings as works of art, some of the great technical and stylistic innovations involved monochrome drawings made with black chalk and charcoal, as has already been seen in examples by Millet and Courbet. *Fusinisme* (from *fusain*, the French word for charcoal) represents another important development in this area, as artists took advantage of the exceptional crumbliness and dustiness of charcoal (which could be smudged, rubbed, erased, scratched, and manipulated in myriad ways and then sometimes heightened with white) to create images of remarkable tonal variety and colorlike richness. Maxime Lalanne was the leading proponent of the technique (pls. 19, 25), not only exploring and pushing in unexpected directions the artistic possibilities offered by the many new types of charcoal that became available to artists toward the middle of the century[10] but also writing a treatise on it, *Le fusain* (Paris, 1869). Equally adept and inventive in his handling of the medium was Adolphe Appian, whose hauntingly beautiful view across a forest pond at dusk (pl. 24) evokes Barbizon and the forest of Fontainebleau where the first experiments with tonal charcoal drawing took place.

The *fusinistes* quickly expanded their subject matter beyond landscapes alone, especially to scenes of genre and everyday life, all the while stretching the boundaries of the medium. Very different from the visions of Lalanne and Appian is *The Conversation* (fig. 4) by the animal painter Rosa Bonheur (1822–1899), in which she draws with unexpected crispness, precision, and sharp focus a charming scene of a shepherd tending his flock and communing with his dog. Still another interpretation of the medium is provided by the realist François Bonvin in his rendering of a peasant woman kneeling before a fireplace in a cottage interior (pl. 28), which is drawn with a quiet restraint and a softness that is consonant with the private nature of the theme. Recalling to some extent Dutch genre painting of the seventeenth century — in the works of Pieter de Hooch (1629–1684), for example — Bonvin's scene is darkly atmospheric and quiet, a true "still" life that shows a side to realism that could hardly be more unlike the assertive subjects and style of his friend Courbet (see fig. 3).

A different but no less important side of realism is presented in the social and political commentaries of Honoré Daumier, Paul Gavarni, and other

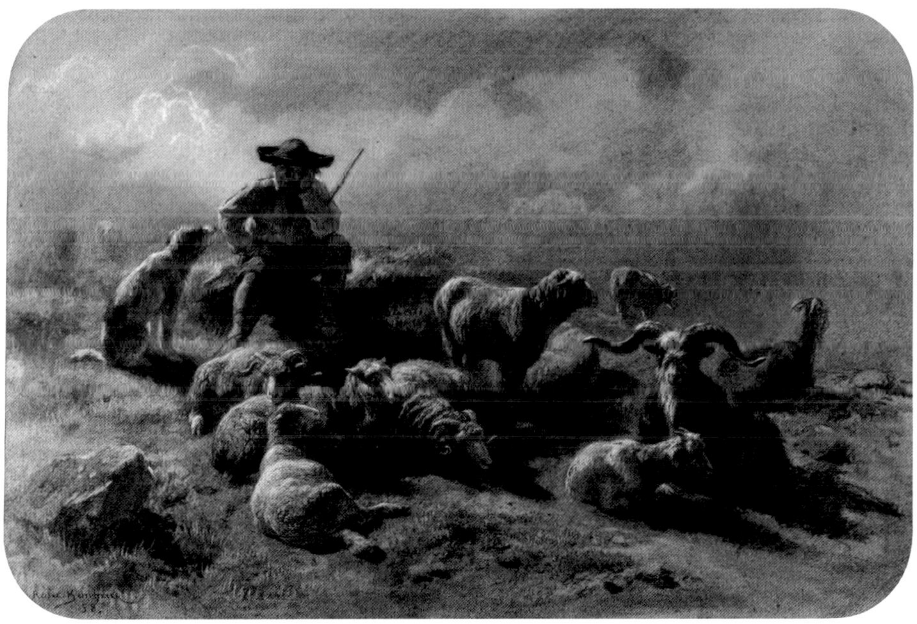

4 Rosa Bonheur, *The Conversation*, 1858, charcoal heightened with white gouache on blue-gray paper, Walters Art Gallery, Baltimore, Acquired by William T. Walters, 1860

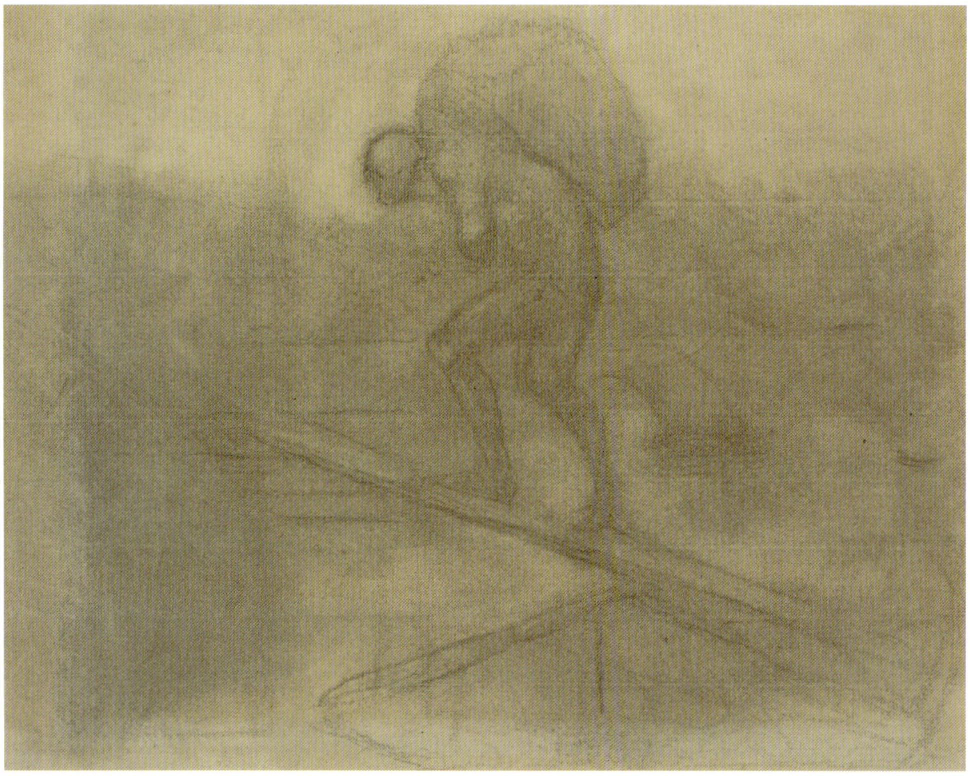

5 Honoré Daumier, *Man Carrying a Sack*, charcoal, National Gallery of Art, Washington, Rosenwald Collection, 1943

equally acerbic observers of the human comedy. The detached objectivity that was expected of realist artists was a major component of the studies they made from life, such as Daumier's *Man Carrying a Sack* (fig. 5), but in their caricatures and political satires exaggerations were both expected and allowed. The humorous intent of Gavarni's *Pierrot's Son Asking Fatherly Advice* (pl. 26) is evident to a certain extent from the masks and brilliant white theater costumes worn by the two protagonists, but the execution of the drawing is perfectly straightforward — and exceptionally refined. The comic punch line of the scene is revealed only in the caption, as Pierrot *fils* asks his father in all seriousness, "Where have you seen a gentleman stick his finger in his nose without pulling up his sleeves?"

Because color is an integral element of nature, no matter what the subject might be, watercolor, like pastel, was a key medium for artists who strove to render the natural landscape in full true-to-life fashion. Several watercolors in the Dyke collection represent the range of achievement in this arena, most notably two landscapes by Henri-Joseph Harpignies (pls. 34, 35) and two others by Gustave Doré (pl. 32) and François-Louis Français (pl. 33). Of these artists, Harpignies ranked as one of the most gifted and successful French watercolorists of the nineteenth century. The classically calm views by Corot served as his first models, tempered later by Rousseau's Barbizon scenes; and Harpignies's watercolors rarely diverged from a neatly representational and tranquil view of nature. Continuing to work almost to the day of his death in 1916 at the age of ninety-seven, he was the artist who carried the legacy of Corot and the Barbizon school into the twentieth century.

Standing apart from the group of watercolor landscapes in the Dyke collection are two extraordinary still lifes, one by Harpignies, *A Potted Fuchsia with Children's Toys* of 1877 (pl. 31), and the other, *A Pot of Chrysanthemums on a Ledge* of 1864 (pl. 30) by Léon Bonvin, half-brother of François. The two are rendered in dissimilar techniques, with Harpignies using a more suggestive style made up of light, varied touches of pure color against a darkly atmospheric background, and Bonvin employing a more tightly descriptive and consciously detailed technique. In keeping with the quiet and pleasant view of nature that generally percolates through

Harpignies's work, his image of vibrant pink fuchsias is cheerful and utterly charming. Bonvin presents a more somber vision, setting his bouquet against a wintry-gray array of leafless trees and portraying flowers that have passed their peak, already browned around the edges. The dark mood of this and other works by Bonvin was certainly affected by the struggles he endured in pursuing his art, burdened by family and job responsibilities that allowed him to draw only at odd hours. When a dealer criticized his pieces as "too dark, not gay enough," the despondent thirty-two-year-old artist hanged himself.[11]

During the last decades of the nineteenth century a new form of realism emerged that focused even more intensely on scenes of everyday reality in the modern world. This new "naturalism" in art coincided with similarly naturalist themes that were expressed in the writings of Émile Zola and other authors and thinkers of the time. As Jules-Antoine Castagnary, its foremost advocate, explained, "The Naturalist school affirms that art is the expression of life in all its modes and varying degrees; its only object is to reproduce nature and lead to its greatest power and intensity. . . . The Naturalist school reestablishes the severed relationship between man and nature. By its double focus on country life . . . and city life . . . it attempts to embrace all forms of the visible world. It already has restored line and color to their proper function, never again to go their separate ways."[12] Key to naturalist painting — and indeed to Zola's writing — was the detailed observation of real people in their local environments and the objective and dispassionate documentation of everyday life.[13]

Representing this movement in memorable fashion in the Dyke collection is Léon Lhermitte's riveting, brilliantly observed, and beautifully rendered *Elderly Peasant Woman* (pl. 29). Using the simplest of means — rich black charcoal and chalk on cream paper — Lhermitte draws an unflinching portrait of old age, the woman's face deeply creviced by time and care. It is an extraordinarily rich landscape of aged flesh, set off in all its detail against the more generalized forms of her headscarf and coat. Adding poignancy to this all-too-human image are the wisps of hay seen at the woman's neck, evidence of the cheap insulation that she has stuffed under her coat to help ward off wind and cold.

More typical of Lhermitte's naturalist style is his *Family by a River* (pl. 38), drawn very late in his career — in 1922 — yet consistent with the type of work he produced for most of his life. Here, too, he adheres to the naturalist vision, but now drawn in the pastel that was his favorite drawing tool and presenting the kind of pastoral vision that recalls the earlier work of Jacque (pl. 27) and Millet.

The development of the new naturalism coincided almost exactly with the rise of impressionism; and several of the impressionists — Édouard Manet, Edgar Degas, Camille Pissarro, and Gustave Caillebotte among them — dealt with subjects that were clearly naturalist. (A particularly powerful example is Degas's *Two Women Ironing*; pl. 45). Although the aims of the two schools intersected in many ways and some proponents of naturalism hoped that the two schools would merge,[14] both personal rifts — one of the leading naturalists Jean-François Raffaelli was loathed by several of the impressionists, though Degas admired his work — and theoretical differences led to a complete rupture in the early 1880s. The naturalists did not skip a beat, however, but carried their deeply realist style and socially conscious subjects well into the first decades of the twentieth century.

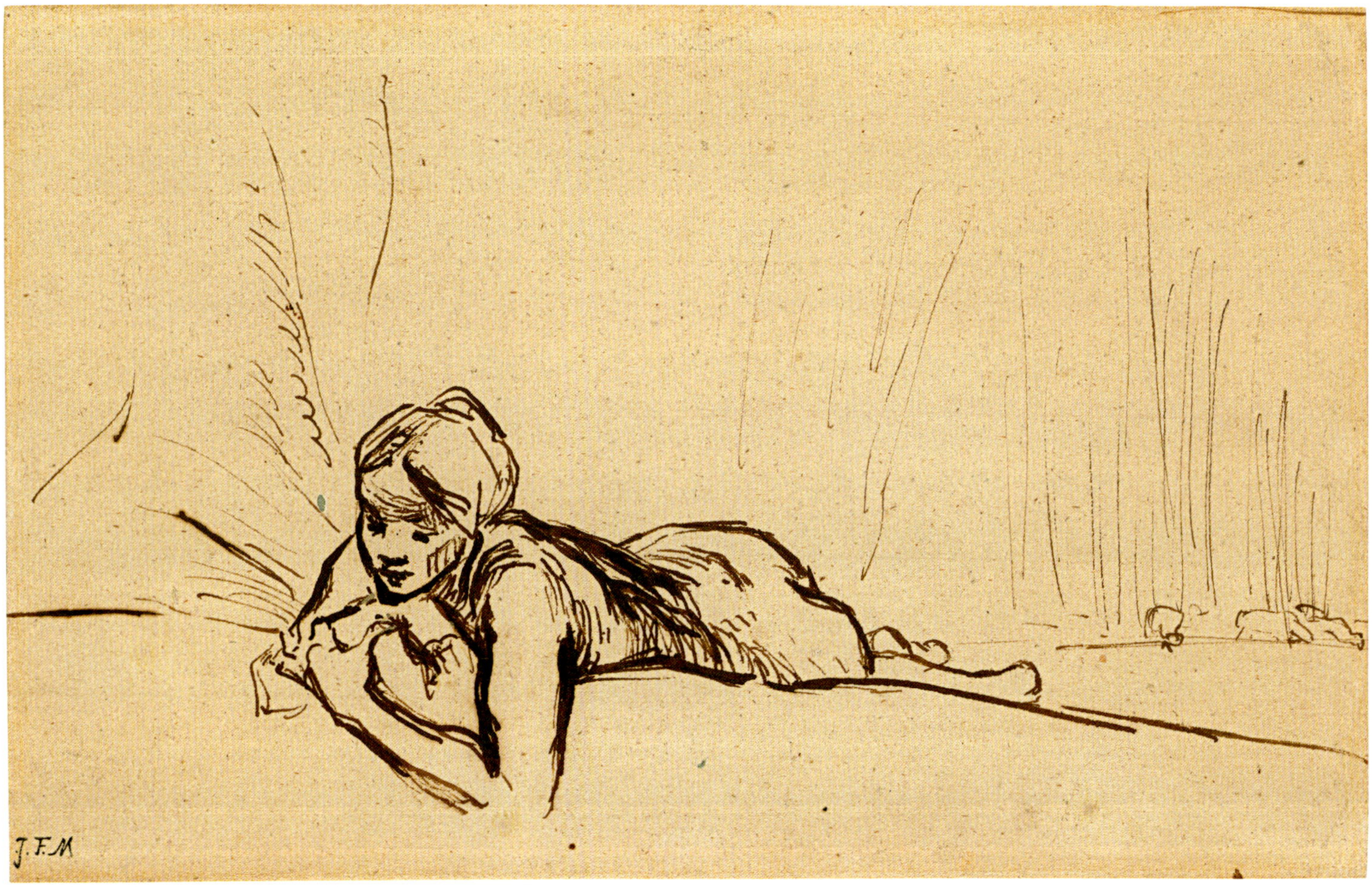

21 Jean-François Millet, *Nude Reclining in a Landscape*, 1844/1845
pen and brown ink, 165 × 256

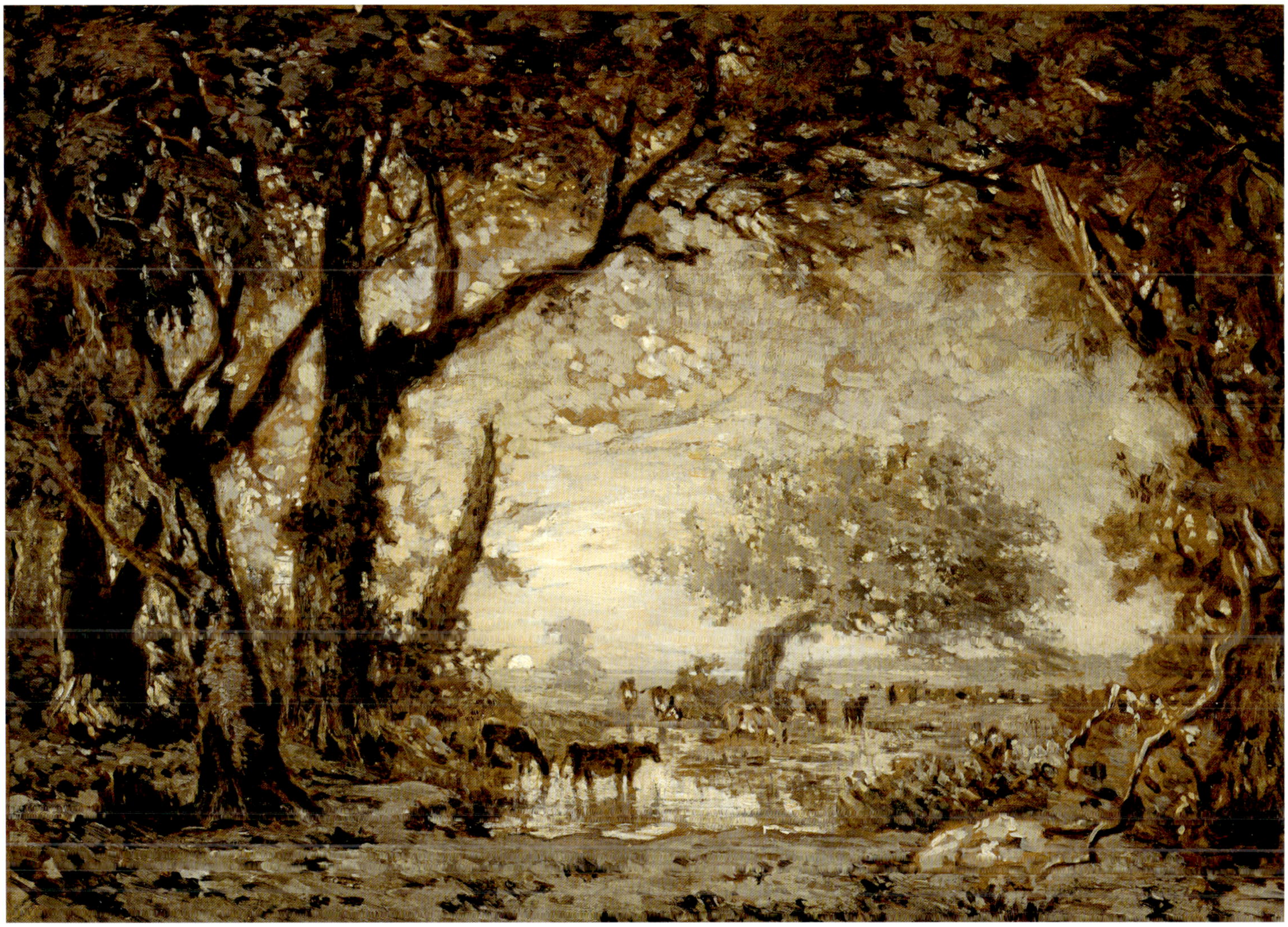

22 Théodore Rousseau, *Sunset from the Forest of Fontainebleau,* 1848/1850
oil on paper, 322 × 459

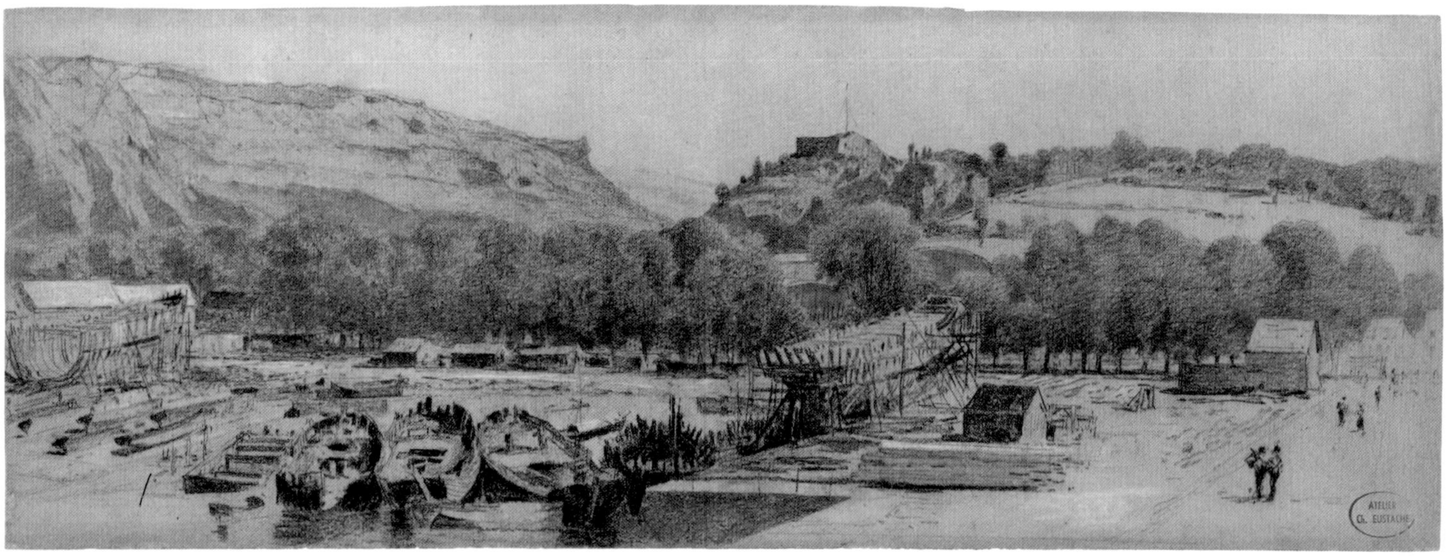

23 Charles-François Eustache, *A Boatyard,* c. 1850
black and white chalk, 222 × 599

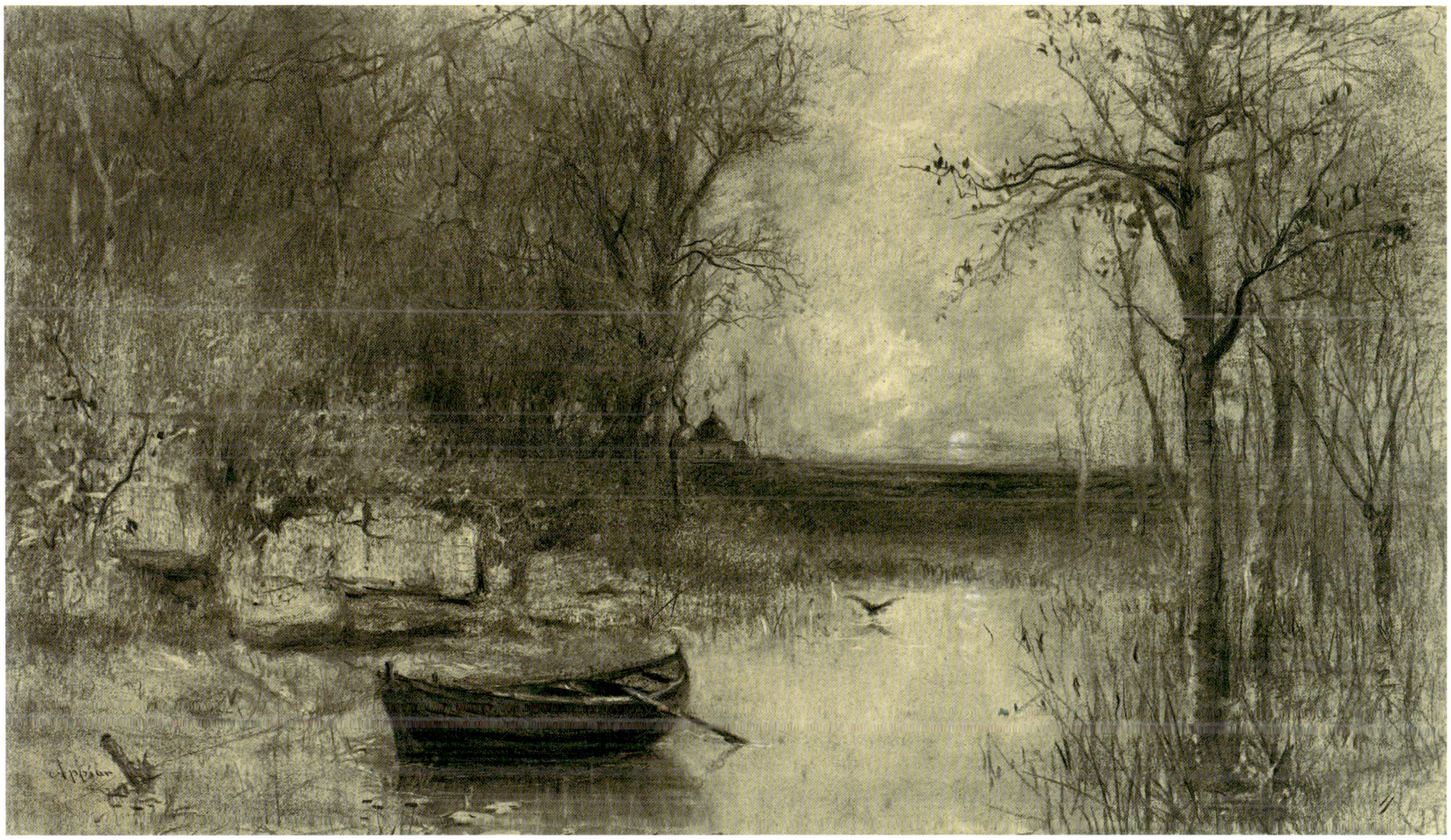

24 Adolphe Appian, *An Empty Rowboat Moored on a Forest Pond,* c. 1855
charcoal with white chalk, 475 × 845

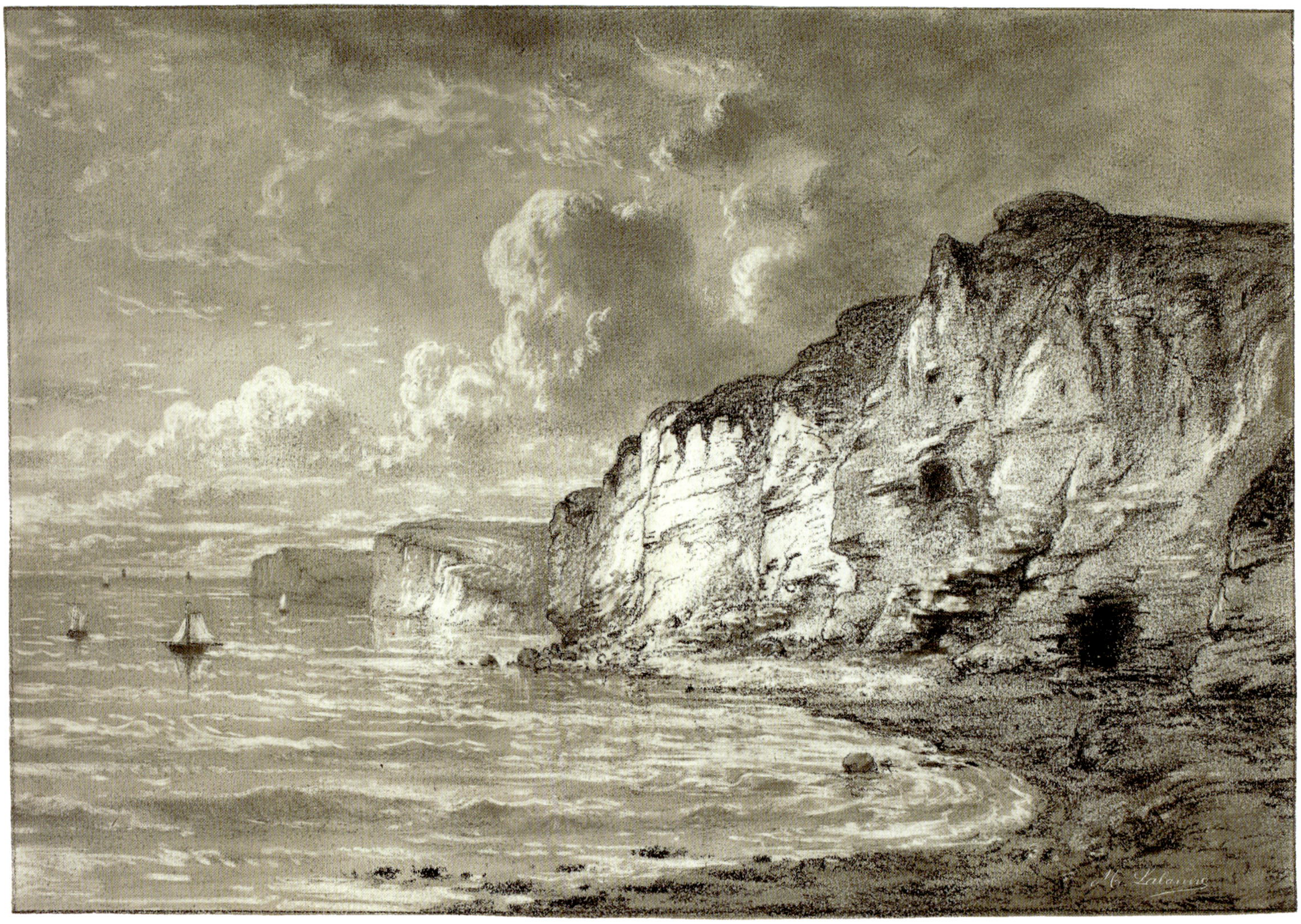

25 Maxime Lalanne, *Cliffs along the Normandy Coast,* 1868
charcoal, 312 × 462

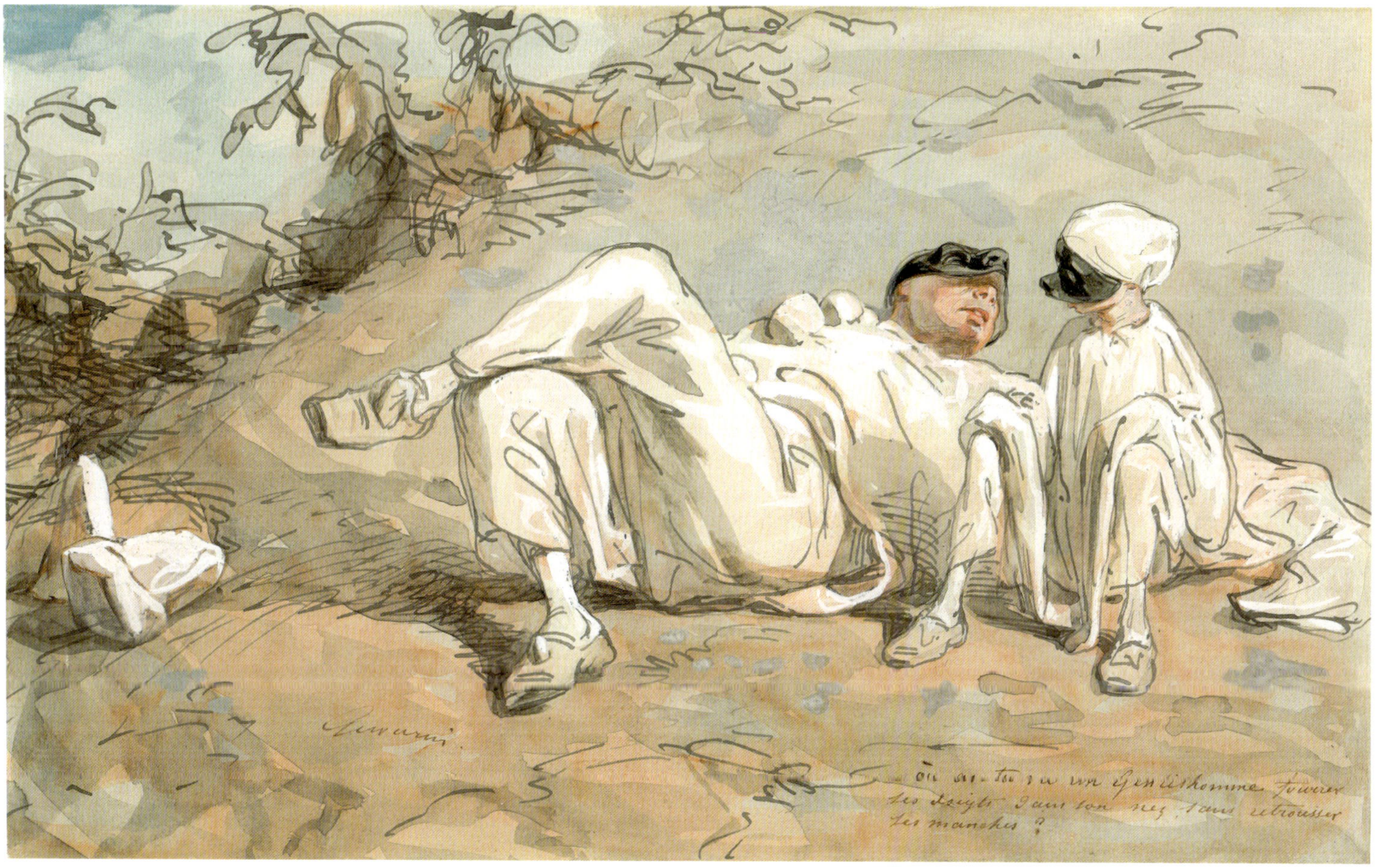

26 Paul Gavarni, *Pierrot's Son Asking Fatherly Advice*, 1850s(?)
pen and ink with watercolor and gouache, 195 × 320

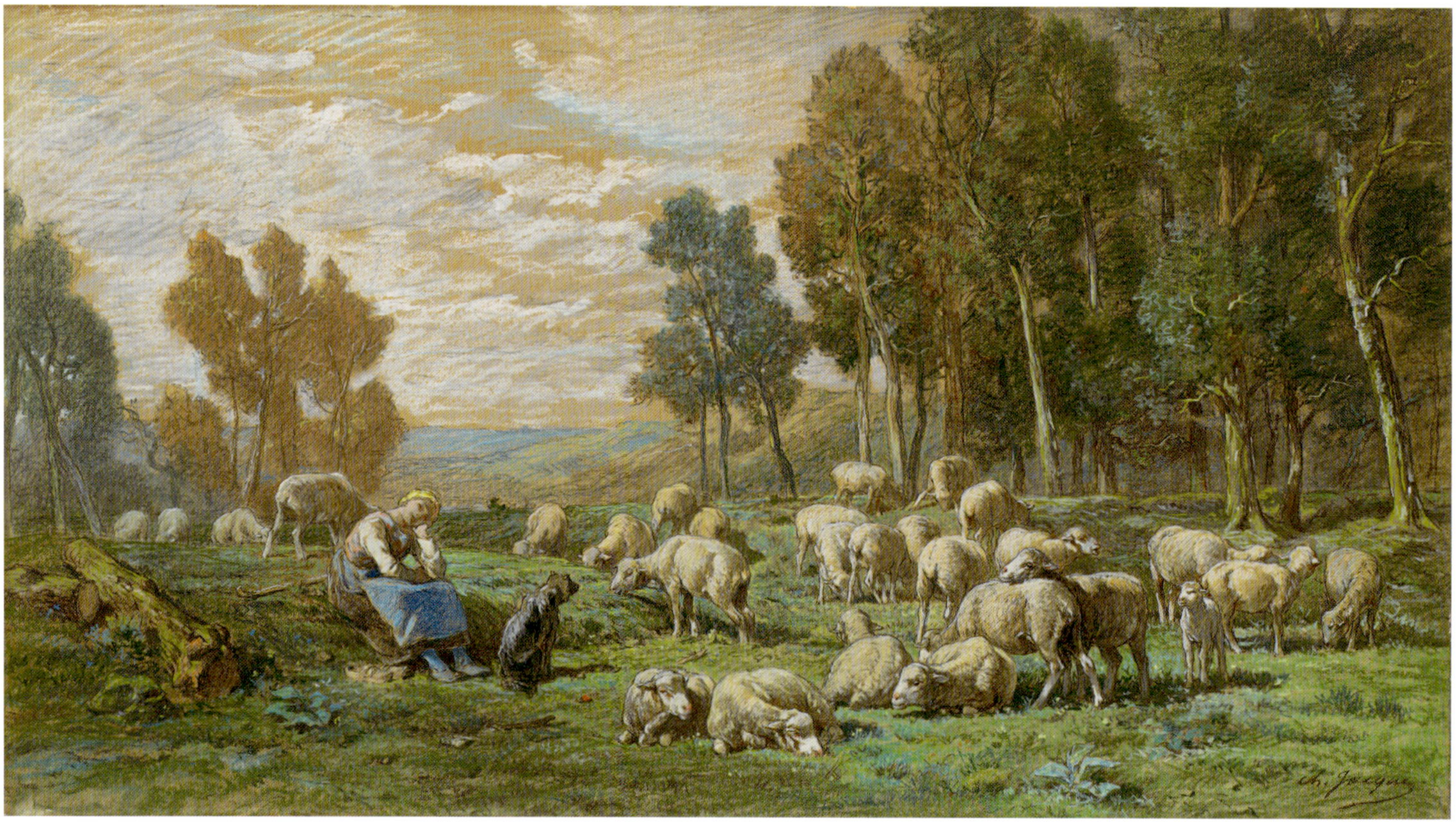

27 Charles-Émile Jacque, *The Shepherdess*, 1869
pastel, 526 × 949

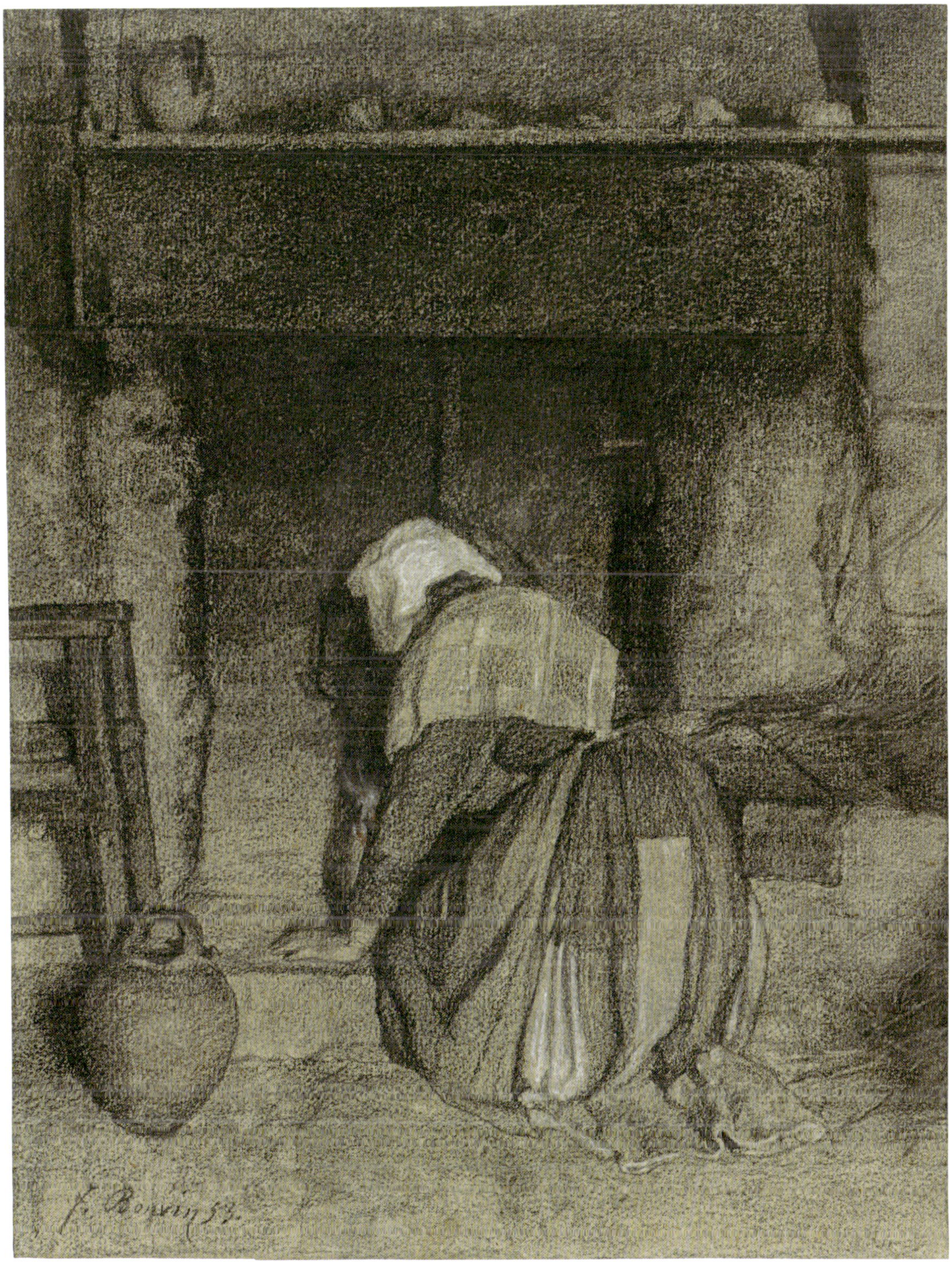

28 François Bonvin, *A Country Woman Tending a Fireplace*, 1853
charcoal with white gouache, 290 × 215

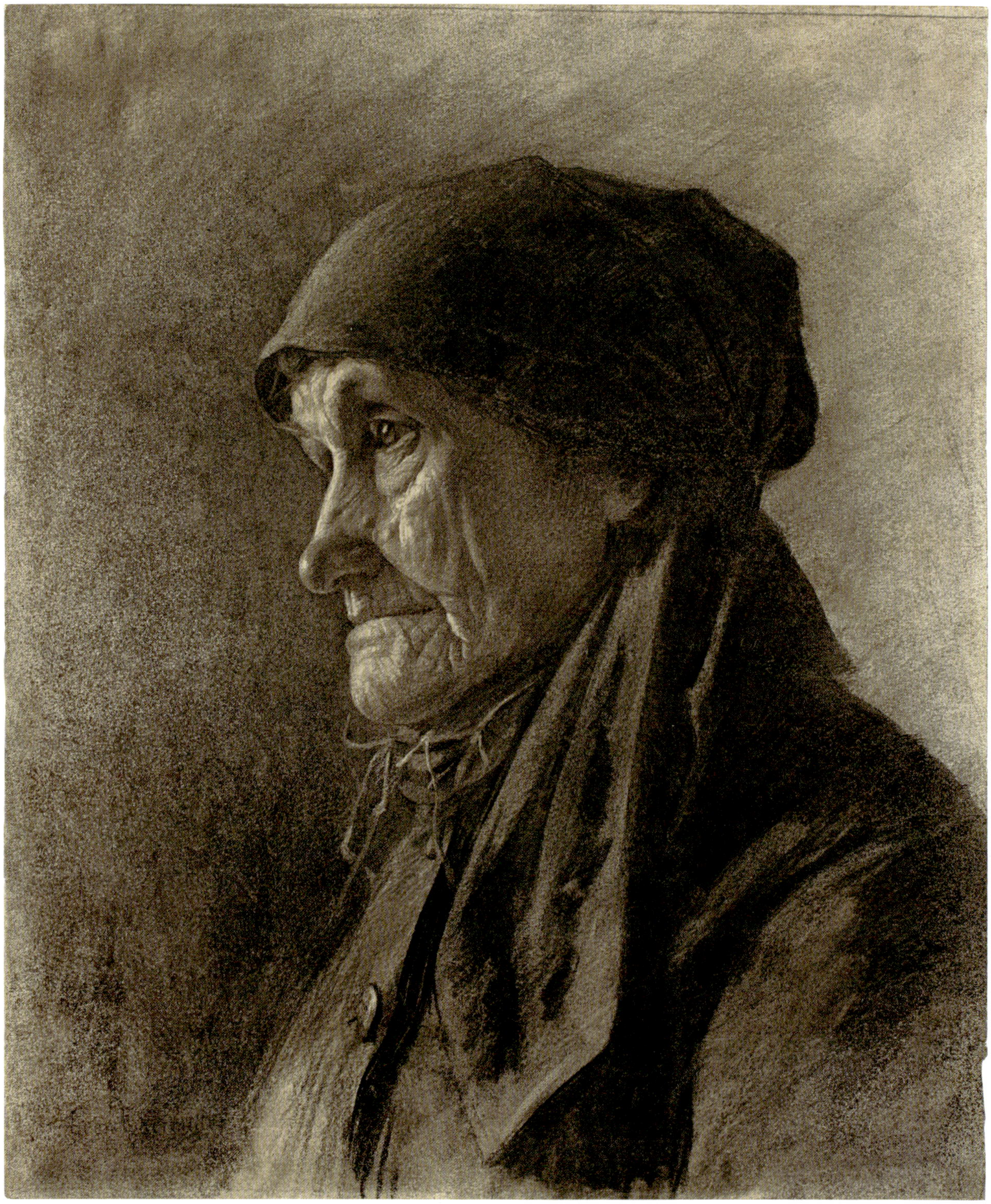

29 Léon Augustin Lhermitte, *An Elderly Peasant Woman,* c. 1878
charcoal, 475 × 396

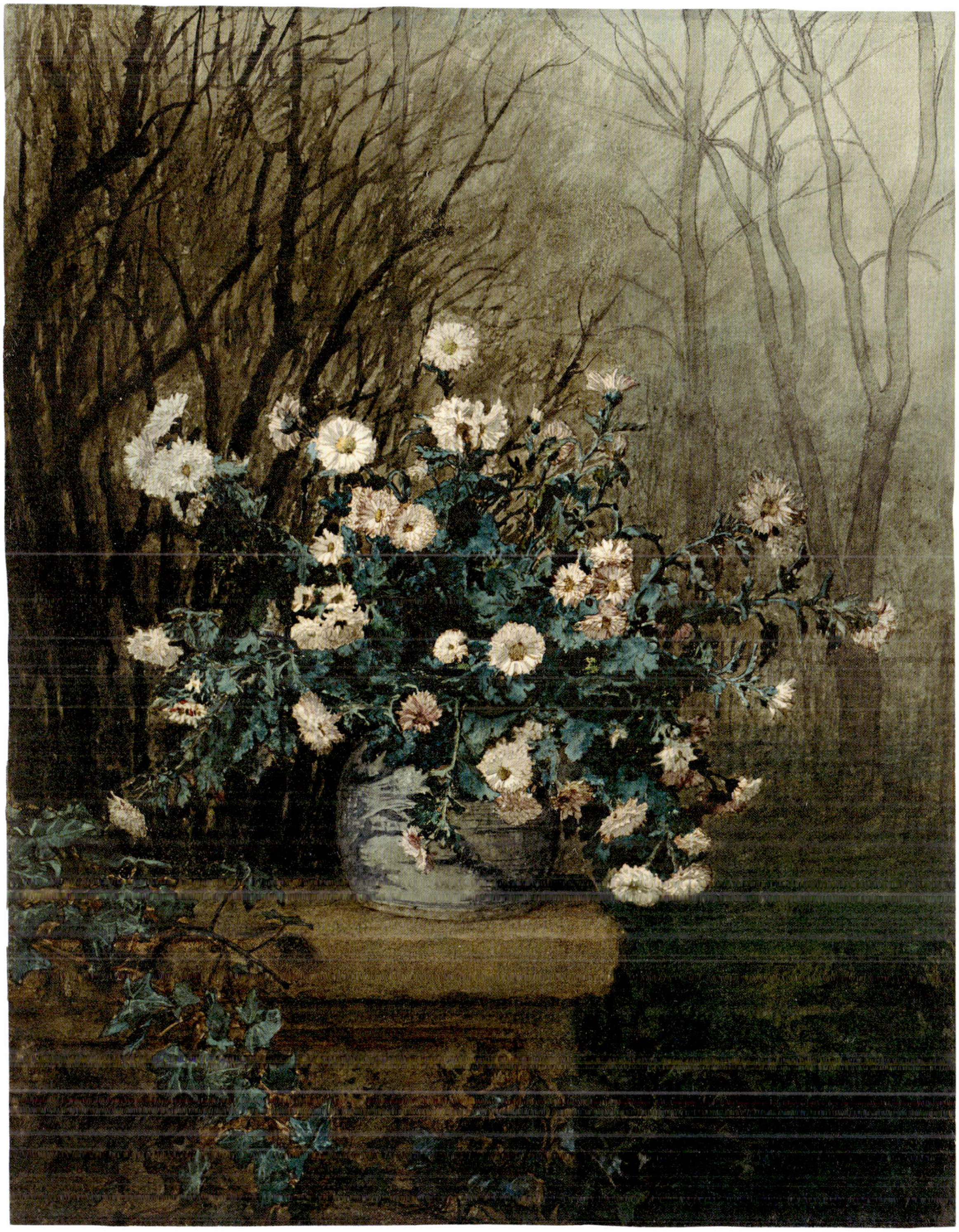

30 Léon Bonvin, *A Pot of Chrysanthemums on a Ledge,* 1864
pen and ink with watercolor and gouache, 247 × 197

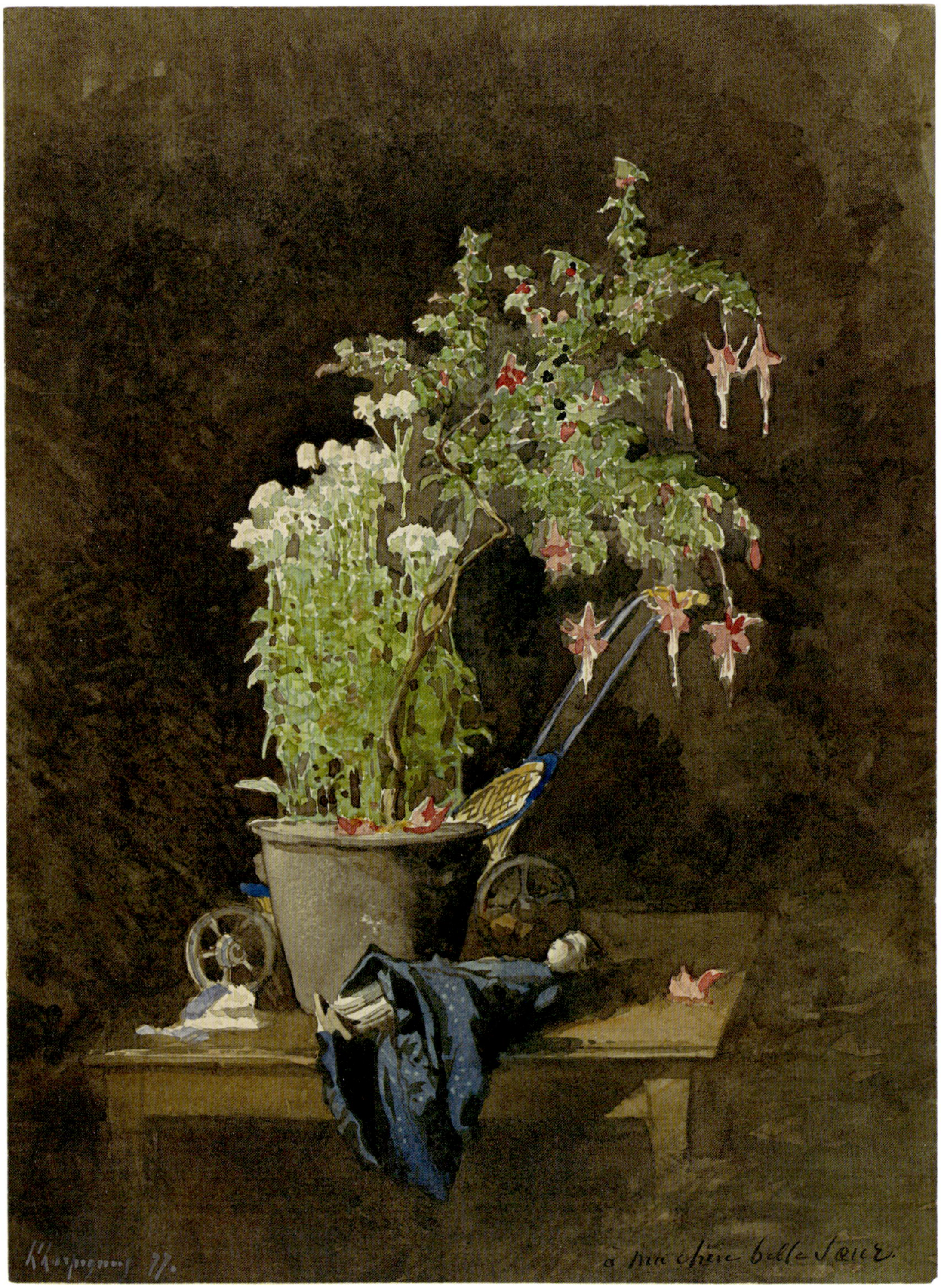

31 Henri-Joseph Harpignies, *A Potted Fuchsia with Children's Toys*, 1877
watercolor, 340 × 250

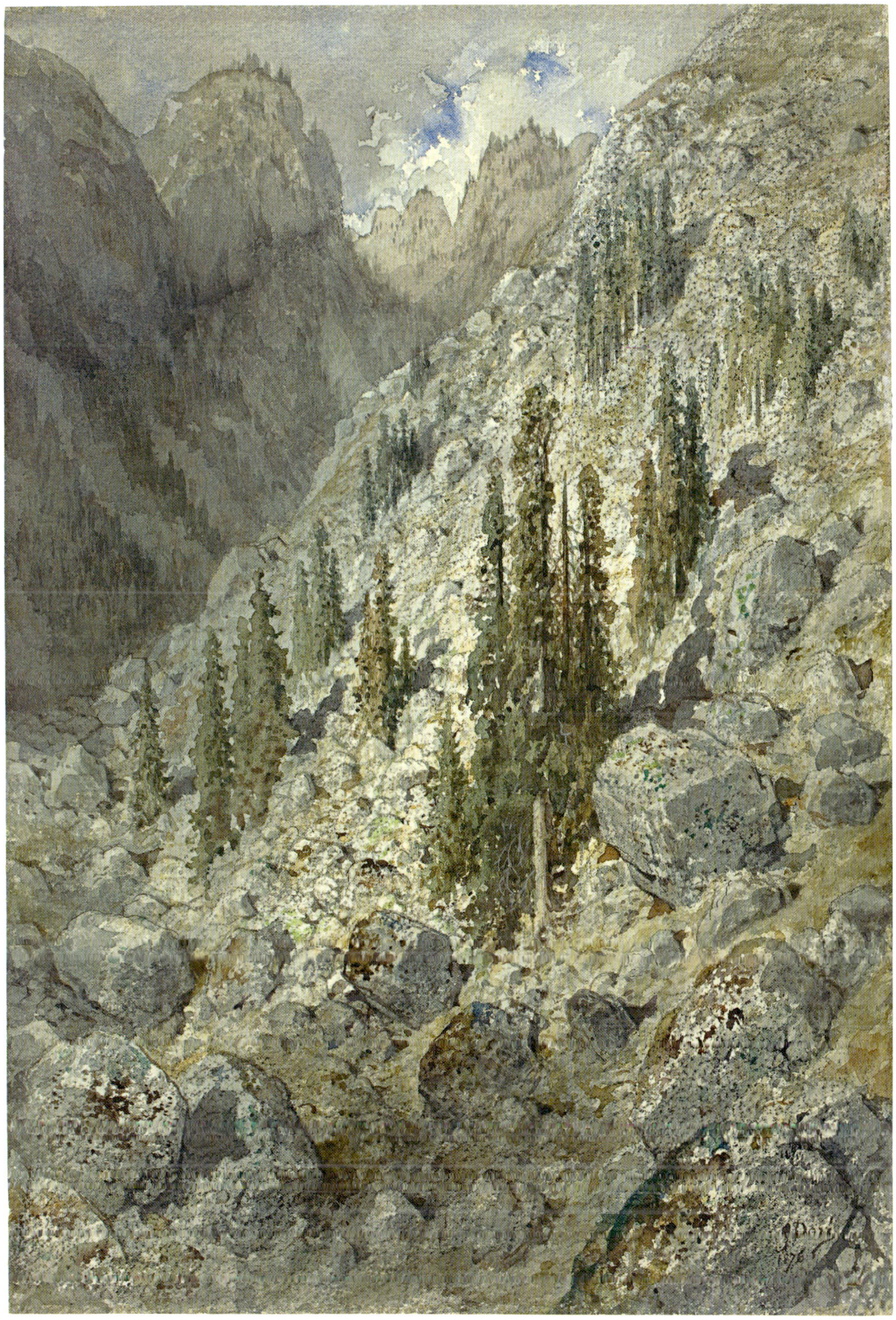

32 Gustave Doré, *An Alpine Valley with Trees and Boulders,* 1876
watercolor, gouache, and charcoal over pen and ink, 451 × 317

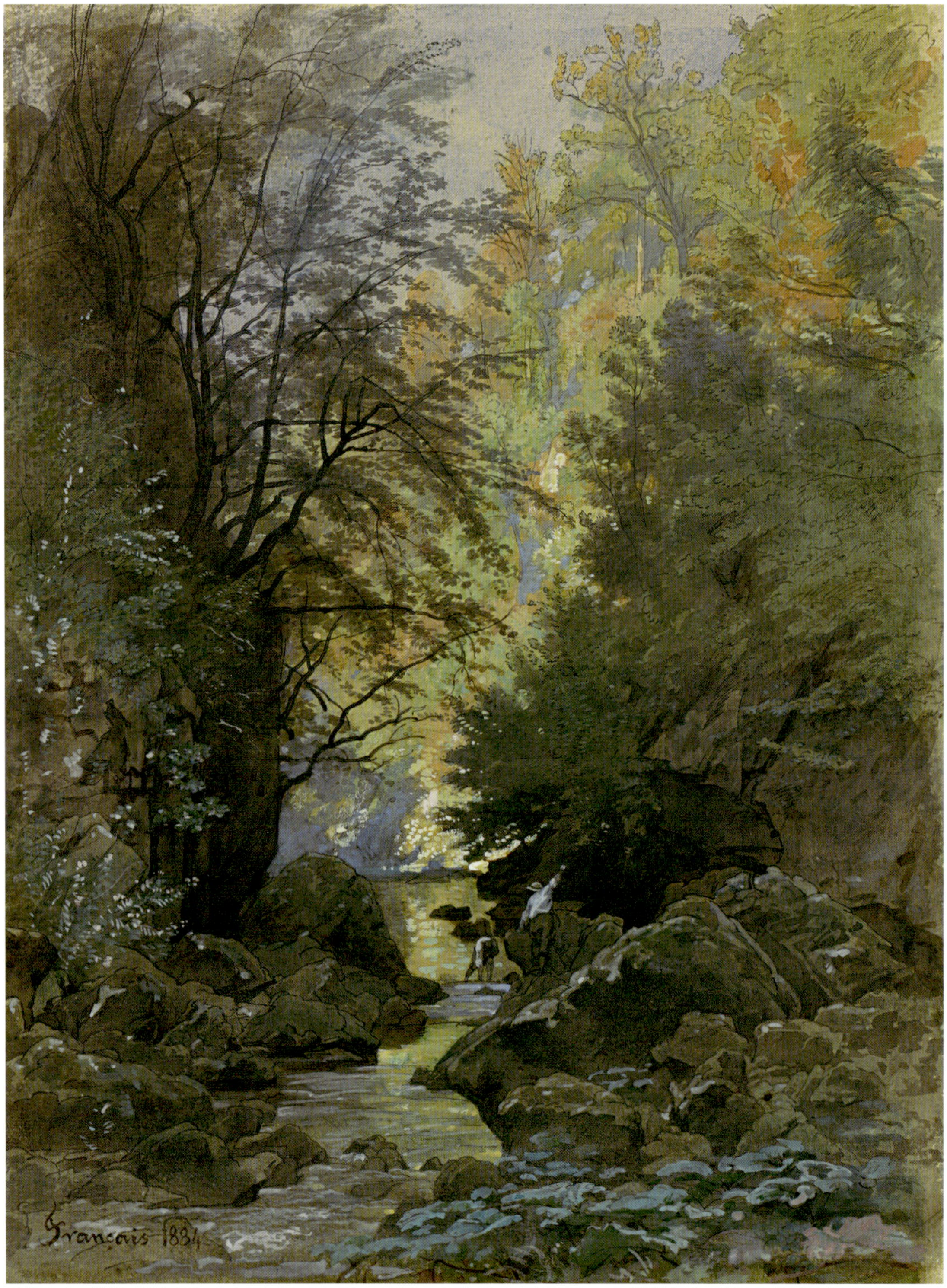

33 François-Louis Français, *A Stream through a Dense Forest,* 1884
watercolor and gouache, 460 × 345

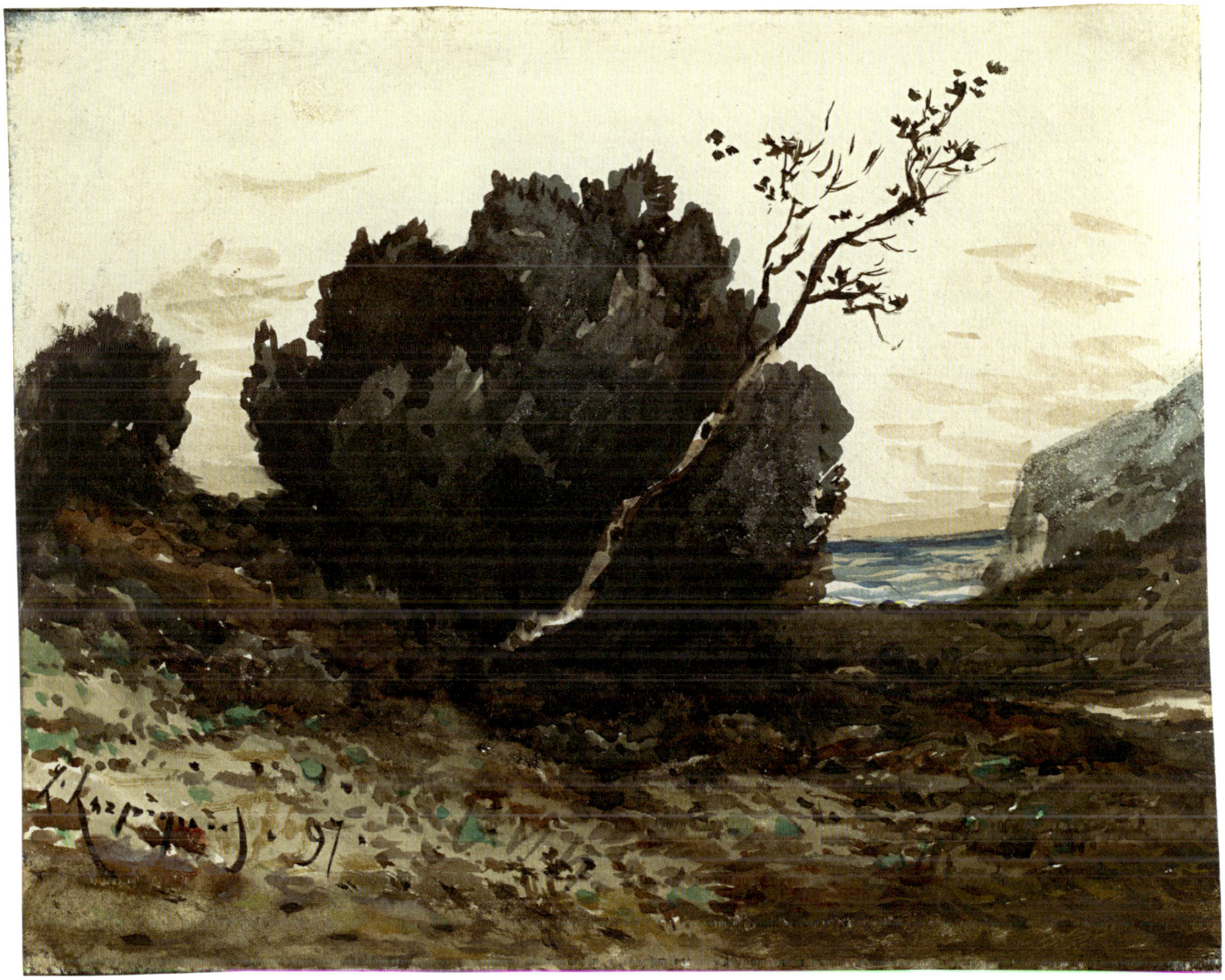

34 Henri-Joseph Harpignies, *Trees along the Coast,* 1897
watercolor, 216 × 257

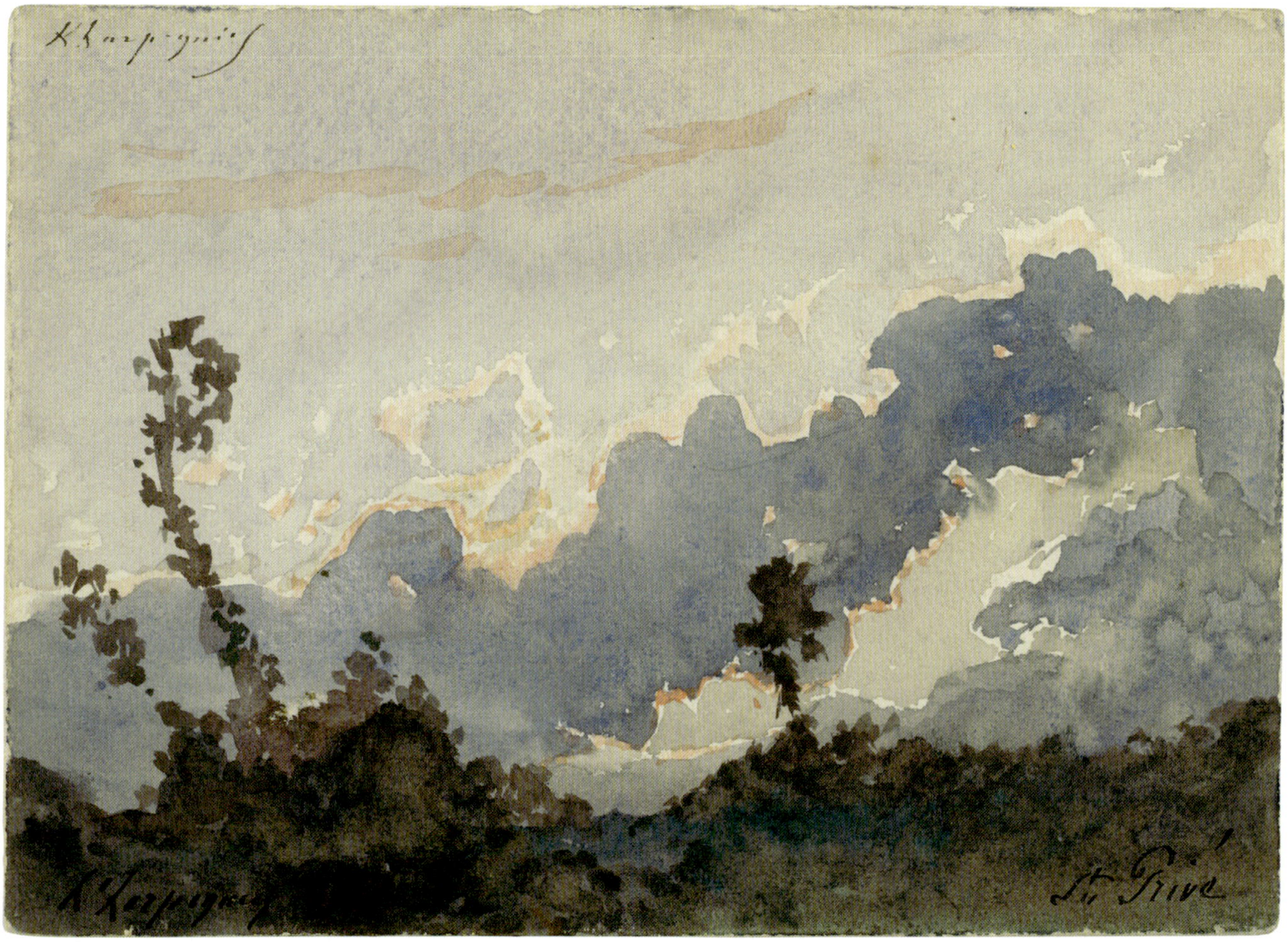

35 Henri-Joseph Harpignies, *Sun behind the Clouds at Saint-Privé,* c. 1900
watercolor, 125 × 175

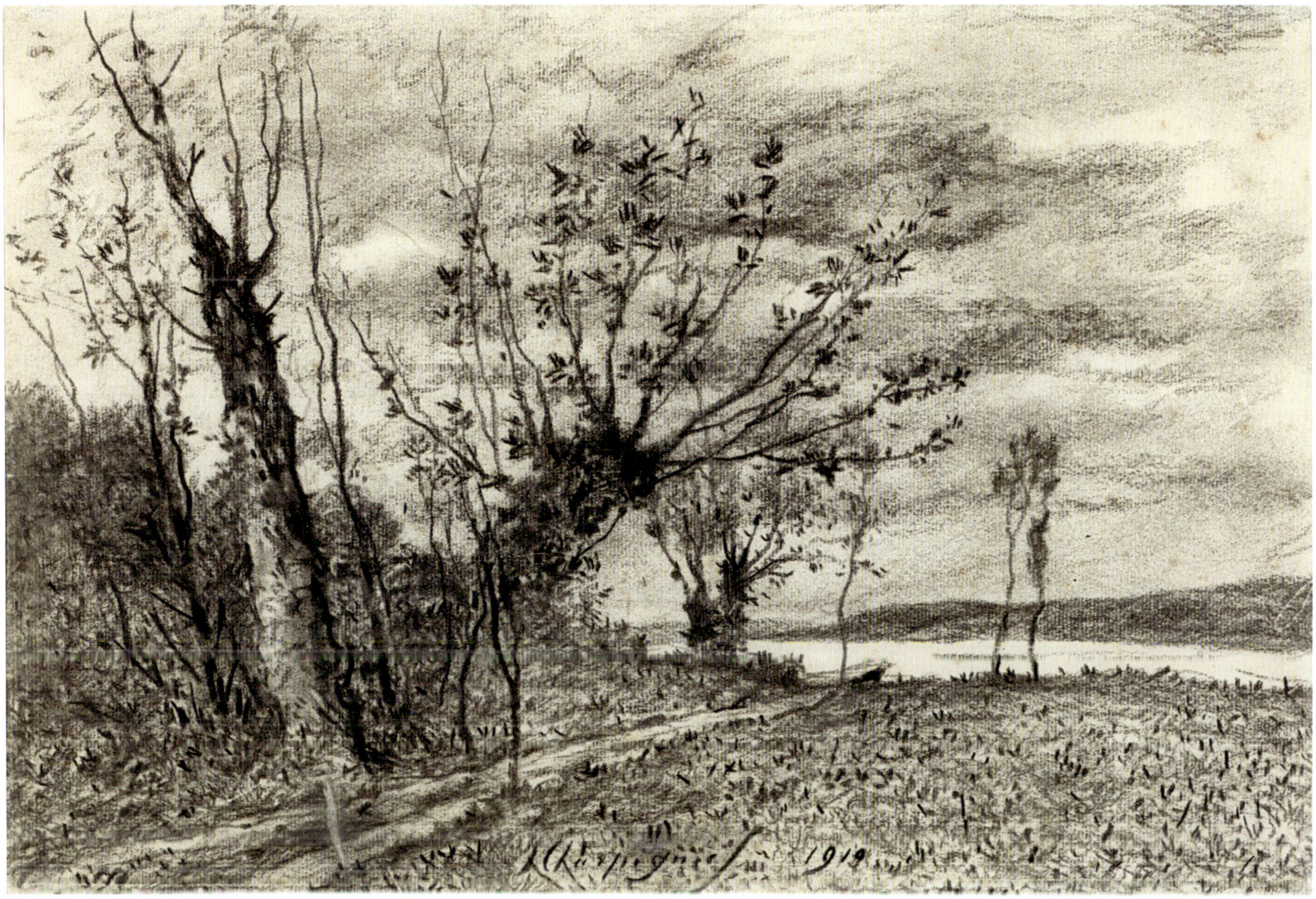

36 Henri-Joseph Harpignies, *Pollard Willows along a Coastal Road,* 1919
charcoal, 270 × 425

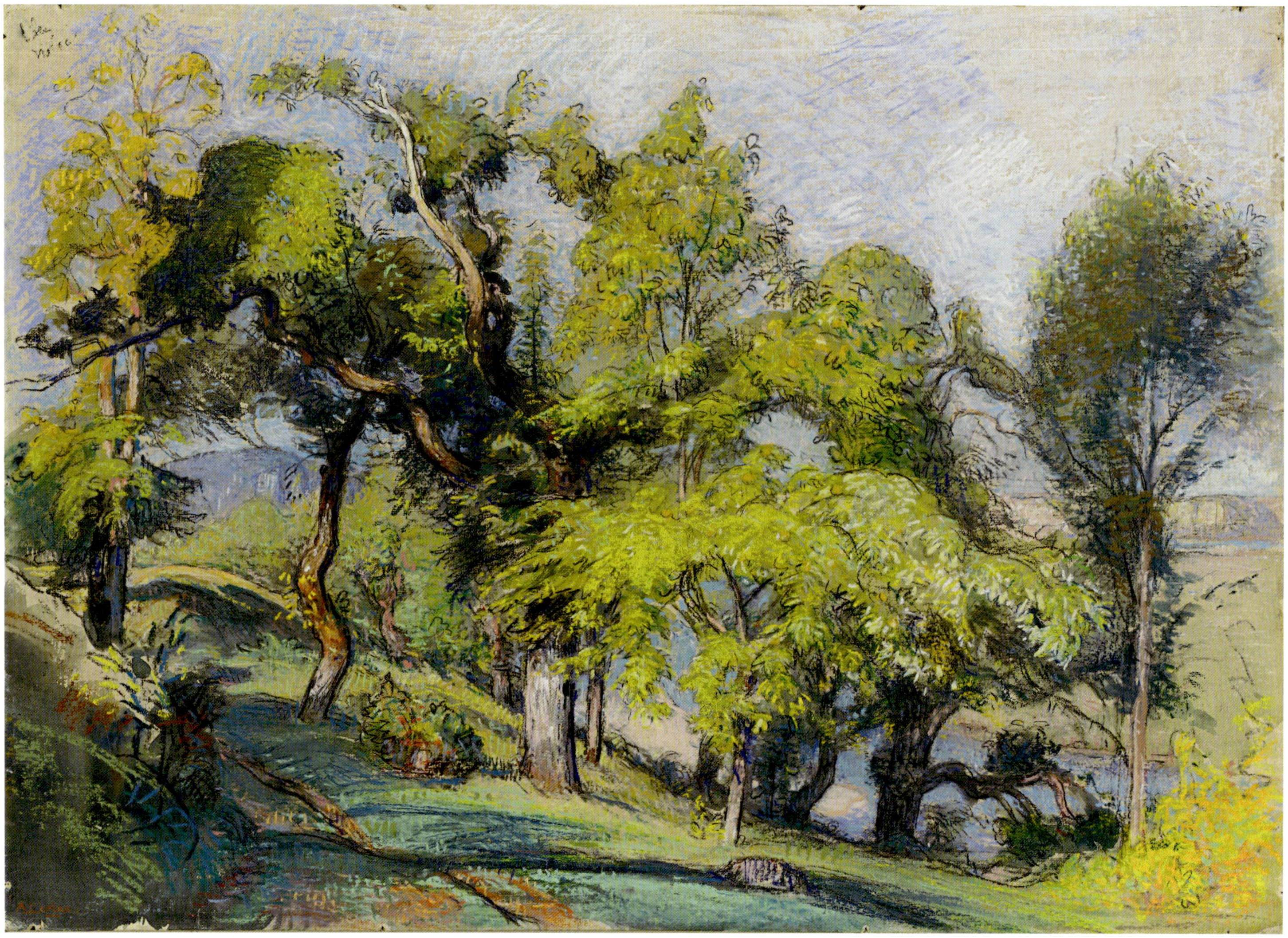

37 Auguste Louis Lepère, *Chestnut Trees above a River,* c. 1900
pastel, 370 × 521

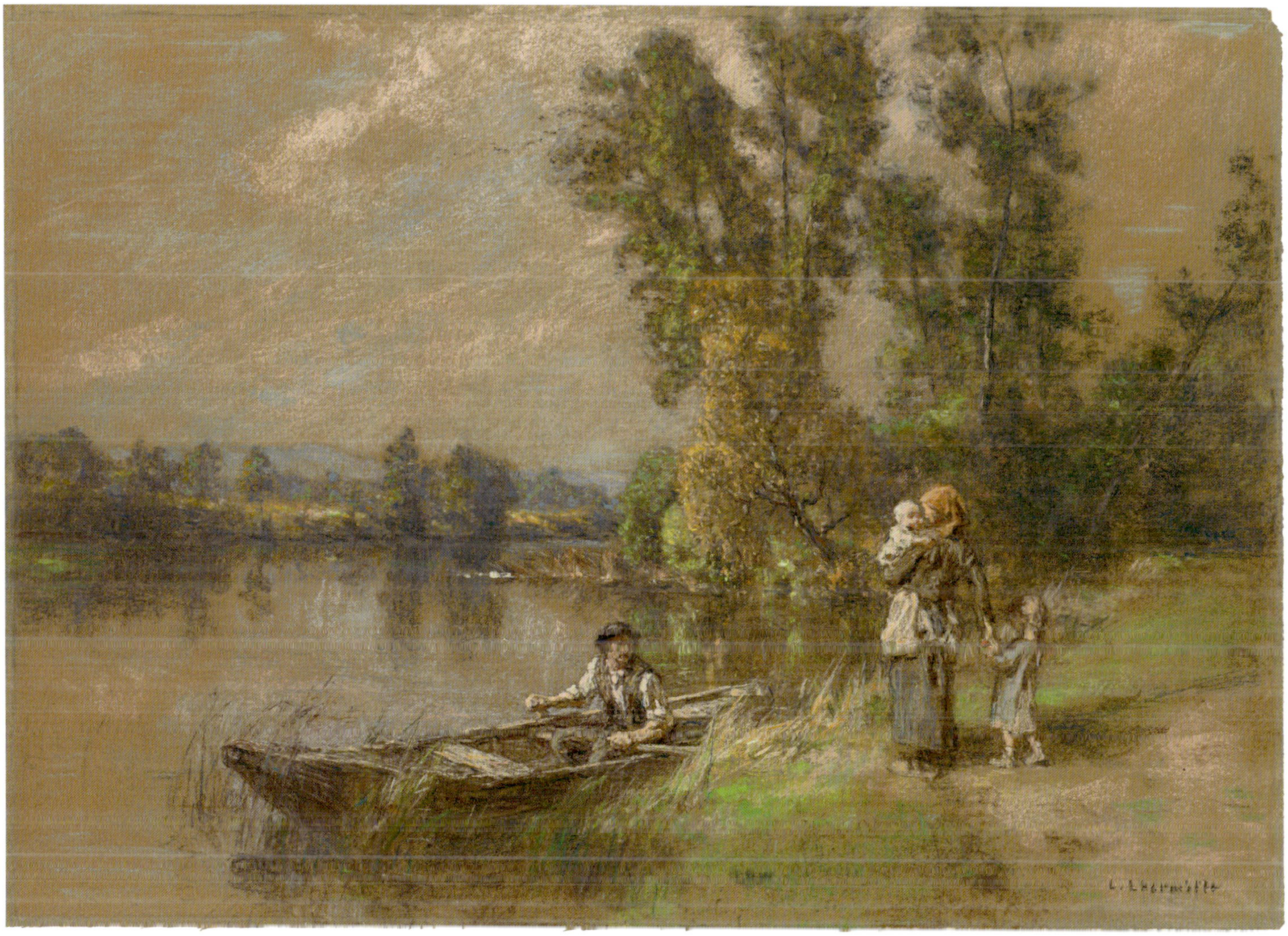

38 Léon Augustin Lhermitte, *Family by a River,* 1922
pastel, 480 × 680

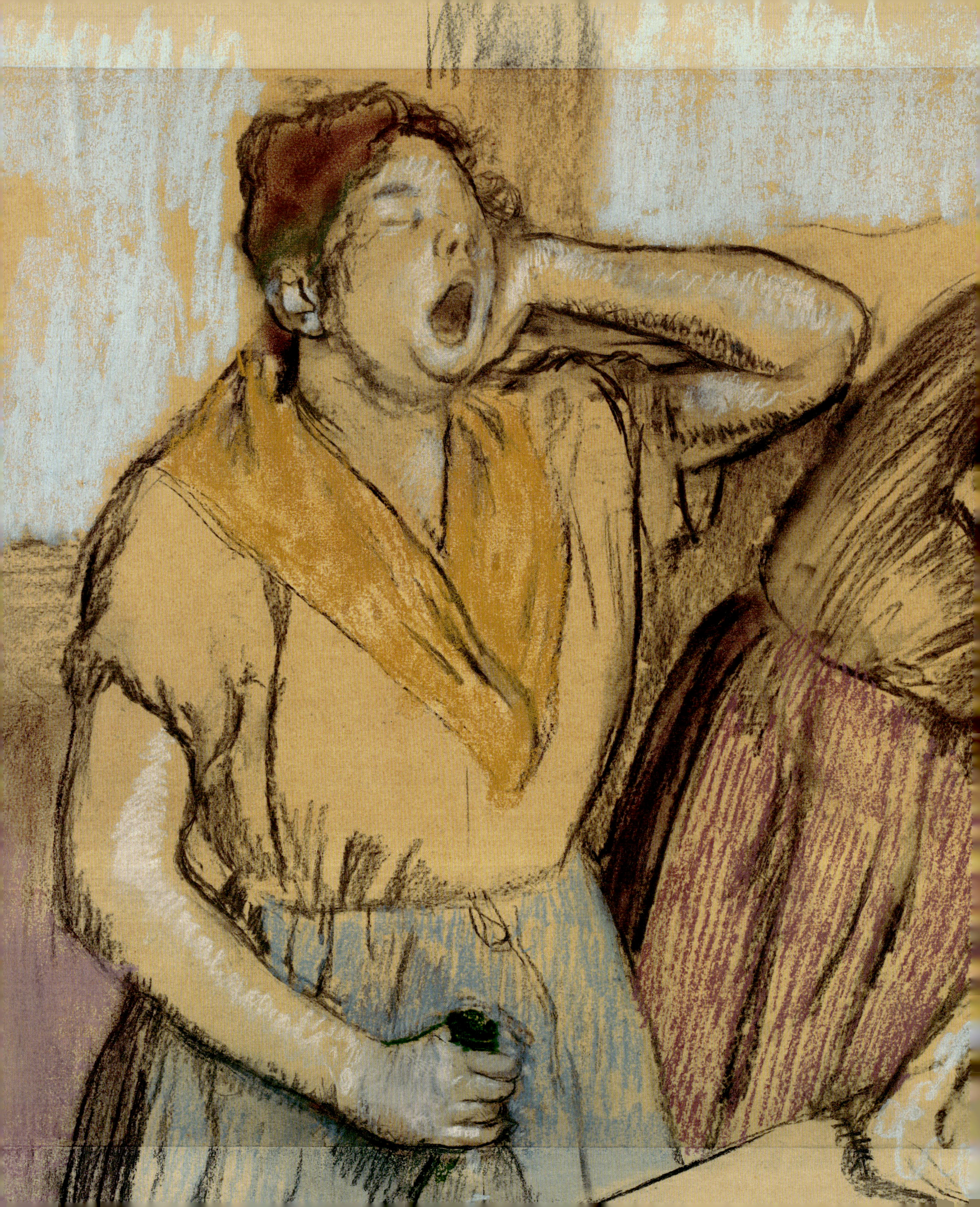

Impressionist Drawings

MARINA FERRETTI BOCQUILLON

FOR MANY YEARS impressionist drawing received little attention, and specialists believed that Edgar Degas was the only artist in the group who drew with passion and talent.[1] The "painter of dancers" exhibited his drawings regularly, and beginning in the 1880s, he devoted himself principally to making "feverish, economical, and powerful" drawings in charcoal and works of rare chromatic intensity in pastel, the latter of which dominates his final production.[2] By contrast, Édouard Manet was an enthusiastic draftsman from his student days but did not disseminate his drawings, preferring to keep them for family and friends. As a result, it was not until the late 1960s that this aspect of his oeuvre was revealed in all its richness.[3] After him, Camille Pissarro, Paul Cézanne, Auguste Renoir, Berthe Morisot, and Claude Monet emerged successively as skillful practitioners of the art of drawing. Unknown sheets that had remained in the hands of the artists' heirs were rediscovered and studied. Research into impressionist drawing reached a high point in 2007 with the publication of *The Unknown Monet: Pastels and Drawings*.[4] And the popular success the following year of the exhibition of pastels presented by the Musée d'Orsay proved that enthusiasm for these works goes far beyond the elite world of connoisseurs and experts.[5]

The impressionist drawings assembled with such acumen by James Dyke constitute a remarkable sampling. Encompassing Manet and Morisot, Cézanne, Monet, and Eugène Boudin, the collection offers a cohesive synthesis. With the exception of Renoir, all of the main proponents of the movement are represented, and the works — in a wide range of graphic techniques involving black and white or color, line or brushstroke — span the period from 1860 to 1901.

The goal of the impressionist painters was to record reality, and they took their inspiration from it as directly as possible. But the singer does not linger long upon the stage, the laundress goes off to make a delivery, the fashionably dressed lady disappears barely glimpsed into the crowd. Nature is equally fluid: the tide rises, the wind picks up, the boats leave the harbor, the sun sets, and a single cloud is enough to end the spectacle that so recently delighted us. Capturing an "impression" is a challenge, especially if the aim is to retain a certain naturalism, to avoid a "freezing" of the original sensation. And therein lies the art. The supreme refinement is to suggest that the result has been obtained without effort, just as the ballerina's grace draws a veil over the arduous work at the bar.

The impressionists had chosen to portray life itself, but when they were observing it, they had time to register only hastily what they saw. Subsequently, it became a matter of memory and documentation, and it was here that drawings often played a crucial role. Degas was continually reworking his paintings and pastels. Rarely satisfied, Cézanne worked extremely slowly. Monet destroyed a good number of his paintings and spent close to ten years working on the *Water Lilies* at the Orangerie in Paris. There are nineteen known preparatory studies, in a variety of media (graphite, chalk, ink, and watercolor), for Renoir's *Large Bathers* of 1884–1887 (The Philadelphia Museum of Art), several of which are consummate masterpieces (see fig. 1).[6]

Oil painting is too slow a technique to capture the fleeting moment, and it also requires a good deal

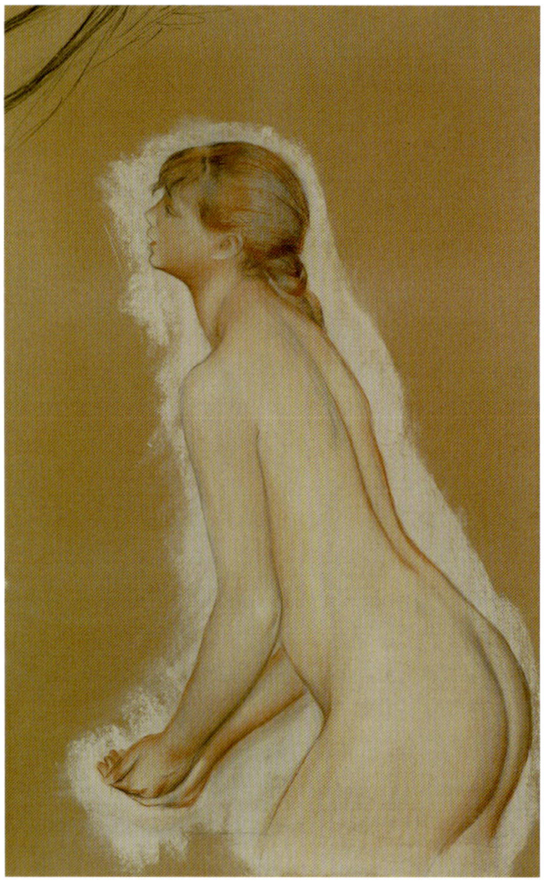

1 Auguste Renoir, *Splashing Figure (Study for "The Large Bathers")*, 1884–1885, red, white, and black chalk and black Conté crayon, with brush and red and white chalk wash on tan tracing paper laid down on canvas, The Art Institute of Chicago, Bequest of Kate L. Brewster

of equipment, which makes working outdoors difficult. Despite the advantages offered by the paint tube and the portable easel (invented in 1841 and 1857, respectively), there were still many other items to be carried into the open air — stool, parasol, palette, thinner, rags — aside from the canvas itself. It is hard to believe that the paintings made by Monet and Renoir at La Grenouillère were executed almost entirely out of doors. And regardless of the account given by Georges Rivière,[7] no one has ever seriously believed that a group portrait as complex as *Dance at Le Moulin de la Galette* from 1876 (Musée d'Orsay, Paris) could have been painted in situ.

Though the impressionists invented a new way of painting, they were all well versed in the art of the past. Many were admirers of Raphael and Jean-Auguste-Dominique Ingres, but they generally felt a greater affinity for Jean Siméon Chardin, François Boucher, and Jean-Honoré Fragonard. The French artists of the eighteenth century had recently regained favor, and like them, the impressionists were concerned with creating paintings that retained a feeling of spontaneity and naturalness. And again like them, they were led by a love of color and light effects to favor red chalk, brown ink, and pastel, which had been abandoned by the painters of neoclassicism and rediscovered by the romantics. They learned, too, from the Barbizon masters — Jean-Baptiste-Camille Corot, Charles-François Daubigny, Théodore Rousseau, Jean-François Millet — all fine draftsmen who sought to establish a direct relationship with nature. As Manet so aptly put it: "To achieve spontaneity, you must be a master of your art."[8] Of Degas, Paul Valéry wrote: "He liked talking of 'scholarly art,' saying that a painting was the result of a 'series of operations.'"[9]

Manet always had pencil in hand when he visited monuments and museums while traveling. In Paris, too, his sketchbook was constantly by his side: "No Parisian idler ever idled to better effect. He sketched in a notebook a trifle, a profile, a hat, whatever happened to strike him at the moment."[10] Each drawing technique was approached with the same blend of authority and freedom (fig. 2). As Antonin Proust wrote in 1899, some years after Manet's death: "Whether these sketches are copied after the old masters or taken directly from nature, there is not a single superfluous stroke, nor any accent that is not precisely right. Everything is composed with a sureness of hand that reveals both a profound ability and the passion for truth that is the hallmark of his genius."[11] Unlike Degas, Manet generally chose not to exhibit his drawings, though on rare occasions he did disseminate them in the form of prints, as with *A Boy Holding a Dog* (pl. 39).

Degas was a merciless observer of those around him, and the major part of his oeuvre is given over to the portrayal of modern life. Always seeking the characteristic pose and demonstrating a penchant for portraying Parisian women of modest means going about their daily activities, he strove to show his subjects as accurately as possible, without embellishing reality. As the Dyke collection's *Dancer at the Bar* (pl. 44) reveals, the beauty of Degas's dancers generally has more to do with the way they are presented — an unusual viewpoint, the intensity of the blacks, a light effect, the delicacy of a tutu — than with the charm of their faces or even their bodies, which are often stocky and muscular. Degas was no kinder in his portrayals of laundresses, such as the one he showed yawning and stretching, bottle in hand (pl. 45). The realism of this scene fascinated him, and he made four slightly different versions of it. The first, an oil now in a private collection, was executed before 1876. Of the three versions that followed in the mid-1880s two are oil paintings, one now at the Musée d'Orsay in Paris (fig. 3) and the other at the Norton Simon Museum of Art in Pasadena. The fourth variant, included in this catalogue, is a pastel drawing. It was thought for some time to be a preparatory study for the painting at the Musée d'Orsay, which it markedly resembles, but there are now those who believe it to be a later repetition.[12] Whatever the case, the artist, known for his perfectionism, was especially proud of this drawing, which he signed very obviously before allowing it to enter the collection of one of his friends, the renowned composer Ernest Chausson (1855–1899).

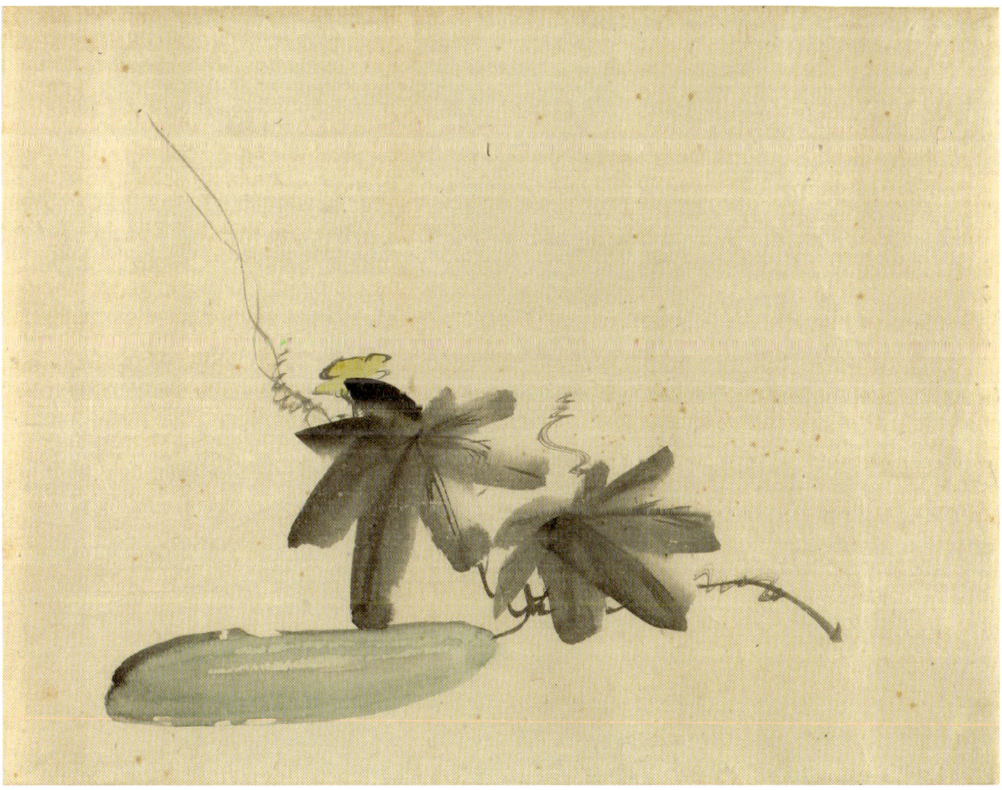

2 Édouard Manet, *Cucumber with Leaves*, c. 1880, watercolor and gray wash, National Gallery of Art, Washington, Collection of Mr. and Mrs. Paul Mellon, 1985

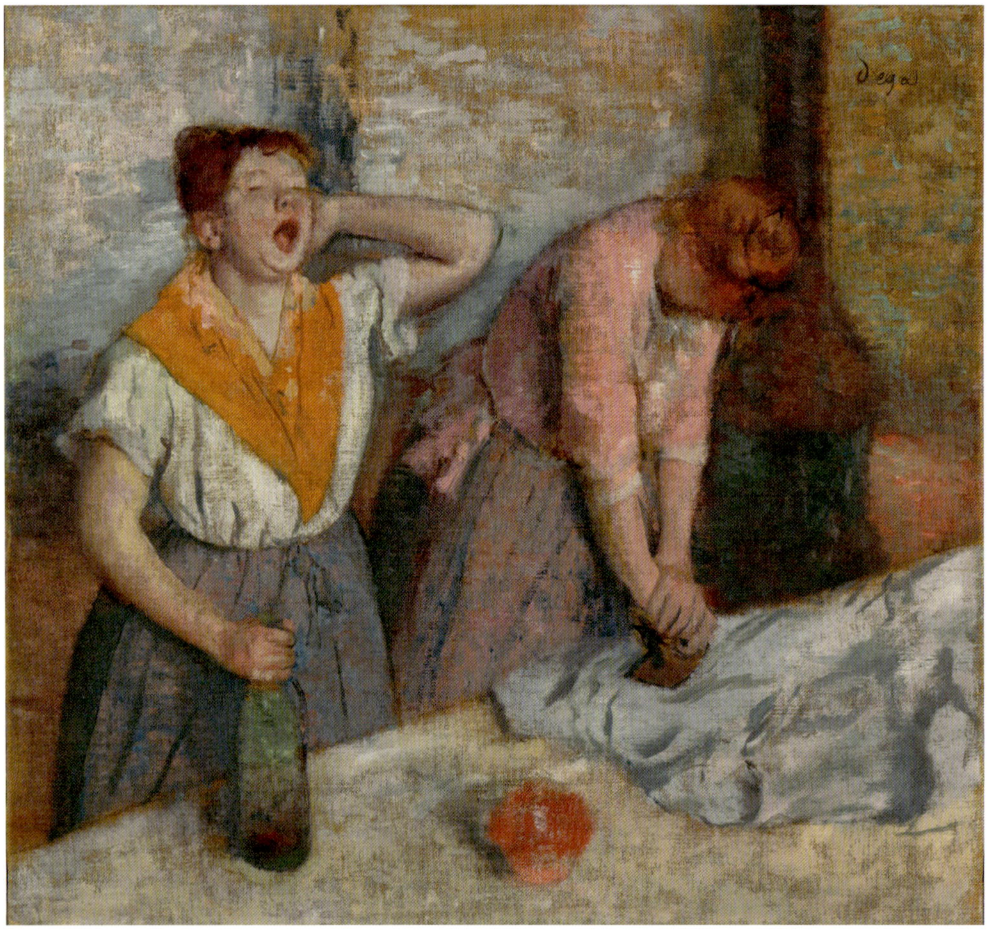

3 Edgar Degas, *Women Ironing*, c. 1884–1886, oil on canvas, Musée d'Orsay, Paris

Each impressionist approached the challenge of capturing the moment in his or her own way: Degas openly affirmed his passion for drawing and constantly experimented with a broad range of media; Renoir turned to the models of the past, declaring that he needed to relearn how to draw and paint; the wise Pissarro had never ceased to draw; Monet strove relentlessly to come to terms with the changeability of things. For all of them, though, the practice of drawing was essential. And they had all benefited from a sound training, even those who had not studied at the École des Beaux-Arts, for the teaching offered in both Charles Gleyre's atelier and the Académie run by Charles Suisse was based principally on drawing.

In fact, in the final quarter of the nineteenth century, drawing epitomized the academic approach — the strict rules of apprenticeship, the studio work after a live model, with all its doubts and hesitations. As this was precisely the approach that the impressionists had rejected, they did not promote this aspect of their art, nor did they often exhibit their preparatory works. Yet beyond the need to assemble "documentation" that would facilitate work in the studio, the impressionists often drew simply for pleasure, with no other goal than to capture a privileged moment or the features of someone dear.

In a dynamic pastel study of his wife and small daughter, Armand Guillaumin was evidently captivated by the contrast between the mother's dark dress and the pale garments of the child (pl. 46). This initial sketch retains all the vigor of a study made from life, but a short while later the artist illustrated the same subject in a more schematic pastel drawing inscribed "St. Cheron 94." In this subsequent work he altered his wife's pose slightly so as to emphasize her profile, bringing it closer to her likeness in the painting *Madame Guillaumin and Her Daughters*.[13]

It was in watercolor that Berthe Morisot chose to make one of her very first images of her daughter Julie Manet (pl. 41). With an exquisitely light brush she defined the features of the baby, who had nothing to recommend her but "her fat cheeks and pretty complexion" and whom her mother judged to be "a Manet to the tips of her fingers."[14] A few strokes of fluid color were all it took to create this delicate harmony of blonde and blue, yet as period photographs prove, the resemblance is striking.

Although the impressionists employed a variety of drawing techniques, often simultaneously, they showed a definite preference for pastel and watercolor. Pastel enabled the artist to draw in color, while the watercolorist could create volume by juxtaposing different tones: the idea of separating form and color seemed to them artificial. Cézanne summarized it thus: "Drawing and color are not distinct from one another; gradually as one paints, one draws; the more harmonious the colors are, the more precise the drawing will be."[15] Nevertheless, for the large majority of his sketchbook studies, Cézanne used monochromatic media like black chalk or graphite (fig. 4).

Following on from Eugène Delacroix and the romantics, Johan Barthold Jongkind did much to enhance the status of watercolor in France. The medium had a rich history, for it was considered an essential tool of travelers, both those pursuing scientific explorations and well-born young men making their Grand Tour. In England, Joseph Mallord William Turner had already transformed it into a full-fledged art form (see p. 22, fig. 4). Jongkind seems to have preferred watercolor to oil. In an excellent monograph on the artist, Paul Signac wrote: "Jongkind's drawings and watercolors represent the most characteristic aspect of his oeuvre, the one that enables us best to understand and appreciate it. It is also the one that he favored, guarding it jealously in portfolios, reserving it for friends rather than dealers. It was the joy of his life."[16] Among Jongkind's extensive production, the view of Avignon presented here (pl. 47) is especially significant, as it is illustrated in the book on Jongkind by Signac, who owned at least twenty-six of the Dutch artist's watercolors.[17] This *Street in Avignon* was apparently among them: when visiting the city Signac executed his own version of the same view, which he titled "Jongkind's motif."[18]

Watercolor — a form that demands decisiveness and speed — also appealed to Cézanne, slow and rough as he was. Discovered on his death, the

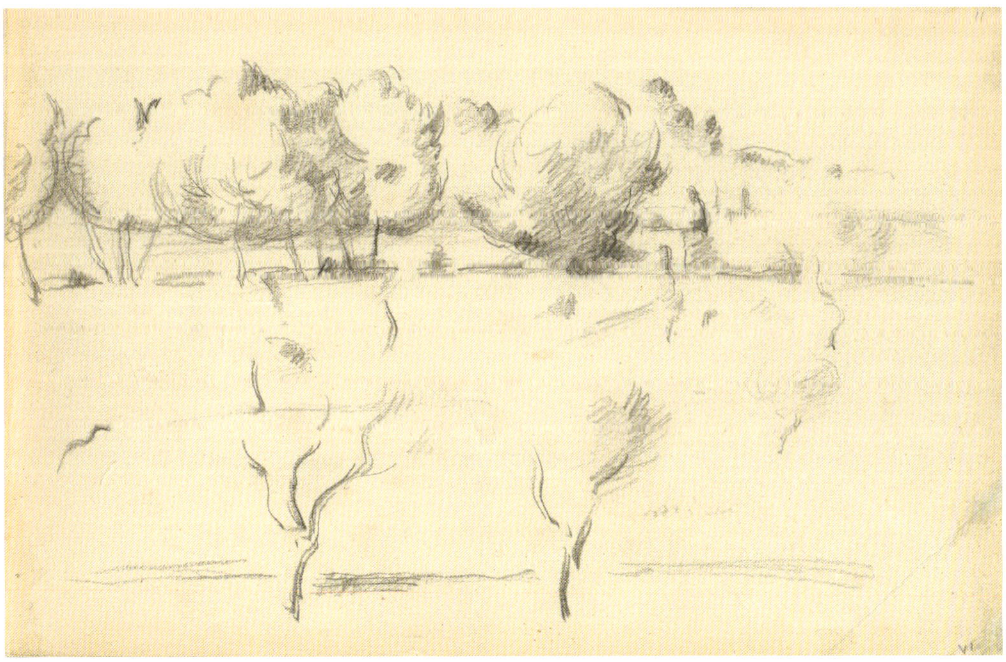

4 Paul Cézanne, *Landscape with Trees*, 1895/1898, graphite, National Gallery of Art, Washington, Collection of Mr. and Mrs. Paul Mellon, in Honor of the 50th Anniversary of the National Gallery of Art, 1992

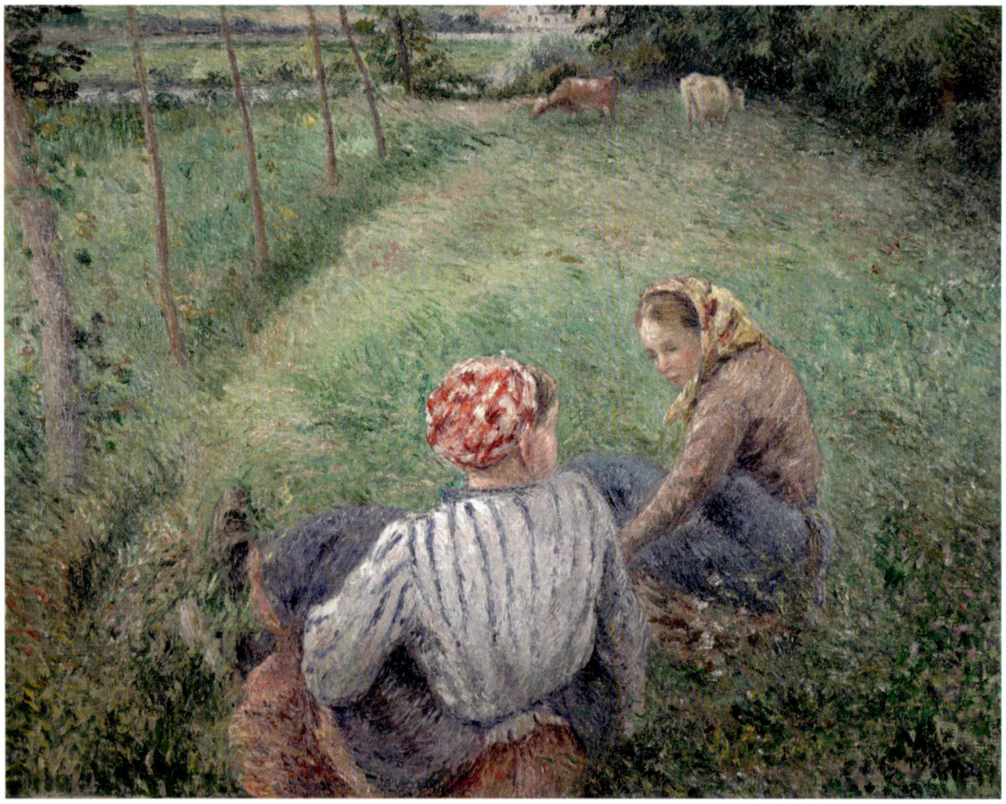

5 Camille Pissarro, *Peasant Women Watching Cows*, 1882, oil on canvas, Collection of Mrs. Paul Mellon, Oak Spring Garden Library, Upperville, Virginia

watercolors made by the painter from Aix were a revelation, immediately snapped up by the ever-astute Ambroise Vollard. The one seen here, *A Stand of Trees along a River Bank* (pl. 50), was singled out by Lionello Venturi, who was especially taken by the subtle tiering of tones in the foliage, which he likened to the "lyrical rhythm of a magnificent waterfall."[19] With rare refinement, the artist has exploited the intrinsic properties of the medium, and the whole image is illuminated by the white of the support, either left in reserve or gleaming through the color.

Under the impact of Pierre Paul Prud'hon and the painters of romanticism, there was also an upswing in the popularity of pastel in France. What really sparked the impressionists' interest, however, were the large black crayon and pastel drawings by Millet, first brought to public attention in 1875 during the Émile Gavet sale (p. 49, fig. 2). Pissarro, a great admirer of Millet, was an excellent draftsman. He was in the habit of methodically preparing his oil paintings, and to this end he drew constantly — *en plein air* and from life. His training in the studio of the Danish artist Anton Melbye had provided him with a solid grounding, which he honed during sojourns in Venezuela and London, before his ultimate move to Eragny in 1884. In the early 1880s Pissarro embarked on a series of canvases featuring large figures of peasant women, represented here by an outstanding pastel and a charcoal work (pls. 42 and 43). The former, a preparatory sketch for *Peasant Women Watching Cows* (fig. 5), is a marvelous fusion of expertise and freedom — a masterpiece in its own right. In this admirably composed image, the artist offers us a rear view of a woman seated on the ground. He juxtaposes black, blue, and red — brightened with touches of pink — with the tone of the paper left in reserve. The artist has also taken full advantage of the contrast between the spiral created by the sinuous contours and the emphatic hatching.

Like watercolor, pastel can be applied quickly and involves no drying time, but in contrast to watercolor, it does allow for correction. This advantage did not escape Degas, who, ever the innovator, would sometimes steam his pastels with boiling water in order to obtain a richer texture. His technique was almost alchemical: "I soak them over and over again," he told Vollard, "and even put them in the sun."[20] The women impressionists, Berthe Morisot, Eva Gonzalès, and the American Mary Cassatt — a great friend of Degas — were also brilliant pastelists, and they exhibited their drawings regularly. Manet, for his part, became interested in the medium around 1878, as his art moved closer to impressionism. It soon became his preferred technique, and in 1880 he exhibited a group of about fifteen pastels in the offices of *La Vie moderne*.

An important role was played as well by Boudin, who began using pastel very early in his career, finding it particularly well suited to his favorite subjects — sky and water (see pl. 40). Around 1858 he began taking the young Monet with him on expeditions to the beaches of Normandy, thereby exerting a decisive influence on the birth of impressionism. Many years later a pastel by Boudin hung in Monet's bedroom at Giverny.[21]

Monet also drew from an early age (with somewhat schoolboyish precision), and it was to the incisive style of his caricatures that he owed his adolescent reputation.[22] In spite of the evident talent of their author, these works offer no hint of the extraordinarily supple, decisive, and elliptical line that characterizes the water lily studies kept at the Musée Marmottan. Yet the pastels from the 1860s are highly accomplished works. The artist was evidently aware of this, as seven pastels by him are listed in the catalogue of the first impressionist exhibition, held in 1874. Nevertheless, he did not exhibit these large and solidly composed sheets again.

Initially, the "poet of nature" worked according to the most classical of methods: "At that time I did what everyone else did; I proceeded bit by bit with studies done from nature which I would then put together in my studio" (fig. 6).[23] But Monet made a greater effort than any of his friends to paint out of doors. After his move to Giverny, this led to the idea of the series, which involved the simultaneous plein-air execution of several canvases that would be subsequently completed and reworked in the studio. Before his final trip abroad, to Venice in 1908, the artist made a series in London devoted to the effects of light in misty weather. The first of these canvases dates from 1900, but it was not until 1904, after several trips to the English capital, that he judged them finished and exhibited them at the Durand-Ruel Gallery.

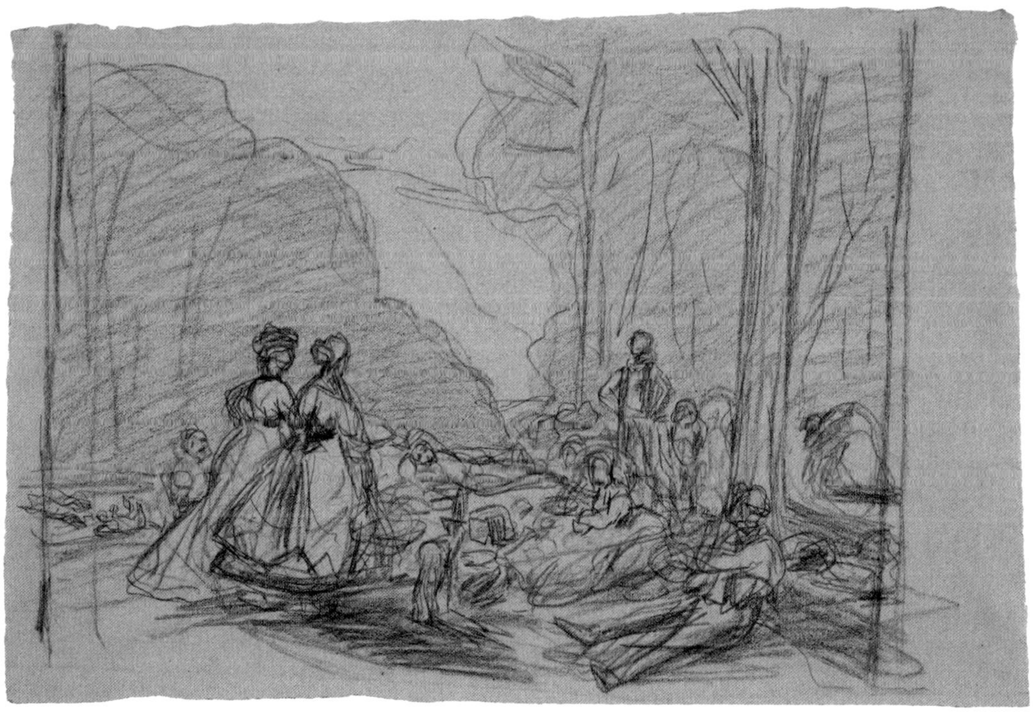

6 Claude Monet, *The Luncheon on the Grass*, c. 1865, black chalk on blue paper, National Gallery of Art, Washington, Collection of Mr. and Mrs. Paul Mellon, 1995

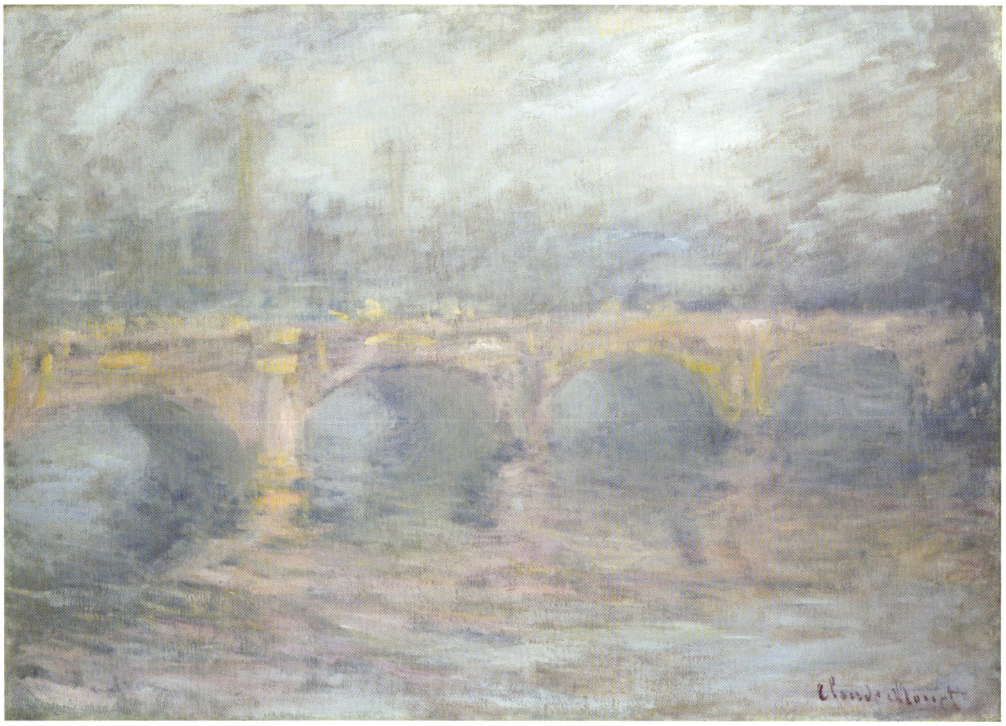

7 Claude Monet, *Waterloo Bridge, London, at Sunset*, 1904, oil on canvas, National Gallery of Art, Washington, Collection of Mr. and Mrs. Paul Mellon, 1983

On one of these visits, in January 1901, Monet rented two rooms at the Savoy Hotel that offered direct views of the Charing Cross and Waterloo Bridges. Eager to get to work but obliged to wait several days for the arrival of the boxes containing his painting material, he decided to lay down his first impressions in pastel: "I'm still trying pastels," he confided to his wife; "I'm really enjoying it, although I've got out of the habit." On February 4, after the luggage had arrived, he wrote: "I'm working hard from my window.... Since I arrived here, aside from the pastels, I've been working exclusively on Waterloo Bridge, about ten canvases. This way, I have fewer pictures to look after, and it works better, but I'll be glad to have a couple more or less finished. It's so difficult."[24] The series of works executed in London eventually consisted of forty-two paintings and twenty-six drawings. In the Dyke collection's beautiful pastel (pl. 51) shades of blue and pink drift across the paper with absolute freedom. This sheet, though likely the basis for the painting at the Art Institute of Chicago, *Waterloo Bridge, Sunlight Effect*, can also be related in both its composition and palette to a canvas at the National Gallery of Art in Washington (fig. 7). But in spite of the evident pleasure afforded the artist by this renewed contact with the medium, no pastels were featured in the 1904 exhibition, and the bulk of them stayed in the artist's possession. For Monet, like most of his fellow impressionists, drawing remained the preserve of intimates and initiates.

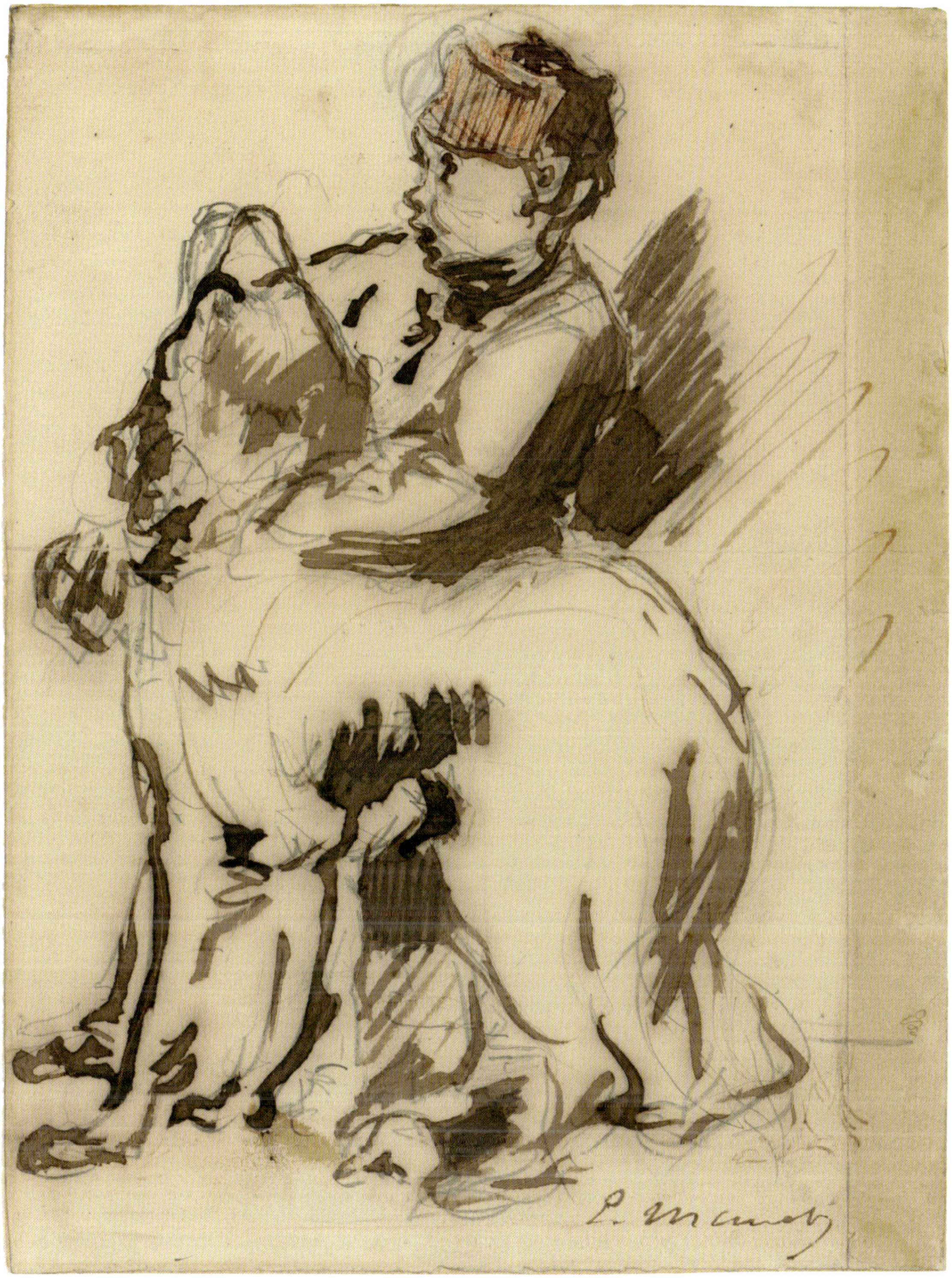

39 Édouard Manet, *A Boy Holding a Dog*, c. 1861
pen and ink with brown wash, graphite, and colored pencil, 212 × 162

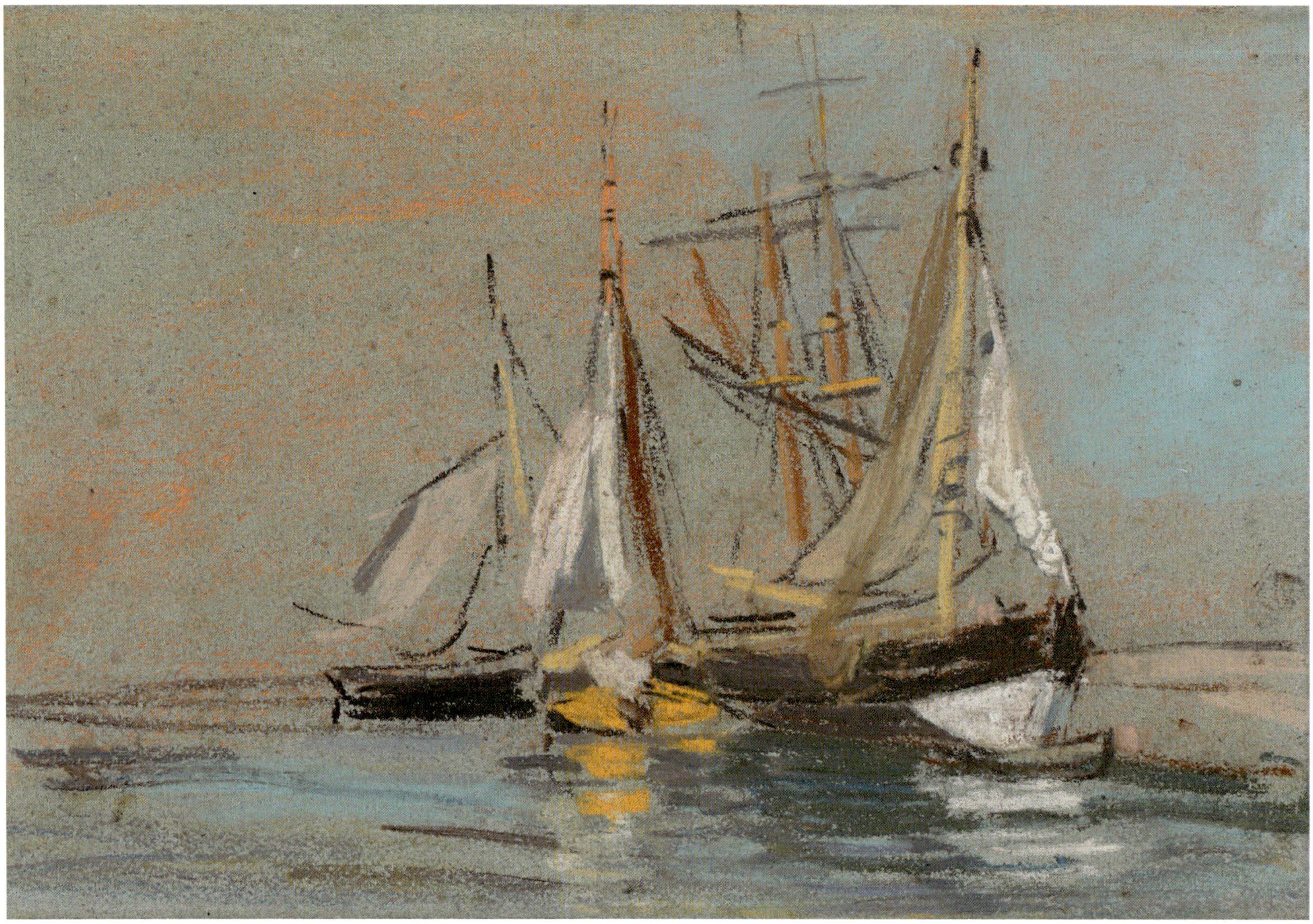

40 Eugène Boudin, *Sailboats,* c. 1860
pastel, 178 × 274

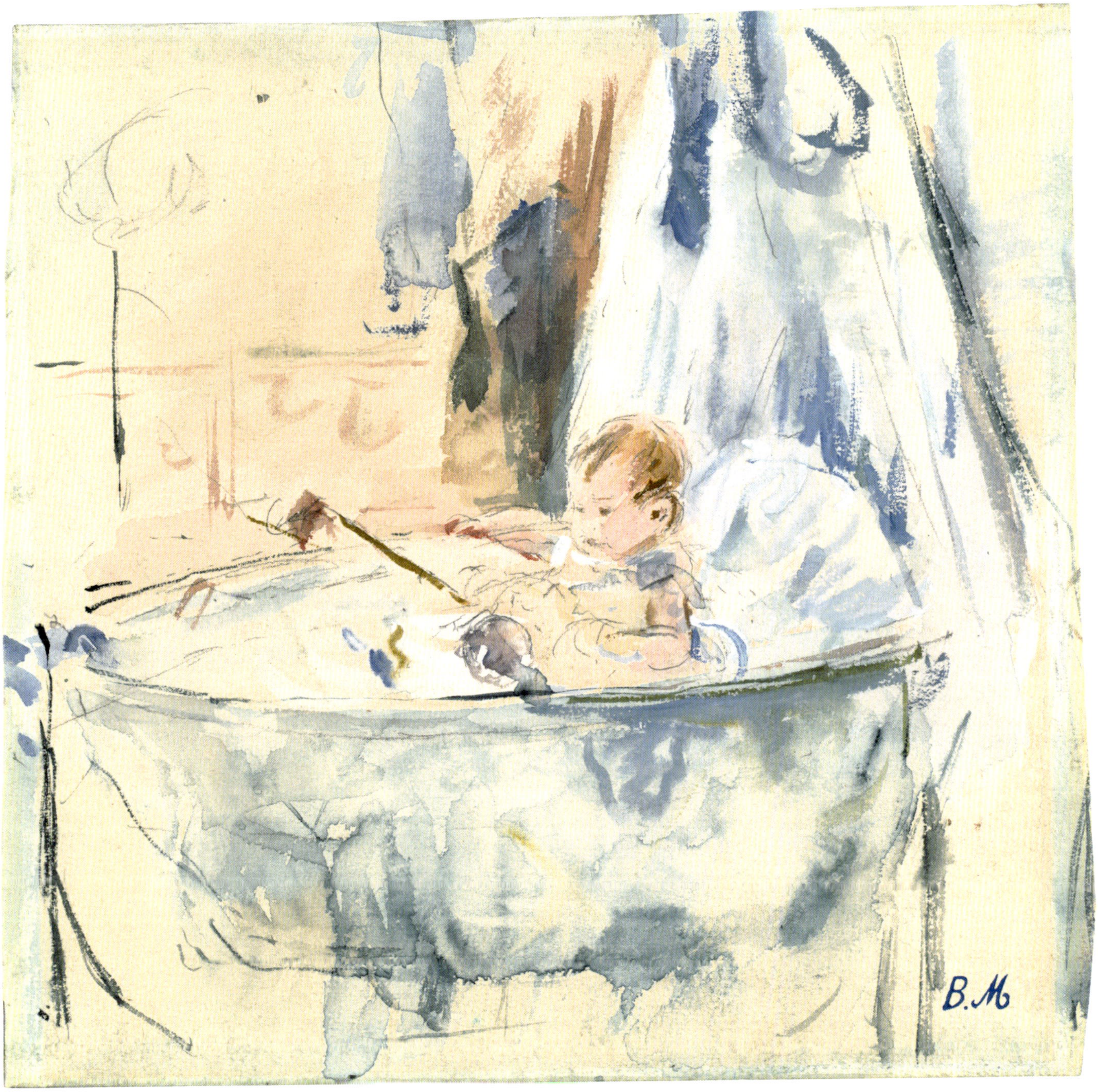

41 Berthe Morisot, *Julie Manet in a Canopied Cradle,* 1879
watercolor and gouache, 180 × 180

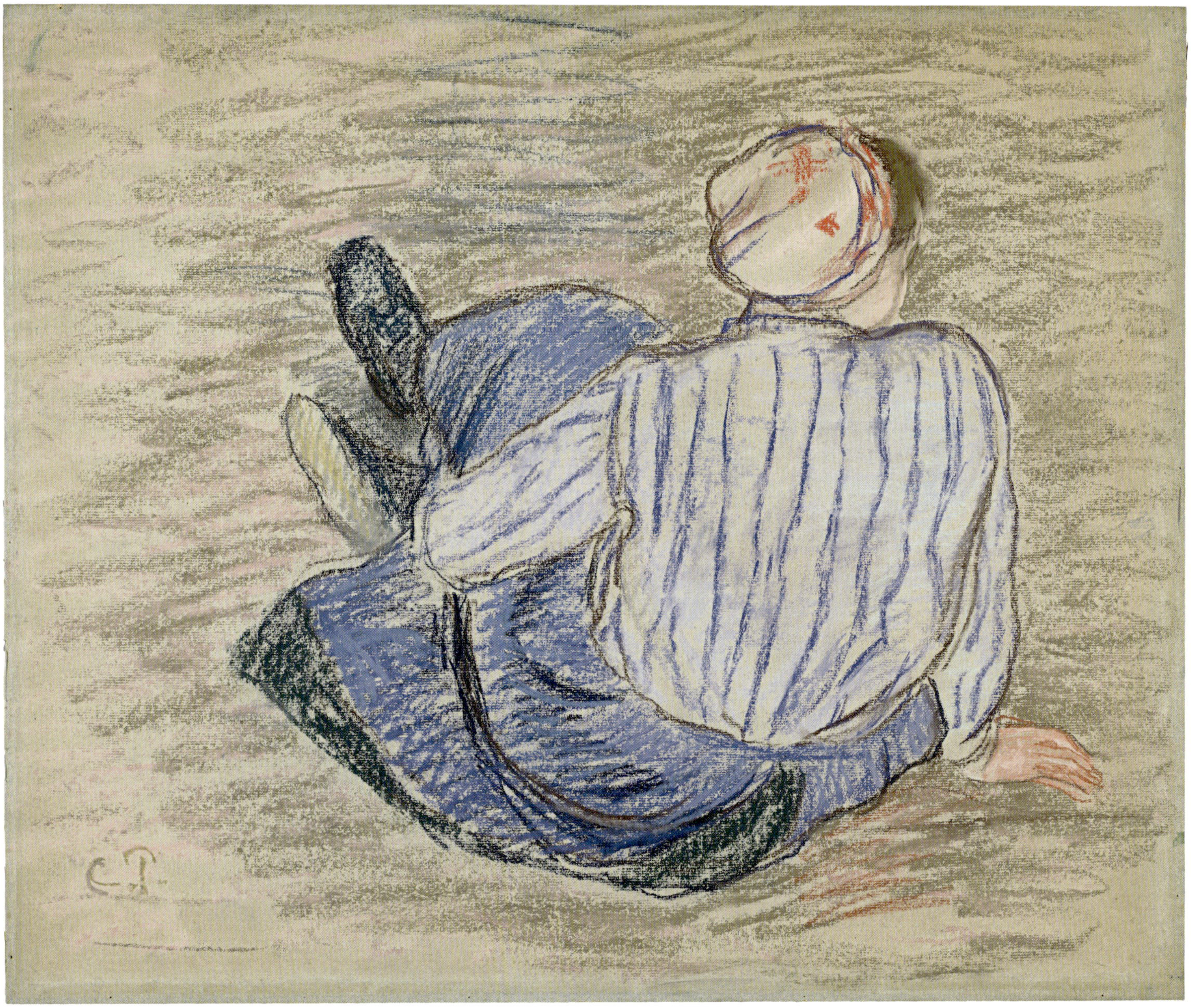

42 Camille Pissarro, *A Country Girl Seated on the Ground,* c. 1880
pastel, 470 × 566

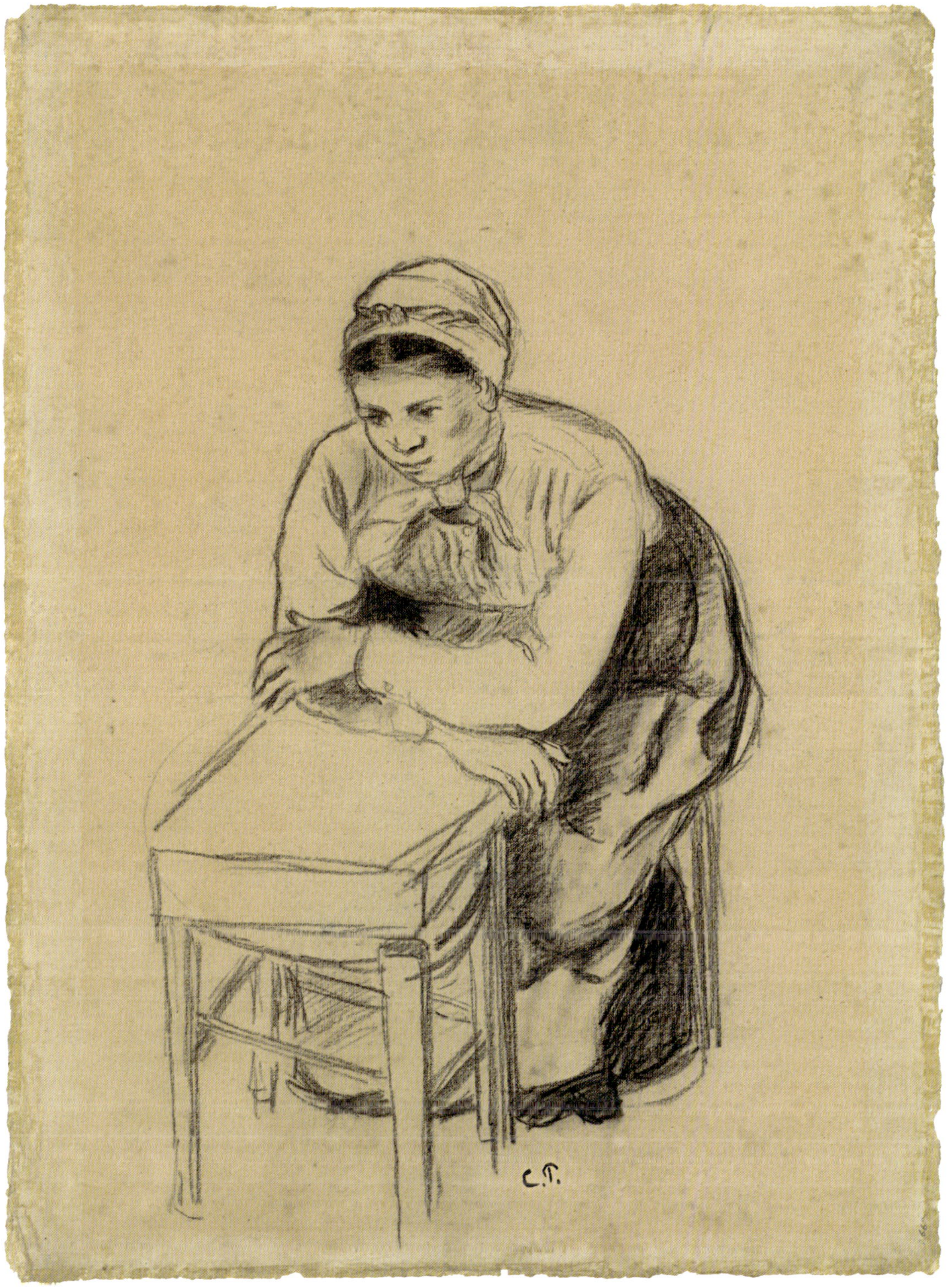

43 Camille Pissarro, *The Pumpkin Seller,* c. 1888
charcoal, 645 × 478

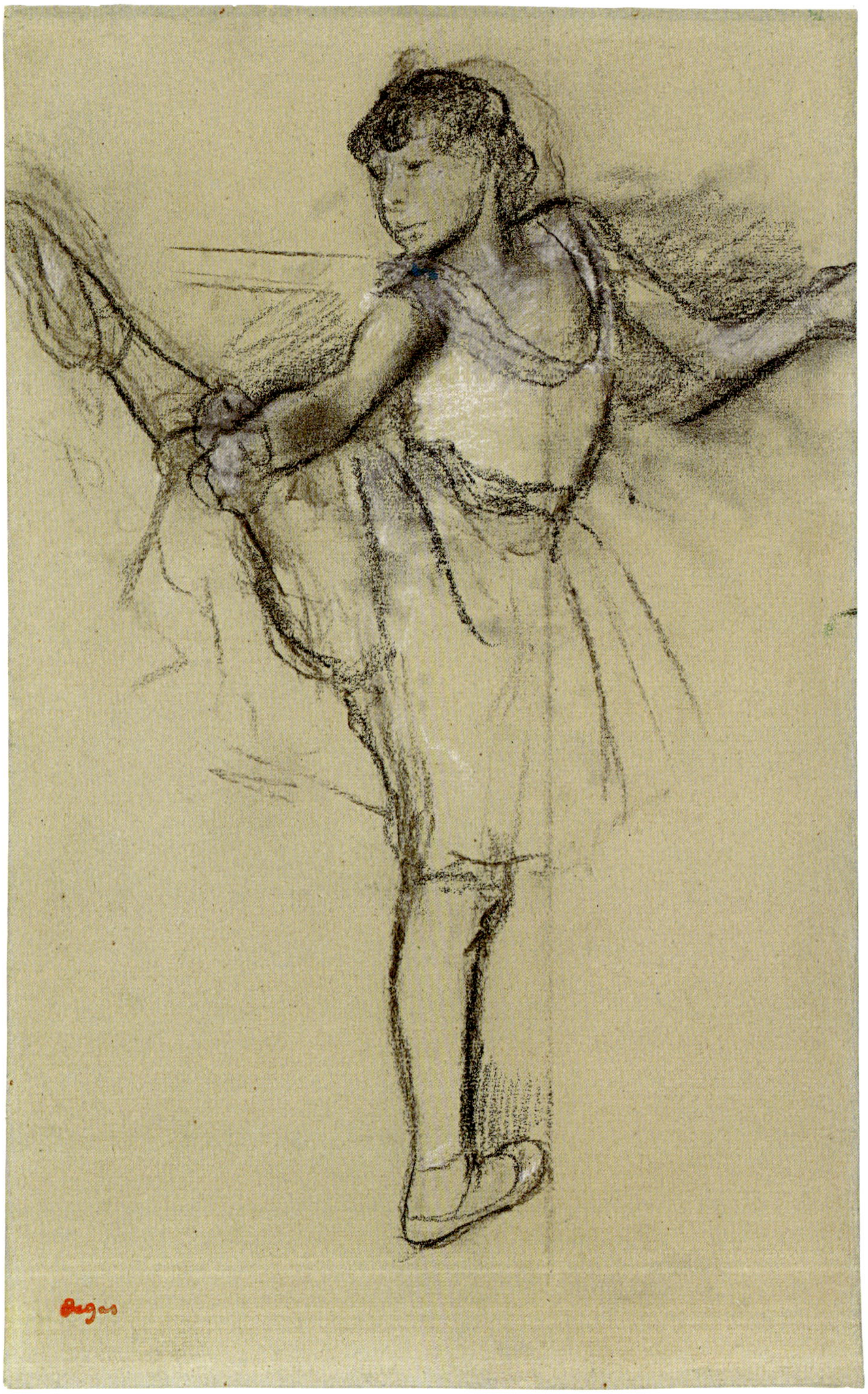

44 Edgar Degas, *A Dancer at the Bar,* 1876/1878
charcoal with white chalk, 457 × 292

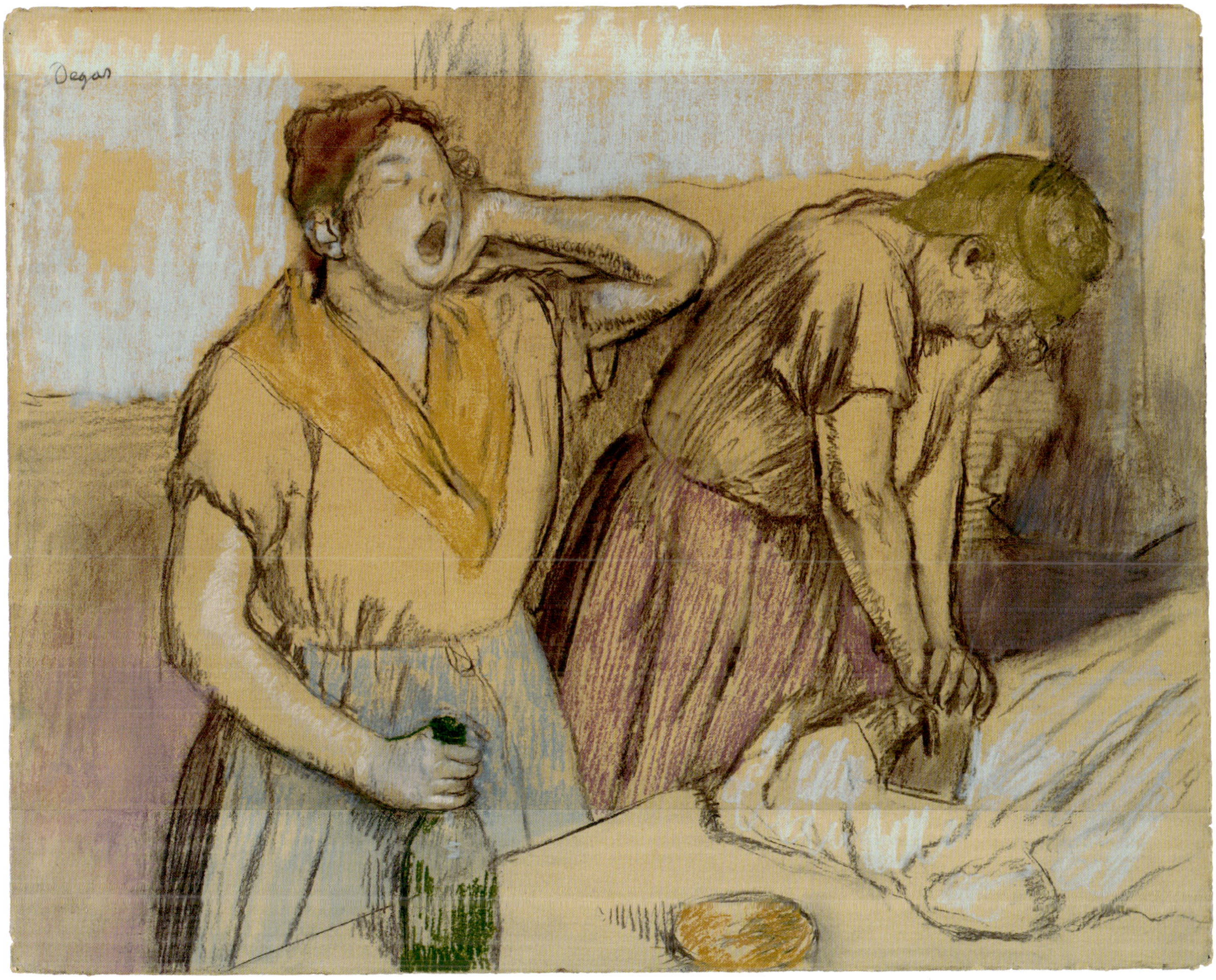

45 Edgar Degas, *Two Women Ironing*, c. 1885
pastel and charcoal, 600 × 760

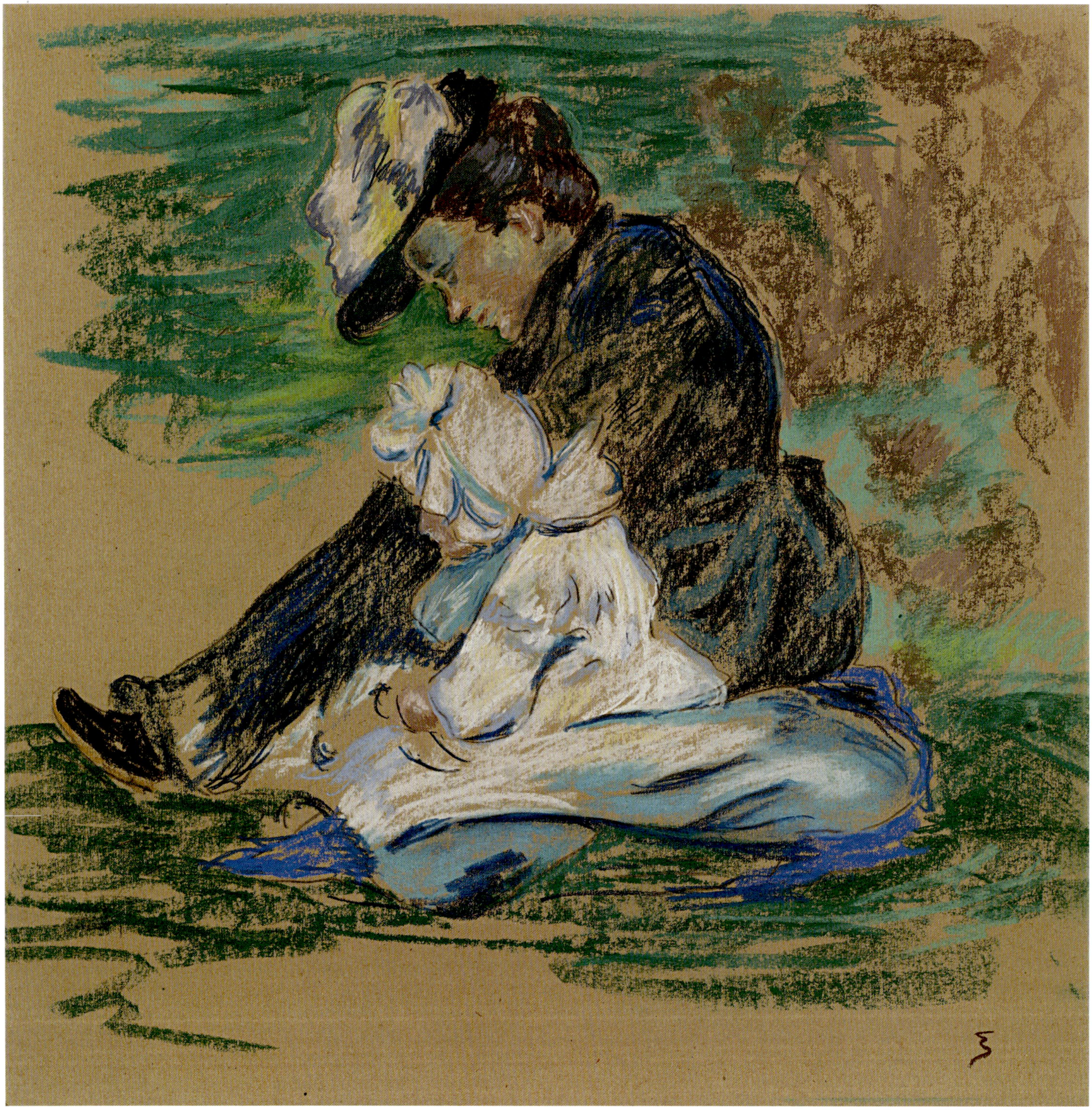

46 Jean-Baptiste-Armand Guillaumin, *Madame Guillaumin with Her Infant Daughter,* 1890/1892
pastel, 530 × 530

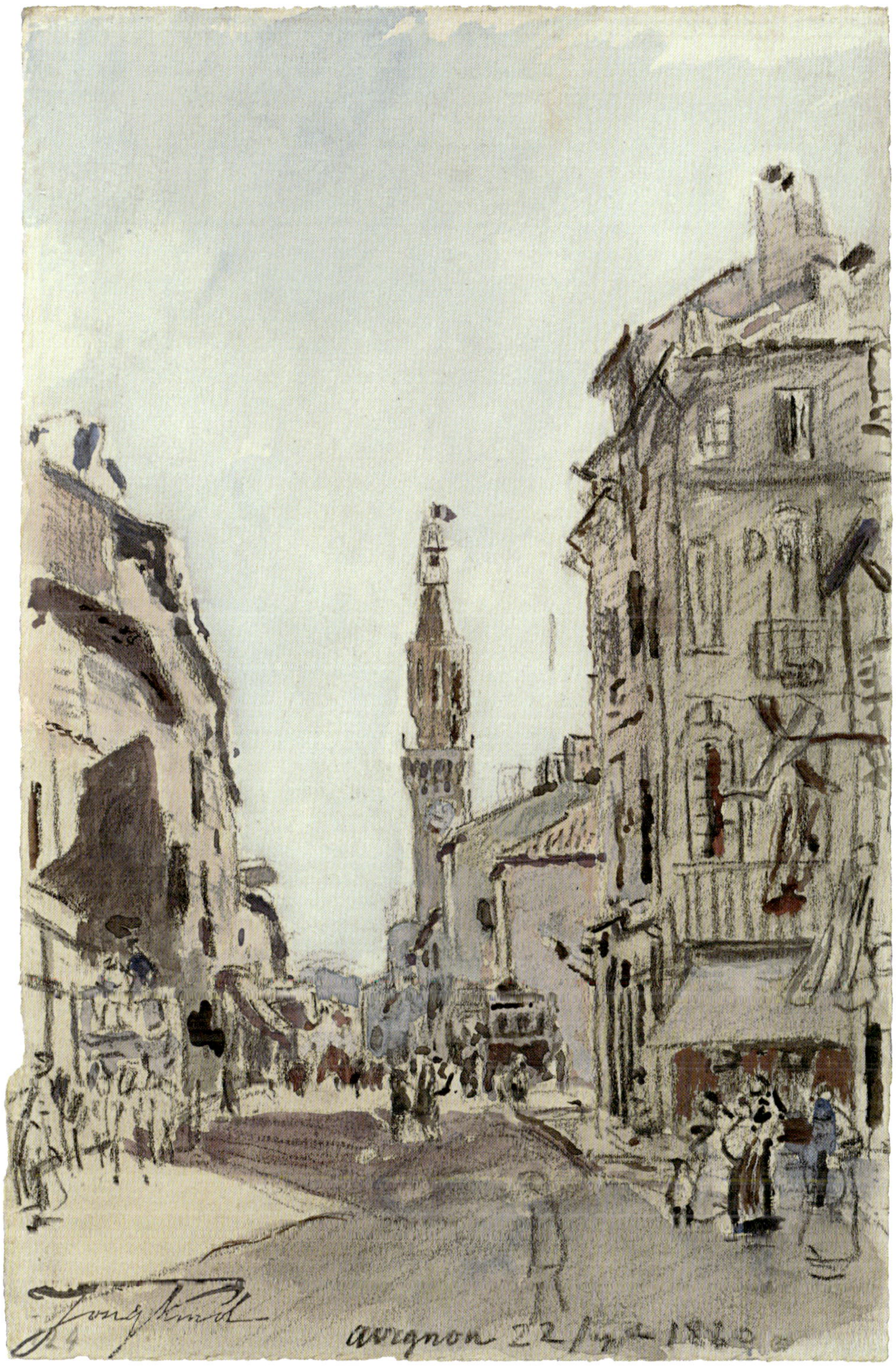

47 Johan Barthold Jongkind, *A Street in Avignon Leading toward the Place de l'Horloge,* 1880
watercolor and gouache, 230 × 150

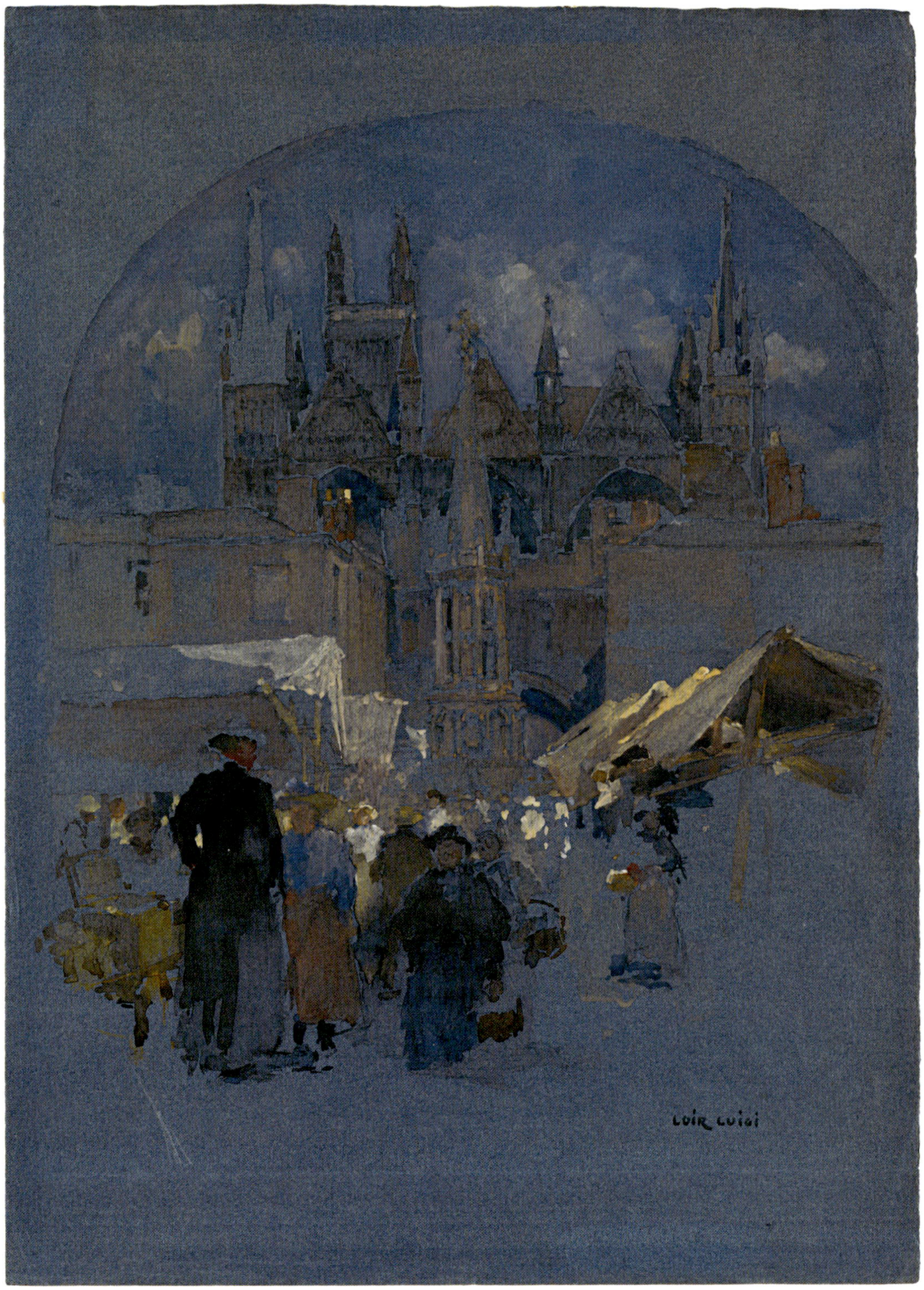

48 Luigi Loir, *A Market Square in Front of a Cathedral,* 1870s/1880s
watercolor and gouache, 389 × 283

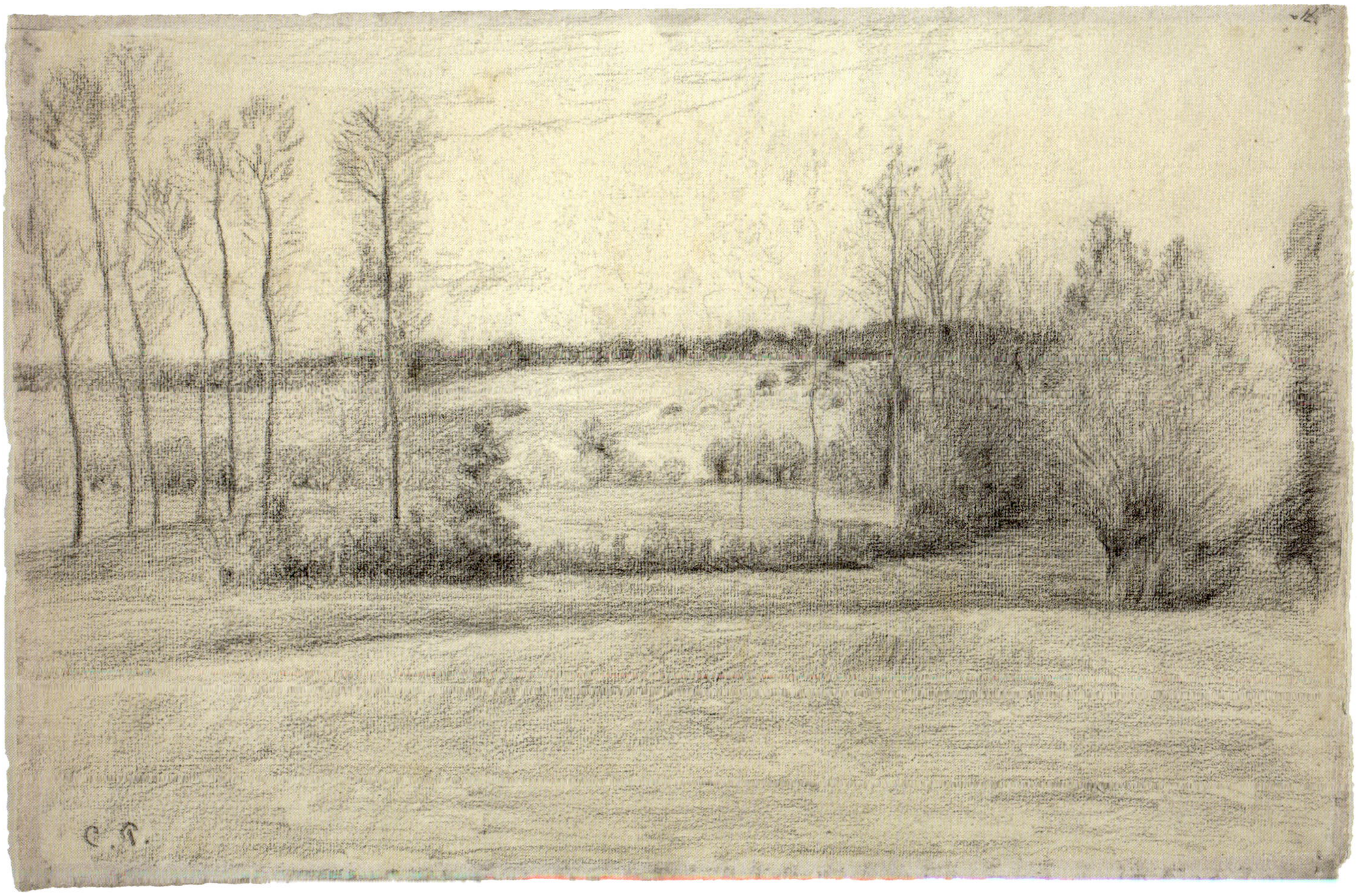

49 Camille Pissarro, *Trees and Meadows at Eragny,* 1895/1900
black chalk, 308 × 475

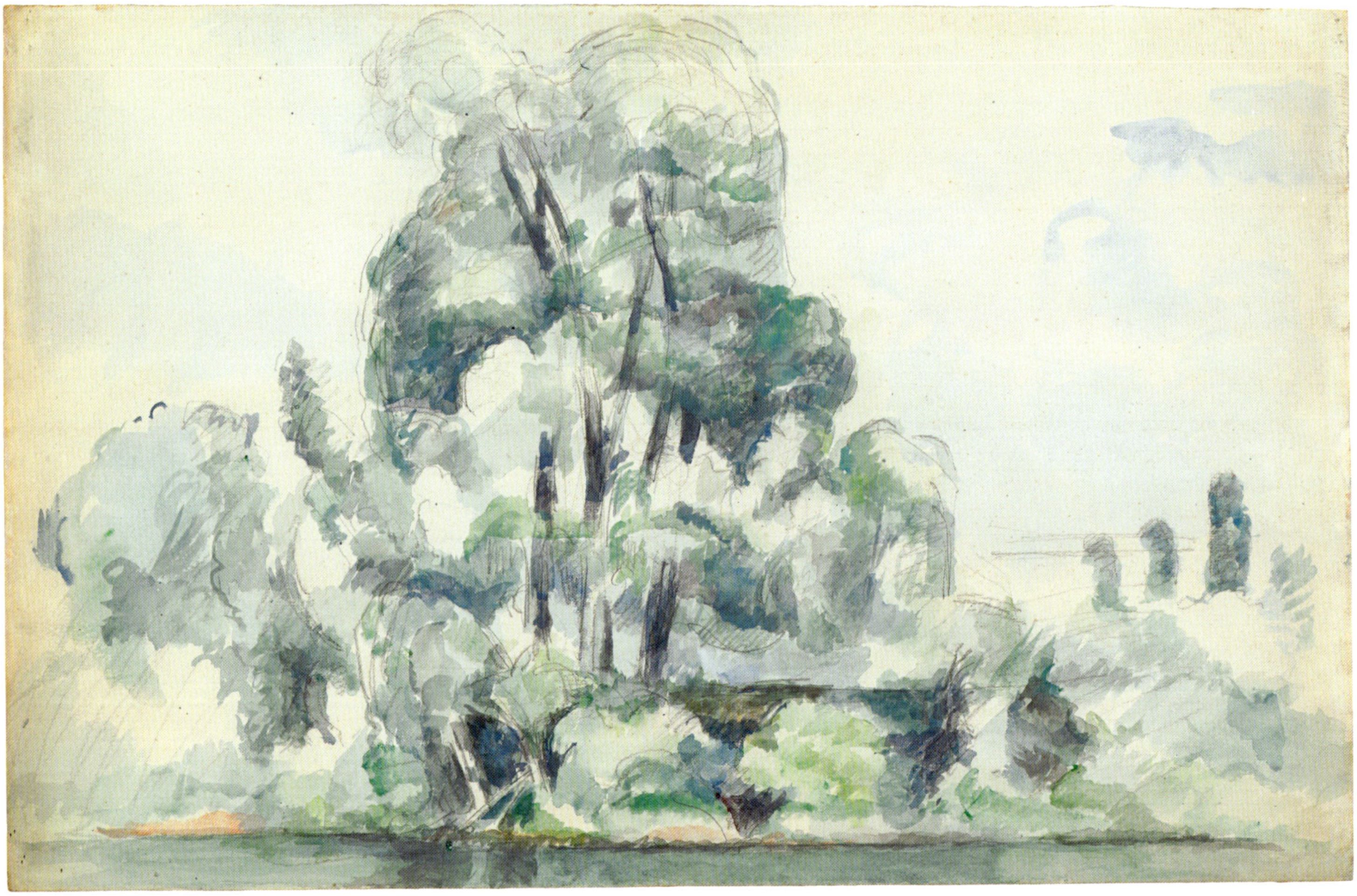

50 Paul Cézanne, *A Stand of Trees along a River Bank,* 1880/1885
watercolor and graphite, 310 × 430

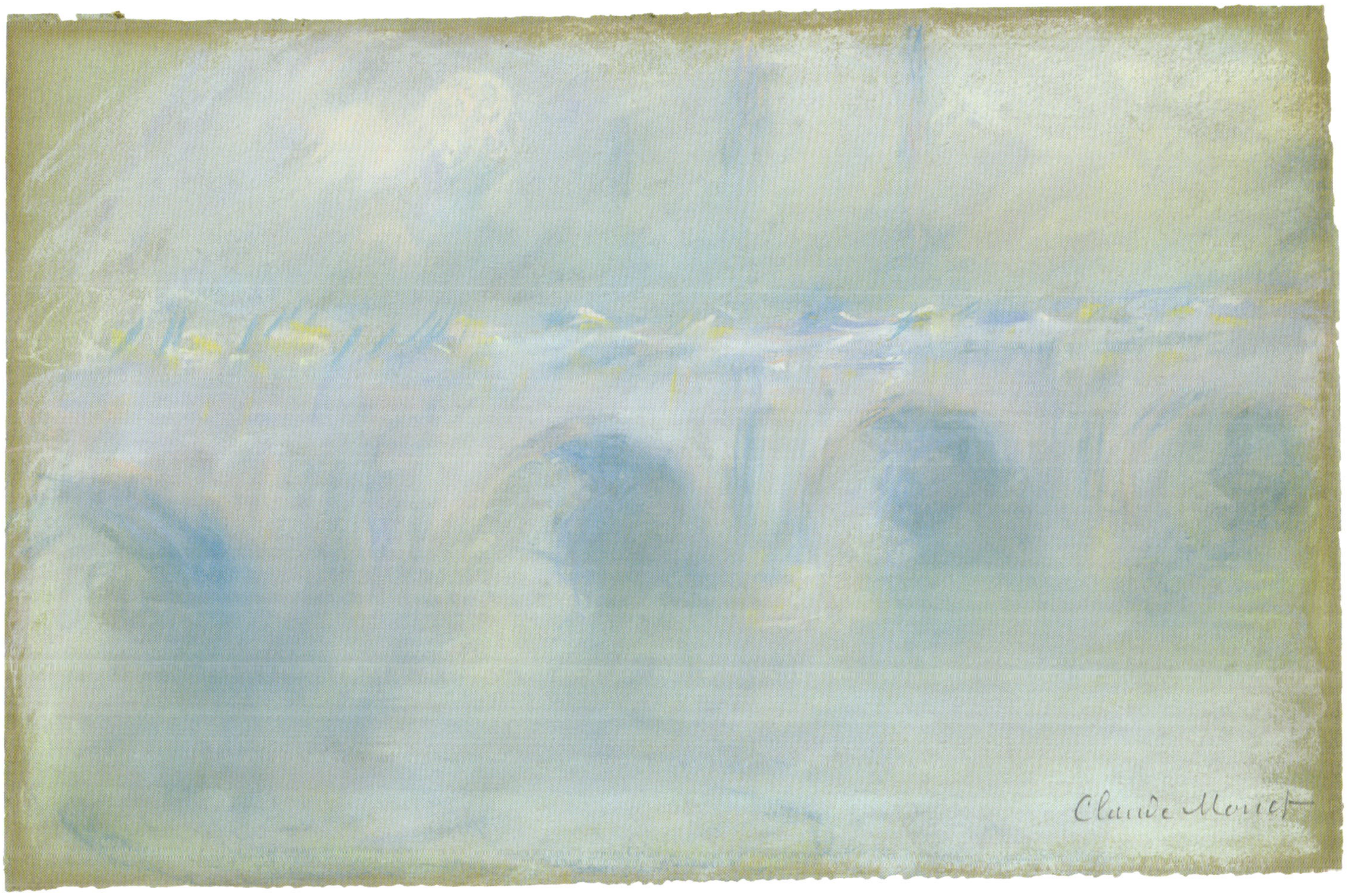

51 Claude Monet, *Waterloo Bridge*, 1901
pastel, 311 × 502

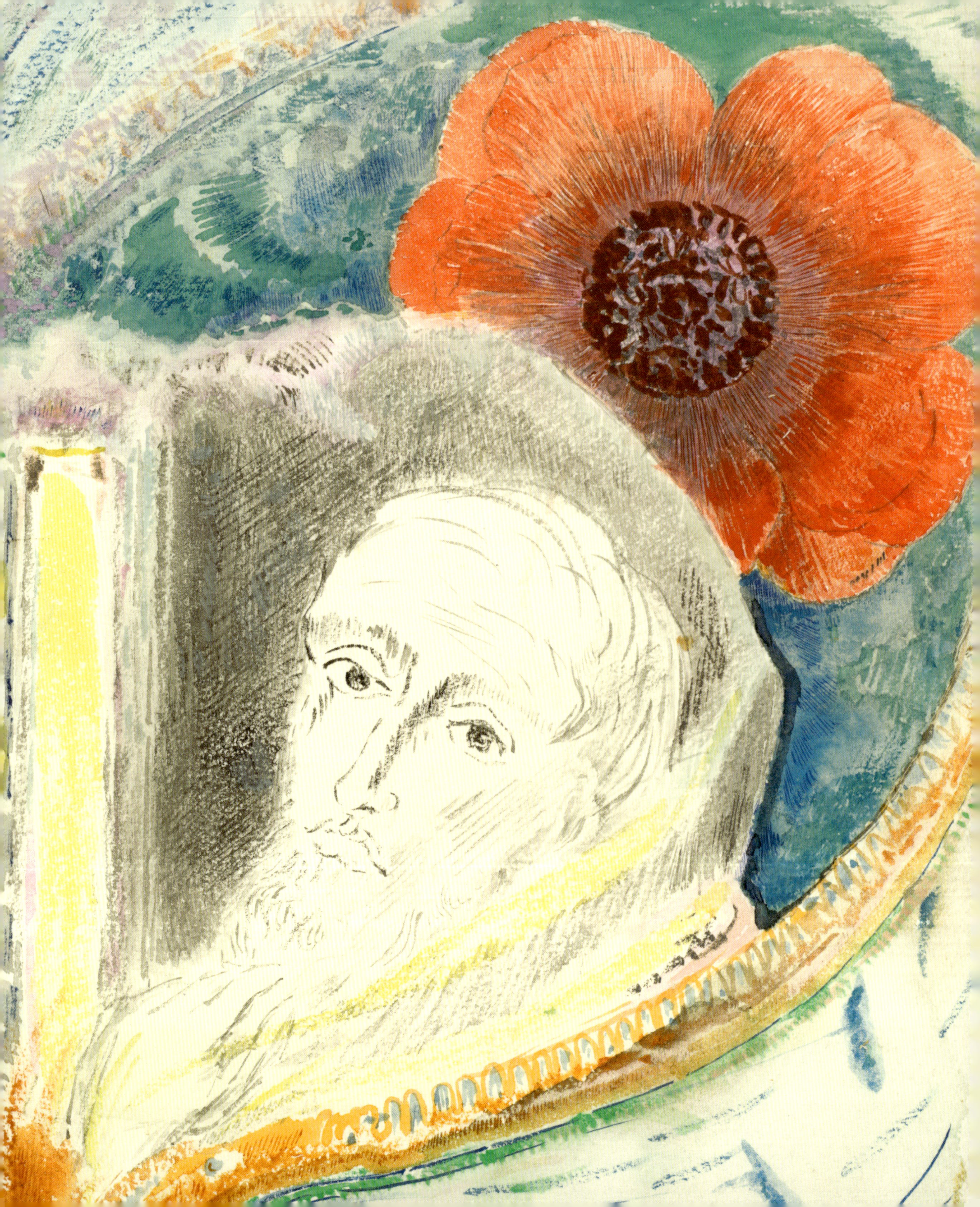

The Nabis and Symbolists

ELIZABETH EASTON

AT THE END OF the nineteenth century a small group of artists calling themselves the "Nabis," after the Hebrew word for "prophets," sought to create a new kind of painting. Inspired by the art of Paul Gauguin, these artists wanted to evoke the sensations of the world around them rather than depict the objective reality that was the core of impressionism. The moment that is most often credited with the consolidation of the Nabi aesthetic was the return of the artist Paul Sérusier from a stay with Gauguin in Pont-Aven, the town in Brittany where the older artist had formed the core of an artistic community. Maurice Denis, Pierre Bonnard, Édouard Vuillard, and others were inspired by a painting by Sérusier on a cigar box cover that depicted a landscape in the Bois d'Amour of Pont-Aven. It was an almost abstract composition, with blotches of bright colors and abstract forms. Labeled the "Talisman," it became the inspirational object of their artistic goals (fig. 1). Denis, whose essays and diaries chronicle the history of the group, recalled Gauguin's words of advice to Sérusier: "How does that tree look to you?...It's a vivid green, isn't it? So take some green, the best green you've got on your palette. And that shadow's blue, really, isn't it? So don't be afraid — make it as blue as you can."[1] This message freed the young painters from the compulsion to paint the objective world, filled with academic rules and conventions, and instead attempt to depict the images in their imagination.

The subject of Nabi drawings embodies an essential paradox that underlies a disparity between "observing," which is central to drawing, and

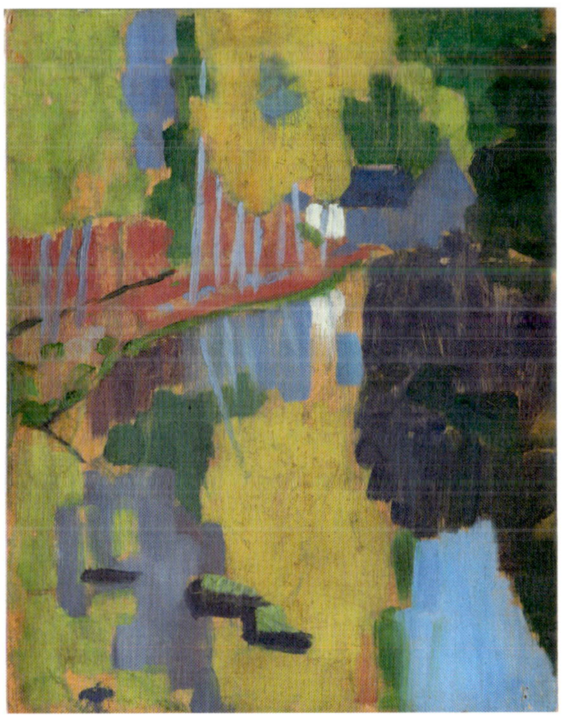

1 Paul Sérusier, *The Talisman, the Aven River at the Bois d'Amour,* 1888, oil on wood, Musée d'Orsay, Paris, Acquired with the participation of M. Philipe Meyer, through Lutèce, 1985

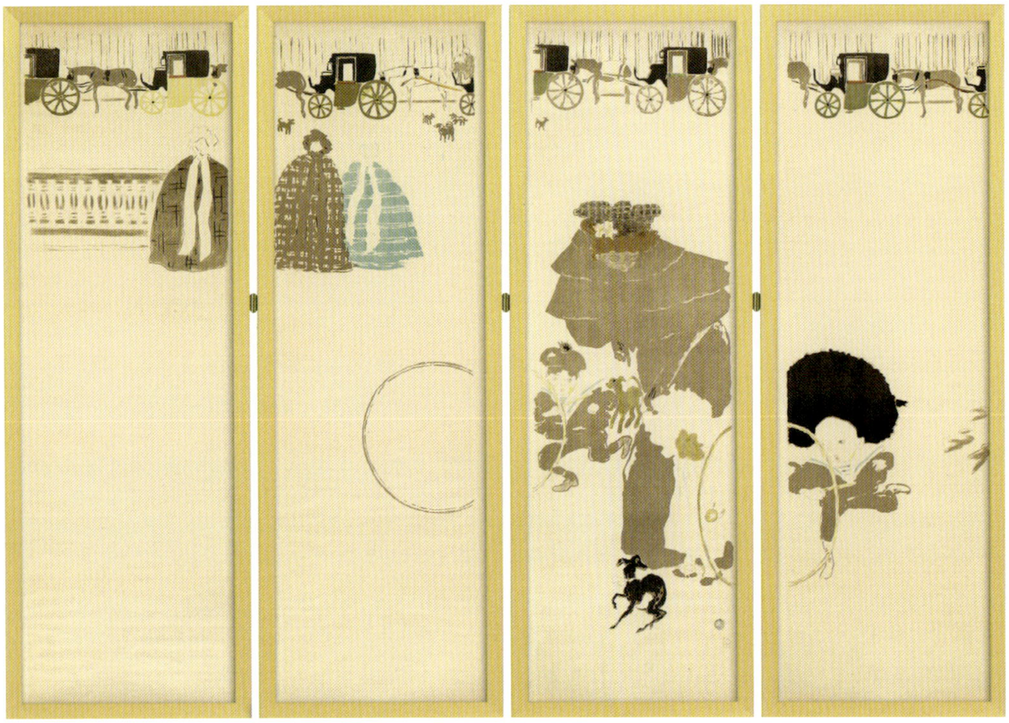

2 Pierre Bonnard, *Promenade des Nourrices, Frise des Fiacres*, 1899, 4-part color lithographic screen, National Gallery of Art, Washington, Virginia and Ira Jackson Collection, 1999

"imagining," which lies at the core of the symbolist aesthetic. To a great extent, and contrary to the recording of daily life that sketching would imply, the Nabis rejected the primacy of direct observation that had dominated the art of the previous generation of impressionists, choosing instead to portray a more imaginary realm in their art. They sought what the symbolist poet and critic Gustave Kahn termed the "essential aim" of art, which was "to objectify the subjective (the exteriorization of an idea) instead of subjectifying the objective (nature seen through a temperament)."[2]

The lofty theoretical basis of their art did not inhibit the Nabis from drawing, printmaking, and myriad other artistic endeavors beyond their main activity of painting with oil on canvas; indeed, this was an intellectual program that the Nabis were eager to apply to a wide range of media or genres. They designed backdrops for theatrical performances, embellished furniture with decorated glazed tiles, made stained-glass windows, carved wood, painted porcelain dinner services, experimented with photography, and embraced the fullest range of artistic expression to decorate their environments — domestic or commissioned, public or private. To this day, remnants of this decorative impulse can still be seen in such places as the Théâtre des Champs-Elysées and the ceilings of the Petit Palais in Paris as well as in the large panel paintings and objects scattered throughout public and private collections, separated from their original functions and the spaces for which they were intended (fig. 2). While these decorative endeavors might at first seem at odds with the group's philosophical aspirations, in fact the two were closely aligned. This was best expressed by the young symbolist critic, Albert Aurier, who wrote in an article on Gauguin that the work of art should be:

> 1. *Idéist,* for its unique ideal will be the expression of the Idea. 2. *Symbolist,* for it will express this Idea by means of forms. 3. *Synthetist,* for it will present these forms, these signs, according to a method that is generally understandable. 4. *Subjective,* for the object will never be considered as an object but as the sign of an idea perceived by the subject. and 5. (it is consequently) *Decorative* — for decorative painting in its proper sense, as the Egyptians and, very probably the Greeks and the Primitives understood it, is nothing other than a manifestation of art at once subjective, synthetic, symbolic and Idéist.[3]

The manner in which the Nabis used drawing to address these artistic challenges was as varied as the purposes of the art: from random sketches in small pocket notebooks that captured vignettes of life directly observed to formal sketches that were intended as preparatory cartoons for tapestries. It seems as if the Nabis were never without a pencil and paper. And if their artistic aims were lofty, direct observation was often the point of departure for their symbolist compositions.

The range of the Nabis' styles, too, was as varied as their artistic goals; while one can discern a generalized chronological evolution from the most radical visual minimalism in their early art to a more descriptive approach in their work of the twentieth century, each artist had a distinctive way of putting pencil or pen to paper and paint to canvas. With Gauguin as the wellspring, the early draftsmanship of the Nabis hovered around a style called *cloisonnisme*, where flat areas of color defined forms that were contained within heavy outlines. Maurice Denis's manifesto of 1890 declared: "It should be remembered that a picture — before being a warhorse, a nude, or an anecdote of some sort — is essentially a flat surface covered with colours assembled in a certain order."[4] This simple statement reflects the reductive style of the Nabis' art in the late 1880s to early 1890s; Vuillard's early pastel of *The Dressmaker* (pl. 54) is a perfect example of cloisonniste style. By the middle to late 1890s many of the artists embraced a more decorative, patterned approach in their work. Denis's *Design for a Fan* (pl. 56), with its colorful flourishes and curving lines, is an example of this style that would influence art nouveau by the end of the century. Bonnard's *Promenade* (pl. 55), the only complete study for his famous screen (see fig. 2) — with its patterning and emphasis on decoration more than on form or on the depiction of perspective or any kind of penetration of the pictorial surface — stems from the same artistic worldview.

The drawings in the Dyke collection offer a rich array of Nabi styles, beginning with a major pastel by Gauguin on yellow paper (pl. 52). Although Gauguin was not a member of the Nabi brotherhood, his art served as the group's seminal inspiration. The figure in the pastel — large in scale, fully realized, and clearly taken from a live model — is the same size as she will appear in the painting *Women Bathing* from the same year (Museum of Mohamed Mahmoud Khalil, Giza, Egypt).[5] In the Dyke collection's pastel, Gauguin gives a stark portrayal of a seated woman, deftly using the yellow paper for her body and surrounding her with a halo of turquoise that isolates her from the rest of the sheet. The sparest lines and shading indicate the muscles and textures of her form. Most striking is the abstraction of the head, shown bent over the torso, which Gauguin has reinforced with heavy, precise, clear lines of bister pastel to articulate the eyelids, eyebrows, and nose. The entire drawing is a masterful reduction to the essentials, with the contrapposto of the figure and the abstracted position of the head suggesting the power and humility of Eve. Gauguin regarded his drawings as private, declaring: "A critic at my house...asks to see my drawings. My drawings! Never! They are my letters, my secrets."[6] But this drawing was exhibited posthumously at the Salon d'Automne, *Oeuvres de Gauguin*, in 1906.

The Nabis who embraced the mystical side of symbolism, such as Denis and Sérusier, were inspired not only by Gauguin but also by Odilon Redon, who was well known to the group and much admired.[7] Redon spent the early years of his artistic career creating what he called *noirs*, or black charcoal drawings, with fanciful creatures and dreamlike settings — depicting images of the visible and the invisible (fig. 3).[8] He invented a potent compositional universe, with acute attention to detail, depicting objects in the natural world juxtaposed with more dreamlike evocations. By the 1890s Redon had introduced color into his work, and although the Dyke watercolor, *A Vision of a Saint with a Poppy* from around 1912 (pl. 69), was made well after the artist's initial contact with and influence on the Nabis, it nevertheless conveys the essence of what appealed to the Nabis in Redon's art. Here the vibrant red poppy in the upper right corner, closely observed, hovers over an evanescent portrait of a bearded man, in grisaille, which occupies the lower part of a decorative lozenge shape that surrounds

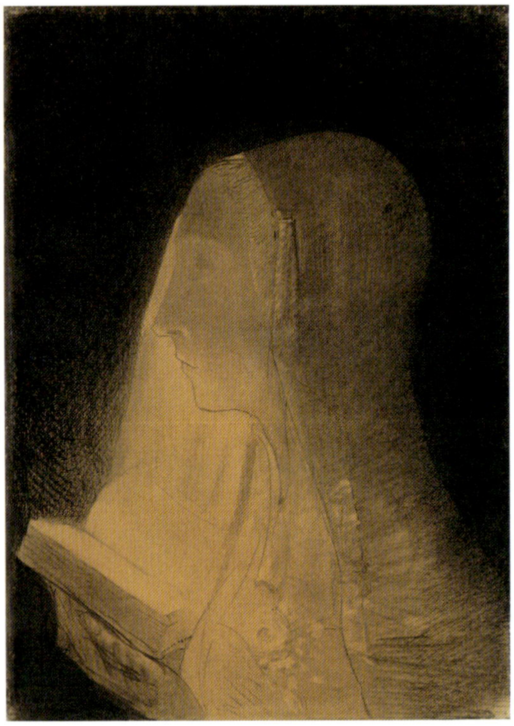

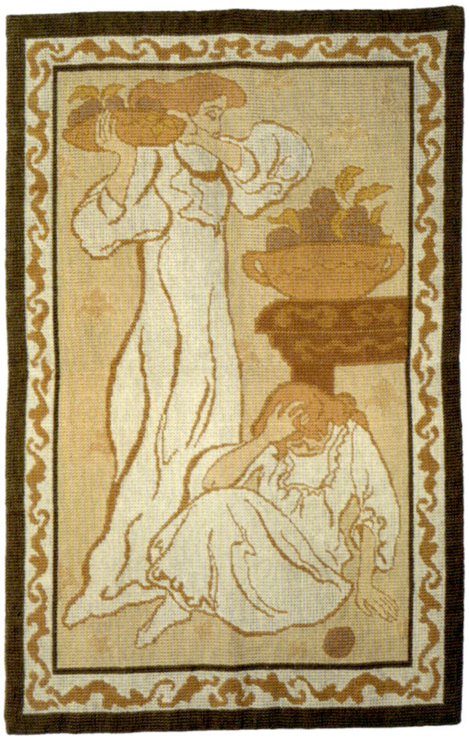

3 Odilon Redon, *The Book of Light*, 1893, charcoal on tan paper, National Gallery of Art, Washington, Rosenwald Collection, 1951

4 Paul Ranson and France Ranson, *Women in White*, c. 1895, wool on canvas, petit-point tapestry, Musée d'Orsay, Paris

them both. Redon recognized the centrality of this seeming paradox to his artistic process: "after trying to copy minutely a pebble, a blade of grass, a hand, a human profile or any other example of living or inorganic forms, I experience the onset of a mental excitement; at that point I need to create, to give myself over to representations of the imaginary. Thus blended and infused, Nature becomes my source, my yeast, and my leaven. I believe that this is the origin of my true inventions. I believe that this is true of my drawings."[9]

Paul Ranson, a founding member of the Nabi group, held meetings at his home, which came to be called the "temple"; he assigned nicknames to the artists, along with a secret language for the "brotherhood." With a sincere interest and commitment to the decorative arts, he made several designs for tapestries that were executed by his wife, France Ranson. In fact, the drawing *After the Fall* (also known as "Women in White") (pl. 59) was a virtual cartoon for the first tapestry (fig. 4). The sinuous outlines of the figures, the simple flowing forms that describe the drapery, the still life on the table, the border of the composition, and the background all look to the aesthetic that would be championed by Siegfried Bing and his Maison de l'Art Nouveau. A final preparatory sketch for the tapestry, this design shows a masterful balance of form and decorative flourish. Its title derives from the foreground figure sitting on the ground with her head in hand, having apparently been hit by an apple that fell from the bowl — a modern-day image of the fall of Eve. In its serpentine lines, reductive form, and the creation of pattern on the surface of the paper (as opposed to the pictorial illusion of depth), this could be considered a quintessential Nabi drawing. The tapestry translates the outlines virtually exactly as drawn, indicating that Ranson used the most limited means possible to prepare this design so that it could easily be translated into another medium.

Another large-scale sheet by Ranson, *Three Women at a Fountain* (pl. 60), is a preparatory drawing for a painting of the same dimensions (there are faint indications of squaring on the upper portion of the paper). Ranson developed a more complex composition in this work, demonstrating an interest in the decorative potential of vegetation, something he would continue to explore in depth for the rest of his career. The simple outlines and arabesques used to indicate form are not unique to Ranson, but the artist nonetheless conveys the essence of the Nabi aesthetic, where Aurier's apotheosis of the decorative reigns supreme.

The Dyke collection has many impressively large sheets that demonstrate serious and carefully worked compositions. Bonnard and Vuillard, the two most important Nabis, represented the more domestic, earthbound approach to subject and meaning in their art. Bonnard's art changed over the course of his career, from flat, densely patterned arrangements in the 1890s to a masterful embrace of color in the twentieth century. Bonnard is represented in the Dyke collection by a vibrant ink and watercolor drawing, *The Promenade* (pl. 55), which shows a complete decorative ensemble on the subject of "La Parisienne," a theme that would occupy the artist for much of the early 1890s. He and Vuillard were seen as the more "intimist" artists, drawing inspiration from daily life rather than from a religious or mysterious source. And Bonnard had a particular affinity for the emblematic observation of Parisian street life. In this drawing he transposed his vision in compelling individualistic graphic detail. In the *Promenade* screen for which the Dyke sheet is a study (see fig. 2), Bonnard combined abstracted versions of figures observed in daily life with a dramatic use of empty space. The largest figure in the four-panel screen is the "Parisienne" and her posse of children, dogs, and hoops, while farther up on the right there is a band of nurses; the entire screen is decorated with a line of carriages that stretches across the tops of all four panels. The dramatic silhouettes of the figures, the play between flatness and depth (indicated by the diminishing sizes of each of the three groups of elements on the screen from bottom to top), and the intention that the screen should function as an actual piece of furniture all attest to the Nabi desire to radicalize forms and pictorial space and to extend creativity to useful objects.

Bonnard's working method relied on the power of his initial confrontation with his subject, through which he believed the painter would achieve "universality." True to the symbolist aims of Gustave Kahn, Bonnard believed throughout his career that "the starting point of a picture is an idea." After that, memory played a central role. As he observed, "if the object is there at the moment he is working, the artist is always in danger of allowing himself to be distracted by the effects of direct and immediate vision, and to lose the primary idea on the way."[10] Thus in the many compositions devoted to the elegant Parisienne, Bonnard abstracts the figure to a strong, articulated graphic presence: a woman bending over, often with an umbrella, accompanied by a small child. In some cases these figures are in silhouette, inspired no doubt by the shadow theater of the Chat Noir; at other times they consist of a mix of patterns, where the figure and the background can be understood only in terms of a transition from checks to dots, splashes to squiggles. The complex relationship of figure to ground, the dramatic shifts in scale between the figure and her surroundings, and the abundance of pattern, at times, or articulated silhouette, at others, all reveal an inspiration from the Japanese prints that earned Bonnard the name "Nabi japonard."

Many of these Parisiennes ended up as posters or prints, where their silhouetted black forms were especially striking. In the Dyke *Promenade* Bonnard must have been working out certain aspects of the composition, as the ink wash is layered over pencil, reinforcing the outline of the forms. Like many of these images, the major figure of the woman bends over, compressed as if to try to fit within the confines of the page. The patterns are so vivid, varied, and lively that it takes a while to note that Bonnard has indicated color in the most sparing way, with brief touches of orange in the hair of the woman and girl, and with a slight indication of yellow in the background. The artist would use similar combinations of patterns to create a symphony of color in painted series of related themes, each woman occupying her own panel (see, for example, fig. 5).

The Dyke collection has an extraordinary selection of works by the Belgian artist Georges Lemmen, who was a close contemporary of the Nabis but was not himself a member of the brotherhood. Many of his drawings from the late 1880s and 1890s, however, demonstrate the strong contours, spatial ambiguity, and symbolic allusiveness that

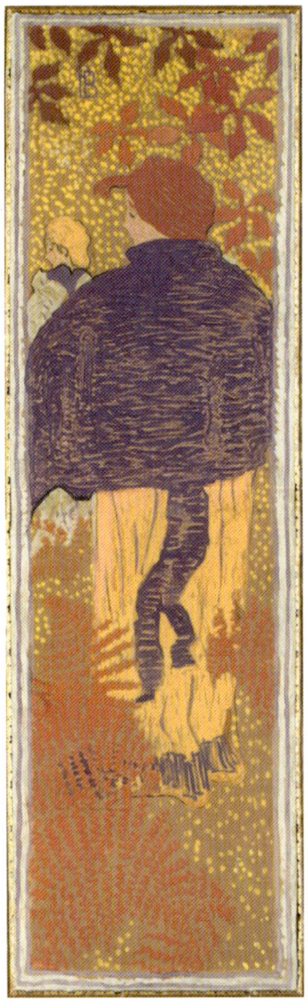

5 Pierre Bonnard, *Women in a Garden: Woman Wearing a Cloak*, 1891, détrempe with glue on canvas, Musée d'Orsay, Paris

are essential characteristics of the work of the early Nabis. A masterful drawing of Madame Lemmen standing (pl. 53) shows the artist's wife twice on the same page. Simply depicted in black chalk, with heavy outlines defining her form, she appears in profile both times, facing the center of the sheet. From the right, extending the whole height of the paper, she reaches across the page, seeming to touch the arm of her shadowy other likeness, which is facing toward her but drawn only on the top half of the sheet. This creates a sense of different scales — large on the right in the foreground; smaller on the left in the distance — with the touching hands, which are in fact both the right hand of the same sitter, miraculously bridging the space and scale. The still, contemplative stance of the woman looks forward to Fernand Khnopff's iconic *Memories (Lawn Tennis)* of 1889 (Brussels Royal Museums of Fine Arts of Belgium) and firmly roots Lemmen in the tradition of Belgian symbolism.

Lemmen was a member of the avant-garde group Les XX (Les Vingt) beginning in 1888. Taking inspiration from the great post-impressionist artists who exhibited with this group in Brussels (including Gauguin and Seurat), Lemmen paid homage in his early work to a heightened pointillism that was embraced by many of the young Belgian painters at this time. His strong drawing of sunflowers from 1892 (pl. 57) could be mistaken for a drawing by Van Gogh, so clearly defined are the individual strokes of ink and so monumental the forms. Two flowers take up the entire expanse of the page, forcefully commanding the variety of depths of the blacks and the articulation of different strokes and dabs of the pen. A different inspiration is seen in his later *Vase of Poppies and Anemones* (pl. 68), which reveals the individual daubs of paint and the serenity of composition for which Seurat was noted. Here Lemmen created a still life of flowers with close tonal relationships between blossoms, tablecloth, and background, adding to the quietude of the scene.

Other compositions by Lemmen from the early years of the twentieth century reveal the influence of Vuillard, with a closely observed chalk drawing study and then oil on cardboard rendition of the artist's wife sewing at tea time (pls. 64 and 65). The dramatic angle, looking down on the figure, which allows the still life on the table to occupy much of the foreground, recalls the intimism of the Nabis. In fact, Lemmen was so intent on creating this rendition of domesticity that he provided more details of the objects on the table than he did the features of his wife's face. The warm palette establishes a halo in which she occupies the central, but not the dominating position.

The most prolific draftsman in the Nabi brotherhood was Vuillard, who drew his entire life and never went anywhere without a small sketchbook. As Jacques Salomon, his biographer and nephew by marriage, observed: "Vuillard hardly ever painted from nature. His paintings almost always came out of a preliminary pencil sketch. When among his friends, he drew continually. Throughout his life, he filled sketchbook after sketchbook. From minute to minute, he noted down whatever took his fancy: his mother at the breakfast table, a bunch of flowers, the view from his window, a street corner, a patch of

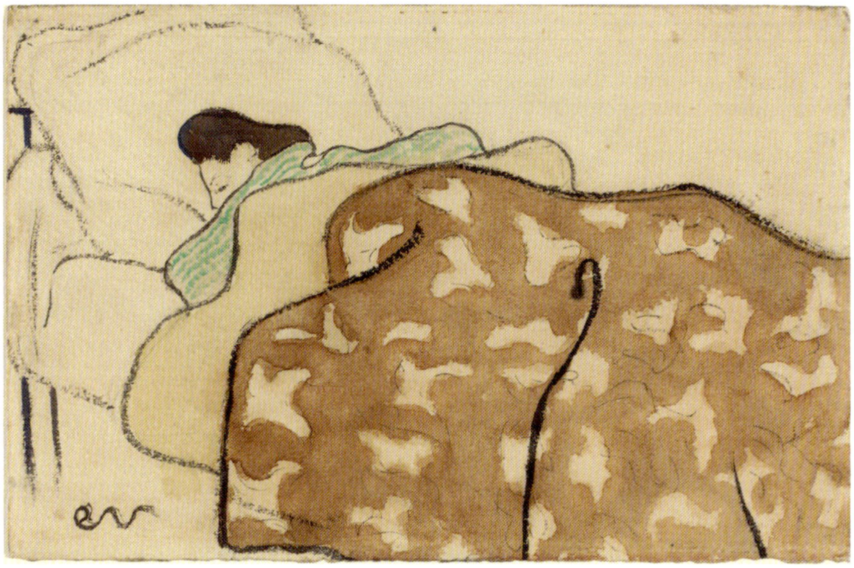

6 Édouard Vuillard, *Woman in Bed*, early 1890s, watercolor and black chalk, National Gallery of Art, Washington, Ailsa Mellon Bruce Collection, 1970

garden, the look of the city at night, and the vaulting of the Parisian subway stations. Often these drawings were so summary as to amount to a kind of private shorthand."[11]

The Dyke collection has several works on paper by Vuillard, which span his career — from the early, Gauguin-inspired cloisonniste compositions such as *The Dressmaker* (pl. 54) to sketches for commissioned portraits in the early decades of the twentieth century such as *Suzanne Després* (pl. 71). The early drawing, which must date from around 1891, has lozenges of color indicating form, much like the stained-glass windows that gave cloisonnisme its name. An outstanding example of this early style of drawing is *Woman in Bed* (fig. 6) in the collection of the National Gallery of Art. With the face barely indicated, Vuillard presented a scene redolent of sleep, layering shape upon shape to define blanket, sheet, nightdress, and pillows. While he painted several compositions on the same subject, most notably a large work in the collection of the Musée d'Orsay, this small work on paper conveys with extremely limited means the "idea" of sleep, thus embracing the symbolist preference for evocation over description.

Many of the artist's later drawings capture the ephemera of an interior with keen attention to detail. In portrait studies such as *Countess Lanskoy* (pl. 75), Vuillard included sharply observed still-life elements to create an environment filled with objects that amplify the personality of the sitter. In this pastel the subject sits awkwardly on a bench and is portrayed in dark tones that harmonize with the background. The only objects in the room that Vuillard touches with bright color are the works of art on the mantel and behind the sitter. As Guy Cogeval observed, perhaps her odd pose reflects her unease at being painted in the home of her lover, Marcel Kapferer, and his family.[12]

The legacy of Nabi drawing is that no matter how abstracted the theoretical goal of the artists to capture an idea, they were keenly observant, rooting their drawings in their study of the old masters at the Louvre or in their embrace of the world around them as the inspiration for their art. And although the Nabi brotherhood existed for only part of one short decade at the end of the nineteenth century, the legacy of a "decorative" aesthetic, as defined by Aurier, was still at the core of their varied artistic production for the rest of their careers.

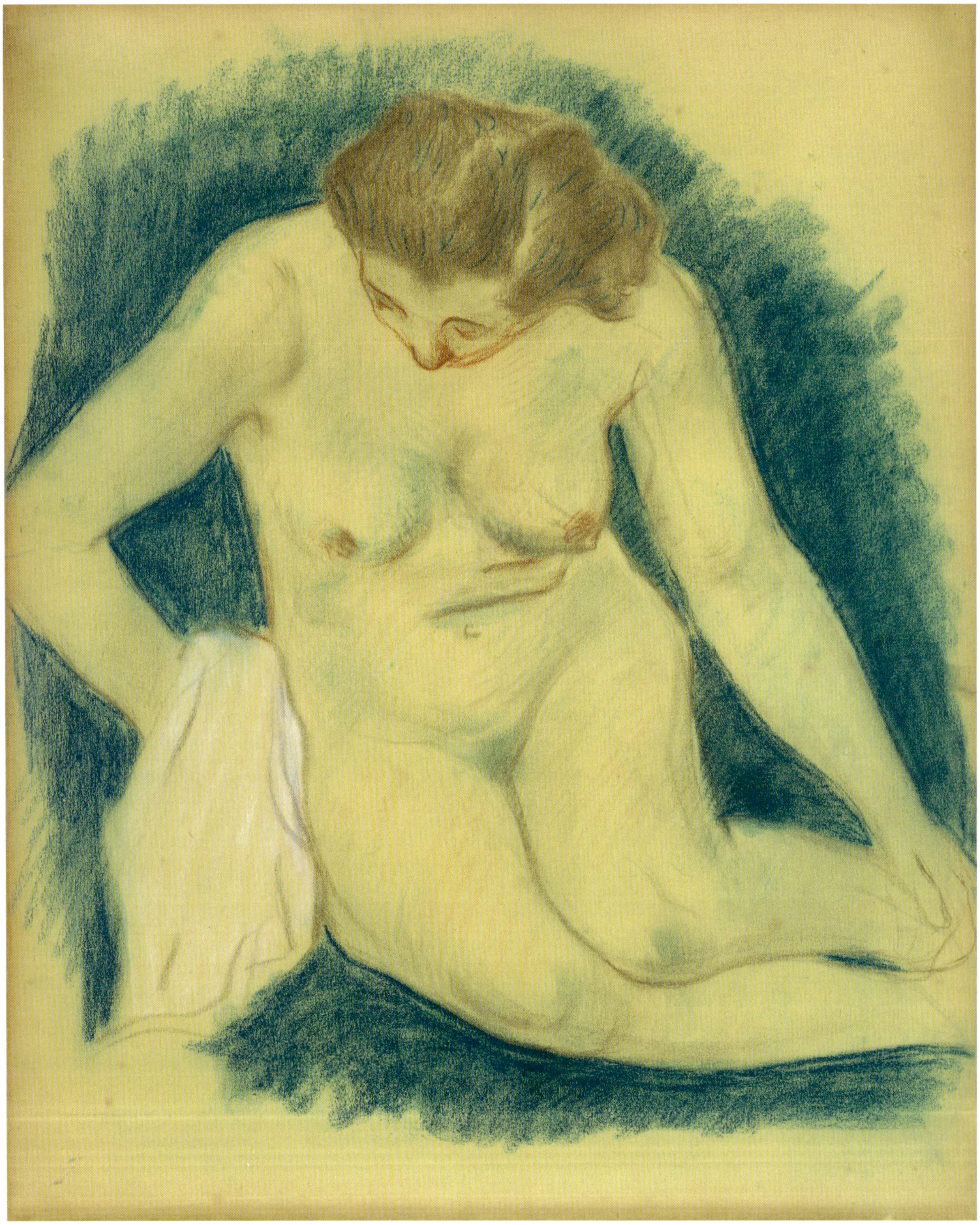

52 Paul Gauguin, *Seated Nude,* 1888/1889
pastel, 616 × 505

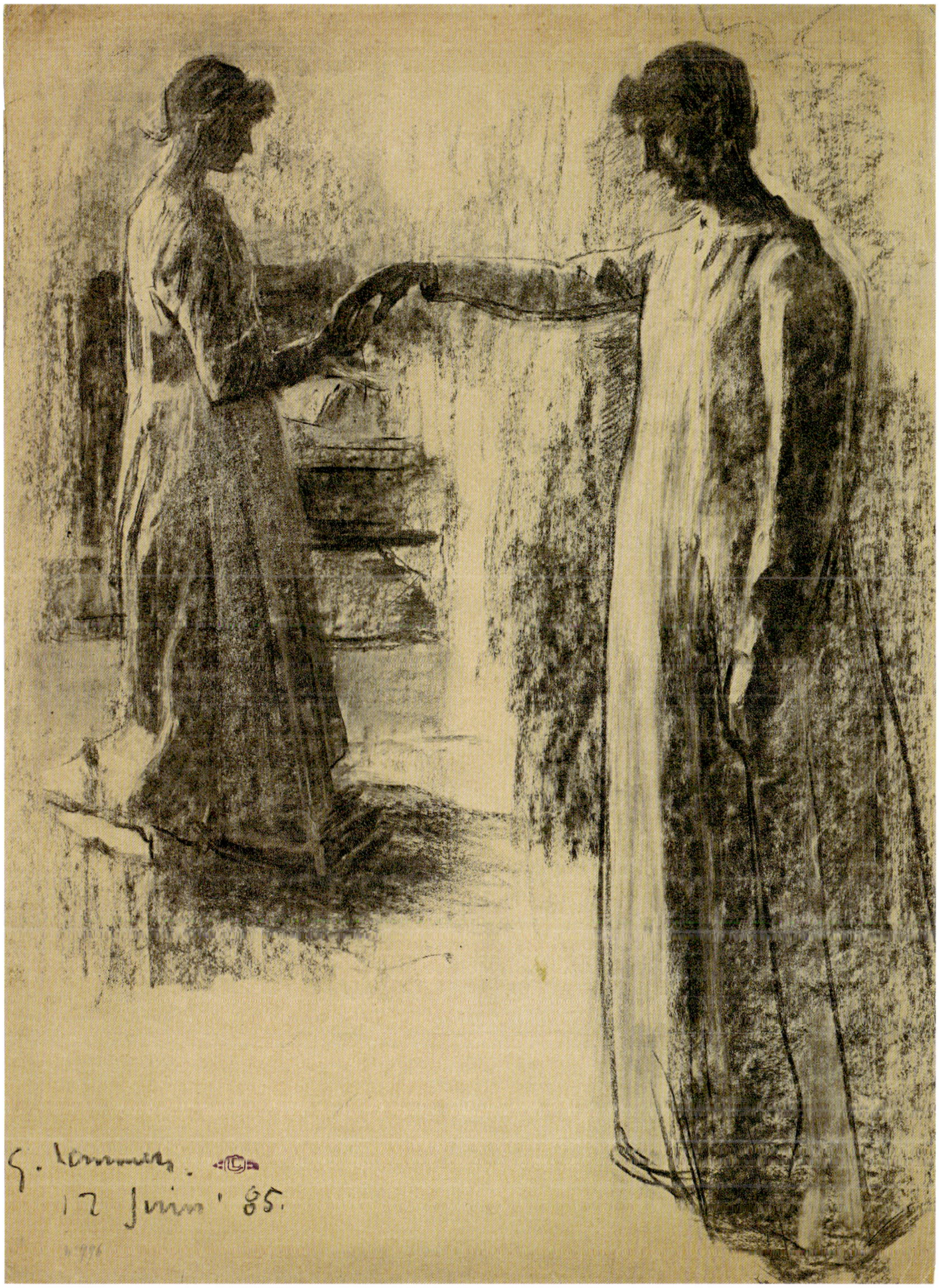

53 Georges Lemmen, *Two Studies of Madame Lemmen,* 1885
black chalk, 655 × 495

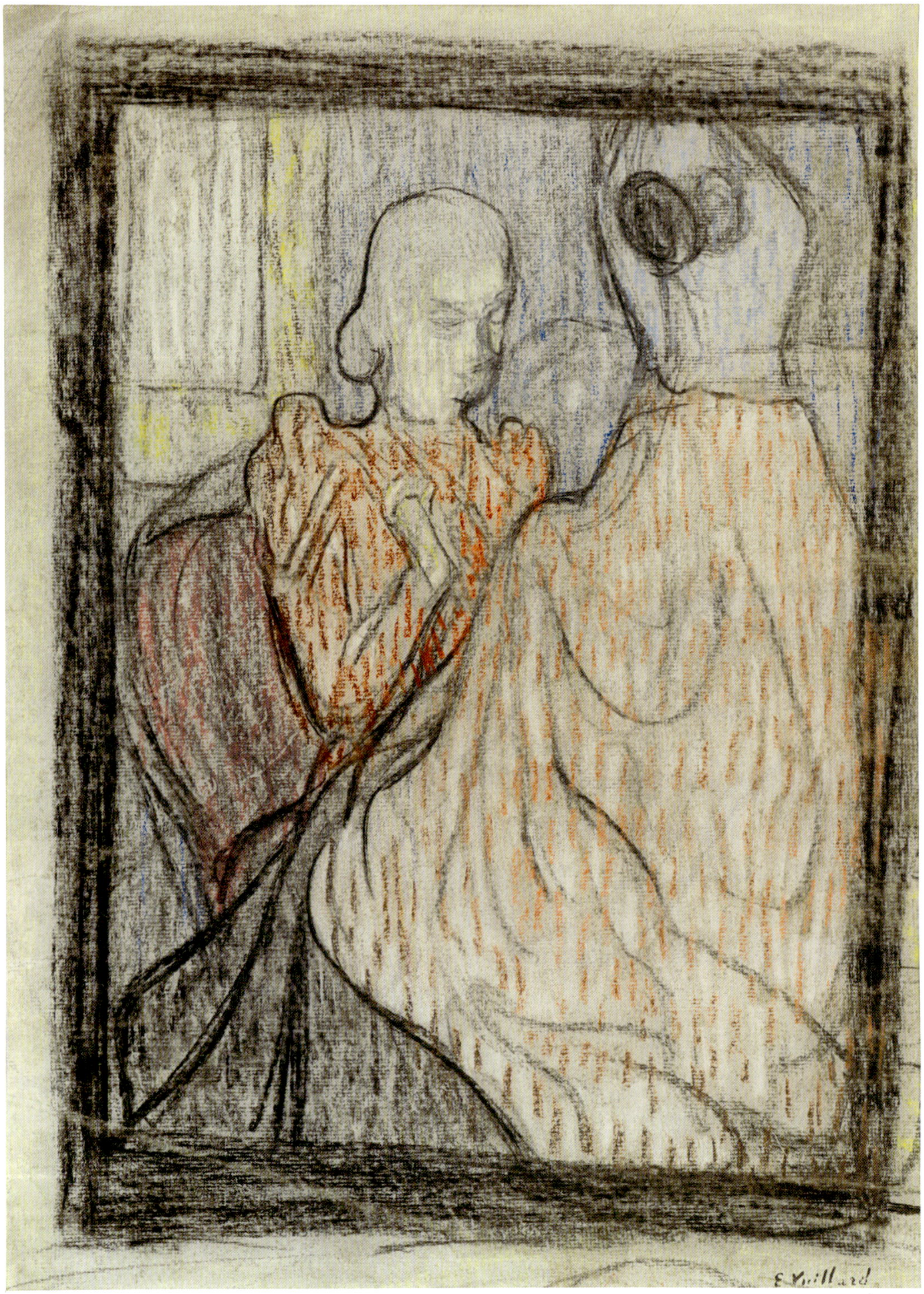

54 Édouard Vuillard, *The Dressmaker,* c. 1890
pastel, 425 × 313

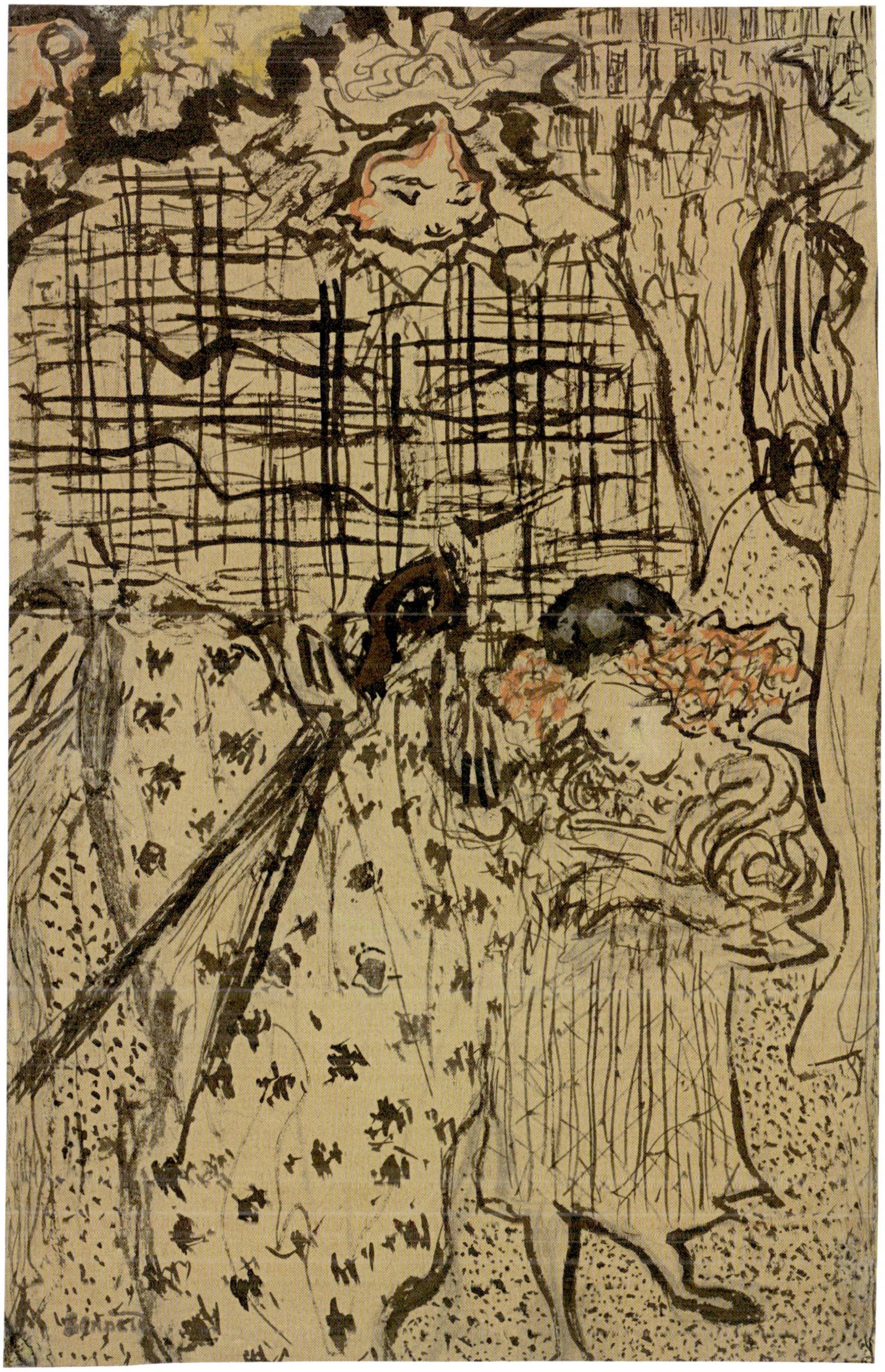

55 Pierre Bonnard, *The Promenade,* c. 1893
pen and ink with wash and watercolor, 473 × 312

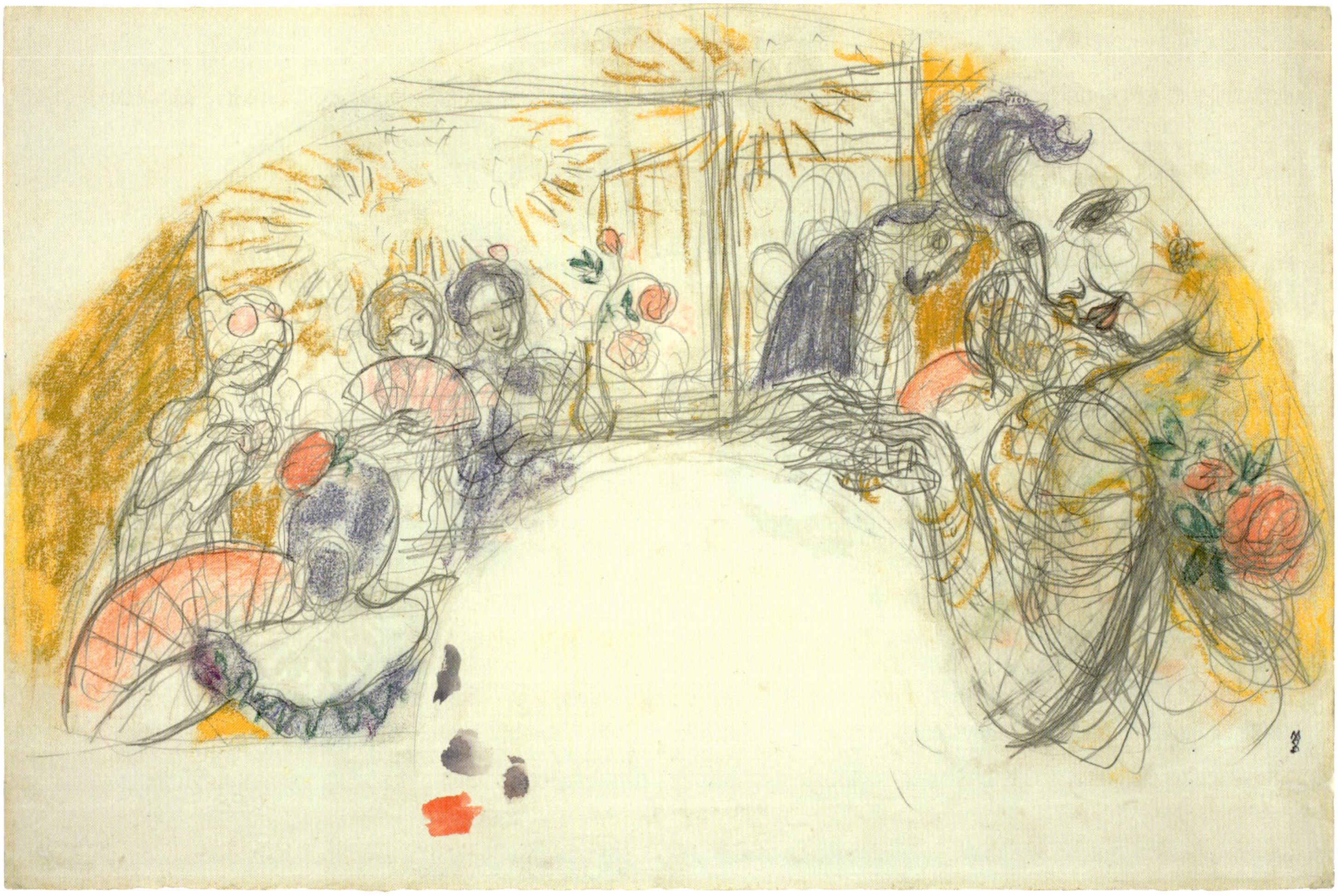

56 Maurice Denis, *Design for a Fan: The Engagement Party of Yvonne Lerolle,* 1898
pastel and black chalk with touches of watercolor, 321 × 492

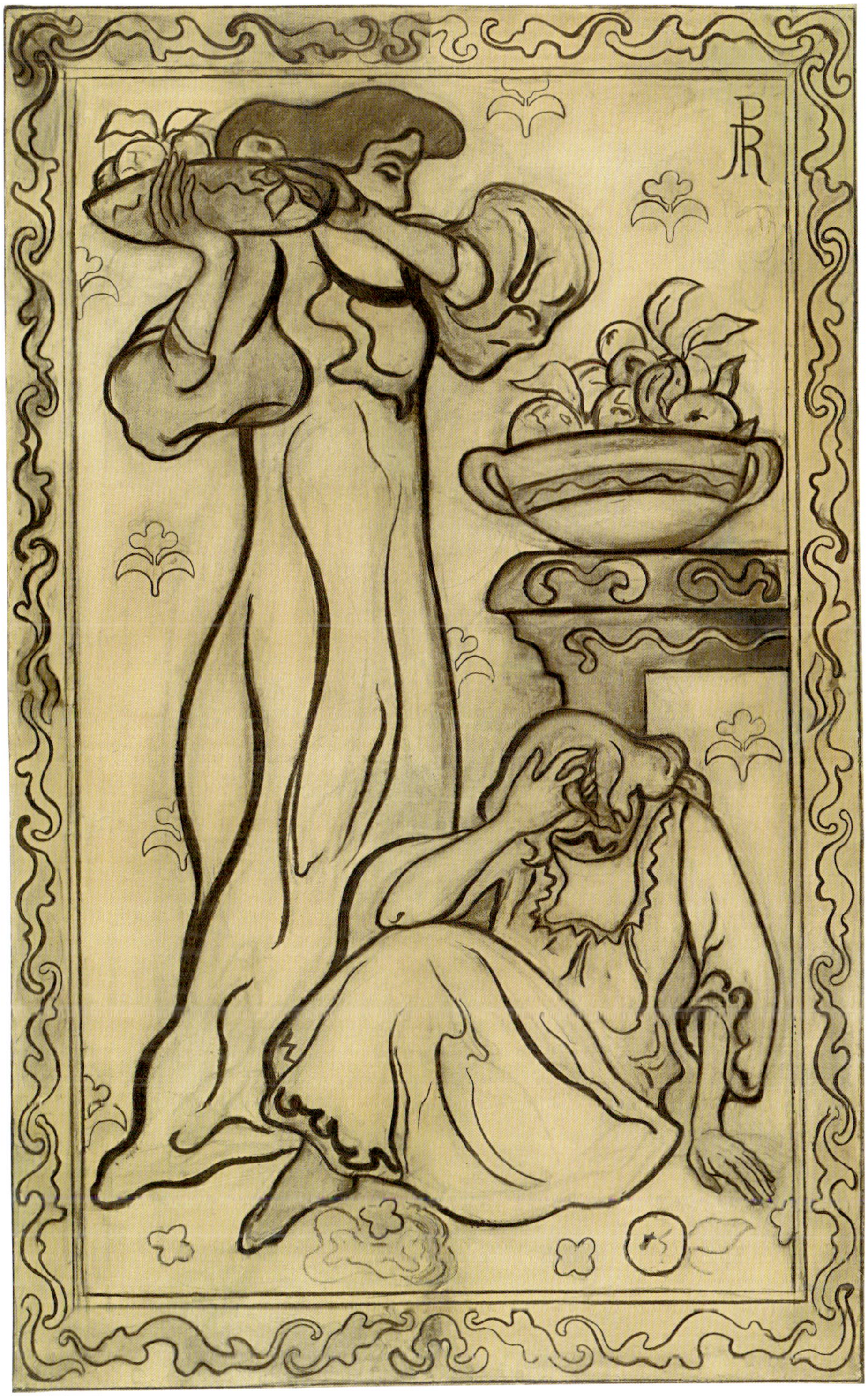

59 Paul Ranson, *After the Fall,* 1892/1893
pastel and charcoal, 1455 × 920

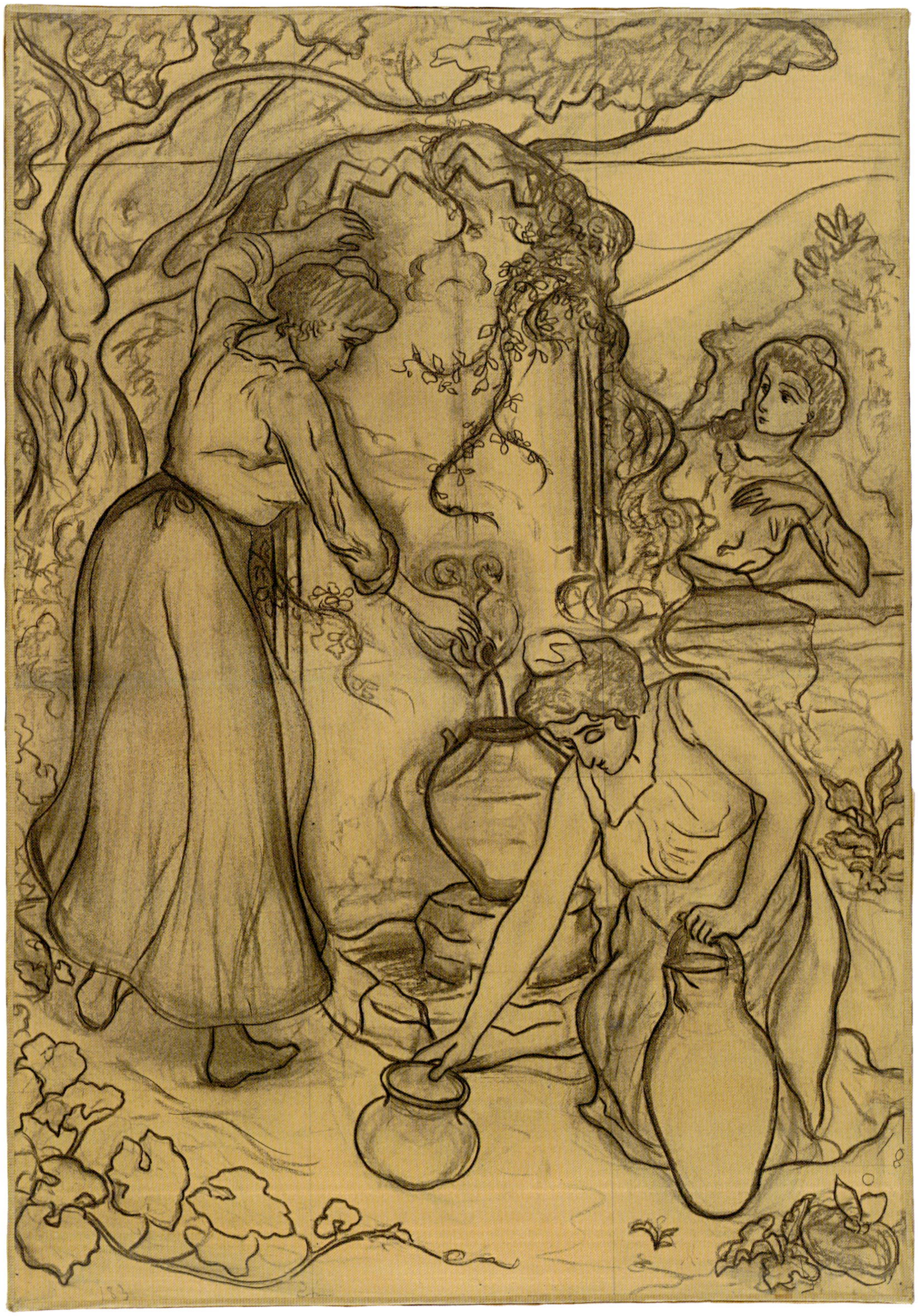

60 Paul Ranson, *Three Women at a Fountain,* 1897
charcoal, 860 × 610

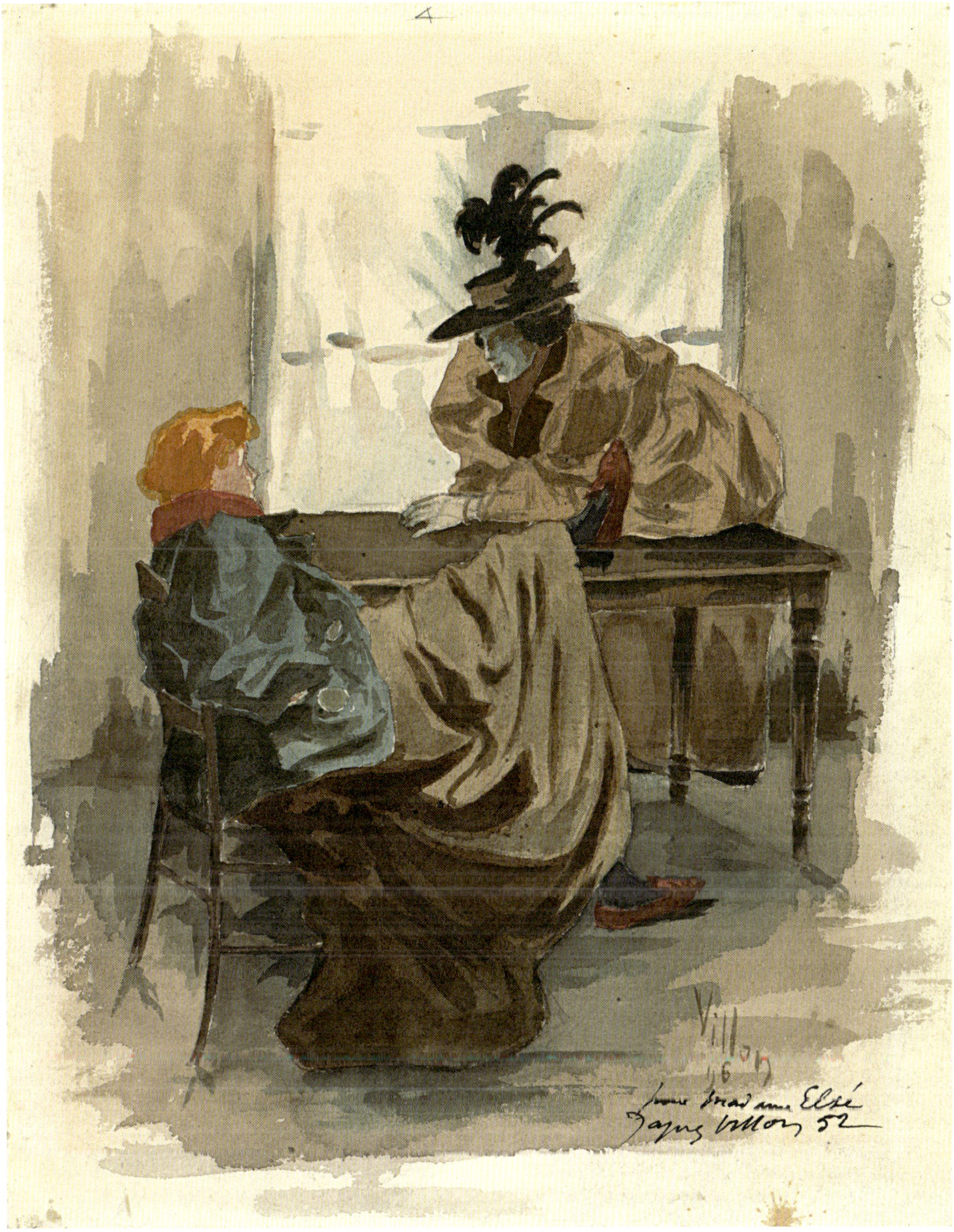

61 Jacques Villon, *The Proposal,* 1896
watercolor, 320 × 253

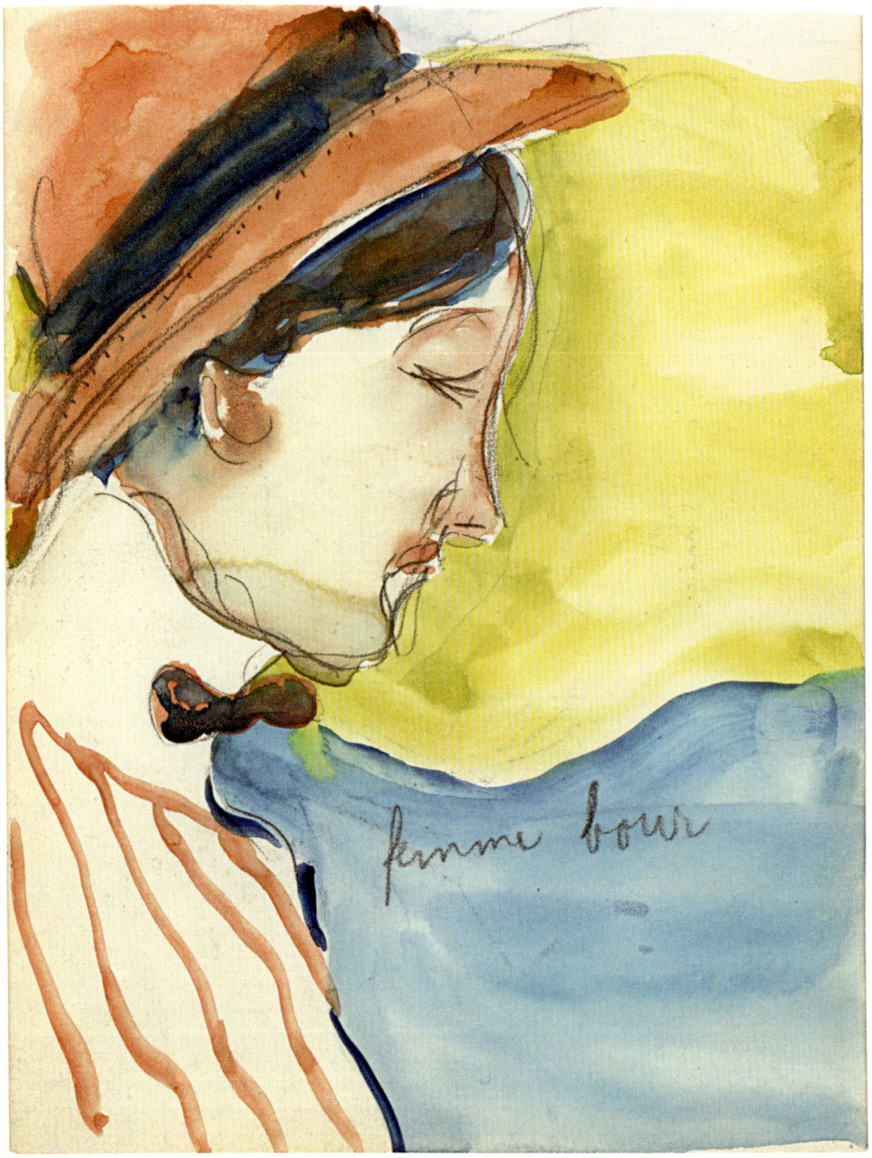

62 Jean-Émile Laboureur, *"Femme bour": The Artist's Sister,* c. 1899
watercolor, 155 × 120

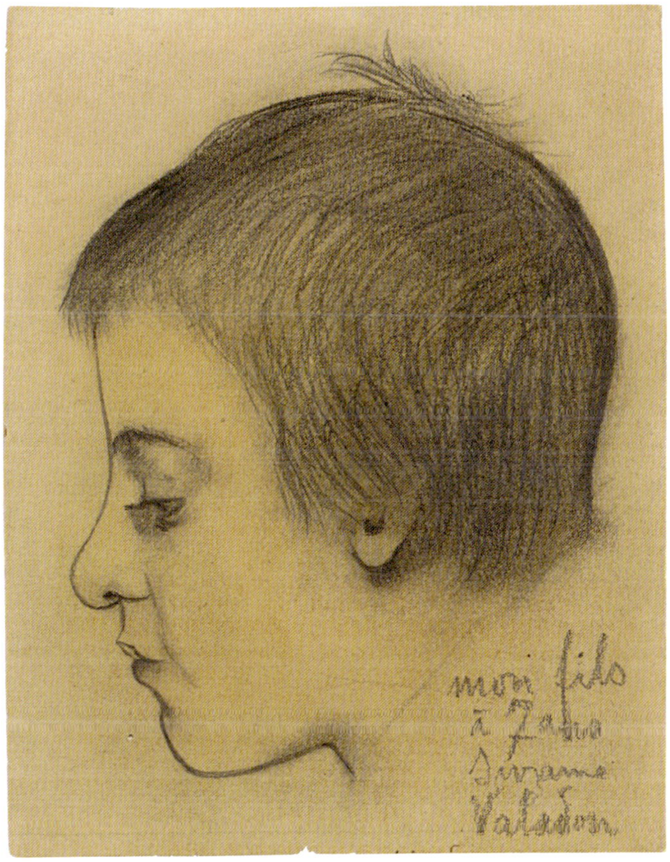

63 Suzanne Valadon, *The Artist's Son, Maurice Utrillo*, c. 1890
graphite, 120 × 90

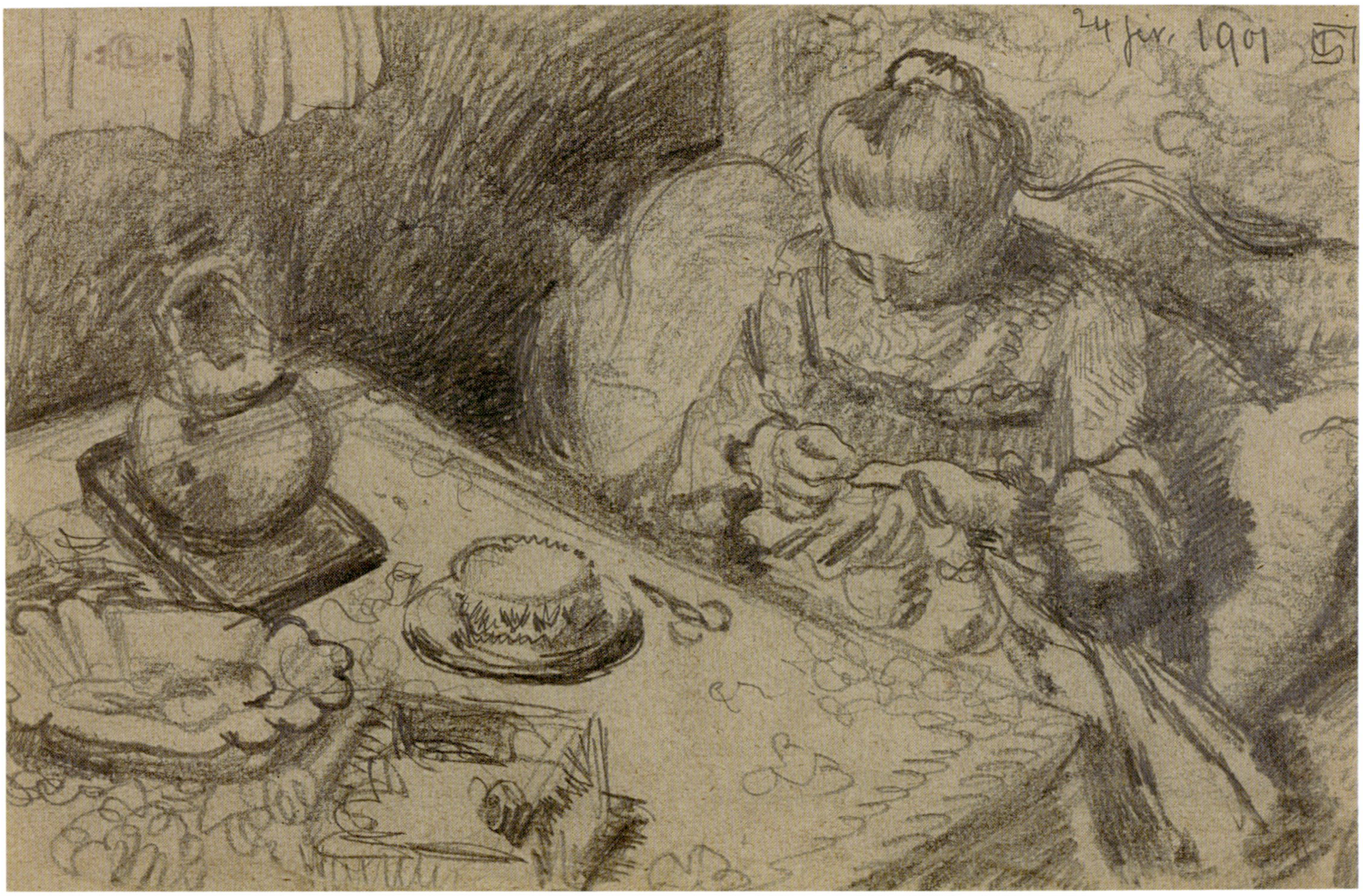

64 Georges Lemmen, *Tea-time with Madame Georges Lemmen Sewing*, 1901
black chalk, 190 × 300

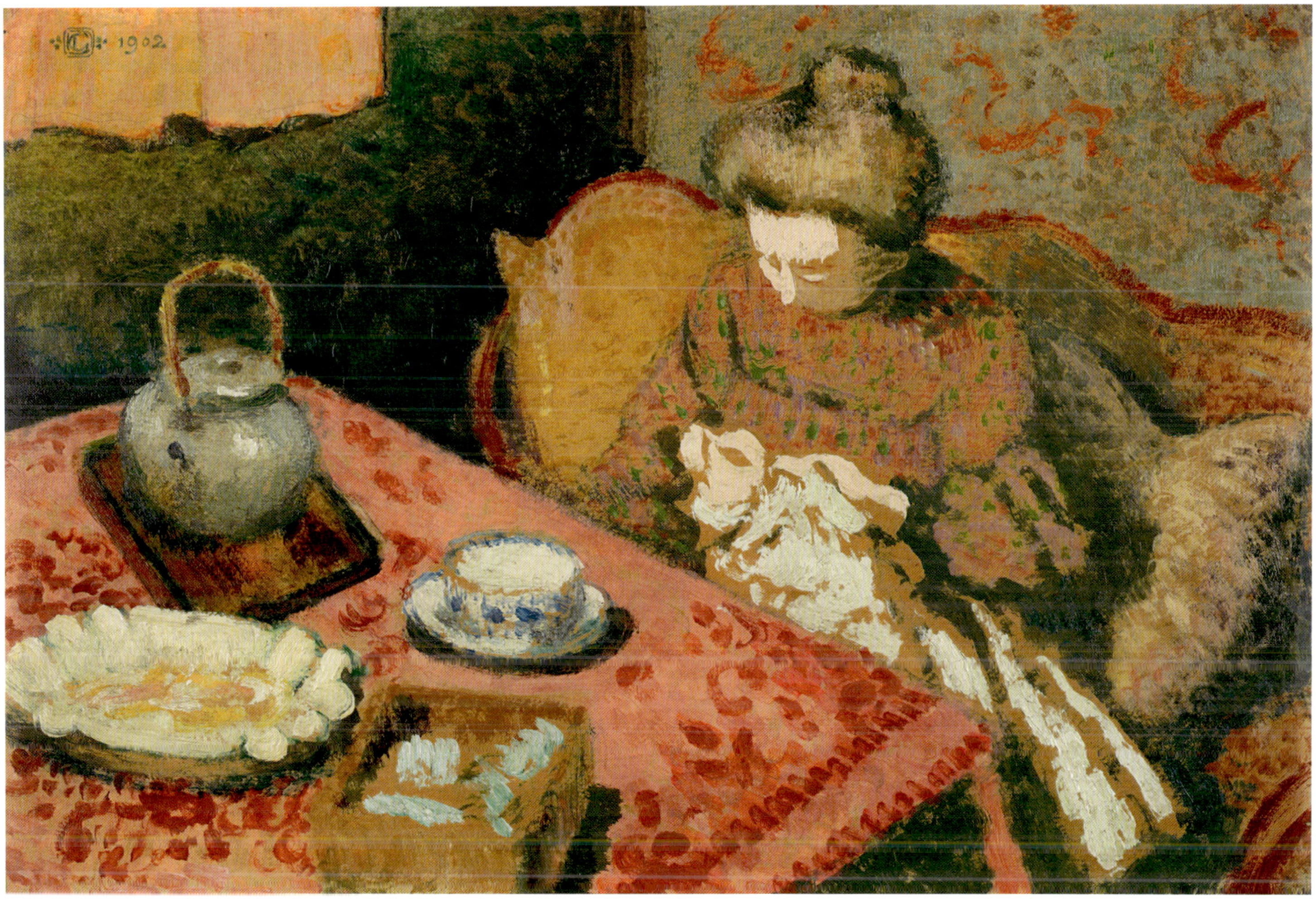

65 Georges Lemmen, *Tea-time with Madame Georges Lemmen Sewing*, 1902
oil on cardboard, 310 × 460

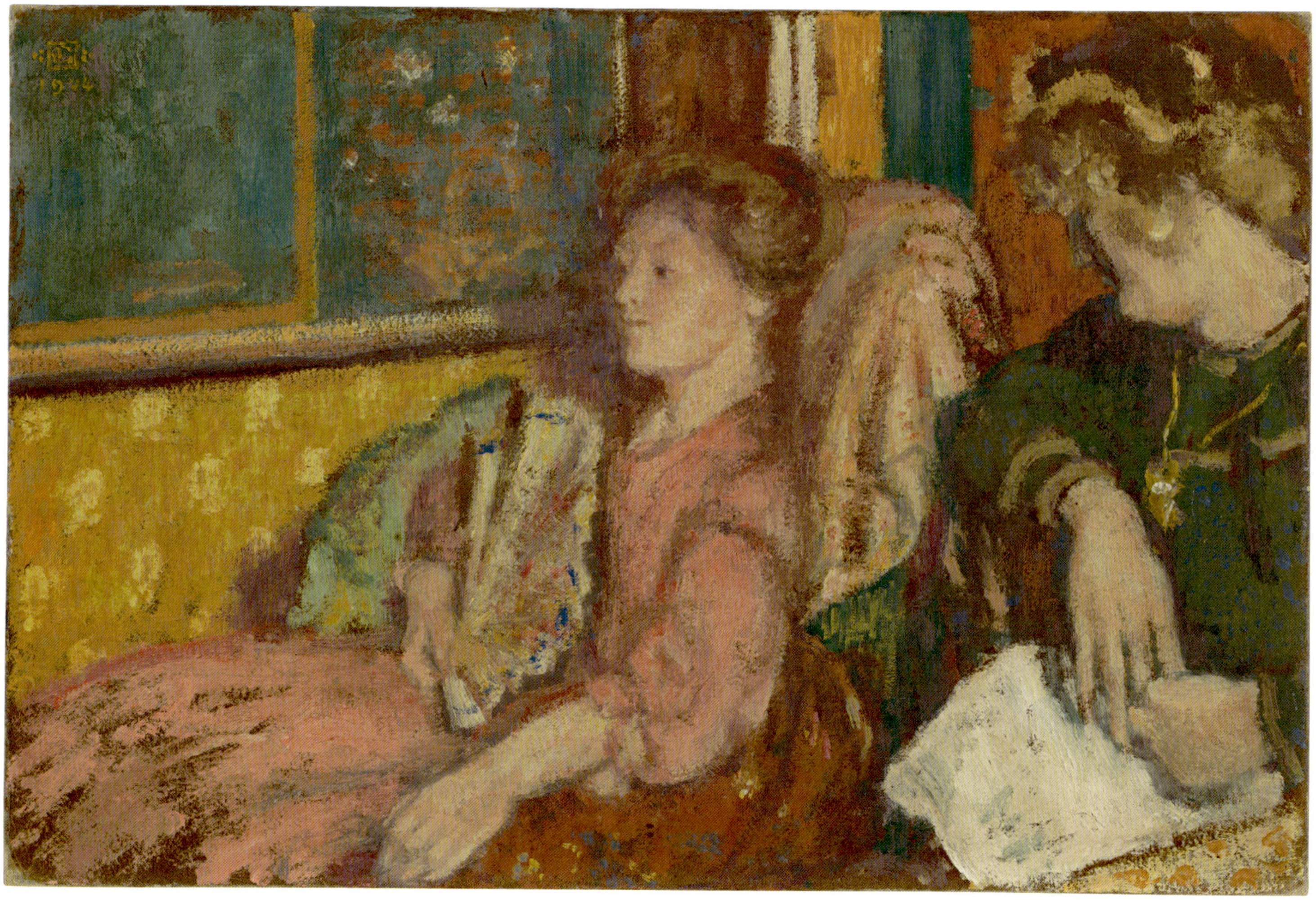

66 Georges Lemmen, *A Visit with Madame Lemmen*, 1904
oil on board, 305 × 432

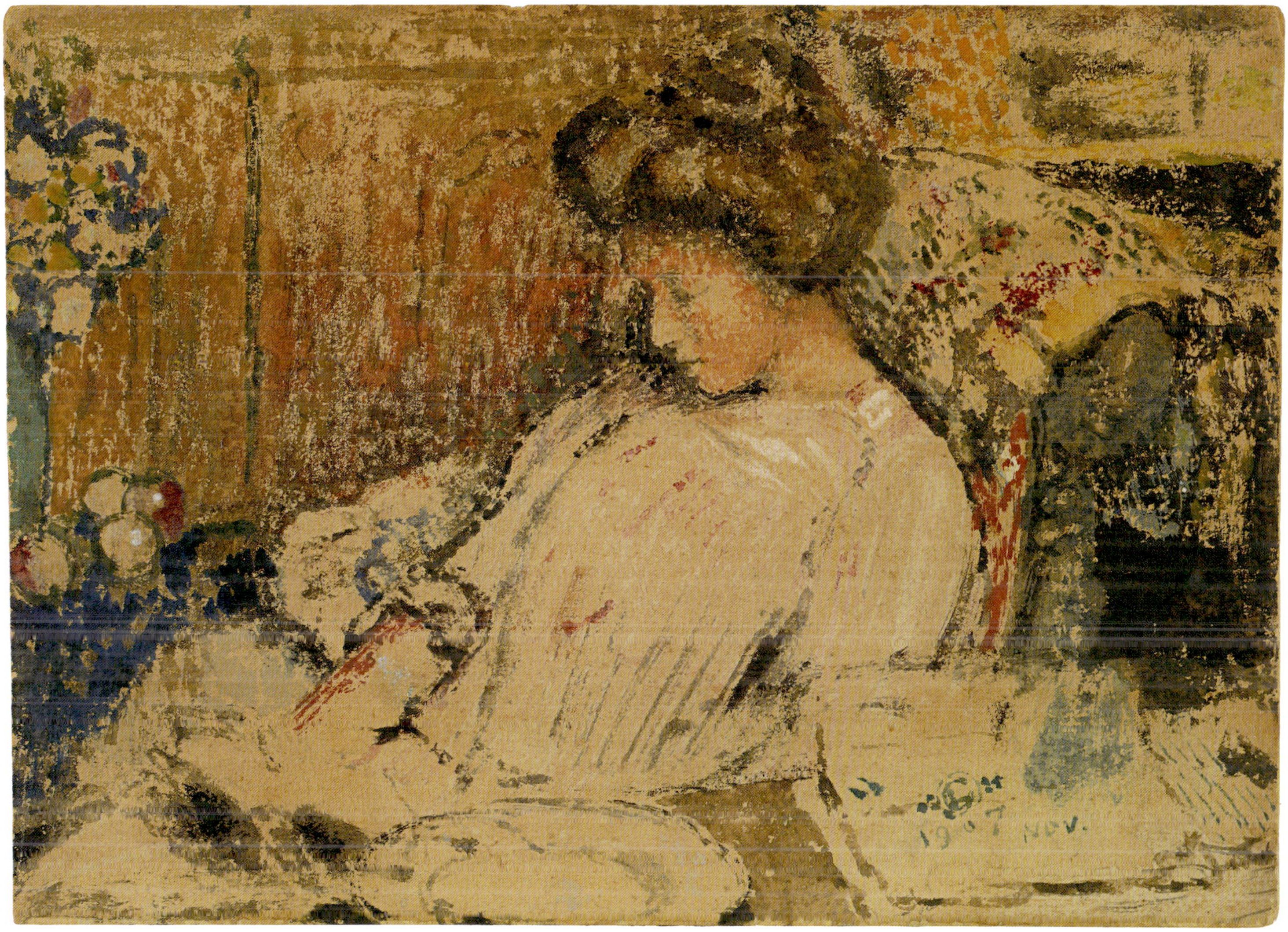

67 Georges Lemmen, *Madame Lemmen Reading*, 1907
watercolor and gouache, 265 × 372

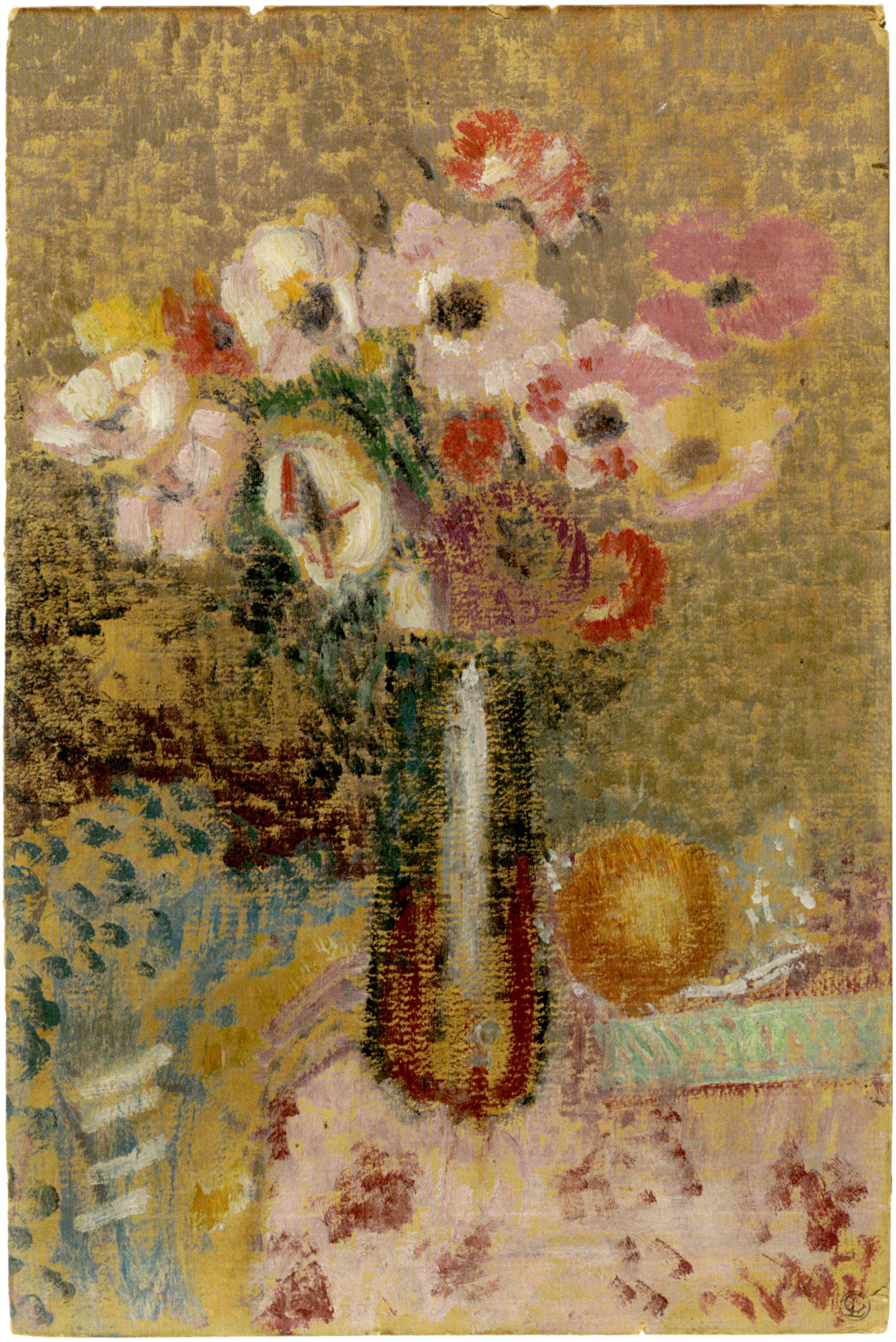

68 Georges Lemmen, *A Vase of Poppies and Anemones*
oil, 513 × 348

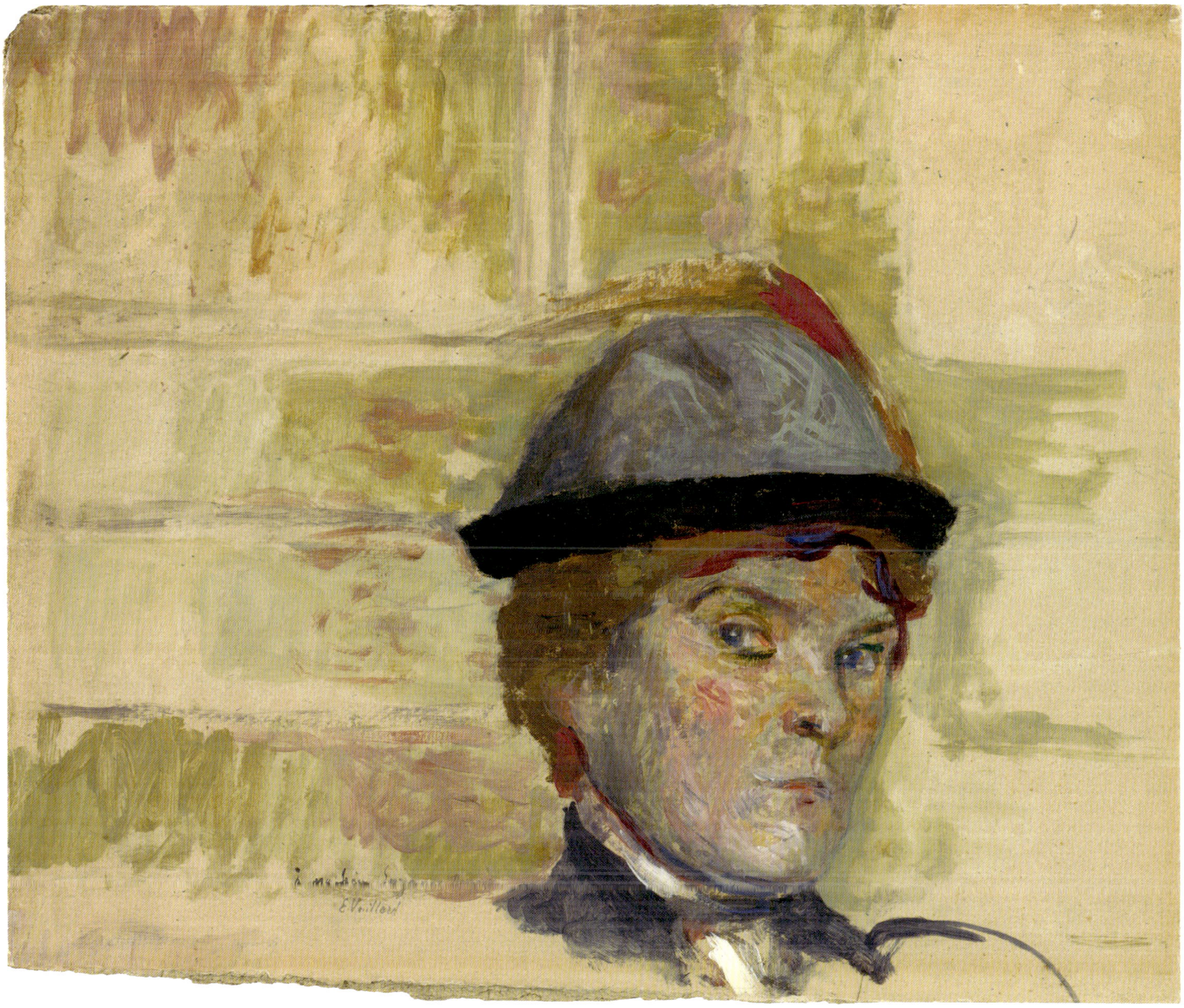

71 Édouard Vuillard, *Suzanne Desprès,* c. 1908
oil on board, 435 × 545

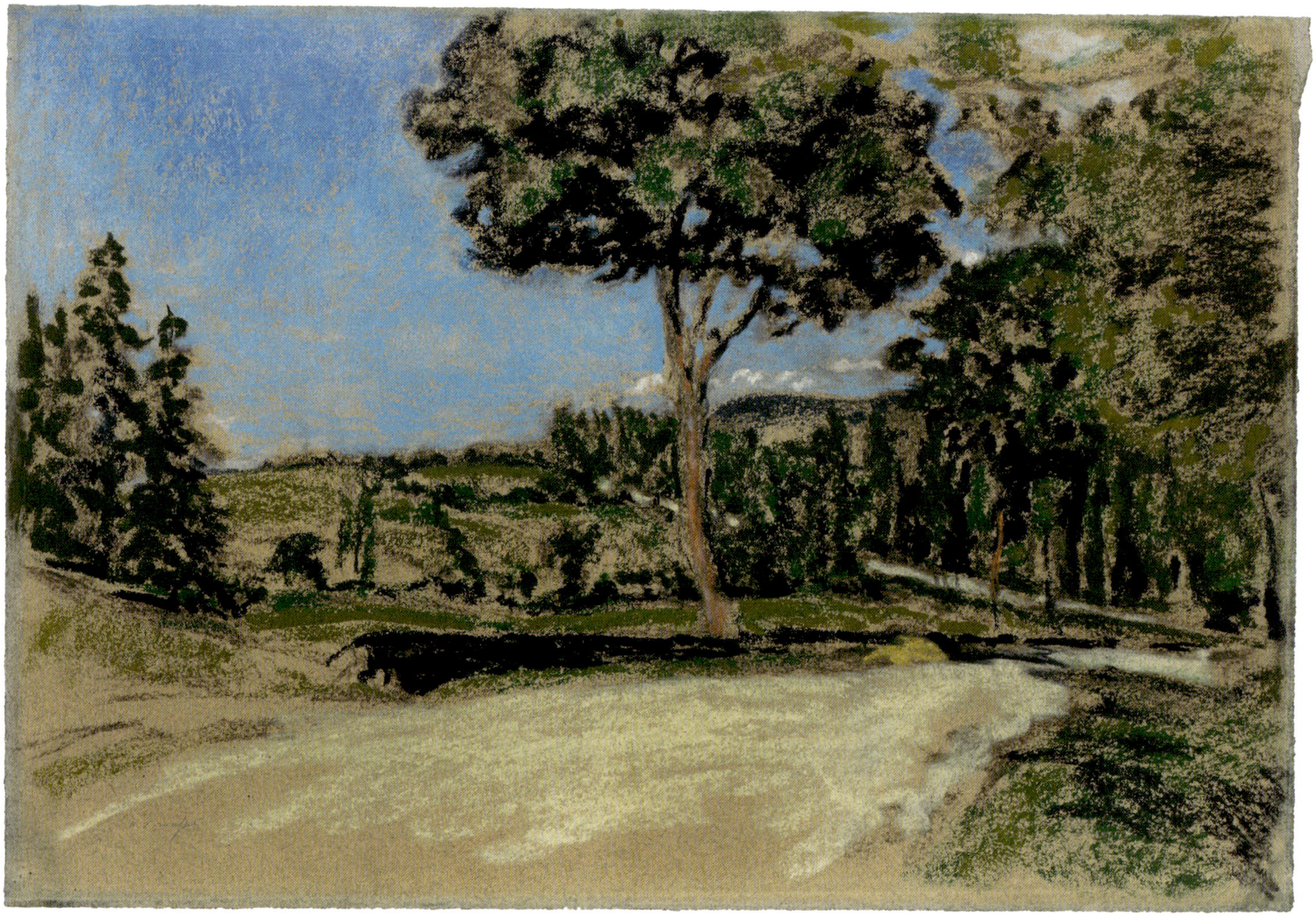

72 Ker Xavier Roussel, *A Road in the French Countryside,* 1915/1920
pastel, 367 × 534

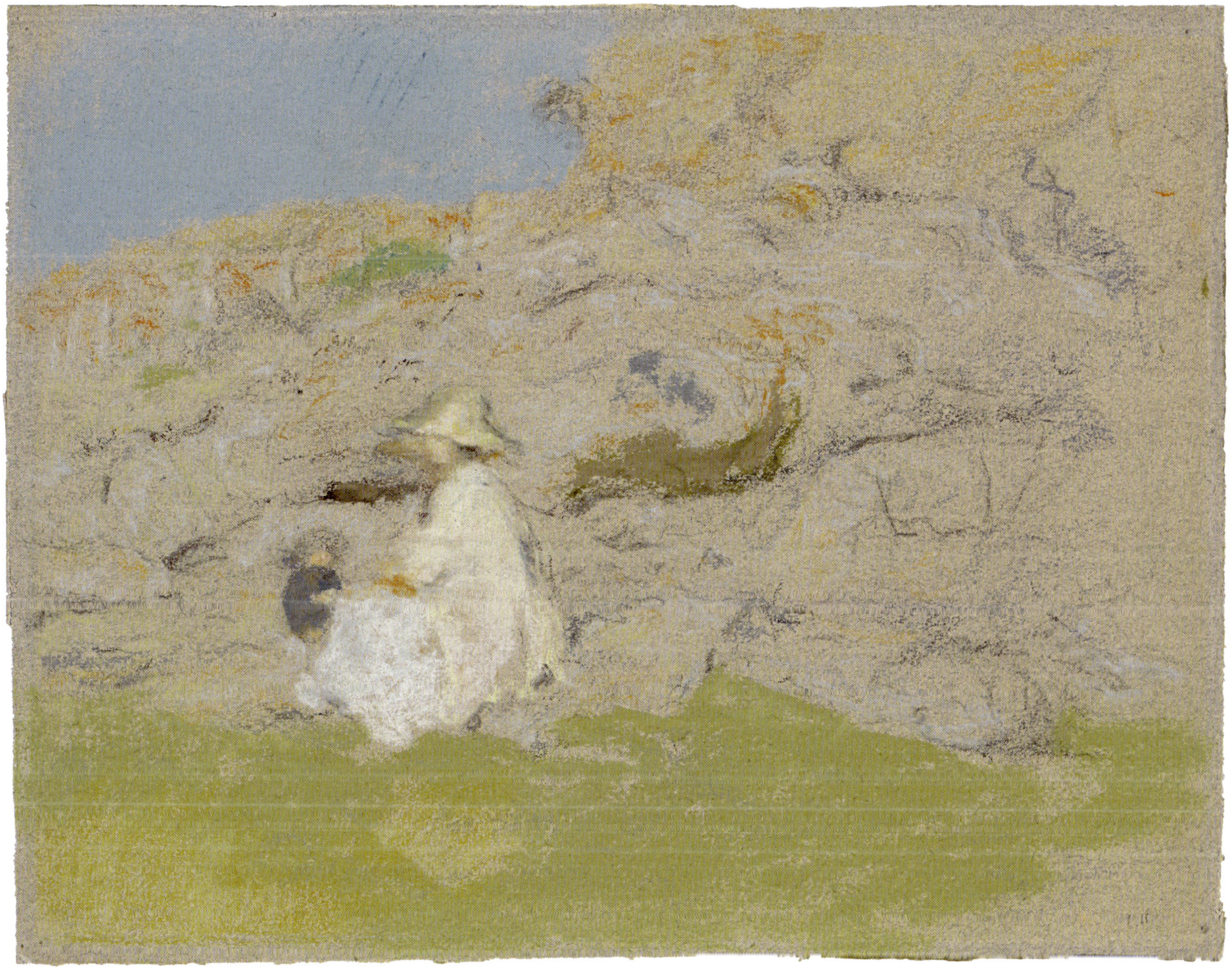

73 Édouard Vuillard, *Mother and Child in a Summer Landscape,* 1919/1920
pastel, 240 × 310

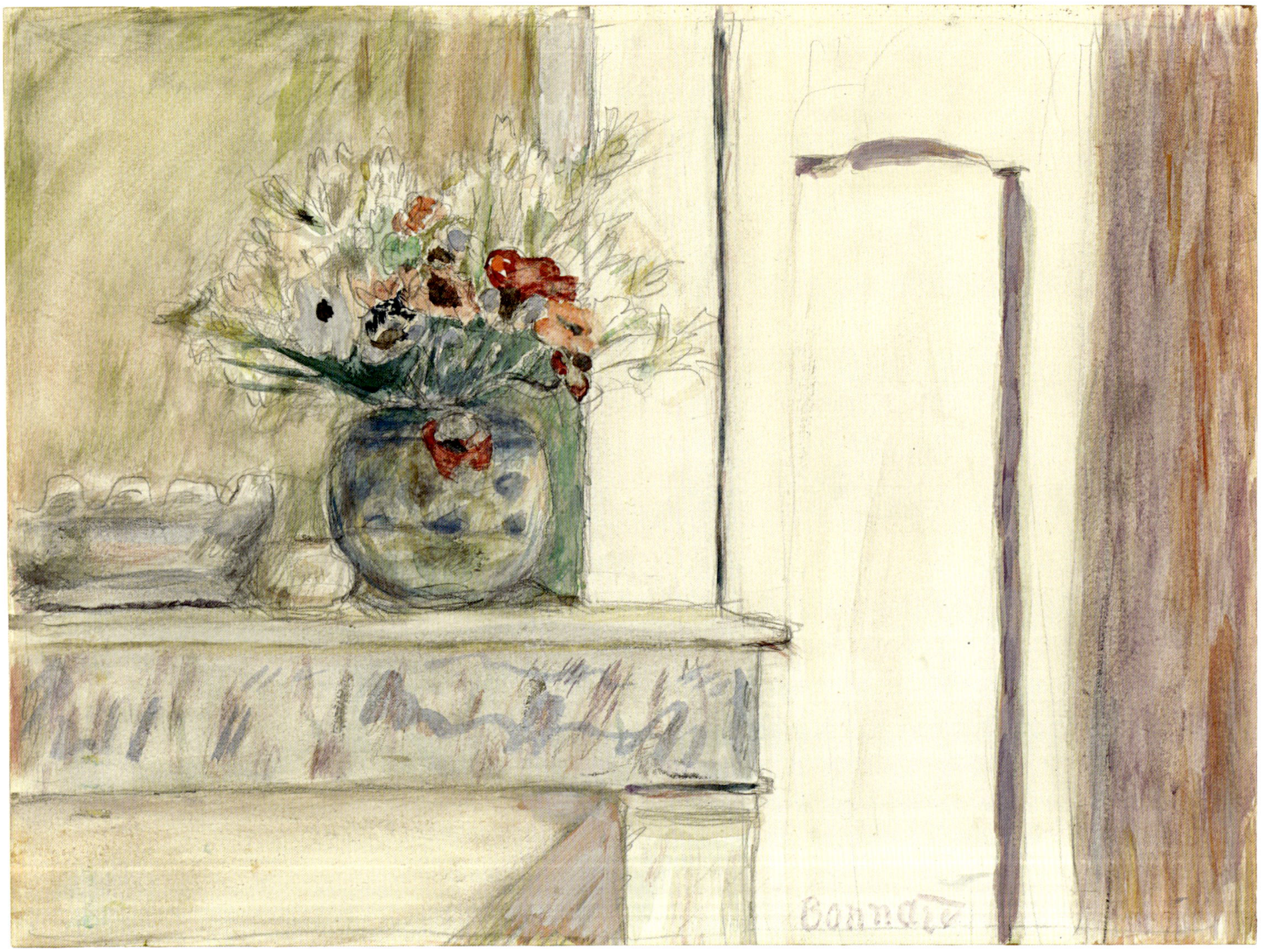

74 Pierre Bonnard, *A Vase of Summer Flowers on a Mantelpiece,* 1920s
watercolor and graphite, 267 × 362

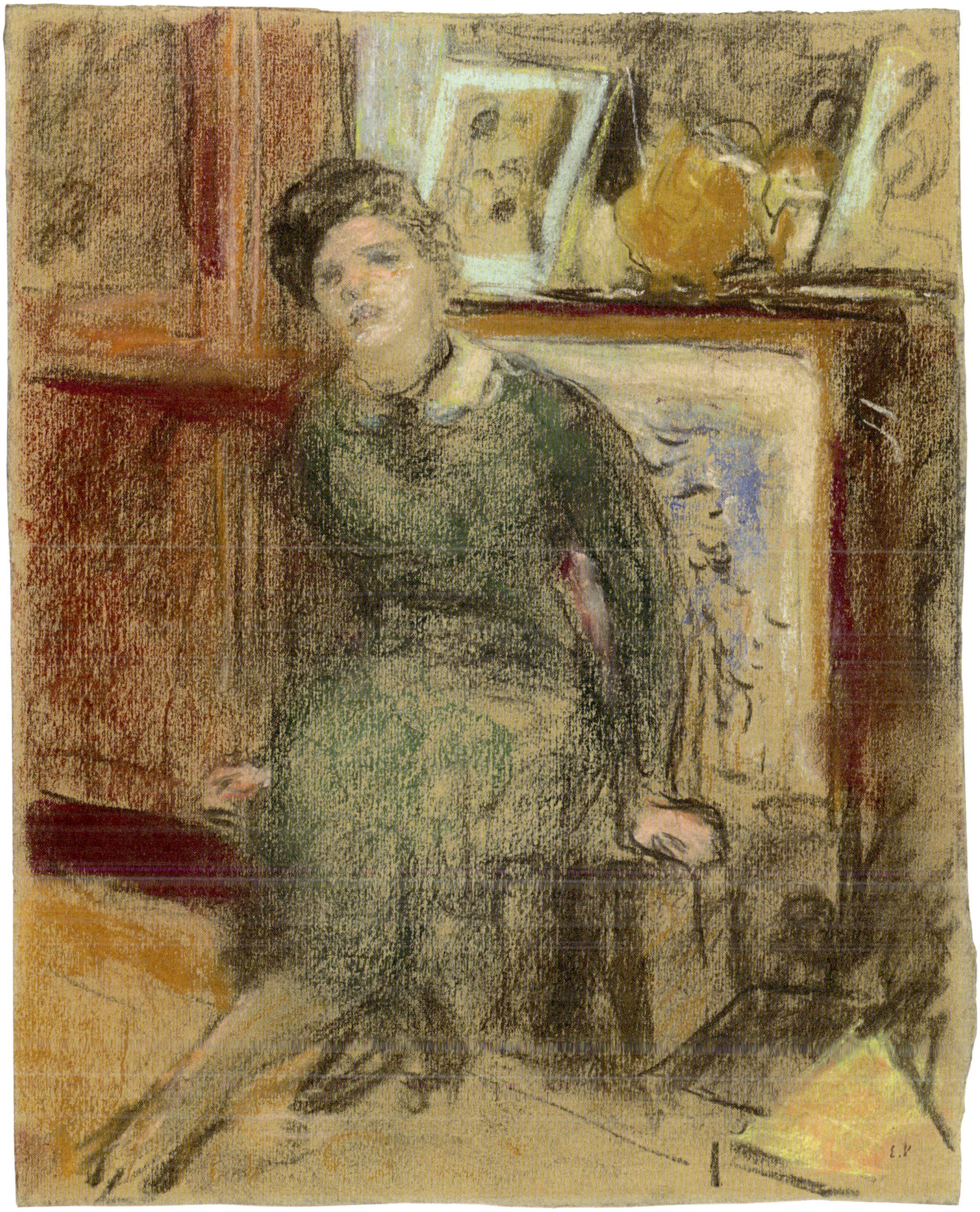

75 Édouard Vuillard, *Countess Lanskoy,* 1934
pastel, 333 × 273

Neo-Impressionist Drawings

MARINA FERRETTI BOCQUILLON

LIKE THE IMPRESSIONISTS, whose heirs they declared themselves to be, the neo-impressionists chose modern life and nature as their principal subjects. But unlike their predecessors, they sought to preserve chromatic purity by working according to infallible rules. In their effort to achieve "a maximum of brightness, color, and harmony,"[1] they invoked science and the theory of optical mixing. The goal was to preserve the brilliance of the pigments employed by juxtaposing small, discrete dots of pure color, leaving the viewer's eye to blend the tones from a distance. As Paul Signac explained, to obtain grays a neo-impressionist "will use pure hues whose optical mixture will give him the desired resultant, so greatly superior to the resultant — not gray, but dirty — obtained by a pigmentary mixture. These intense and brilliant colorations will be still further heightened, when the painter sees fit, by gradation and contrast."[2] The uniformity of the brushstrokes instilled the painted surface with a subtle vibration and permitted a delicate modulation of tones. But it was a slow technique, and the neo-impressionists recognized from the outset the impossibility of painting outdoors. The beauty of their works lay not in any sense of spontaneity or movement, but in the harmony of the synthesized forms and, above all, the intensification of color.

The first of the neo-impressionist painters, Georges Seurat, who had studied at the École des Beaux-Arts, put the emphasis once more on composition and revived the monumental format. In conceiving such works as *A Sunday on La Grande Jatte* of 1884–1886 (The Art Institute of Chicago) — which he referred to as his *toiles de luttes,* or "canvases of struggle" — the artist's goal was to make impressionism an art of museums. He sketched outdoors and executed oil studies *en plein air,* but it was in the studio that these notations from nature were turned into paintings. Employing the most classical of methods, he would make preliminary studies (either drawn or painted) that he would then transpose and rework into the final composition.

The neo-impressionists made systematic use of drawing, then, both in recording the details of everyday life and in working out the composition of a picture. But they also practiced it independently of their oil paintings. Seurat's Conté crayon sheets alone would have been enough to make him one of the greatest talents of his century. These drawings, at once simple and mysterious, are the fruit of a highly personal alchemy (fig. 1 and pl. 76). Eschewing detail, the artist concentrates on the essential — the emergence of forms through the contrast between light and shade. Jean-François Millet took a comparable approach, but usually in charcoal; Seurat, by using the greasy Conté crayon medium, succeeded in giving his blacks their particularly alluring velvetiness and depth. To arrive at these contourless drawings, Seurat sometimes employed a tangle of fluid lines, sometimes a light rubbing over the textured weave of the paper, and sometimes — for a more defined effect — hatching. The earliest sheets of this type date from 1881, five years before the official birth of neo-impressionism in 1886, and Seurat would continue to draw with fervor until the end of his short life.

Curiously, these black-and-white drawings today appear as one of the highest expressions of neo-impressionist art, in which color otherwise plays such an essential role. But the contradiction is only illusory, for as Signac recalled: "The result of Seurat's studies was his judicious and productive

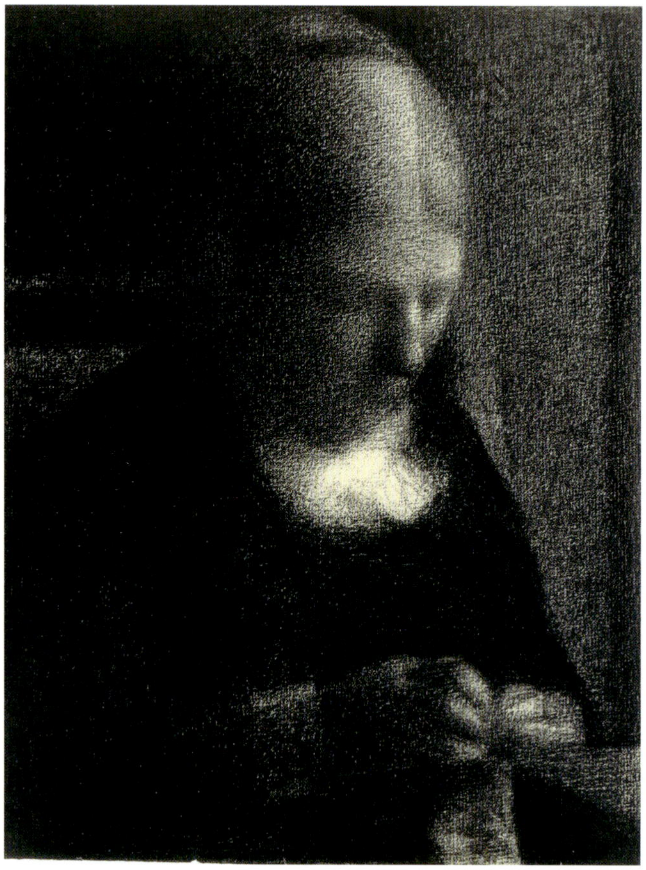

1 George Seurat, *Embroidery; The Artist's Mother,* 1882–1883, Conté crayon, The Metropolitan Museum of Art, Purchase, Joseph Pulitzer Bequest, 1951; acquired from The Museum of Modern Art, Lillie P. Bliss Collection

theory of contrast.... He applied this, first of all, to chiaroscuro: with these simple means, the white of a sheet of Ingres paper and the black of a Conté crayon, skillfully gradated and contrasted, he would execute some four hundred drawings, the most beautiful 'drawings by a painter' that exist."[3]

The Dyke collection's *Strolling Woman with a Muff* (pl. 76), which had once belonged to Signac, beautifully illustrates this idea. It dates precisely from the heroic moment when Seurat undertook *A Sunday on La Grande Jatte*, the "laboratory" work that would become the manifesto of neo-impressionism. This sheet conveys all the young artist's amusement at the deformations that the fashion of the time imposed on the silhouettes of contemporary women, a theme he would soon thereafter immortalize in the most important figure of that painting, the instantly famous woman with a monkey. But beyond Seurat's detached irony, the synthetic treatment of the forms and the admirable handling of the light diffused throughout the sheet confer an inimitable grace on this unknown passer-by.

Signac was impressed by the originality of Seurat's work when the two first met in 1884 at the gatherings that led to the founding of the Société des Artistes Indépendants, and they became close friends. Signac did not alter his painting approach right away, continuing to make canvases in the impressionist manner until the spring of 1886. But he did immediately begin experimenting with Conté crayon, and with very fine results. Although Signac was self-taught (in contrast to Seurat), he drew regularly throughout his life, both in black and white and in color. He possessed unquestionable talent as a draftsman, and in 1885 began producing Conté crayon sheets that from the start showed signs of a singular artistic vision (fig. 2). Though lacking the monolithic focus of his mentor, the fiery Signac was already expressing in these works all the energy and vivacity that would become his hallmark. In his study for *The Milliners* nothing has been rendered in detail aside from the slender scissors, and light takes complete precedence. It glows from beneath the dark lampshade, glances off the hatmaker's brow, and reflects on the fabric she is fashioning. From 1892 on Signac began gradually replacing Conté crayon with india ink. In 1907 he undertook the first of his large wash cartoons, executed on the same scale as the final paintings. In the outstanding example presented here, *Les Andelys on a Summer Morning* (pl. 92), the lines unfurl broadly across the page and give rhythm to the composition through a measured balance between whites and blacks.

The most typical neo-impressionist drawings nevertheless remain the many Conté crayon sheets executed in the manner of Seurat. On the artist's death in 1891 his drawings and panels were distributed among his friends, and black-and-white works were displayed alongside the paintings in both the posthumous exhibitions devoted to him in 1892, held at the Salon des XX in Brussels and the Salon des Indépendants in Paris. As the remarkable selection of Conté crayon and charcoal works in the Dyke collection reveals, Seurat's drawings had a lasting influence on his admirers.

Along with Signac, Charles Angrand had been one of Seurat's closest friends, and the two painted together on the island known as La Grande Jatte. One of Angrand's most explicit memories, however, concerned the drawings: "I recall going with him to his mother's house and seeing hanging on the wall a number of his black drawings — *Man Dining*, for example — which were his first studies."[4] Angrand exhibited drawings for the first time at the Salon des Indépendants of 1892, where three works in crayon hung alongside his paintings. "They are intimate subjects," he wrote, "vaguely derived from Millet."[5] They also owed a great deal to Seurat. Drawing would gradually come to dominate Angrand's production, and when he retreated permanently to Saint-Laurent-en-Caux, in Normandy, in 1896, the local surroundings provided him with an inexhaust-

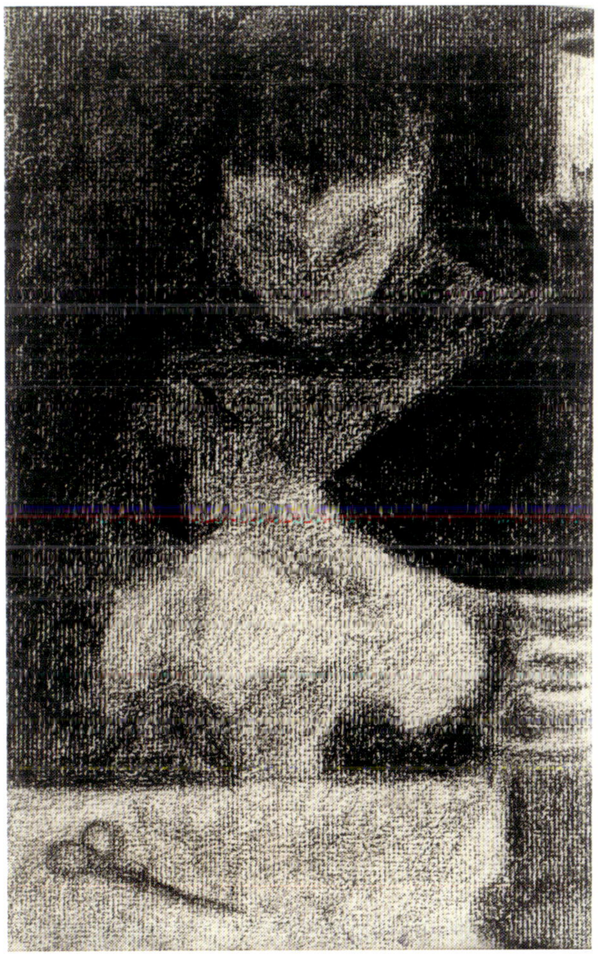

2 Paul Signac, *Study for "The Milliners,"* 1885, Conté crayon, private collection

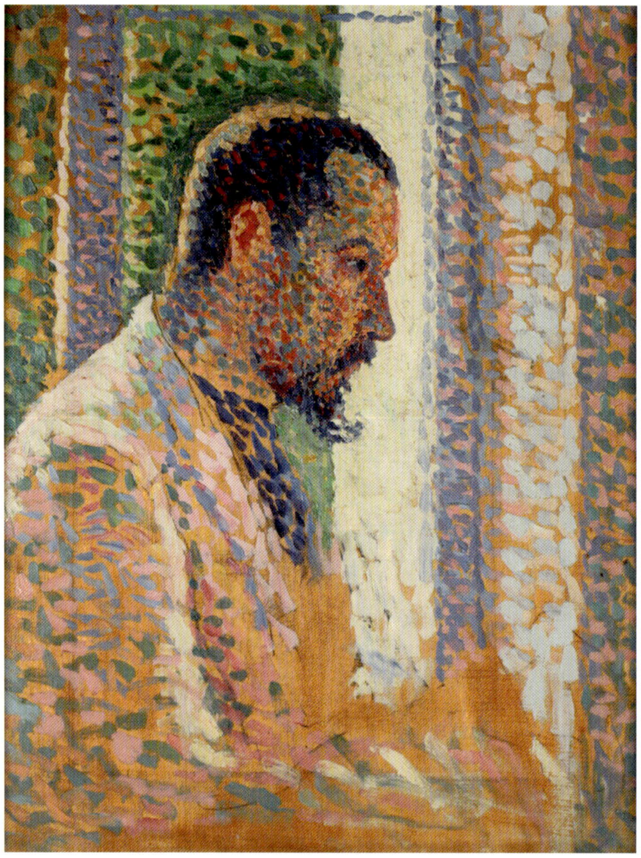

3 Maximilien Luce, *Portrait of Paul Signac*, c. 1890, oil on wood, private collection

ible source of inspiration. Sometimes — *The Annunciation to the Shepherds* (pl. 81) is an example — the mysterious balance between light and shade imbues a rural subject with an almost mystical quality. Though he explored pastel for a time, Angrand devoted most of his creative energy to the contrasts of black and white, tirelessly reworking and perfecting the equilibrium between the two. "The drawings are all I'm about," he disclosed in 1899. "I get up, have breakfast, plant my easel near the window, and pick up my crayon. In the afternoon, another identical session. And it is this exclusive re-beginning that makes up my life."[6]

Like Angrand, Achille Laugé lived for several years in Paris, where he studied in the atelier of Alexandre Cabanel. He returned to his native region of Aude in 1888. Though not actually a member of the neo-impressionist group, Laugé was interested in Seurat's theories and subsequently interpreted them in a highly personal way in the genres of landscape, still life, and portraiture. His works, which are often imprinted with a certain naïveté, are characterized by a powerful luminosity and a marked geometry. In the figural works, nevertheless, the simplified contrasts do not preclude a sensitive psychological study. *The Artist's Mother* (pl. 80) is a case in point: Catherine Laugé's serene and radiant presence owes much to the intensity of the gaze she directs toward her son. This beautifully preserved sheet, with its contrasts of light and dark fully intact, is without doubt one of the masterpieces of neo-impressionist drawing. Yet it could hardly be more different from Seurat's interpretation of the same theme in one of his most famous works, *Embroidery; The Artist's Mother* (see fig. 1).

Maximilien Luce was also an excellent portraitist, and like most of the neo-impressionists, he drew his inspiration mainly from friends and family. Here again James Dyke has chosen a particularly significant image: a drawing depicting the profile of a youthful Signac (pl. 77), the man Thadée Natanson would humorously refer to as "the St. Paul of neo-impressionism." Luce's study, executed in 1889 at Herblay, on the banks of the Seine, is a preliminary sketch for a portrait of the painter that shows him in silhouette, deeply absorbed in the canvas on which he is working (fig. 3). Signac, whom Luce had met some two years earlier, had introduced Luce to his circle of friends and initiated him into the subtleties of tonal division. Made in the very earliest phase of neo-impressionism, the painting reflects the close friendship of two men linked by a shared artistic ideal.

Better known as a portraitist than any of the artists so far mentioned was the Belgian painter Théo Van Rysselberghe. Academically trained and schooled in the Flemish tradition, he was especially skilled at conveying the individuality of his models and adapting to different drawing techniques. Whether executed in charcoal or red chalk, his works reveal a consummate mastery of the balance between light and shade. As seen in his portrait of Augustine de Rothmaler (pl. 78), Van Rysselberghe's Conté crayon works show Seurat's enduring influence, despite his greater attention to detail. In general, Van Rysselberghe's drawings are characterized by a fluid line, subtle shifts from dark to light, and an elegance that was also evident in his innovative typographic design work.

Albert Dubois-Pillet occupied a special place within the neo-impressionist group. Notwithstanding the demands of his military career and the army's disapproval of his artistic activities, he played a crucial role in the founding of the Société des Artistes Indépendants. He was also one of the pioneers of neo-impressionism, adopting a pointillist technique in the winter of 1886–1887 after having seen Seurat's *Grande Jatte*. The application of neo-impressionist principles to drawing was an early preoccupation as well, and like Camille Pissarro, Signac, and (rarely) Seurat, Dubois-Pillet experimented with drawing in dots. Although most of the group used this technique to make reproductions of their divisionist paintings for magazines printed in black and white, he also practiced it outdoors, producing works like *The Pont des Arts and the Île de la Cité, Seen from the Quai du Louvre* (fig. 4). In this work, the dots of india ink — applied in varying sizes with a pen — are distributed unevenly across the surface according to the requirements of light and color. In spite of the refined, almost immaterial charm of this type of drawing, however, it would not endure beyond the deaths of Dubois-Pillet in 1890 and Seurat in 1891. At this period Pissarro, who had (like his friend Louis

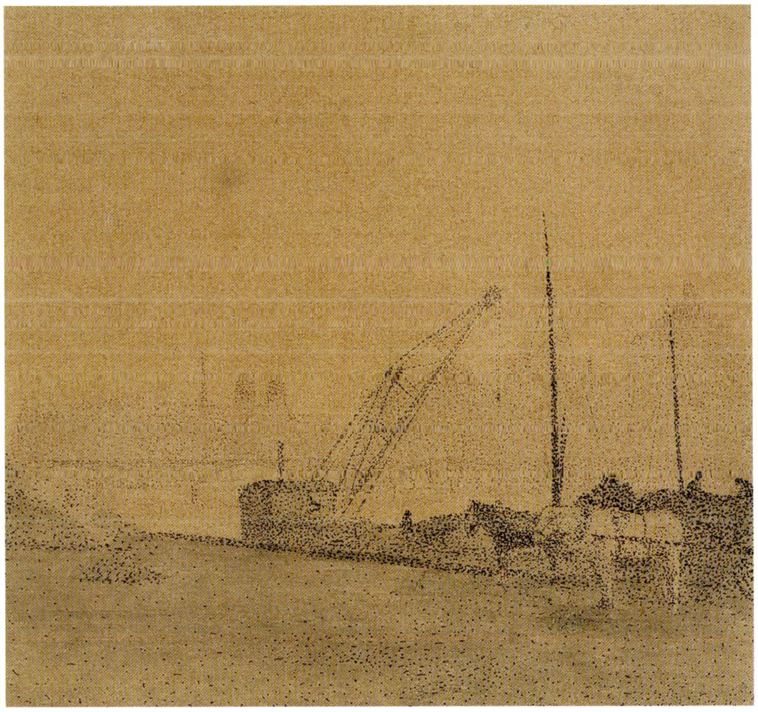

4 Albert Dubois-Pillet, *The Pont des Arts and the Île de la Cité, Seen from the Quai du Louvre*, c. 1888, pen and brown ink, private collection

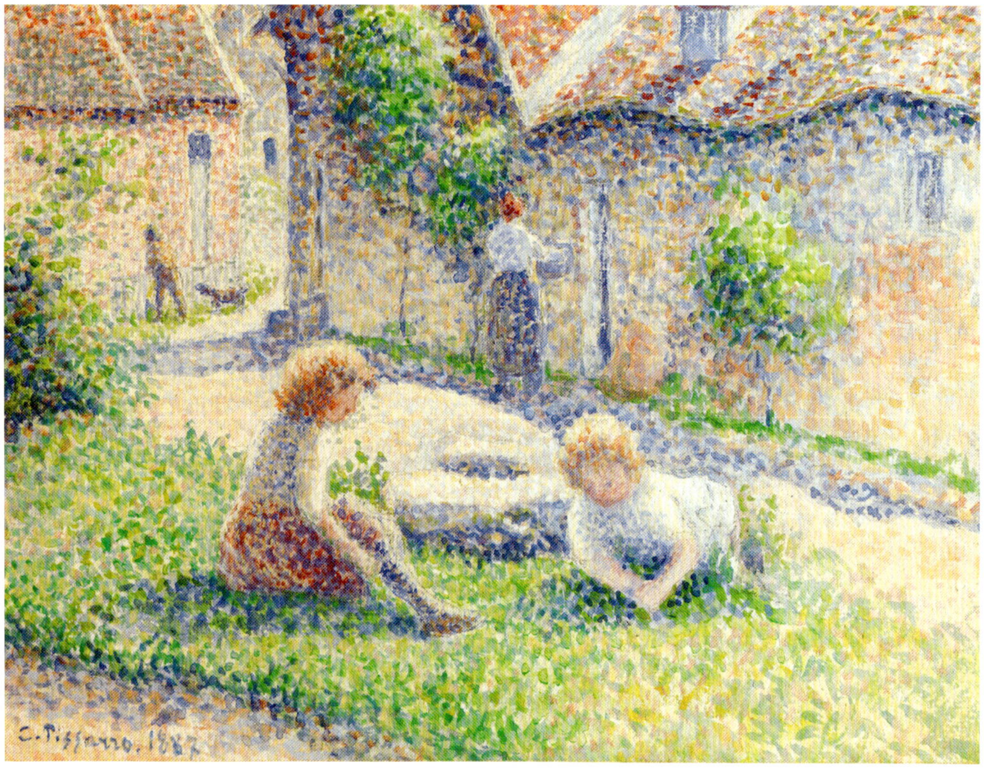

5 Camille Pissarro, *Village Children*, 1887, gouache, private collection

Hayet) experimented with the pointillist touch in watercolor or gouache (fig. 5), was moving away from divisionism and would soon return to a more orthodox form of impressionism.

The idea of making pointillist watercolors would be taken up again by Hippolyte Petitjean. Like many painters of his time, this student of Alexandre Cabanel was an admirer of Pierre Puvis de Chavannes. He began exhibiting mythological scenes at the Salon in 1880, but the earliest documentary evidence of his links to the neo-impressionists dates from the start of the following decade. Close to Pissarro and his son Lucien as well as to Luce (whose anarchist political views he shared), Petitjean participated in events organized by the Indépendants beginning at this time. He exhibited at the Barc de Boutteville Gallery in 1892 and at the Salon des XX in Brussels the next year, adapting the divisionist stroke of neo-impressionism to a Puvis-like theme. As with most of his works, his watercolors are not dated, nor are their locations identified. In executing them, he employed the divided color technique very freely, applying dabs of color in a loose network that allows the white of the paper to show through. Although his watercolors are reminiscent of those made by the Pissarros in the 1886–1890 period, Robert Herbert dates them to later in Petitjean's career, after his 1912 return to the neo-impressionist technique he had abandoned around the turn of the century.[7] Several depicting riverside strollers obviously allude to Seurat's *A Sunday on La Grande Jatte* (pls. 85 and 86). But in his pure landscapes the artist takes a more individual approach, subtly modulating the different areas of color to suggest gradual spatial recession and the light effects of a setting sun (pl. 84).

Of all the neo-impressionists, it was Henri-Edmond Cross and Signac who employed the watercolor medium with the most freedom. Although it served for both as a precious tool for making studies, they also practiced it as an art in its own right — and one in which they abstained from the pointillist touch. Cross applied watercolor in long, sinuous strokes, like small sticks of pure color, while from the outset Signac adopted an impressionist flick, short and energetic.

As recent research has revealed, Cross was a talented draftsman, and he left a very fine series of Conté crayon drawings that show a particularly harmonious use of the arabesque.[8] In the plein-air watercolor on view here, *A Villa on the Mediterranean Coast* (pl. 87), the freely handled pigment has been applied over a rapidly executed graphite sketch. It can be compared to *Provençal Coastline* (1907, Musée Malraux, Le Havre), which represents the same landscape seen from an opposite point of view. The handling recalls that of such early watercolors by Signac as *Barges on the Seine at Samois* (pl. 88), where the paint has been applied in juxtaposed strokes of pure color.

Signac was the neo-impressionist who practiced watercolor most consistently. He first began experimenting with the medium at the prompting of Pissarro in 1892, on his first visit to Saint-Tropez, and was immediately captivated by what had traditionally been considered the art of the traveler. For him, watercolor was a seductive alternative to the demanding labor of studio painting, a zone of freedom that suited his restless temperament and love of the outdoors.[9] It gradually took over from his work in oil, and he ultimately wrote a treatise on watercolor that was included in his monograph on Johan Barthold Jongkind, published in 1927.[10]

James Dyke is unquestionably one of the greatest collectors of Paul Signac's graphic oeuvre,[11] and the works presented here allow us to follow the stages of Signac's artistic development. Following the impressionist watercolor painted around the turn of the century in Samois, on the edge of the forest of Fontainebleau (pl. 88), there are two remarkable sheets with significant work in pen and ink: *The Calanque at Saint-Tropez*, executed in 1906 with a fauve-like latitude, contrasts with the exquisitely delicate portrayal of eucalyptus trees beside the sea at Antibes, made in 1910 (pls. 89 and 90). Also notable are three outstanding still lifes, a genre Signac practiced only rarely (pls. 91, 93, and 95). Finally, with its unusually close-up view of a fountain in a public square, *The Fountain in the Rue Grande at Saint-Paul de Vence* (pl. 94) is a masterpiece of the artist's mature period. Painted around 1924, it seems to anticipate these words: "There can be no beautiful shades of watercolor unless one brings the white of the paper into play — not only through transparency, but by using it sparingly, in varying proportions, around each stroke. This luminous intermediary intensifies each color and harmonizes it with its neighbors."[12]

Even in his latest works Signac never strayed from the essential tenets of the neo-impressionist theories. For Signac, like all his fellow neo-impressionist artists, light and contrast remained the basic principles of his art, and he continued to celebrate them in his watercolors and black ink drawings to the end of his career.

76 Georges Seurat, *Strolling Woman with a Muff*, c. 1884
Conté crayon, 300 × 230

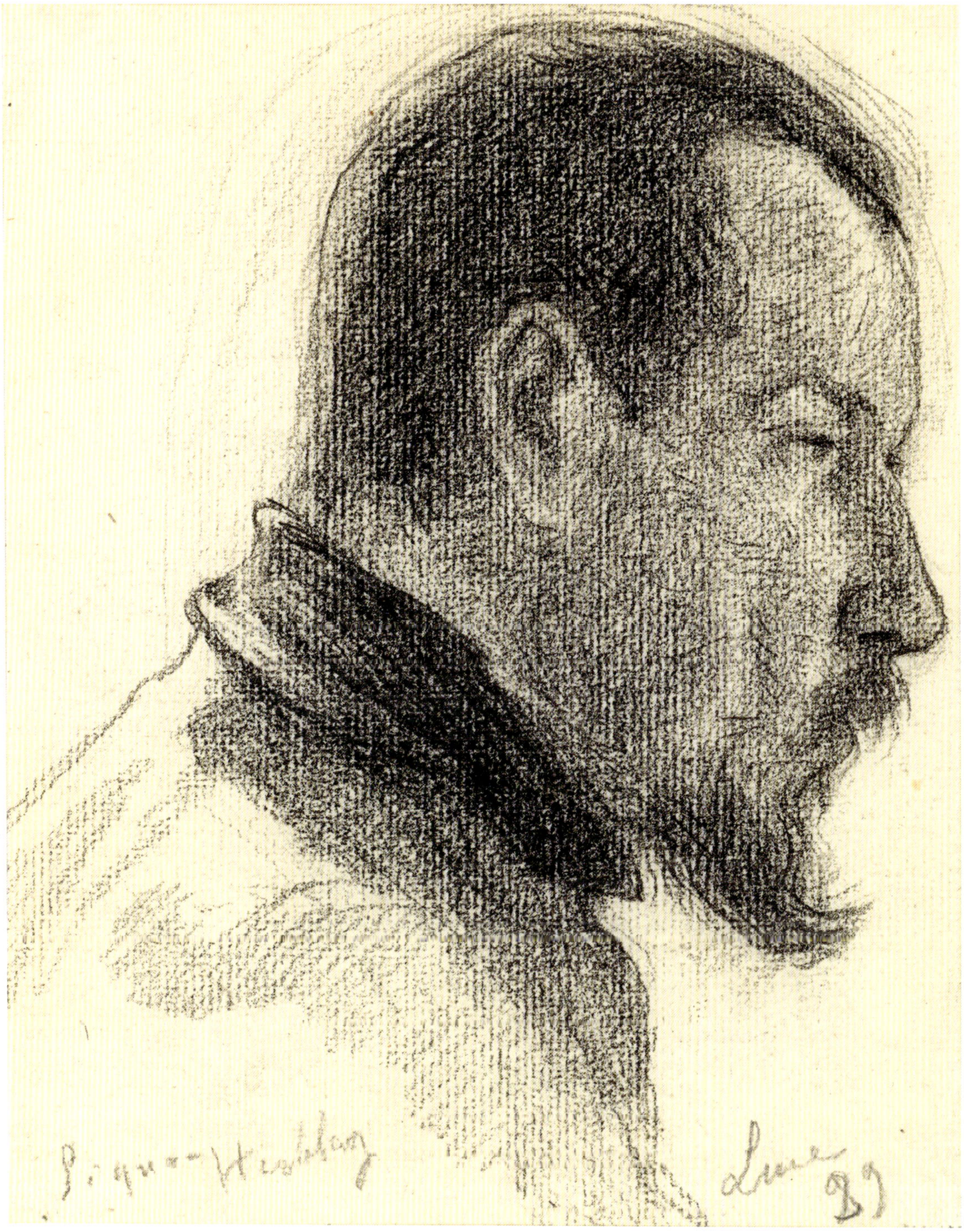

77 Maximilien Luce, *Paul Signac,* 1889
charcoal, 190 × 159

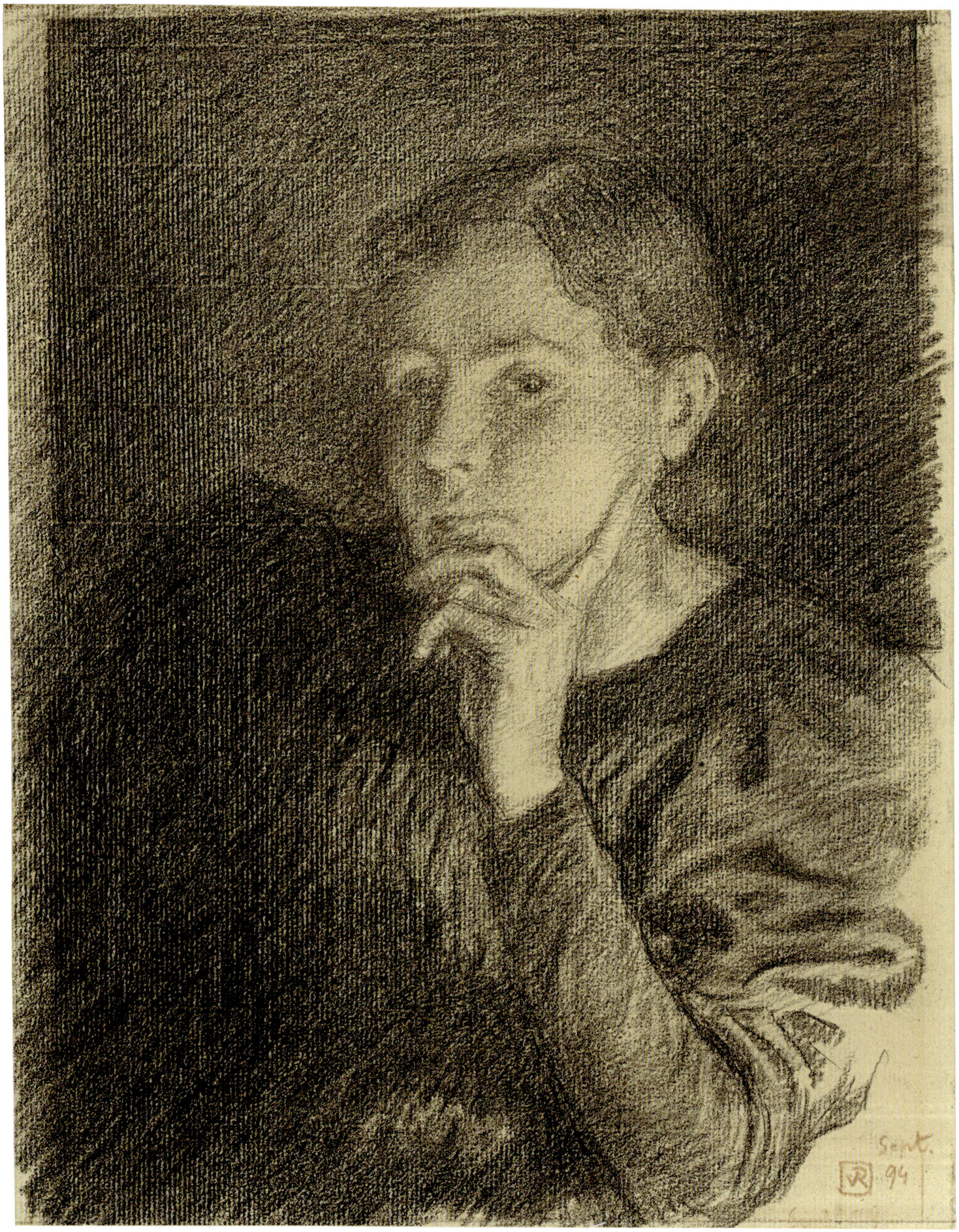

78 Théo van Rysselberghe, *Augustine de Rothmaler,* 1894
Conté crayon, 320 × 250

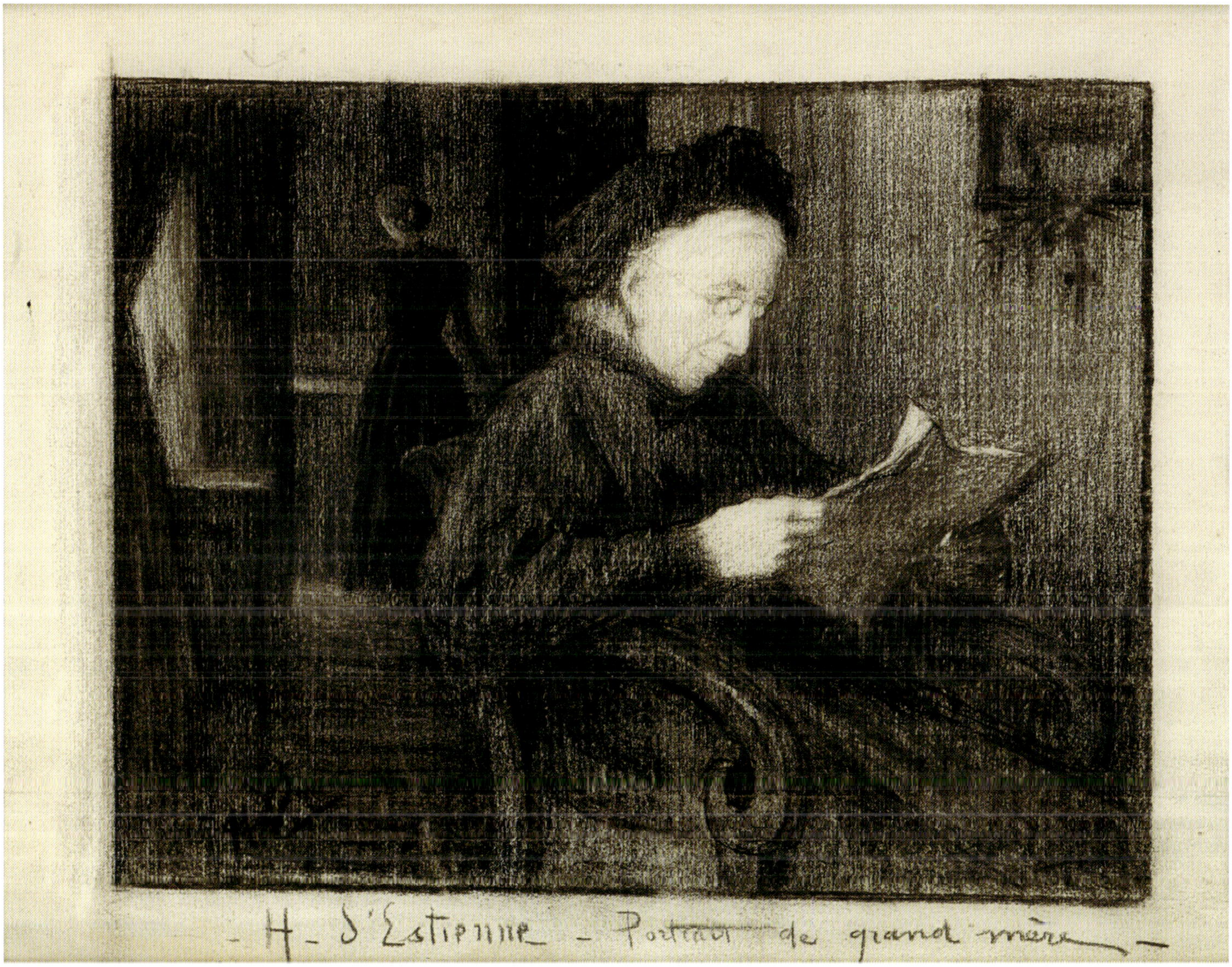

79 Henry d'Estienne, *Grandmother Reading,* 1890s
black chalk, 280 × 370

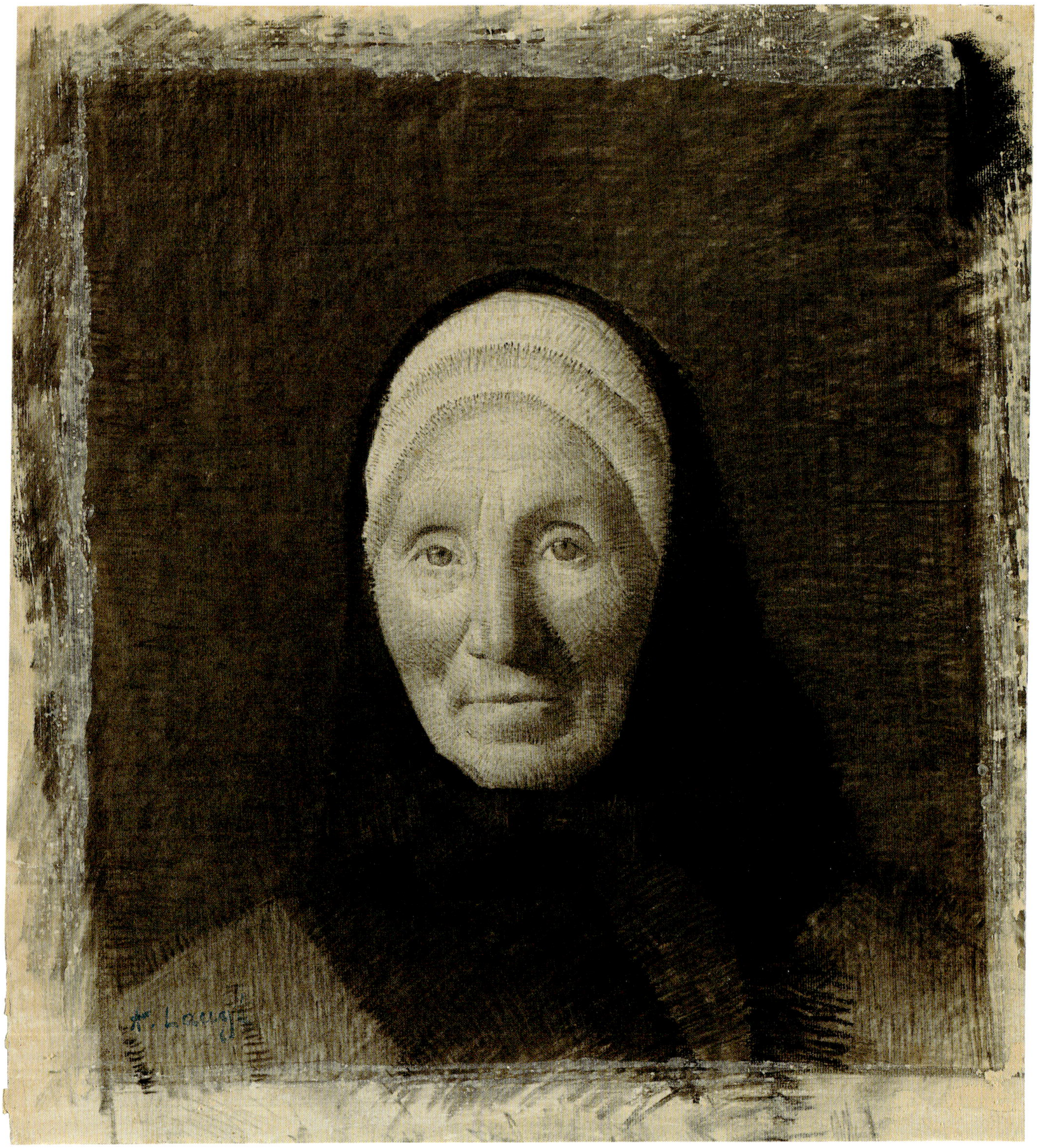

80 Achille Laugé, *The Artist's Mother,* 1893/1896
charcoal, 450 × 400

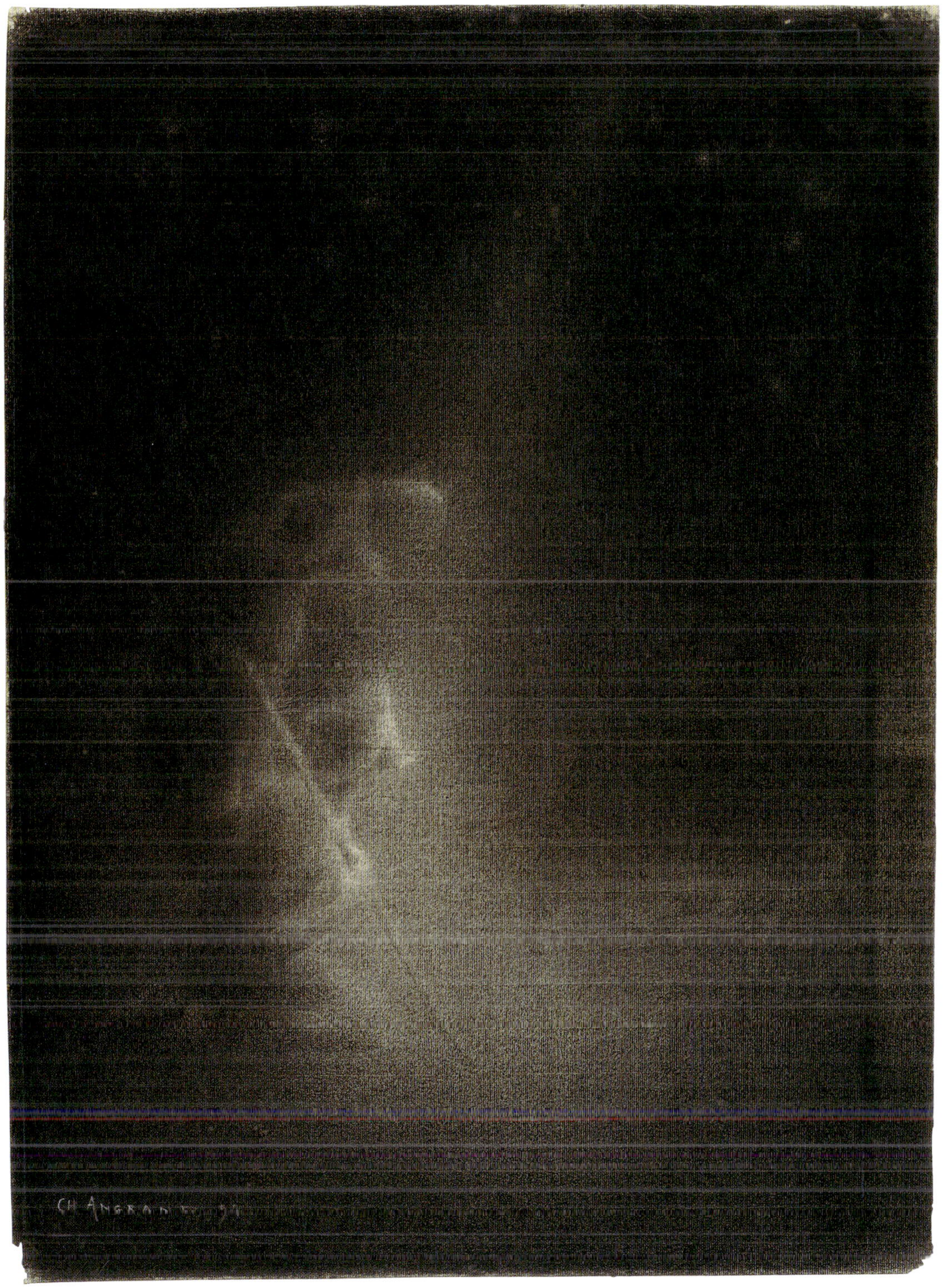

81 Charles Angrand, *The Annunciation to the Shepherds,* 1894
charcoal with Conté crayon, 943 × 700

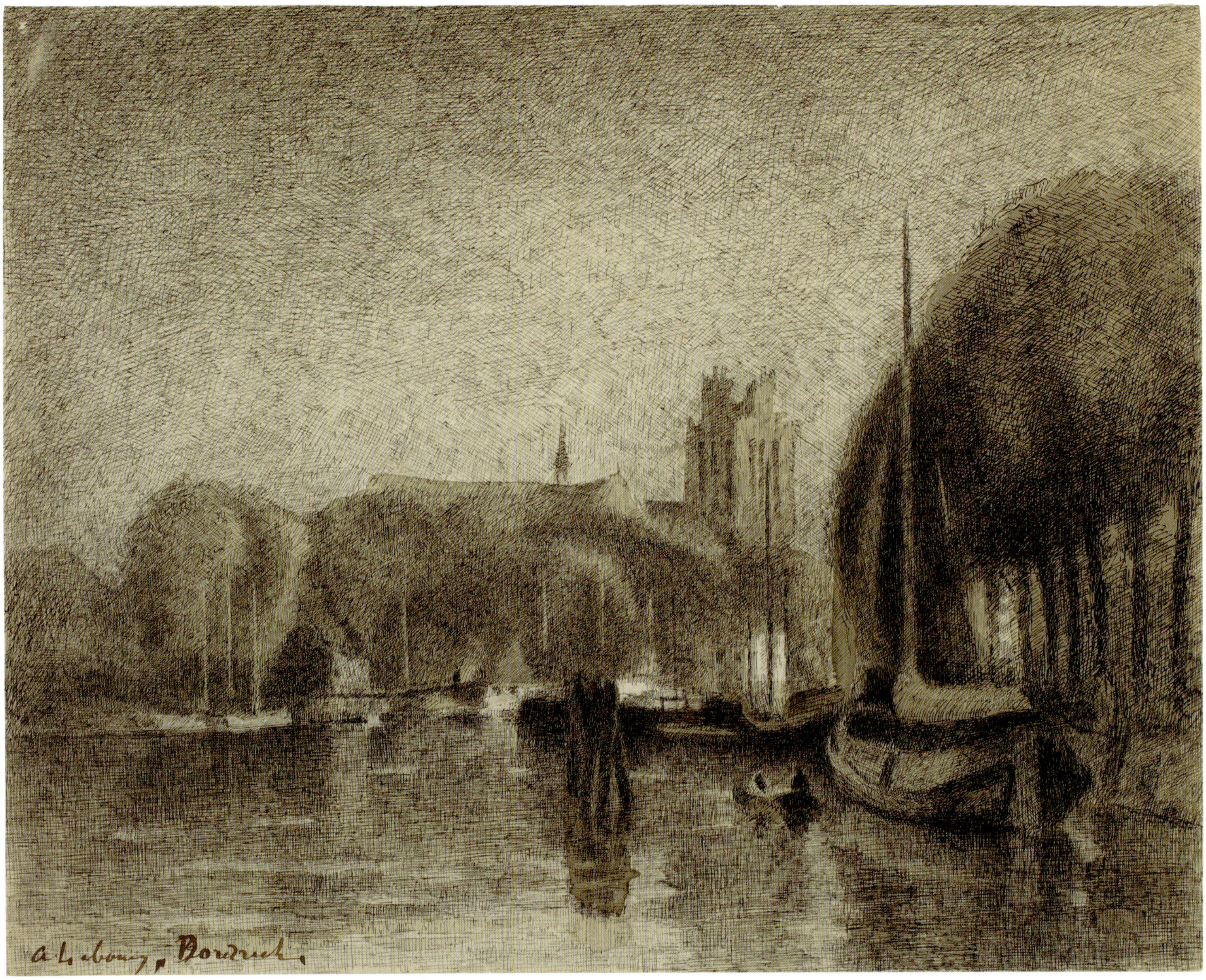

82 Albert Lebourg, *The Harbor at Dordrecht,* 1895/1897
pen and ink with gray-brown wash, 225 × 284

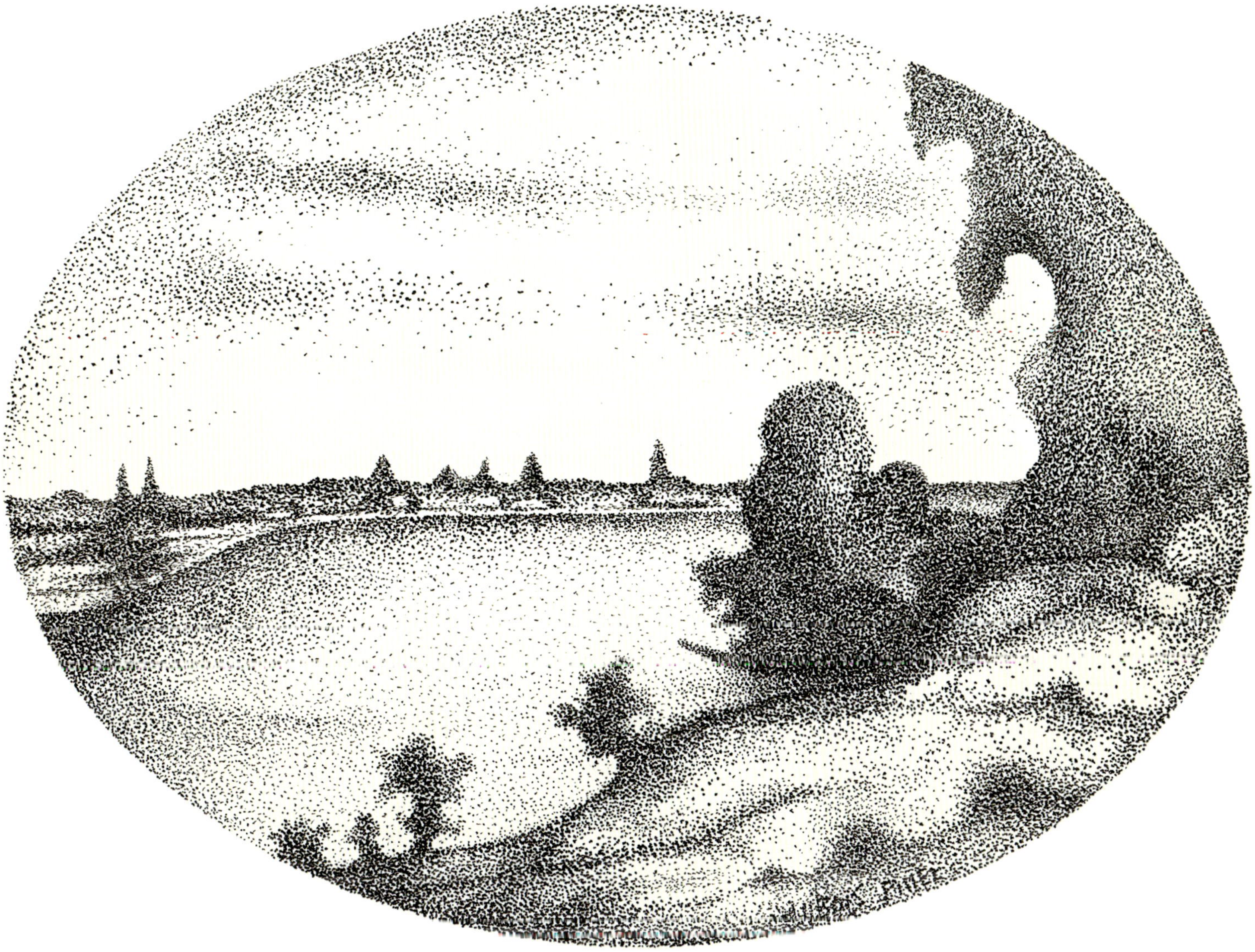

83 Albert Dubois-Pillet, *A River Landscape,* c. 1888
black ink, 290 × 390 (oval)

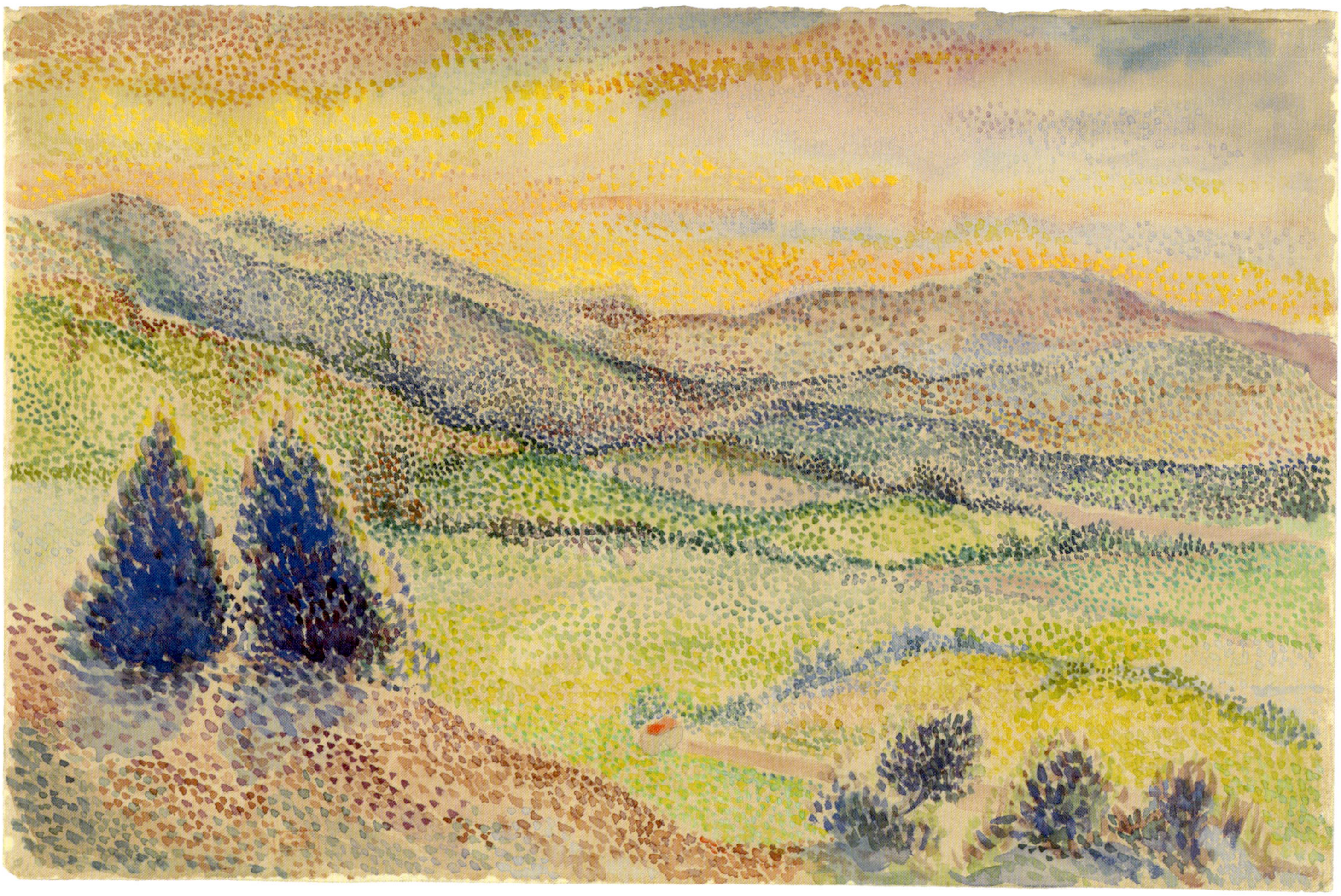

84 Hippolyte Petitjean, *A Broad Valley at Sunset,* c. 1897
watercolor, 320 × 500

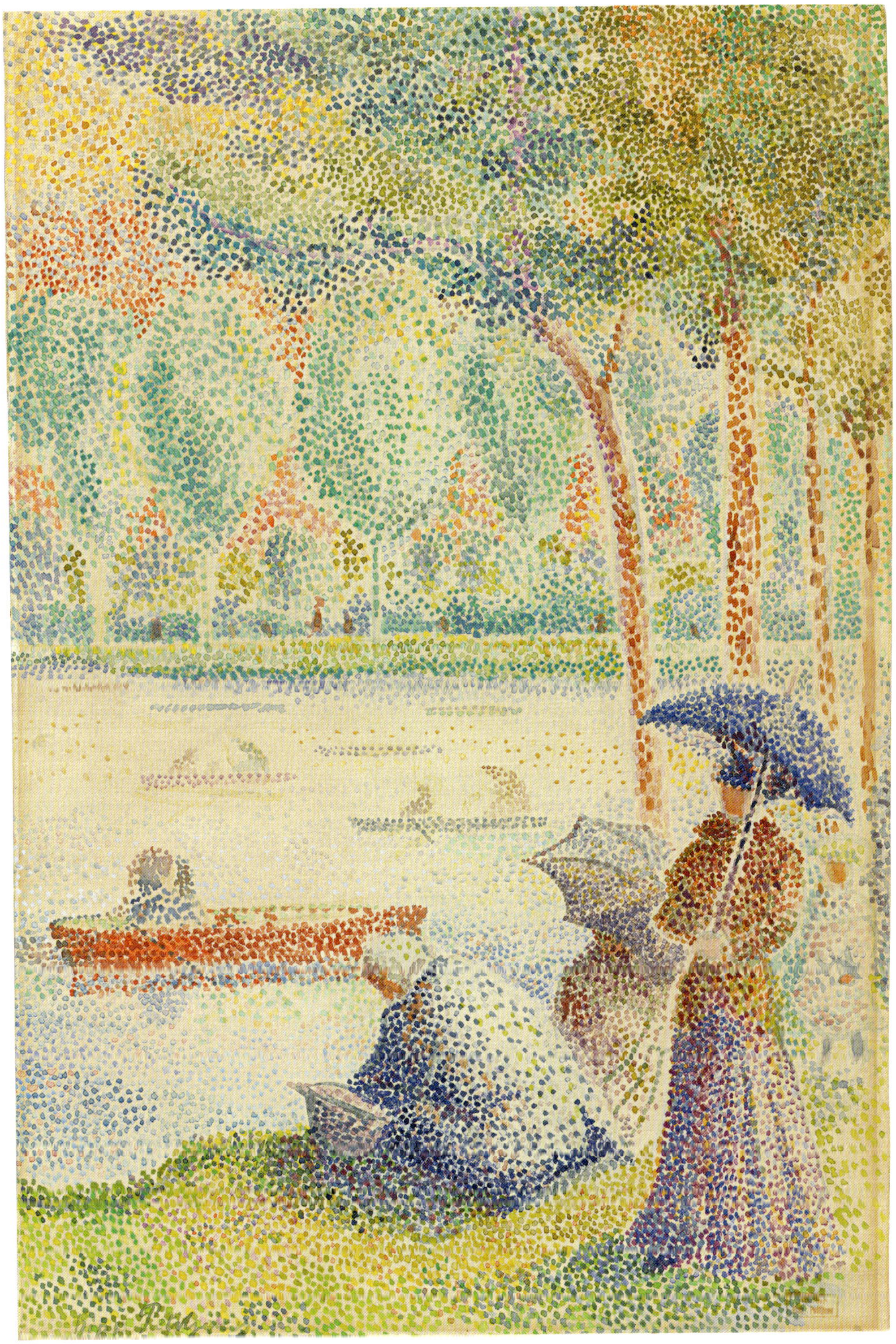

85 Hippolyte Petitjean, *Promenade by a Lake,* 1890s
watercolor, 438 × 293

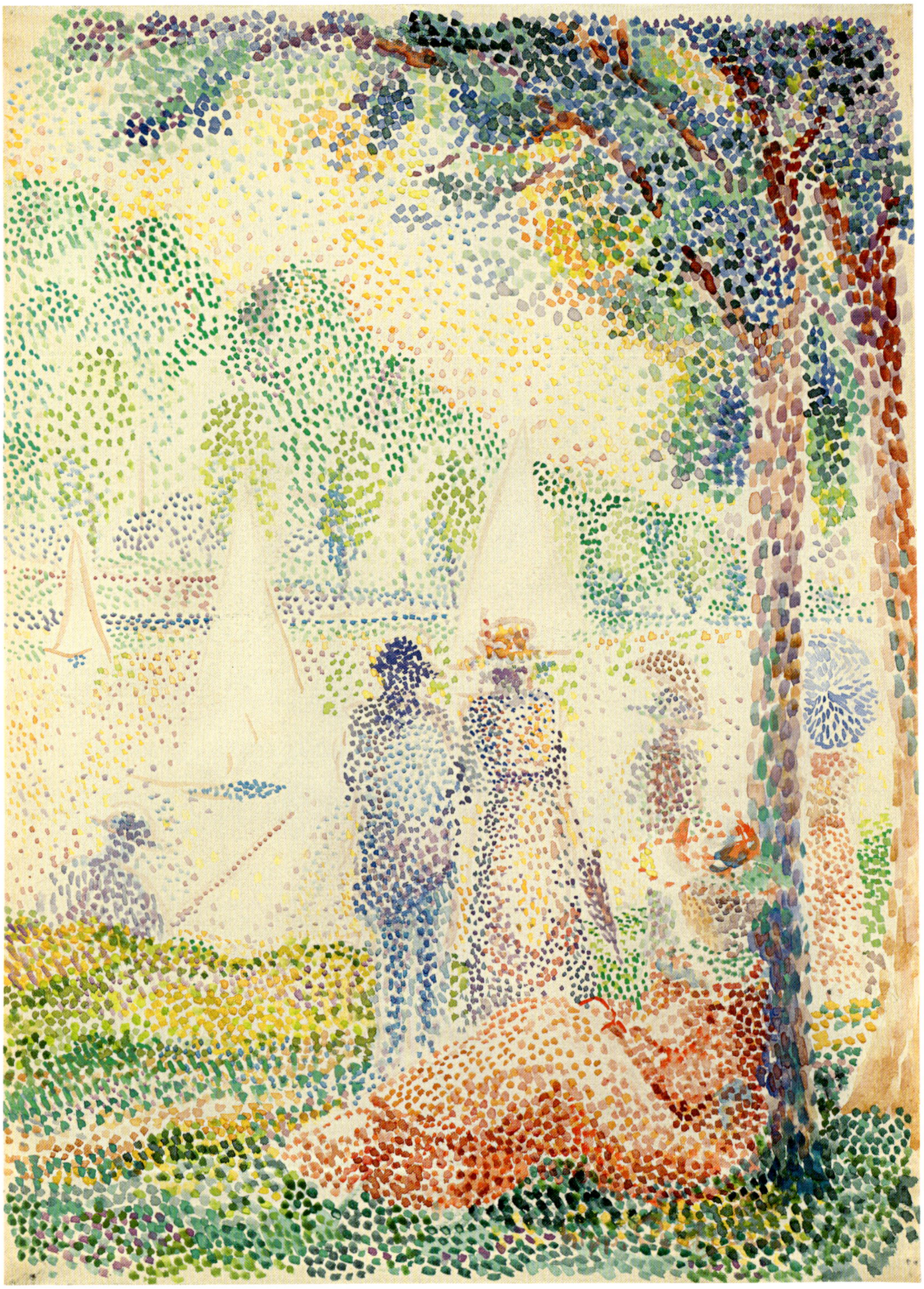

86 Hippolyte Petitjean, *An Afternoon by a Lake,* 1890s
watercolor, 365 × 267

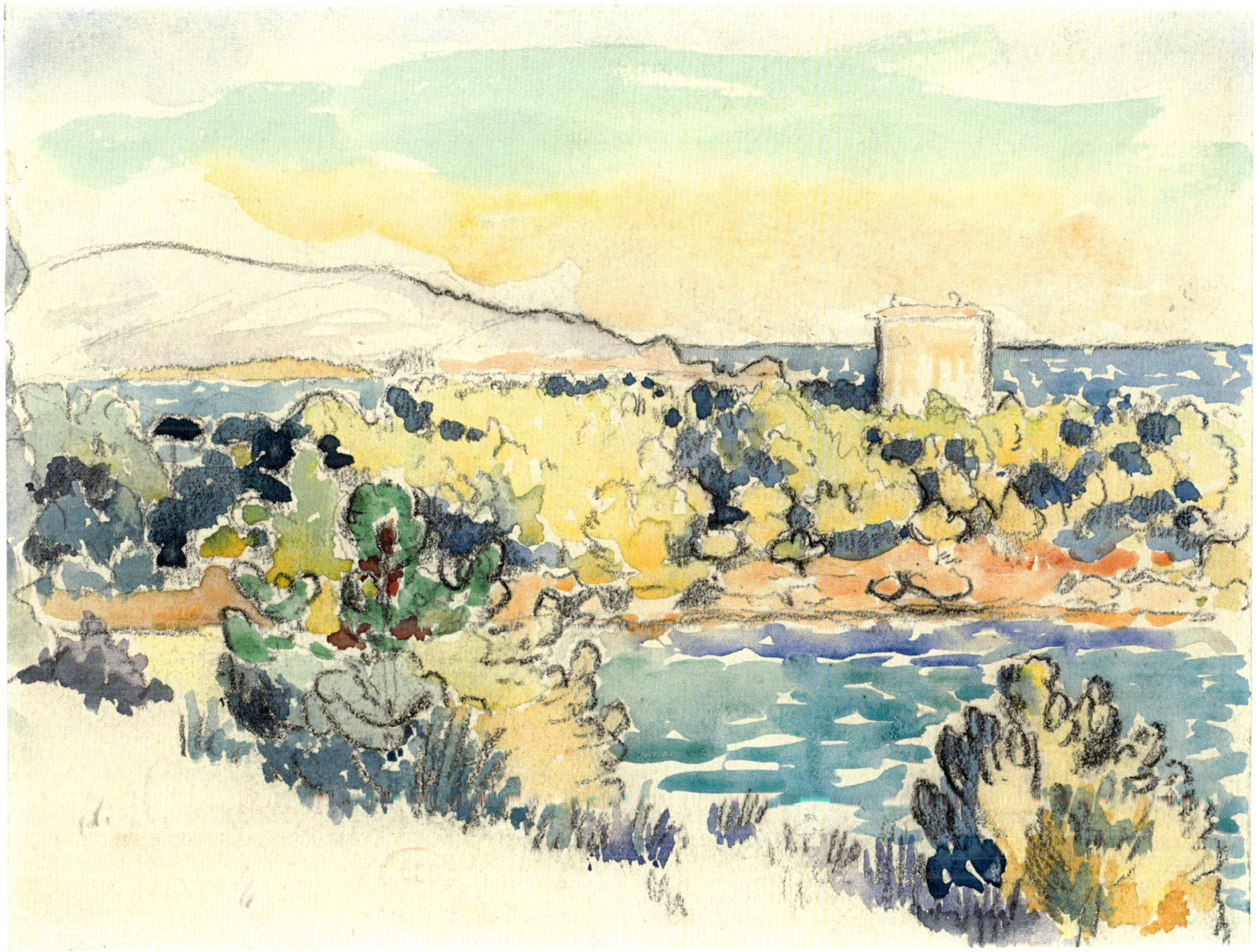

87 Henri Edmond Cross, *A Villa on the Mediterranean Coast,* c. 1907
watercolor and black chalk, 173 × 232

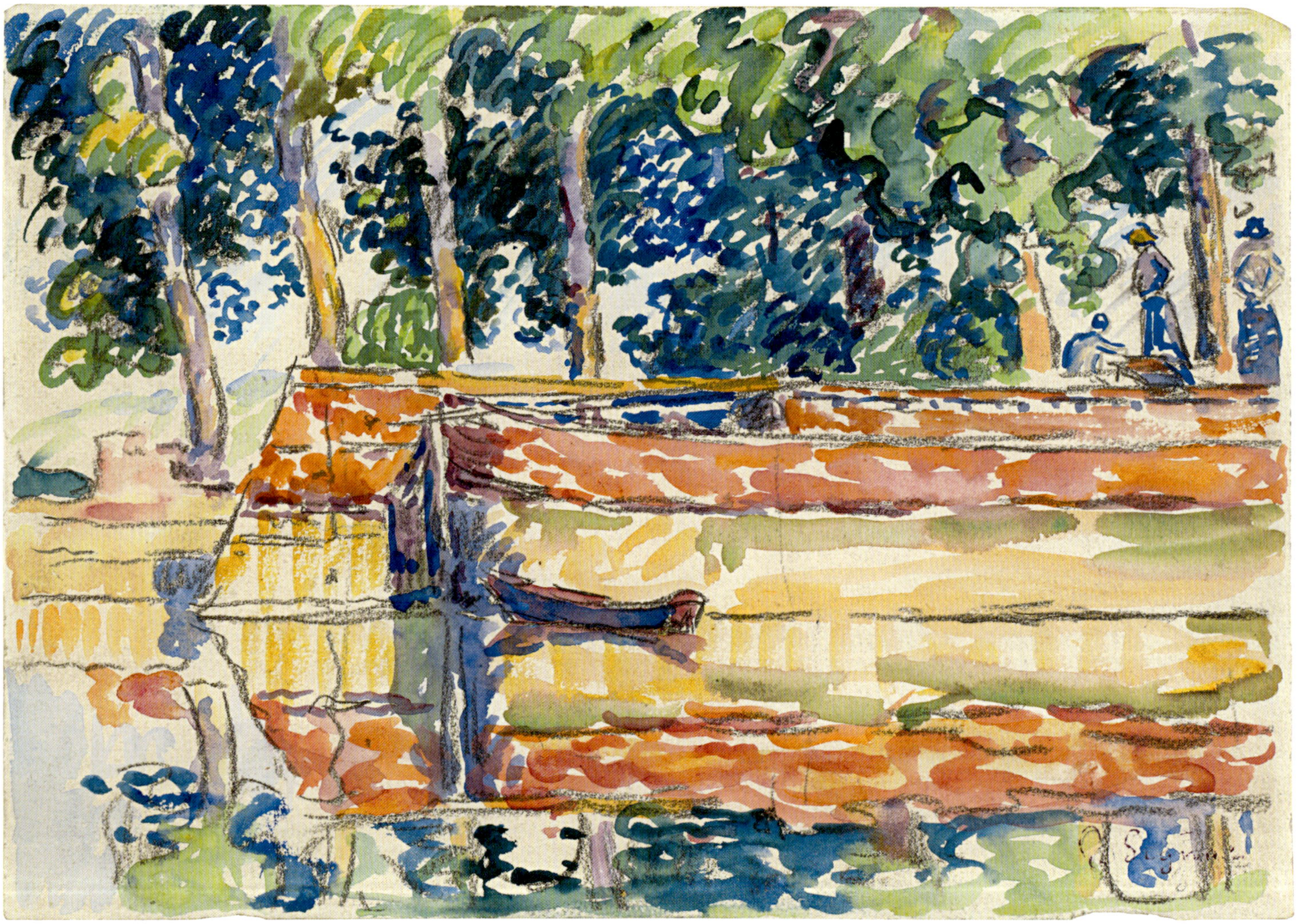

88 Paul Signac, *Barges on the Seine at Samois,* 1900
watercolor and gouache over black chalk, 173 × 250

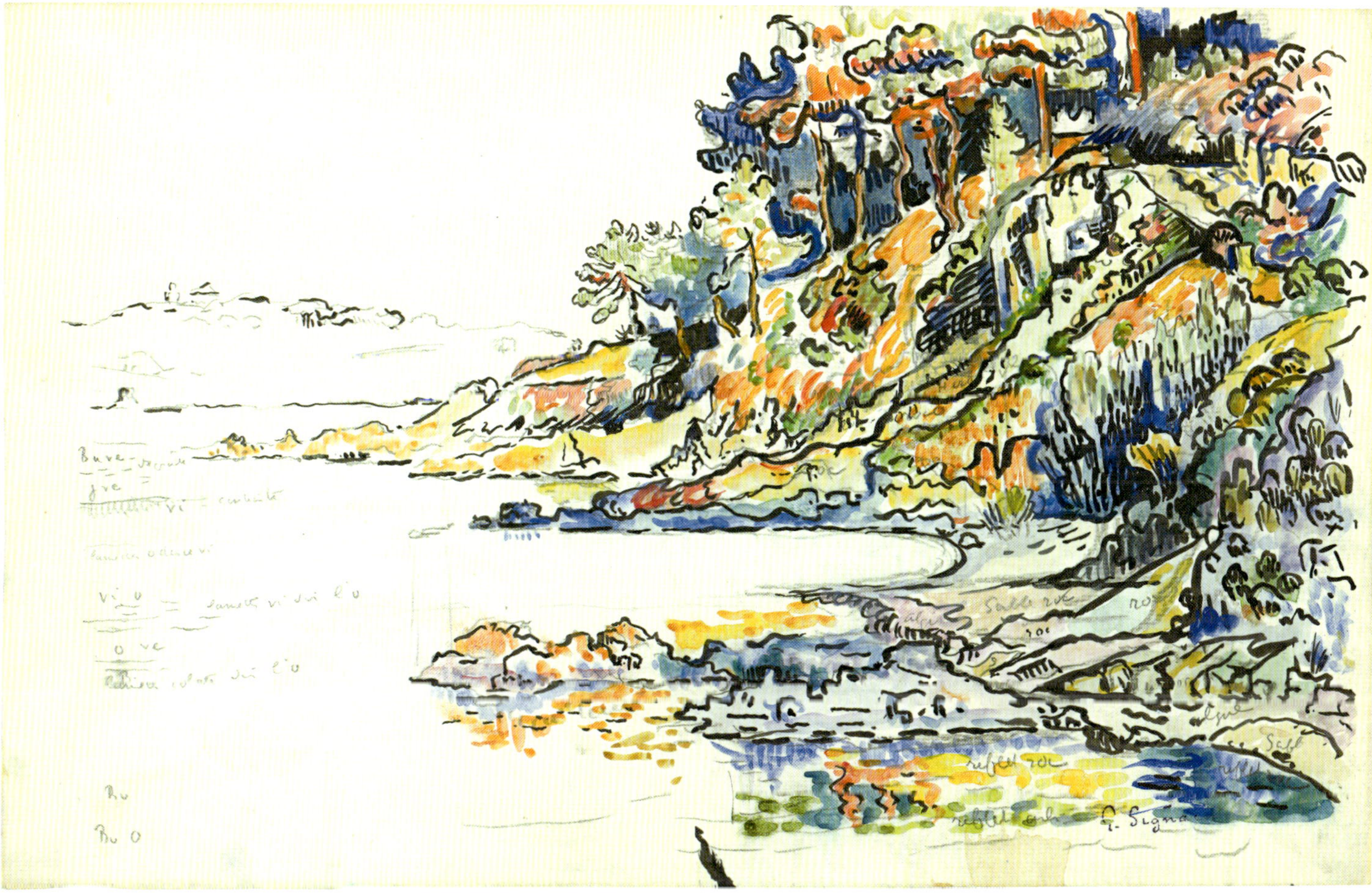

89 Paul Signac, *The Calanque at Saint-Tropez,* 1906
watercolor and graphite, 280 × 437

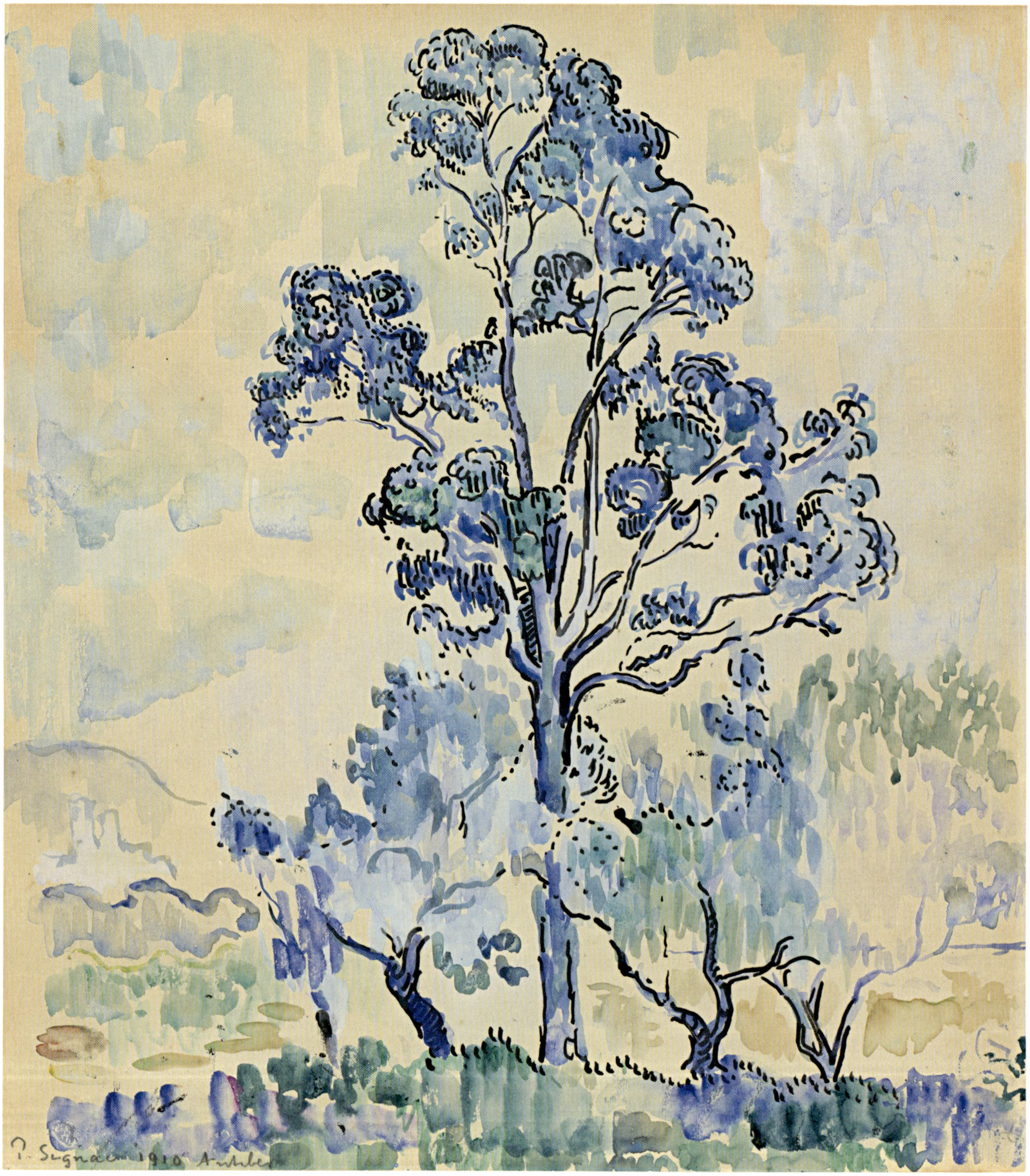

90 Paul Signac, *Eucalyptus Trees at Antibes,* 1910
black ink with watercolor and gouache, 390 × 345

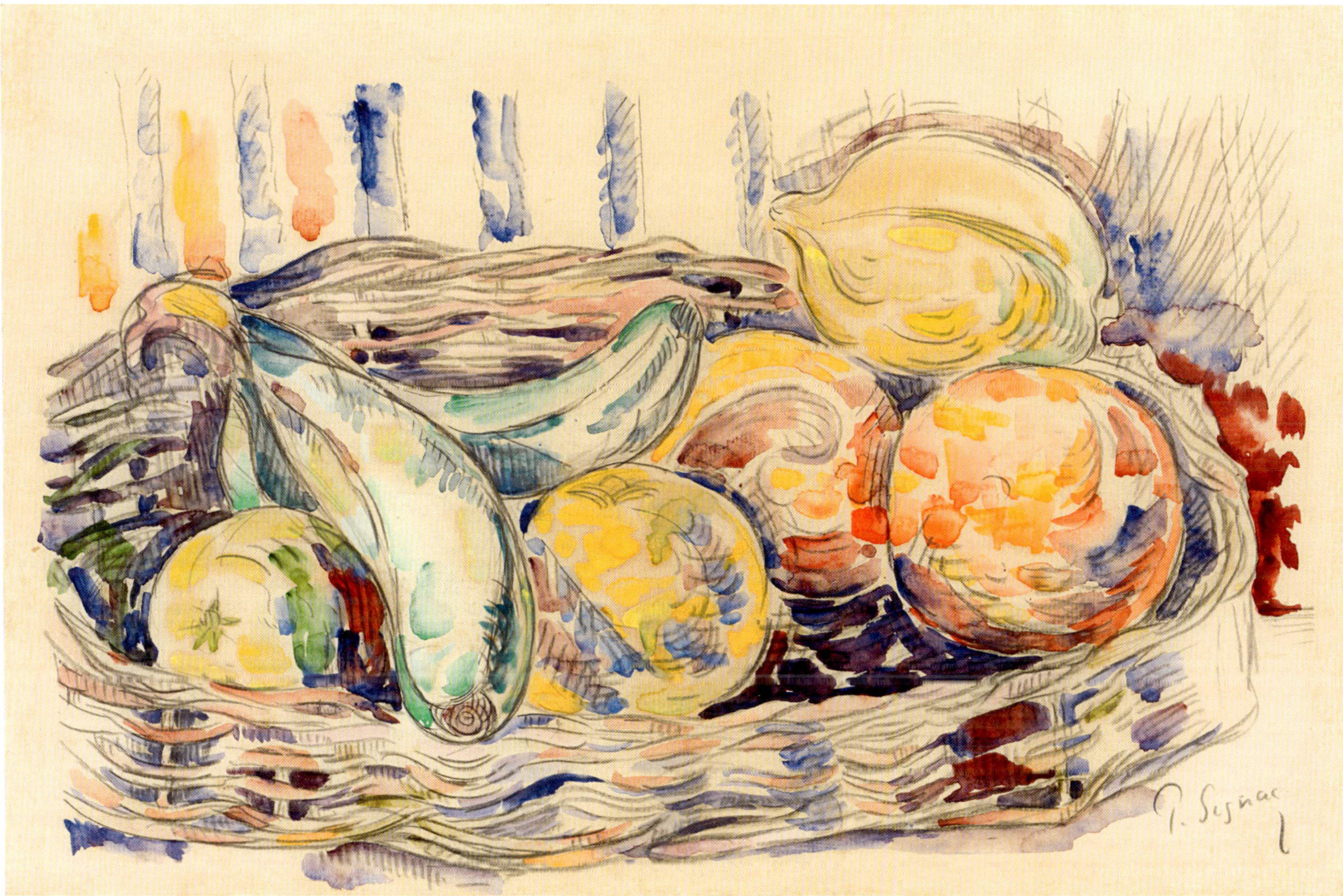

91 Paul Signac, *A Basket of Fruit,* 1920s
watercolor and black chalk, 292 × 445

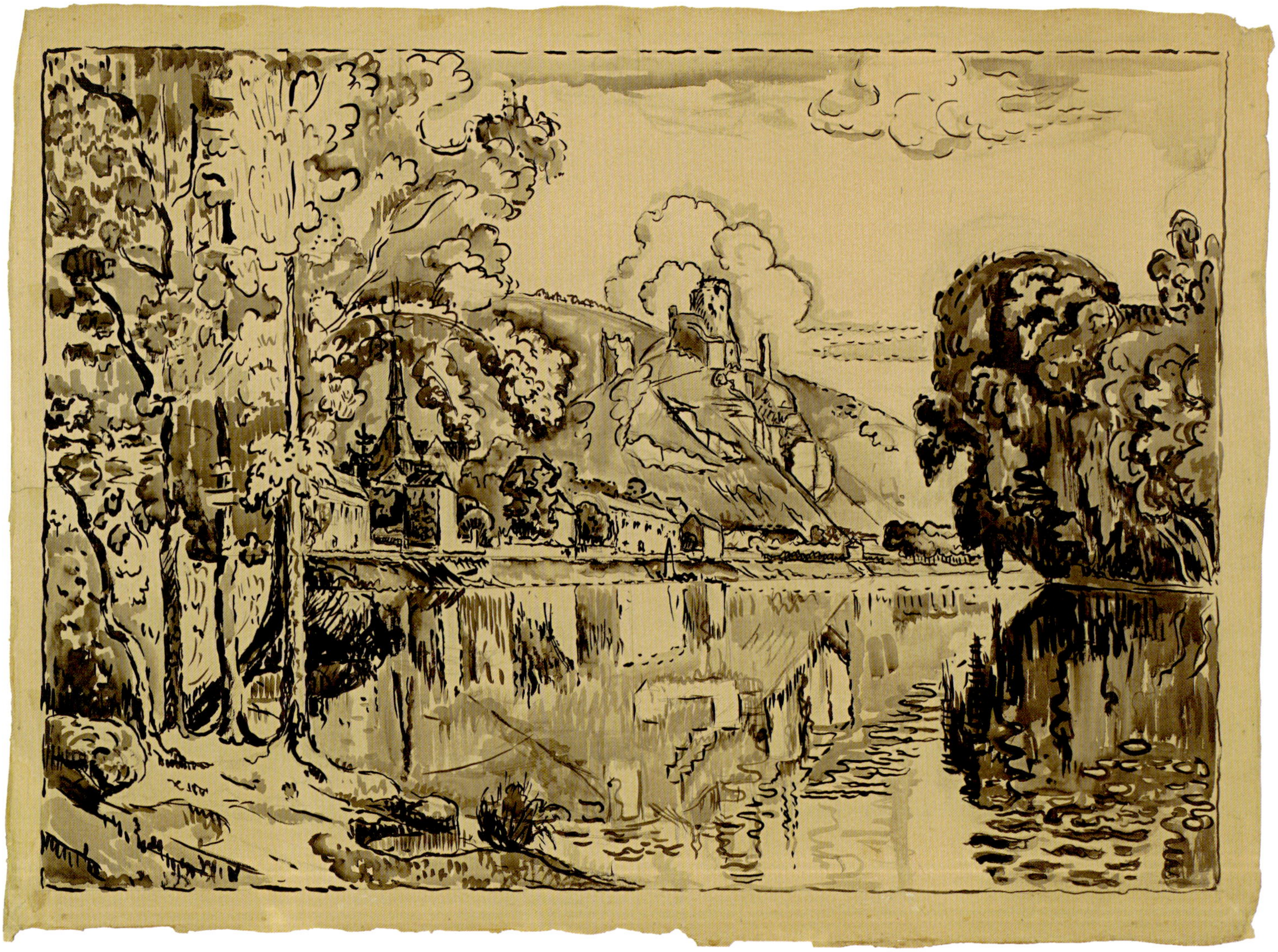

92 Paul Signac, *Les Andelys on a Summer Morning*, 1923
black ink, 695 × 950

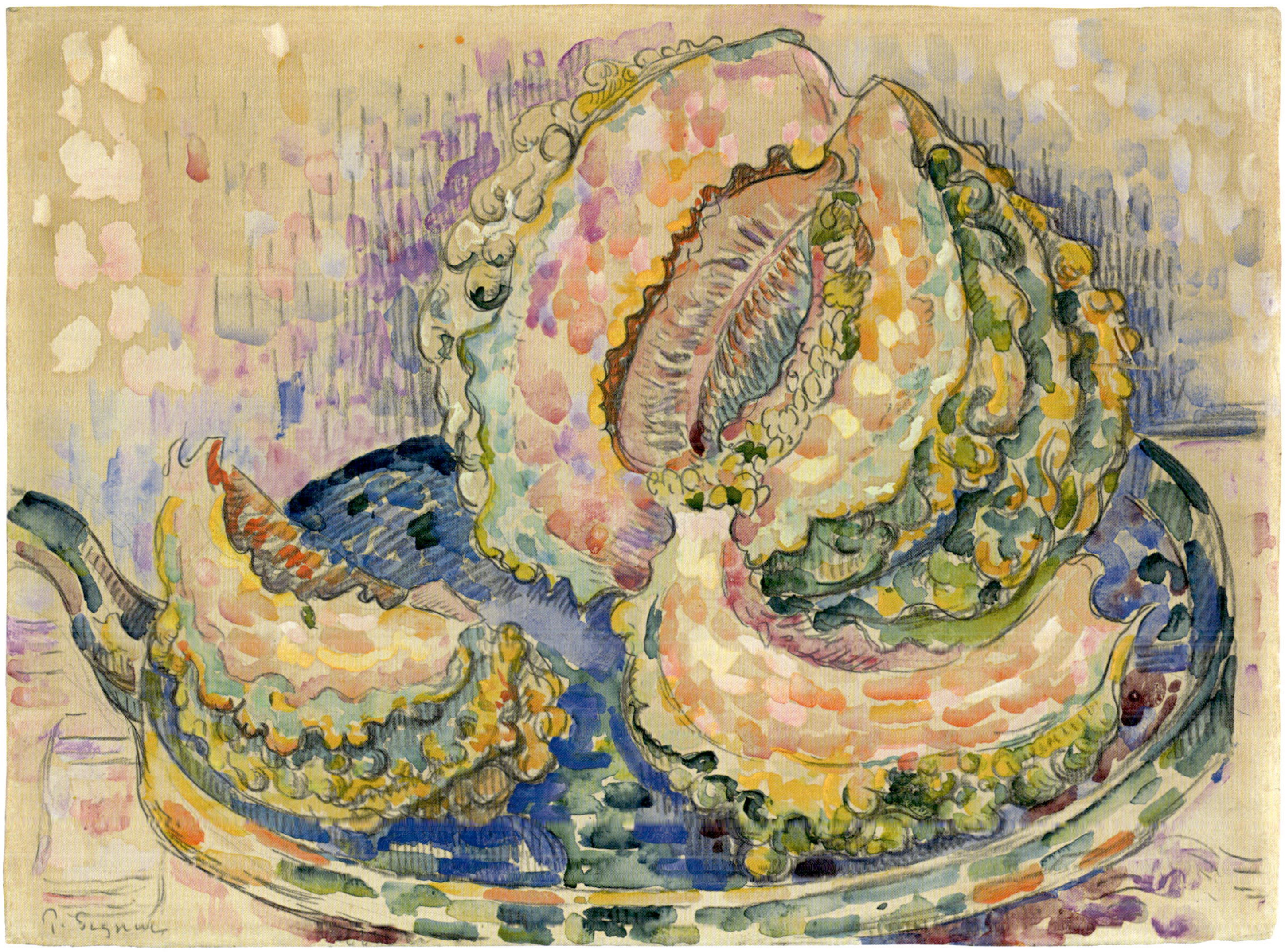

93 Paul Signac, *A Melon on a Plate,* c. 1918
watercolor and gouache, 324 × 450

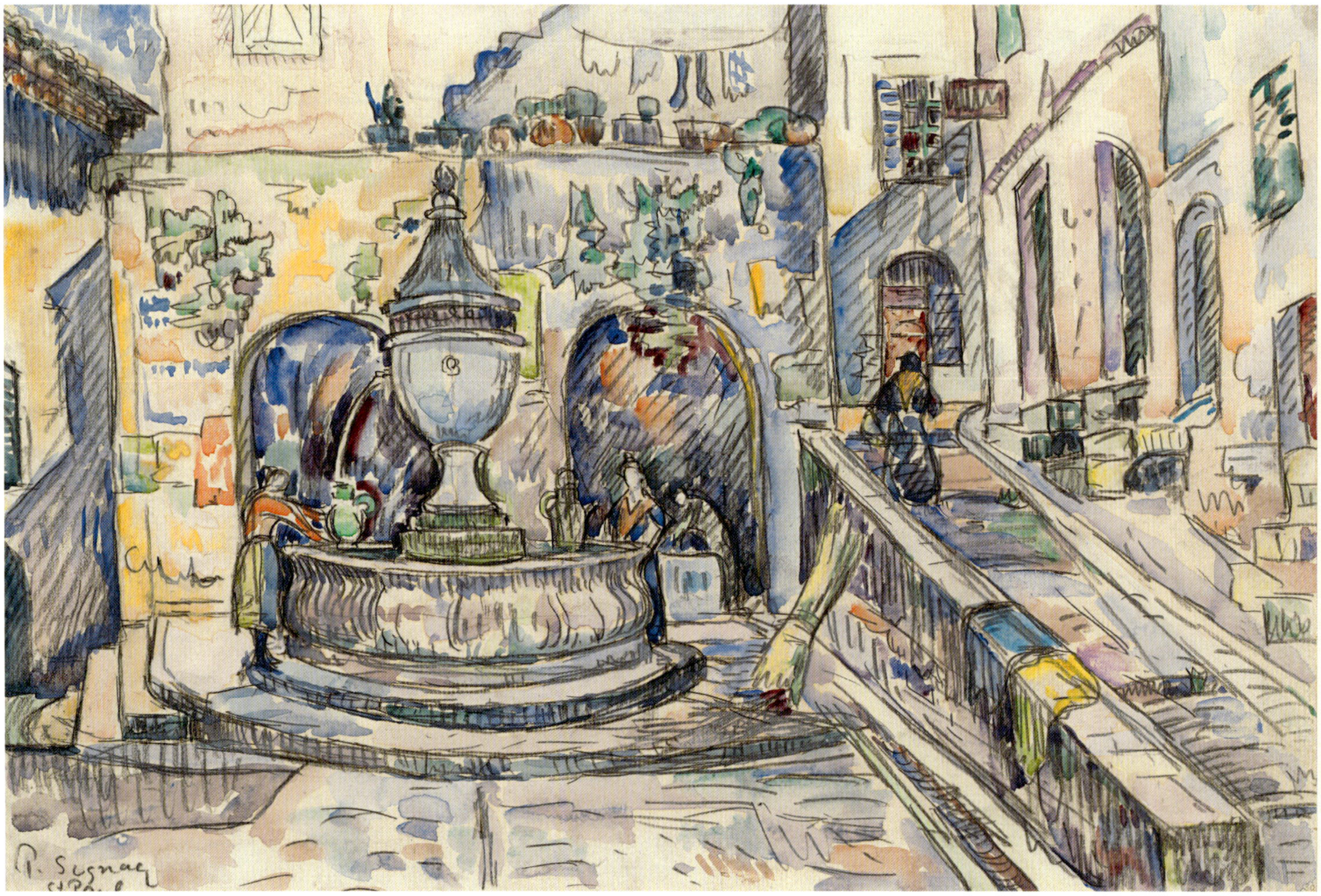

94 Paul Signac, *The Fountain in the Rue Grande in Saint-Paul de Vence,* c. 1924
watercolor and graphite, 290 × 437

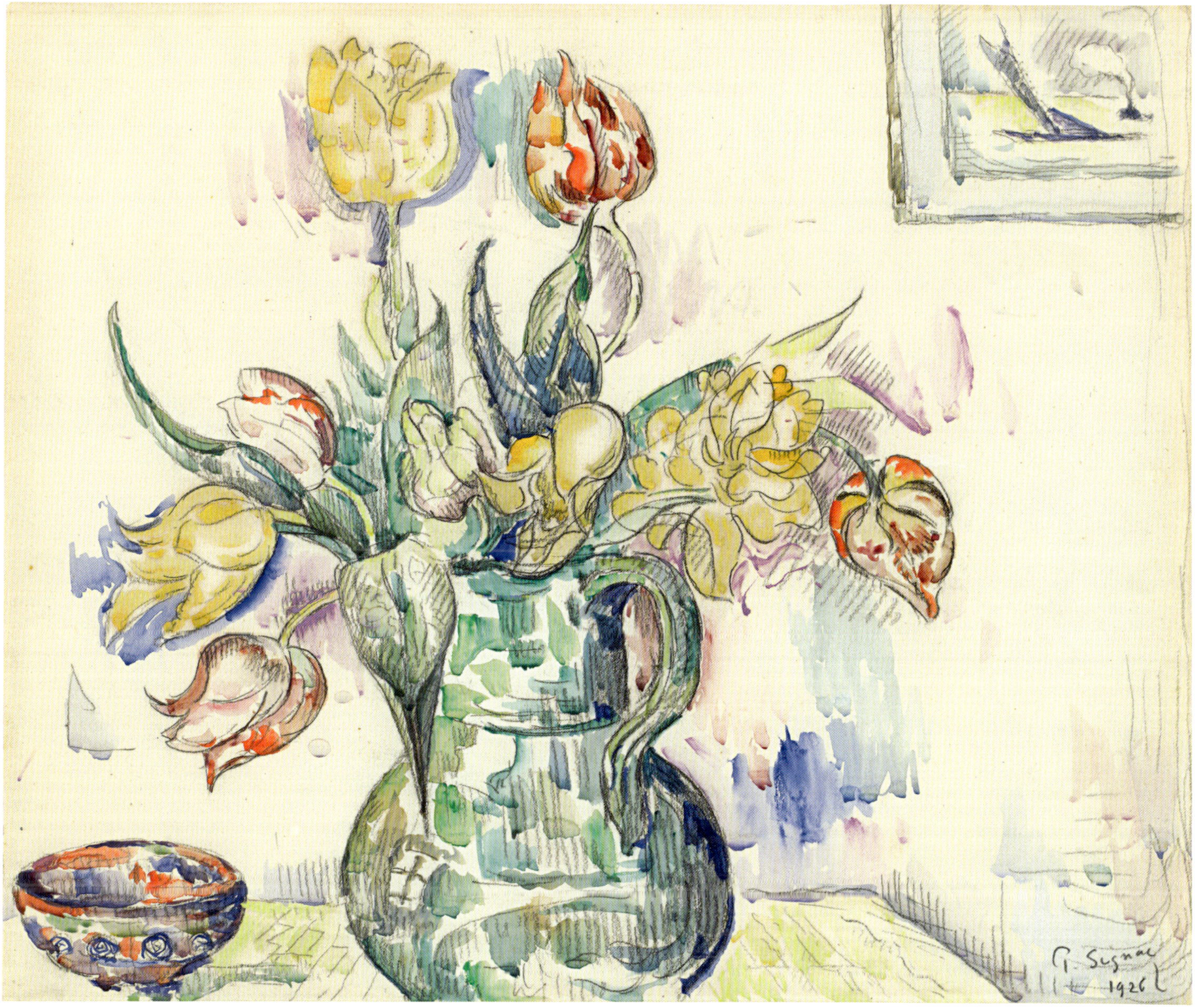

95 Paul Signac, *A Pitcher of Tulips,* 1926
watercolor and gouache over black chalk, 475 × 675

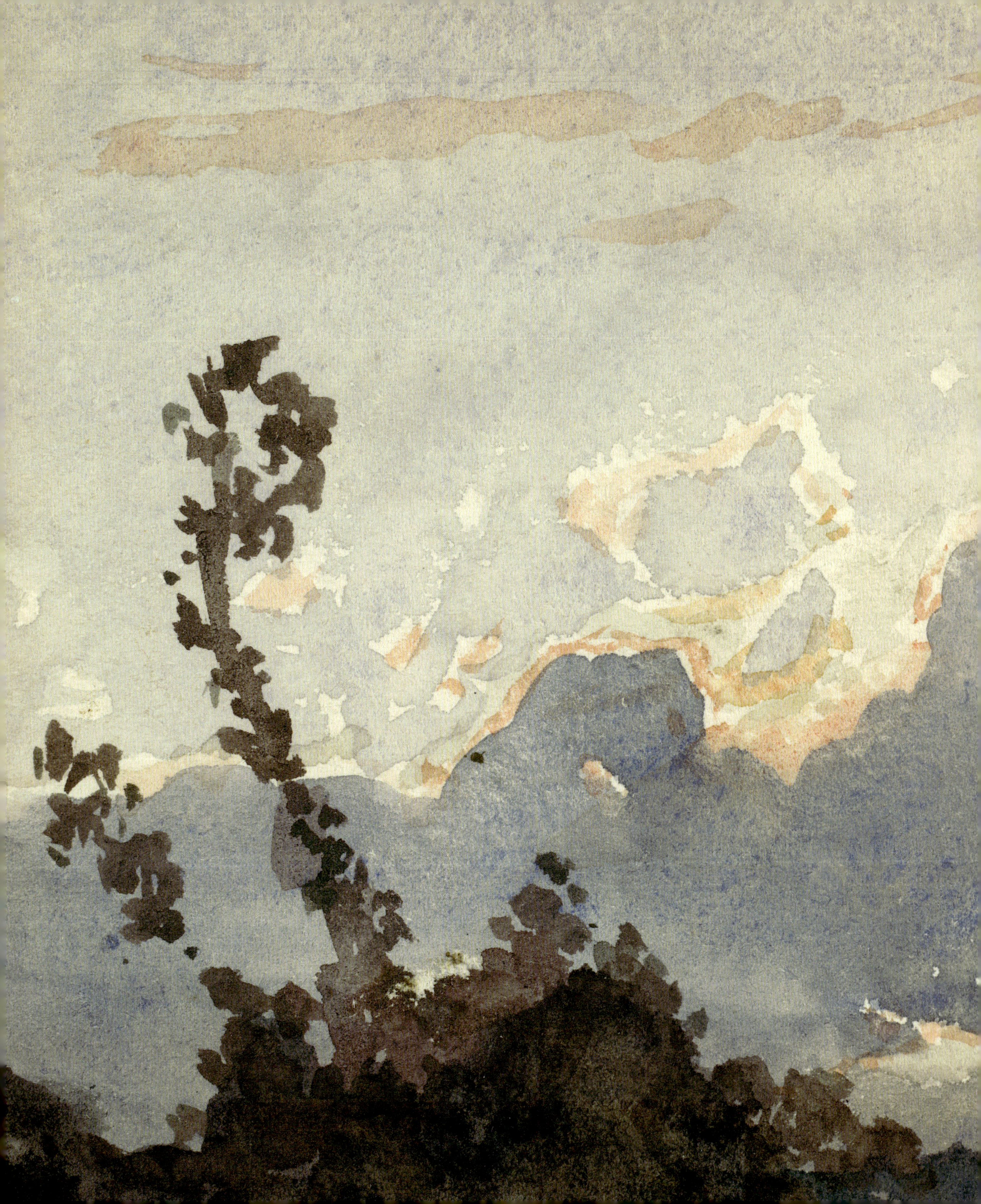

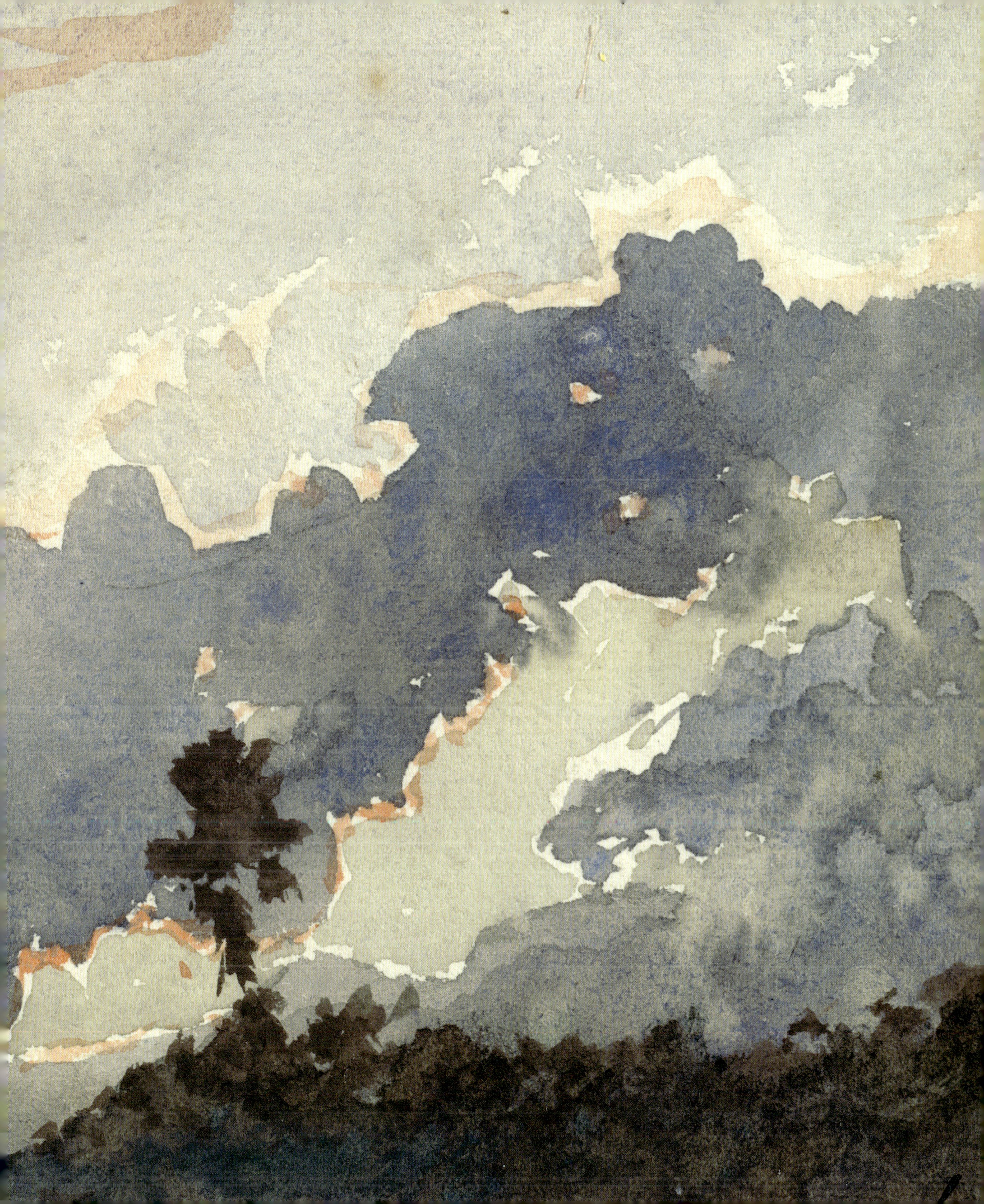

Notes

The Romantic Impulse

1 For the changing meanings of the word "romanticism" in nineteenth-century France, see Maurice Z. Shroder, "France/Roman-Romanesque-Romantisme," in Hans Eichner, ed., *"Romantic" and Its Cognates: The European History of a Word* (Toronto and Buffalo, 1972), 268–292.

2 Madame [Anne-Louise-Germaine] de Staël, *De l'Allemagne* (London, 1813).

3 David Wakefield, *The French Romantics: Literature and the Visual Arts, 1800–1840* (New York, 2007), 21.

4 See de Staël 1813, chap. 11: "De la poésie classique et de la poésie romantique."

5 Charles Baudelaire, *Salon de 1846*, ed. David Kelley (Oxford, 1975), 125; translation from Hugh Honour, *Romanticism* (London, 1979), 14, 55.

6 Anonymous [Arnold Scheffer], "Salon de 1827," *Revue française*, no. 1 (January 1828), 196.

7 The definitive study of the painting is Lorenz Eitner, *Géricault's Raft of the Medusa* (London, 1972). See also Charles Clément, *Géricault. Étude biographique et critique avec le catalogue raisonné de l'oeuvre du maître* (Paris, 1868), 130–132.

8 Translation from Wakefield 2007, 192.

9 Patrick Noon, "Colour and Effect: Anglo-French Painting in London and Paris," in *Crossing the Channel: British and French Painting in the Age of Romanticism* (Minneapolis Institute of Arts; New York, 2003), 12–27.

10 Translation from New York 2003, 196.

11 Claude Allemand-Cosneau, "Le Salon à Paris de 1815–1850," in *Les années romantiques. La peinture française de 1815 à 1850* (Musée des Beaux-Arts, Nantes; Paris, 1995), 106.

12 Kimberly Schenck, "Crayon, Paper, and Paint: An Examination of Nineteenth-Century Drawing Materials," in Jay McKean Fisher et al., *The Essence of Line: French Drawings from Ingres to Degas* (Baltimore Museum of Art and Walters Art Museum, Baltimore; University Park, PA, 2005), 57–85. Also Marjorie B. Cohn, "Wash and Gouache," in *Wash and Gouache: A Study of the Development of the Materials of Watercolor* (Fogg Art Museum, Cambridge, MA, 1977), 9–64.

13 Sir Walter Scott, *Woodstock, or, The Cavalier: A Tale of the Year Sixteen Hundred and Fifty-One* (Edinburgh, 1826).

14 This identification is the suggestion of Professor Beth Wright in a letter to W. M. Brady & Co., courtesy of W. Mark Brady.

15 Arlette Sérullaz, "Chronicle of an Adventure," in *Delacroix in Morocco*, trans. Tamara Blondel (Institut du monde arabe, Paris and New York, 1994), 135.

16 Translation from Wakefield 2007, 195.

17 Alain de Leiris et al., *From Delacroix to Cézanne: French Watercolor Landscapes of the Nineteenth Century* (University of Maryland Art Department Gallery, College Park, MD, 1977), cat. 92.

18 *The Journal of Eugène Delacroix: A Selection*, intro. by Hubert Wellington, trans. Lucy Norton (London and New York, 1995), 407.

19 Translation from Wakefield 2007, 148.

20 Jean-Jacques Lerrant, "Du romantisme à la modernité," in *François-Auguste Ravier, 1814–1895* (Musée des Beaux-Arts de Lyon, Paris, 1996), 10–12.

21 Louis-Antoine Prat, "Théodore Chassériau, oeuvres réapparues. Études, portraits, ambiguïtés," *Revue de l'art*, no. 171 (2011), 45, fig. 13.

22 Vincent Pomarède, "The Cour des Comptes Years," in *Théodore Chassériau, 1819–1856: The Unknown Romantic* (The Metropolitan Museum of Art, New York, 2002), 187–192, cats. 115–133. The Dyke drawing is mentioned in Louis-Antoine Prat, *Théodore Chassériau, 1819–1856. Dessins conservés en dehors du Louvre* (Paris, 1988), 17, no. 65.

23 Théophile Gautier's review of the 1852 Salon included a laudatory assessment of Raffet's work; see Hector Giacomelli, *Raffet, son oeuvre lithographique et ses eaux-fortes...* (Paris, 1862), xxvii, 149.

24 Harriet K. Stratis, "Beneath the Surface: Redon's Methods and Materials," in *Odilon Redon, 1840–1916: The Prince of Dreams* (The Art Institute of Chicago, Cologne and New York, 1994), 358.

25 Honoré de Balzac, "Des Artistes" (1830); translation from Stephen Prickett and Simon Haines, eds., *European Romanticism: A Reader* (London and New York, 2010), 86–87. I would like to thank Professor Tim Blanning for his help with this reference.

Rendering Reality: The Natural Landscape and Everyday Life

1 Vincent Pomarède, "Realism and Recollection," in Philip Conisbee et al., *In the Light of Italy: Corot and Early Open-Air Painting* (National Gallery of Art, Washington; New Haven and London, 1996), 104.

2 For extensive information about the forest of Fontainebleau and the artists who worked there, see Kimberly Jones, *In the Forest of Fontainebleau: Painters and Photographers from Corot to Monet* (National Gallery of Art, Washington; New Haven and London, 2008), 4–27.

3 See Alfred Sensier, *Souvenirs sur Th. Rousseau* (Paris, 1872), 359.

4 The fine line that separates these two aspects of French landscape drawing is also evident in the Dyke collection in pieces by Gustave Doré (pls. 16, 18, 32) and Maxime Lalanne (pls. 19, 25), whose works appear in both of the first two sections of this catalogue.

5 See Alexandra Murphy et al., *Jean-François Millet: Drawn into the Light* (Sterling and Francine Clark Art Institute, Williamstown, MA; New Haven and London, 1999), nos. 1–4. The model in the Dyke drawing has been identified by Murphy as Catherine Lemaire (according to the dealer, W. M. Brady, New York), a Breton serving woman who became Millet's second wife.

6 Drawings had long since ceased to be made only in preparation for finished works in other media and were frequently exhibited at the official Salons. See the discussion by Richard Brettell, 7–10.

7 See Kimberly Schenck, "Crayon, Paper, and Paint: An Examination of Nineteenth-Century Drawing Materials," in Jay McKean Fisher et al., *The Essence of Line: French Drawings from Ingres to Degas* (Baltimore Museum of Art and Walters Art Museum, Baltimore; University Park, PA, 2005), 67–69.

8 The term "realism" was first used in connection with the art of another painter, Adolphe Leleux, in 1844. See Dominique de Font-Réaulx, "Les ambiguïtés du réalisme pictural de Gustave Courbet," in *Gustave Courbet* (Musée d'Orsay, Paris, 2007), 31–32.

9 Francis Wey, in an article published in *La Lumière* (30 March 1851), 1st year, 8: 31 (cited by Font-Réaulx 2007, 31). This translation by Margaret Morgan Grasselli.

10 See Schenck 2005, 63–66. See also Victor Carolson's essay in the present catalogue, p. 24.

11 Philippe Burty, "Léon Bonvin," *Harper's New Monthly Magazine* 75 (January 1886), 48.

12 Quoted and translated in Gabriel P. Weisberg, *Beyond Impressionism: The Naturalist Impulse* (New York, 1992), 13.

13 See Weisberg 1992, 22.

14 See Weisberg 1992, 48–61.

Impressionist Drawings

Unless otherwise noted, quoted material in this essay was translated by Judith Terry.

1 Jean Leymarie, *Dessins de la période impressionniste de Manet à Renoir* (Geneva, 1969).

2 Paul Valéry, *Degas, Danse, Dessin* (Paris, 1949 [1938]).

3 Alain de Leiris, *The Drawings of Édouard Manet* (Berkeley, 1969).

4 James A. Ganz and Richard Kendall, *The Unknown Monet: Pastels and Drawings* (Royal Academy of Arts, London; Williamstown, MA, 2007).

5 *Le mystère et l'éclat. Pastels du Musée d'Orsay* (Musée d'Orsay, Paris, 2008).

6 Barbara Ehrlich White, "The Bathers of 1887 and Renoir's Anti-impressionism," *The Art Bulletin* 55, no. 1 (1973): 125–126.

7 Georges Rivière, *Renoir et ses amis* (Paris, 1921), 131–140.

8 Quoted in Antonin Proust, "Édouard Manet: Souvenirs," *La Revue blanche* 12 (February–May 1897), 427.

9 Paul Valéry 1949 (1938), 10; this translation by Helen Burlin taken from *Degas, Dance, Drawing* (New York, 1948), 10.

10 Quoted in Leymarie 1969, 7; this translation by Robert Allen taken from *Impressionist Drawings from Manet to Renoir* (Geneva, 1969), 8.

11 Letter from Antonin Proust to Suzanne Manet, 1899, quoted in Louis-Antoine Prat, "Monsieur Manet, qui dessine assez bien...," in *Manet inventeur du Moderne* (Paris, 2011), 96.

12 Gary Tinterow, in *Degas*, ed. Jean Sutherland Boggs (Galeries nationales du Grand Palais, Paris; New York and Ottawa, 1988), 426–428.

13 Sale, Sotheby's, London, April 13, 1972, lot 113.

14 Quoted in Alain Clairet, Delphine Montalant, and Yves Rouart, with Waring Hopkins and Alain Thomas, *Berthe Morisot, 1841–1895. Catalogue raisonné de l'oeuvre peint* (Montolivet, 1997), 53 (89 for the English translation).

15 Quoted in Émile Bernard, "Paul Cézanne," *L'Occident* (July 1904); republished in P. M. Doran, *Conversations avec Cézanne* (Paris, 1978), 36; this translation by Julie Lawrence Cochran taken from *Conversations with Cézanne*, ed. Michael Doran (Berkeley and London, 2001), 39.

16 Paul Signac, *Jongkind* (Paris, 1927), 61.

17 Signac, 1927, ill. 47. For a discussion of Signac's collection of works by Jongkind, see Marina Ferretti Bocquillon, "Paul Signac collectionneur," in *Signac, 1863–1935* (Galeries nationales du Grand Palais, Paris, 2001), 61–62.

18 Georges Besson, *Signac* (Paris, 1950), 11, ill. as "Avignon, le motif de Jongkind."

19 Lionello Venturi, quoted in Jean Leymarie, *Les Aquarelles de Cézanne. Catalogue raisonné* (Paris, 1984), 125.

20 Ambroise Vollard, *Degas* (Paris, 1924), 69; this translation by Randolph T. Weaver taken from Ambroise Vollard, *Degas: An Intimate Portrait* (New York, 1986 [1937]), 63.

21 Ganz and Kendall 2007, 115.

22 Daniel Wildenstein, *Claude Monet. Catalogue raisonné* (Lausanne, 1991), 5: 59.

23 Quoted in Duc de Trévise, "Le Pélérinage de Giverny," *La Revue de l'art ancien et moderne* (January 1927): 122; this translation taken from an English version of the essay published in Charles F. Stuckey, ed., *Monet: A Retrospective* (New York, 1985), 334.

24 This and the preceding quotation from letters that Claude Monet wrote to Alice Hoschedé, in Wildenstein 1991, 4: 350–351.

The Nabis and Symbolists

1 Maurice Denis, "The Influence of Paul Gauguin," *L'Occident* (October 1903); cited in John Russell, *Édouard Vuillard: 1868–1940* (Art Gallery of Ontario, Toronto, 1971), 72.

2 Gustave Kahn, "Réponse des symbolistes," *L'Événement*, September 28, 1886; quoted in Sven Loevgren, *The Genesis of Modernism* (Bloomington, IN, 1971), 83–84.

3 G.-Albert Aurier, "Symbolisme en peinture: Paul Gauguin," *Mercure de France* (Paris, 1891), 2: 162–163; translation of the passage from H. B. Chipp, ed., *Theories of Modern Art* (Berkeley and Los Angeles, 1968), 92.

4 Maurice Denis, "Définition du néo-traditionnisme" (1890), in Denis, *Théories, 1890–1910. Du symbolisme et de Gauguin vers un nouvel ordre classique* (Paris, 1920), 9–10.

5 Vojtěch Jirat-Wasiutynski and H. Travers Newton Jr., *Technique and Meaning in the Paintings of Paul Gauguin* (Cambridge and New York, 2000), 142–144. Another contemporary drawing, *The Breton Eve*, less a study from a model than a development from a Peruvian mummy Gauguin saw at the Trocadero, served as a study for the other figure in the composition, though its final incarnation in paint shows a figure much attenuated and revised from the sketch.

6 Paul Gauguin, *Avant et après* (Tahiti, 1903).

7 Maurice Denis's painting *Homage to Cézanne* of 1900, now at the Musée d'Orsay, Paris, shows Redon occupying pride of place on the left of the canvas, with all the Nabi artists and writers facing him

8 *Saint George and the Dragon*, a deeply meditative *noir* by Redon in the collection of the National Gallery (2000.14.1), began as a charcoal drawing and was later embellished by the artist with pastel. This approach would be amplified and refined throughout Redon's career.

9 Odilon Redon, "Confidences d'artiste," in *L'Art moderne* (June 1894). This translation by Elizabeth Easton.

10 Colta Ives, "An Art for Everyday," in Colta Ives, ed., *Pierre Bonnard: The Graphic Art* (Metropolitan Museum of Art, New York, 1990), 13.

11 Jacques Salomon, *Auprès de Vuillard* (Paris, 1953).

12 Antoine Salomon and Guy Cogeval, *Édouard Vuillard: Critical Catalogue of Paintings and Pastels* (Milan and Paris, 2003), 3: 1516.

Neo-Impressionist Drawings

Unless otherwise noted, quoted material in this essay was translated by Judith Terry.

1 Paul Signac, *D'Eugène Delacroix au néo-impressionnisme*, intro. Françoise Cachin (Paris, 1987 [1899]), 33; this translation by Willa Silverman taken from Floyd Ratliff, *Paul Signac and Color in Neo-Impressionism* (New York, 1992), 205.

2 Signac 1987 (1899), 45; this translation from Ratliff 1992, 213.

3 Signac 1987 (1899), 109.

4 Quoted in Gustave Coquiot, *Seurat* (Paris, 1924), 38–39.

5 Letter to Monsieur Dezerville, April 1892, in François Lespinasse, ed., *Charles Angrand. Correspondances 1883–1926* (Rouen, 1988), 48.

6 Letter to Monsieur Dezerville, January 14, 1899, in Lespinasse 1988, 102.

7 Robert Herbert, *Neo-impressionism* (The Solomon R. Guggenheim Museum, New York, 1968), 79.

8 Annette Haudiquet, *De Delacroix à Marquet. Donation Senn-Foulds. Dessins* (Musée André Malraux, Le Havre, 2011).

9 Marina Ferretti Bocquillon, *Signac aquarelliste* (Paris, 2001); published in English as *Signac Watercolors* (Paris, 2001).

10 Paul Signac, *Jongkind* (Paris, 1927).

11 James Dyke continues to acquire Signac's works on paper, after having generously donated 133 of them to the Arkansas Arts Center in Little Rock, Arkansas, in 1999 and 2001. See Marina Ferretti Bocquillon and Charles Cachin, *Paul Signac. Dessins et aquarelles. Collection inédite* (Paris, 2000); published in English as *Paul Signac: A Collection of Watercolors and Drawings* (New York, 2000).

12 Ferretti Bocquillon and Cachin 2000, 106.

Exhibition Checklist

The Romantic Impulse

1 Eugène Delacroix, *An English Cavalier,* 1826/1830, watercolor over graphite with traces of gouache and gum arabic, 210 × 150. Dyke Collection

PROVENANCE: Emmanuel Bénézit (1854–1920), Paris, thence by descent; W. M. Brady & Co., New York; purchased in 2011

2 Eugène Delacroix, *The Moroccan Courier,* 1832, watercolor, 175 × 115. Dyke Collection

PROVENANCE: Delacroix sale, 1864 (Lugt 838a); Ernest Rouart; Tony Mayer; sale, Galerie Charpentier, Paris, 1957; private collection; Galerie Hopkins-Thomas-Custot, Paris; purchased in 2000

3 Théodore Chassériau, *Auguste Ottin,* 1833, graphite with stumping on oatmeal paper, 408 × 295; signed and dated in black chalk at lower right: *Chasseriau 1833.* National Gallery of Art, Washington, Helen Porter and James T. Dyke Fund, 2006.17.1

PROVENANCE: Salamander Fine Arts Limited, London; NGA purchase in 2006

4 Théodore Caruelle d'Aligny, *Traveler in a Rocky Landscape,* c. 1830, pen and brown ink with brown and gray wash and watercolor, 282 × 389. Dyke Collection

PROVENANCE: private collection; Jill Newhouse, New York; purchased in 2002

5 Paul Huet, *An Abbey by a Wooded Lake at Twilight,* c. 1831, pastel, 230 × 375. National Gallery of Art, Washington, Helen Porter and James T. Dyke Fund, 2011.44.1

PROVENANCE: artist's posthumous sale (Lugt 1268); Galerie de Bayser, Paris; NGA purchase in 2011

6 Jean-Paul Flandrin, *Sunlit Trees in a Valley near Lacoux,* 1840, black chalk heightened with white chalk on blue paper with added strips at left and right, 289 × 267. National Gallery of Art, Washington, Gift of Helen Porter and James T. Dyke, 2011.59.1

PROVENANCE: Pierre Miquel, Paris; W. M. Brady & Co., New York; Charles Ryskamp, New York, 2005 (sale, Sotheby's, New York, January 25, 2011, lot 96); Helen Porter and James T. Dyke, 2011; gift to NGA in 2011

7 Jean-Achille Benouville, *Sunset from a Rocky Coastline,* 1842, watercolor with pen and brown ink and touches of white gouache over graphite on blue-gray paper, 201 × 289; dated faintly in graphite at lower right: *1842.* National Gallery of Art, Washington, Helen Porter and James T. Dyke Fund, 2011.58.1

PROVENANCE: the artist's atelier (stamped with both versions of the Bénouville atelier stamp, one close to Lugt 228a and the other identified as Lugt 228b) (atelier sale, Hôtel Drouot, Paris, January 16, 1901, probably as part of lot 259 or lot 260); Paul Prouté S.A., Paris, 2007; Christine Bethenod, Paris; Stephen Ongpin Fine Art, London; NGA purchase in 2011

8 Paul Huet, *A Meadow at Sunset,* pastel, 135 × 195. Dyke Collection

PROVENANCE: artist's atelier sale (Lugt 1268); Galerie Antoine Laurentin, Paris; purchased 2003

9 François-Auguste Ravier, *A Marsh at Sunset* , watercolor, 175 × 250. Dyke Collection

PROVENANCE: Galerie de Bayser, Paris; purchased in 2006

10 François-Auguste Ravier, *Sunset over a Pond* , watercolor with touches of gouache on pale gray paper, 200 × 230. Dyke Collection

PROVENANCE: Colnaghi Drawings, London; purchased in 2001

11 Gabriel-Hippolyte Lebas, *Sunset in an Oriental Landscape,* c. 1845, watercolor, gouache, and gum arabic on cardboard, 446 × 308; signed in brown ink at lower left: *Hip. Lebas.* National Gallery of Art, Washington, Helen Porter and James T. Dyke Fund, 2009.74.1

PROVENANCE: Paul Prouté S.A., Paris; NGA purchase in 2009

12 Alexandre Calame, *An Ancient Pine Forest with a Mountain Stream,* 1847, watercolor and gouache over charcoal, 612 × 842; signed at lower left on rock: *A. Calame.* National Gallery of Art, Washington, Gift of Mr. and Mrs. James T. Dyke, 1999.126.1

PROVENANCE: August Laube, Zurich; NGA purchase in 1999

13 Eugène Isabey, *Fishing Boats Tossed before a Storm,* c. 1840, watercolor and gouache over black chalk, 639 × 933; signed in watercolor at lower right: *E. Isabey.* National Gallery of Art, Washington, Gift of Mr. and Mrs. James T. Dyke, 2001.79.1

PROVENANCE: Didier Aaron Inc., New York; NGA purchase in 2001

14 Théodore Chassériau, *Drover with Oxen Pulling a Cart,* 1840/1841, watercolor, 250 × 306. National Gallery of Art, Washington, Gift of Helen Porter and James T. Dyke, 2002.29.1

PROVENANCE: artist's atelier sale (Lugt 443), Paris, March 16–17, 1857; Elizabeth Molnar, New York (sale, Parke-Bernet Galleries, New York, November 24, 1965, lot 45); Norbert L. H. Roesler, New York (sale, Christie's, New York, May 31, 1990, lot 58); Flavia Ormond, London; NGA purchase in 2006

15 Eugène Delacroix, *The Normandy Cliffs,* 1849/1852, watercolor and graphite, 175 × 225. Dyke Collection

PROVENANCE: private collection, France; Jill Newhouse, New York; purchased 2001

16 Gustave Doré, *Coastal Landscape,* watercolor, 130 × 205. Dyke Collection

PROVENANCE: Galerie Antoine Laurentin, Paris; purchased in 2003

17 Paul Huet, *Rock Cliffs along the Romanche,* 1858, watercolor over graphite, 303 × 484; inscribed by the artist at lower left in graphite: *a Sechilienne/route de l'Oisans/Isère.* National Gallery of Art, Washington, Gift of Helen Porter and James T. Dyke, 2001.80.1

PROVENANCE: atelier stamp (Lugt 1268); private collection (sale, Christie's, London, December 15, 2000, no. 203); Emmanuel Moatti, Inc., New York; NGA purchase in 2001

18 Gustave Doré, *A River Gorge in a Mountain Landscape* , watercolor, 387 × 305. Dyke Collection

PROVENANCE: artist's atelier stamp (Lugt 681a); Paul Prouté S.A., Paris; purchased in 2002

19 Maxime Lalanne, *Alpine Castle above a Wooded Lake,* c. 1870, charcoal with stumping and white chalk on beige paper, 690 × 1030; signed in black ink at lower left: *Maxime Lalanne.* National Gallery of Art, Washington, Helen Porter and James T. Dyke Fund, 2006.153.1

PROVENANCE: John Mitchell and Son, London; NGA purchase in 2006

20 Gustave Doré, *The Shades of French Soldiers from the Past Exhort the Army to Victory,* 1870, brush with brown ink and brown wash with white gouache over graphite, 655 × 910; signed and inscribed by the artist in brown gouache at lower left: *à mon ami Bourdelin/ G Doré.* National Gallery of Art, Washington, Helen Porter and James T. Dyke Fund, 2006.62.1

PROVENANCE: M. Bourdelin, Paris; Mme Joseph Michel, niece of the artist, Paris; her daughter, Mme Jouaust, thence by descent (sale, Sotheby's, London, November 19, 2001, no. 137); Richard L. Feigen & Co., New York; NGA purchase in 2006

Rendering Reality: The Natural Landscape and Everyday Life

21 Jean-François Millet, *Nude Reclining in a Landscape,* 1844/1845, pen and brown ink, 165 × 256. Dyke Collection

PROVENANCE: artist's estate (Lugt 1460); Hazlitt, Gooden & Fox, London, 1995; private collection, England; W. M. Brady & Co., New York; purchased in 2011

22 Théodore Rousseau, *Sunset from the Forest of Fontainebleau,* 1848/1850, oil and graphite on paper, laid down on canvas, 322 × 459. National Gallery of Art, Washington, Gift of Helen Porter and James T. Dyke, 2003.70.1

PROVENANCE: private collection, Sweden; Salander-O'Reilly Galleries, New York; NGA purchase in 2003

23 Charles-François Eustache, *A Boatyard,* c. 1850, black and white chalk on blue paper, 222 × 599. Dyke Collection

PROVENANCE: by descent in the family of the artist; W. M. Brady & Co., New York; Charles Ryskamp, 1991 (sale, Sotheby's, New York, January 25, 2011, lot 96); purchased via Jill Newhouse, New York, in 2011

24 Adolphe Appian, *An Empty Rowboat Moored on a Forest Pond,* c. 1855, charcoal with stumping and scratching out, heightened with white chalk, 475 × 645. Dyke Collection

PROVENANCE: David Tunick, Inc., New York; purchased in 2001

25 Maxime Lalanne, *Cliffs along the Normandy Coast,* 1868, charcoal with stumping, erasure, and scratching out, 312 × 462; signed in white gouache at lower right: *M. Lalanne.* National Gallery of Art, Washington, Gift of Helen Porter and James T. Dyke, 2006.143.1

PROVENANCE: Paul Prouté S.A., Paris, Helen Porter and James T. Dyke, 2003; gift to NGA in 2006

26 Paul Gavarni, *Pierrot's Son Asking Fatherly Advice,* 1850s(?), pen and brown and gray ink with watercolor and white gouache, 195 × 320. Dyke Collection

PROVENANCE: Galerie Hopkins-Thomas, Paris; purchased in 1994

27 Charles-Émile Jacque, *The Shepherdess,* 1869, pastel on brown paper, 526 × 949; signed in brown pastel at lower right: *Ch. Jacque.* National Gallery of Art, Washington, Gift of Mr. and Mrs. James T. Dyke, 1996.45.1

PROVENANCE: private collection, Florida (sale, Christie's, New York, May 22, 1996, lot 162); NGA purchase via Hazlitt, Gooden & Fox in 1996

28 François Bonvin, *A Country Woman Tending a Fireplace,* 1853, charcoal heightened with white gouache on buff paper, 290 × 215. Dyke Collection

PROVENANCE: Galerie Berès, Paris; purchased in 2005

29 Léon Augustin Lhermitte, *An Elderly Peasant Woman,* c. 1878, charcoal, 475 × 396; signed in black chalk at lower left: *Léon Lhermitte.* National Gallery of Art, Washington, Gift of Mr. and Mrs. James T. Dyke, 1996.30.1

PROVENANCE: Weiss collection; Charles Jerdein, London, until 1979; Josey and Toby Tanenbaum, Canada: Peter Nahum, London; NGA purchase in 1996

30 Léon Bonvin, *A Pot of Chrysanthemums on a Ledge,* 1864, pen and black ink with watercolor and gouache over black chalk, 247 × 197; signed and dated in pen and brown ink at lower left: *Léon Bonvin/1864.* Dyke Collection

PROVENANCE: W. M. Brady & Co., New York; purchased in 2011

31 Henri-Joseph Harpignies, *A Potted Fuchsia with Children's Toys,* 1877, watercolor, 340 × 250; signed and dated at lower left: *Harpignies 77*; inscribed at lower right: *à ma chère belle soeur.* Dyke Collection

PROVENANCE: the artist's sister-in-law (according to the inscription); private collection; Stoppenbach & Delestre Ltd., London; purchased in 2010

32 Gustave Doré, *An Alpine Valley with Trees and Boulders,* 1876, watercolor, gouache, and charcoal over pen and brown ink, 451 × 317; signed and dated in watercolor at lower right: *GDoré/1876.* National Gallery of Art, Washington, Gift of Helen Porter and James T. Dyke, 2003.144.1

PROVENANCE: sale, Christie's East, New York, November 2, 1999, no. 55; private English collection; Jill Newhouse, New York; NGA purchase in 2003

33 François-Louis Français, *A Stream through a Dense Forest,* 1884, watercolor and gouache, 460 × 345. Dyke Collection

PROVENANCE: Galerie Terrades, Paris; purchased in 2003

34 Henri-Joseph Harpignies, *Trees along the Coast,* 1897, watercolor, 216 × 257; signed and dated at lower left: *H. Harpignies 97.* Dyke Collection

PROVENANCE: Jill Newhouse, New York; purchased in 2006

35 Henri-Joseph Harpignies, *Sun behind the Clouds at Saint-Privé,* c. 1900, watercolor, 125 × 175; signed twice at upper left and lower left: *h. harpignies*; inscribed at lower right, *Saint-Privé.* Dyke Collection

PROVENANCE: Emmanuel Moatti, Paris; purchased in 1998

36 Henri-Joseph Harpignies, *Pollard Willows along a Coastal Road,* 1910, charcoal, 270 × 425; signed and dated at lower center: *h. harpignies 1919.* Dyke Collection, Promised Gift to the National Gallery of Art

PROVENANCE: Galerie Hopkins-Custot, Paris; purchased in 2002

37 Auguste Louis Lepère, *Chestnut Trees above a River,* c. 1900, pastel on paperboard, 370 × 521. Dyke Collection

PROVENANCE: David and Constance Yates, New York; purchased in 2002

38 Léon Augustin Lhermitte, *Family by a River,* 1922, pastel on brown paper, 480 × 680. Dyke Collection

PROVENANCE: Noortman, Amsterdam; purchased in 2000

Impressionist Drawings

39 Édouard Manet, *A Boy Holding a Dog*, c. 1861, pen and brown ink with brown wash, graphite, and colored pencil, 212 × 162; signed at lower right: *E Manet*. Dyke Collection

PROVENANCE: Curt Glaser, Berlin, by 1922; Gustav Nebehay, Berlin; Mr. and Mrs. Ernst Eichenwald, Berlin and New York, c. 1935; by descent in the family (sale, Christie's, New York, May 2, 2012, lot 101); purchased via Martha Parrish in 2012

40 Eugène Boudin, *Sailboats*, c. 1860, pastel on blue paper, 178 × 274. Dyke Collection

PROVENANCE: Brame & Lorenceau, Paris; private collection; returned to Brame & Lorenceau, Paris; purchased in 2011

41 Berthe Morisot, *Julie Manet in a Canopied Cradle*, 1879, watercolor and gouache, 180 × 180. Dyke Collection

PROVENANCE: Julie Manet Rouart (daughter of the artist); Clément Rouart (her son); Galerie Hopkins-Thomas, Paris; purchased in 1995

42 Camille Pissarro, *A Country Girl Seated on the Ground*, c. 1880, pastel, 470 × 566; initialed at lower left: *C.P.* Dyke Collection

PROVENANCE: Louis Stern Galleries, New York; JPL Fine Arts, London; purchased in 1995

43 Camille Pissarro, *The Pumpkin Seller*, c. 1888, charcoal, 645 × 478; stamped with initials at lower center. Dyke Collection

PROVENANCE: Neffe-Degandt, London; purchased in 1998

44 Edgar Degas, *A Dancer at the Bar*, 1876/1878, charcoal heightened with white chalk on blue-gray paper, 457 × 292. Dyke Collection

PROVENANCE: atelier stamp (Lugt 658); atelier sale, Galerie Georges Petit, Paris, 2nd sale, December 11–13, 1918, lot 352; Browse and Darby, London; private collection, Illinois; sale, Sotheby's, New York, May 2, 1996, lot 118 (bought in); purchased after the sale via Martha Parrish and James Reinish, Inc., New York, in 1996

45 Edgar Degas, *Two Women Ironing*, c. 1885, pastel and charcoal on three joined sheets of brown paper, 600 × 760; signed in charcoal at upper left: *Degas*. Dyke Collection

PROVENANCE: Ernest Chausson (1855–1899), Paris; by inheritance to his widow (sale, Hôtel Drouot, Paris, June 5, 1936, lot 8); Hector Brame, Paris; César M. de Hauke, Paris; Robert M. Levy, New York, 1938; Hervé Odermatt, Paris, 1973; private collection, Japan; private collection, Greenwich, Connecticut; Noortman Master Paintings, Amsterdam; purchased in 2005

46 Jean-Baptiste-Armand Guillaumin, *Madame Guillaumin with Her Infant Daughter*, 1890/1892, pastel, 530 × 530. Dyke Collection

PROVENANCE: Neffe-Degandt, London; purchased in 1997

47 Johan Barthold Jongkind, *A Street in Avignon Leading toward the Place de l'Horloge*, 1880, watercolor and gouache, 230 × 150; stamped at lower left with the artist's signature and inscribed and dated by the artist at lower center: *avignon 22 Sept 1880*. Dyke Collection

PROVENANCE: Galerie Hopkins-Thomas, Paris; purchased in 1994

48 Luigi Loir, *A Market Square in Front of a Cathedral*, 1870s/1880s, watercolor and white gouache on dark blue paper, 389 × 283; signed in black at lower right: *LOIR LUIGI*. Dyke Collection

PROVENANCE: Jean-Luc Baroni, Ltd., London; purchased in 2011

49 Camille Pissarro, *Trees and Meadows at Eragny*, 1895/1900, black chalk, 308 × 475; initialed at lower left: *C.P.* National Gallery of Art, Washington, Gift of Helen Porter and James T. Dyke, 2006.113.1

PROVENANCE: Jeanne Marguerite Pissarro Bonin; sale, Hôtel Drouot, Paris, June 26, 1931, no. 92; private collection, Switzerland; Jill Newhouse, New York; Helen Porter and James T. Dyke, 1999; gift to NGA in 2006

50 Paul Cézanne, *A Stand of Trees along a River Bank*, 1880/1885, watercolor and graphite, 310 × 430. Dyke Collection

PROVENANCE: Ambroise Vollard, Paris; Alex Reid & Lefevre Galleries, London; Mrs. Chester Beatty, London; Paul Rosenberg, New York; Norton Simon, Los Angeles; Yayoi Gallery, Tokyo; private collection, Japan, from 1972; Noortman Master Paintings, Amsterdam; purchased in 2006

51 Claude Monet, *Waterloo Bridge*, 1901, pastel, 311 × 502. Dyke Collection

PROVENANCE: Galerie Montag, Zurich; to Guy de Portalès, 1912; sale, Christie's, London, March 29, 1988, lot 306; Richard Green, London; to a private collection, 1988; returned to Richard Green, 2009; purchased in 2009

The Nabis and Symbolists

52 Paul Gauguin, *Seated Nude*, 1888/1889, pastel on yellow paper, 616 × 505. Dyke Collection

PROVENANCE: Olivier Sainsère, Paris; private collection, Paris, thence by descent; sale, Christie's, New York, May 5, 2011, lot 112; purchased via Martha Parrish and James Reinish, Inc., New York, in 2011

53 Georges Lemmen, *Two Studies of Madame Lemmen*, 1885, black chalk, 655 × 495; signed and dated *G. Lemmen/12 Juin '85*. Dyke Collection, Promised Gift to the National Gallery of Art

PROVENANCE: artist's studio (atelier stamp at lower left); Kunsthandel Schlichte Bergen, Amsterdam; purchased in 2007

54 Édouard Vuillard, *The Dressmaker*, 1891, pastel, 425 × 313. Dyke Collection

PROVENANCE: artist's studio (stamped at lower right); Neffe-Degandt, London; purchased in 1999

55 Pierre Bonnard, *The Promenade*, c. 1893, pen and black ink with black wash and watercolor on paper laid down on canvas, 473 × 312; signed at lower left: *Bonnard*. Dyke Collection

PROVENANCE: Aline and Marguerite Bowers; Pierrette Vernon, Paris; Galerie Berès, Paris; purchased in 2010

56 Maurice Denis, *Design for a Fan: The Engagement Party of Yvonne Lerolle*, 1898, pastel and black chalk with touches of watercolor, 321 × 492; width of the fan: 150. National Gallery of Art, Washington, Helen Porter and James T. Dyke Fund, 2010.33.1.a

PROVENANCE: artist's atelier (stamp MAUD not in Lugt); Paul Prouté S.A., Paris; NGA purchase in 2010

57 Georges Lemmen, *Sunflowers*, 1892, pen and brush and black ink, 450 × 590; dated at upper right: *25 août 1892*. Dyke Collection

PROVENANCE: Galerie Hopkins-Thomas, Paris; purchased in 1992

58 Georges Lemmen, *Women at a Seaside Well at Heyst*, 1893, brush and black ink, 250 × 185; dated and inscribed at lower right: *Heyst –11 sept 93*. Dyke Collection

PROVENANCE: atelier stamp; Galerie Patrick Derom, Brussels; private collection, Belgium; Galerie Hopkins-Thomas, Paris; purchased in 1997

59 Paul Ranson, *After the Fall*, 1892/1893, pastel, charcoal, and stumping on paper laid down on canvas, 1455 × 920; initialed at upper right: *PR*. Dyke Collection

PROVENANCE: Brigitte Ranson-Bitker, Paris; Galerie Berès, Paris; purchased in 2007

60 Paul Ranson, *Three Women at a Fountain*, 1897, charcoal, 860 × 610; stamped with the artist's signature at lower right. Dyke Collection

PROVENANCE: private collection; Galerie Hopkins-Custot, Paris; purchased in 2003

61 Jacques Villon, *The Proposal*, 1896, watercolor over graphite, 320 × 253; signed and dated at lower right: *Villon/96*; later inscribed by the artist below that: *pour Madame Elsé/Jacques Villon 52*. Dyke Collection

PROVENANCE: given by the artist to Madame Elsé, 1952 (according to the inscription); JPL Fine Arts, London; purchased in 1990

62 Jean-Émile Laboureur, *"Femme bour": The Artist's Sister*, c. 1899, watercolor, 155 × 120; inscribed across the image: *femme bour*. Dyke Collection

PROVENANCE: Suzanne Laboureur; private collection, Paris; Galerie Antoine Laurentin, Paris; purchased in 2007

63 Suzanne Valadon, *The Artist's Son, Maurice Utrillo*, c. 1890, graphite, 120 × 90; signed and inscribed in graphite at lower right: *mon fils / à 7 ans / Suzanne Valadon*. Dyke Collection

PROVENANCE: Galerie Hopkins-Thomas, Paris; purchased in 1994

64 Georges Lemmen, *Tea-time with Madame Georges Lemmen Sewing*, 1901, black chalk, 190 × 300; signed with monogram and dated: *24 fév. 1901*. Dyke Collection

PROVENANCE: Noortman Master Paintings, Amsterdam; purchased in 2003

65 Georges Lemmen, *Tea-time with Madame Georges Lemmen Sewing*, 1902, oil on cardboard, 310 × 460; signed with monogram and dated at upper left: *GL1902*. Dyke Collection

PROVENANCE: F. Buyle; Noortman, Amsterdam; purchased in 1998

66 Georges Lemmen, *A Visit with Madame Lemmen*, 1904, oil on board, 305 × 432; signed with monogram and dated: *1904*. Dyke Collection

PROVENANCE: F. Buyle; private collection, France; sale, Sotheby's, New York, November 18, 1998, lot 489; purchased via Martha Parrish & James Reinish, Inc., New York, in 1998

67 Georges Lemmen, *Madame Lemmen Reading*, 1907, watercolor and gouache on paper, 265 × 372; signed with monogram and dated lower right: *1907 NOV*. Dyke Collection

PROVENANCE: the artist's family; Patrick Derom Gallery, Brussels; purchased in 2004

68 Georges Lemmen, *A Vase of Poppies and Anemones*, oil on panel, 513 × 348; signed with monogram at lower right: *GL*. Dyke Collection

PROVENANCE: Pierre Lemmen, Belgium; Jacqueline van Hoey, granddaughter of the artist; Galerie Berès, Paris; purchased in 2008

69 Odilon Redon, *A Vision of a Saint with a Poppy*, c. 1912, watercolor and graphite, 203 × 152, signed at lower right: *ODILON REDON*. Dyke Collection

PROVENANCE: Galerie Hopkins-Thomas, Paris; purchased in 1998

70 Albert Besnard, *Partially Draped Nude from Behind*, 1910/1911, charcoal, black chalk, and stumping, 463 × 307; signed in charcoal at lower right: *ABesnard*. Dyke Collection

PROVENANCE: Paul Prouté S.A., Paris; purchased in 2011

71 Édouard Vuillard, *Suzanne Desprès*, c. 1908, oil on board, 135 × 545; signed and inscribed at lower left: *à Madame Suzanne Després/ E. Vuillard*. Dyke Collection

PROVENANCE: Neffe-Degandt, London; purchased in 1997

72 Ker Xavier Roussel, *A Road in the French Countryside*, 1915/1920, pastel on brown paper, 367 × 534. Dyke Collection

PROVENANCE: Hill-Stone, New York; purchased in 2011

73 Édouard Vuillard, *Mother and Child in a Summer Landscape*, 1919/1920, pastel, 240 × 310; initialed lower right: *EV*. Dyke Collection

PROVENANCE: Galerie de L'Elysée, Paris (Alex Maguy); private collection, Milwaukee, 1965; Achim Moeller Fine Art, New York; Martha Parrish & James Reinish, Inc., New York; purchased in 1993

74 Pierre Bonnard, *A Vase of Summer Flowers on a Mantelpiece*, 1920s, watercolor and graphite, 267 × 362; signed at lower right: *Bonnard*. Dyke Collection

PROVENANCE: Galerie Druet, Paris; George Waechter Memorial Foundation (sale, Sotheby's, New York, May 2, 1996, no. 154); purchased via Martha Parrish & James Reinish, Inc., New York, in 1996

75 Édouard Vuillard, *Countess Lanskoy*, 1934, pastel, 333 × 273. stamped with signature at lower right. Dyke Collection

PROVENANCE: Neffe-Degandt, London; purchased in 1997

Neo-Impressionist Drawings

76 Georges Seurat, *Strolling Woman with a Muff*, c. 1884, Conté crayon, 300 × 230. Dyke Collection

PROVENANCE: Paul Signac, Paris; Jacques Rodrigues-Hendriqués; Princesse de Bassiano, Paris; Georges Bernheim, Paris; Lucien Demotte, New York; private collection, Geneva; Moeller Fine Art Ltd., New York; John C. Whitehead, New York; purchased via Moeller Fine Arts, Ltd., New York, in 2011

77 Maximilien Luce, *Paul Signac*, 1889, charcoal, 190 × 159; signed and dated at lower right: *Luce 89*; identified at lower left: *Signac Herblay*. Dyke Collection

PROVENANCE: Félix Fénéon, Paris; Jacques Rodrigues-Henriqués, Paris; Arthur G. Altschul, New York, 1961; Galerie Hopkins-Custot, Paris; purchased in 2003

78 Théo van Rysselberghe, *Augustine de Rothmaler*, 1894, Conté crayon, 320 × 250; signed with monogram and dated at lower right: *JR* [in a square] *Sept./1894*. Dyke Collection

PROVENANCE: JPL Fine Arts, London; purchased in 1990

79 Henry d'Estienne, *Grand-mother Reading*, 1890s, black chalk, sheet: 280 × 370; image, 225 × 295; signed and inscribed across bottom: *H. d'Estienne—Portrait de grand mère*. Dyke Collection

PROVENANCE: Galerie Chantal Kiener, Paris; purchased in 2000

80 Achille Laugé, *The Artist's Mother*, 1893/1896, charcoal with stumping, 450 × 400; artist's studio stamp in blue at lower left. Dyke Collection

PROVENANCE: artist's studio sale, Hôtel Drouot, Paris, March 11, 1977, lot 21 (reproduced on the cover); bought by M. Lucien Solanet, Paris, thence by descent; W. M. Brady & Co., New York; purchased in 2011

81 Charles Angrand, *The Annunciation to the Shepherds,* 1894, charcoal with Conté crayon, 943 × 700; signed and dated at bottom left: *Ch Angrand '94*. Dyke Collection

PROVENANCE: Kunsthandlung Michael Voggenaur, Cologne, by 1980; private collection; Kate Ganz USA LTD, New York; purchased in 2009

82 Albert Lebourg, *The Harbor at Dordrecht,* 1895/1897, pen and black ink with gray-brown wash, 225 × 284; signed in brown ink at lower left: *A Lebourg, Dordrecht*. National Gallery of Art, Washington, Gift of Helen Porter and James T. Dyke, 2006.143.2

PROVENANCE: Jill Newhouse, New York; Helen Porter and James T. Dyke, Arkansas, 2003; gift to NGA in 2006

83 Albert Dubois-Pillet, *A River Landscape,* c. 1888, black ink, 290 × 390 (oval); signed at lower right: *duBOIS-PillEt*. Dyke Collection

PROVENANCE: Galerie de la Présidence, Paris; purchased in 2007

84 Hippolyte Petitjean, *A Broad Valley at Sunset,* c. 1897, watercolor, 320 × 500. Dyke Collection, Promised Gift to the National Gallery of Art

PROVENANCE: JPL Fine Art, London; Neffe-Degandt, London; purchased in 2000

85 Hippolyte Petitjean, *Promenade by a Lake,* 1890s, watercolor, 438 × 293; signed lower left: *Hipp Petitjean*; atelier stamp at lower right. Dyke Collection

PROVENANCE: artist's atelier (Lugt 2022c); Stoppenbach & Delestre Ltd., London; purchased 2006

86 Hippolyte Petitjean, *An Afternoon by a Lake,* 1890s, watercolor, 365 × 267; signed at lower right: *Hipp. Petitjean*. Dyke Collection

PROVENANCE: Wally Findlay Galleries, Palm Beach; Frances Moore, Los Angeles (estate sale, Abell Auction Co., Los Angeles, 2005); private collection, USA; Stoppenbach & Delestre Ltd., London; purchased in 2011

87 Henri Edmond Cross, *A Villa on the Mediterranean Coast,* c. 1907, watercolor and black chalk, 173 × 232; atelier stamp, lower center. Dyke Collection

PROVENANCE: Galerie Vallotton, Lausanne; Galerie Wilhelm Grosshennig, Düsseldorf; private collection, Germany; Stoppenbach & Delestre Ltd., London; purchased in 2011

88 Paul Signac, *Barges on the Seine at Samois,* 1900, watercolor and gouache over black chalk, 173 × 250; stamped with artist's signature at lower right. Dyke Collection

PROVENANCE: artist's atelier (Lugt 2285b); Galerie Lucie Weill, Paris; private collection, 1965; Galerie Berès, Paris; purchased in 2004

89 Paul Signac, *The Calanque at Saint-Tropez,* 1906, watercolor and graphite, 280 × 437. Dyke Collection

PROVENANCE: by descent in the family of the artist; purchased in 1999

90 Paul Signac, *Eucalyptus Trees at Antibes,* 1910, black ink with watercolor and gouache, 390 × 345; stamped with the artist's signature at lower left; dated and located by the artist at lower left: *1910 Antibes*. Dyke Collection

PROVENANCE: artist's atelier; Galerie Berès, Paris; purchased in 2009

91 Paul Signac, *A Basket of Fruit,* 1920s, watercolor and black chalk, 292 × 445; signed at lower right: *P. Signac*. Dyke Collection

PROVENANCE: Galerie de la Présidence, Paris; purchased in 2009

92 Paul Signac, *Les Andelys on a Summer Morning,* 1923, brush and black ink, 695 × 950; inscribed and dated: *les Andelys Matin d'été 1923*. Dyke Collection

PROVENANCE: by descent in the family of the artist; purchased in 2000

93 Paul Signac, *A Melon on a Plate,* c. 1918, watercolor and gouache, 324 × 450; signed at lower left: *P. Signac*. Dyke Collection

PROVENANCE: Doctor Roudinesco and by descent; Galerie Antoine Laurentin, Paris; purchased in 2001

94 Paul Signac, *The Fountain in the Rue Grande in Saint-Paul de Vence,* c. 1924, watercolor and graphite, 290 × 437; signed and identified in black chalk at lower left: *P Signac/St Paul*. Dyke Collection

PROVENANCE: Mr. and Mrs. Preston Harrison, USA; Los Angeles County Museum of Art; Hammer Galleries, New York; Stoppenbach & Delestre Ltd., London; purchased in 2011

95 Paul Signac, *A Pitcher of Tulips,* 1926, watercolor and gouache over black chalk, 475 × 675; signed and dated at lower right, *P. Signac/1926*. Dyke Collection, Promised Gift to the National Gallery of Art

PROVENANCE: Stoppenbach & Delestre Ltd., London; purchased in 2004

Artists in the Catalogue

Index

Note: Page numbers in bold type indicate illustrations.

Photography Credits

Cover: Detail pl. 13, Image courtesy of the Board of Trustees, National Gallery of Art, Washington, photographer Ric Blanc

Plates

pls. 1–7, 10–15, 17–35, 37, 38, 40–53, 55–63, 66–76, 78, 80–90, 92–95: Images courtesy of the Board of Trustees, National Gallery of Art, Washington; pls. 1, 5–7, 21, 30, 40, 48, 80, 86, 87, 94: photographer Lea Ingold; pls. 2, 4, 10–13, 15, 19, 20, 23, 26, 27, 34, 35, 37, 38, 41, 42, 45–47, 51, 52, 57, 59–63, 67–70, 72, 74, 75, 78, 81, 83, 84, 88, 92: photographer Ric Blanc; pls. 3, 14, 17, 25, 29, 32, 49, 56, 82: photographer Adam Davies; pls. 18, 24, 28, 31, 33, 43, 44, 53, 55, 58, 66, 71, 73, 85, 89, 90, 93, 95: photographer Lee Ewing; pl. 22: photographer Greg Davis; pl. 50: photographer Lorene Emerson

pls. 8, 9, 16, 36, 54, 64, 65, 77, 79, 91: © André Morin

pl. 39: Photo © Christie's Images / The Bridgeman Art Library

Comparative illustrations

PROLOGUE

figs. 1–5: Images courtesy of the Board of Trustees, National Gallery of Art, Washington; fig. 1: photographer Lee Ewing; figs. 2–5: photographer Adam Davies

THE ROMANTIC IMPULSE

fig. 1: Imaging Department © President and Fellows of Harvard College; fig. 2: © Trustees of the British Museum; figs. 3–5: Images courtesy of the Board of Trustees, National Gallery of Art, Washington; figs. 3, 5: photographer Adam Davies; fig. 4: photographer Ric Blanc; fig. 6: courtesy of Andrea Woodner, New York

RENDERING REALITY

figs. 1, 5: Images courtesy of the Board of Trustees, National Gallery of Art, Washington, photographer Adam Davies; fig. 2: Photograph © 2012 Museum of Fine Arts, Boston; fig. 3: courtesy of Andrea Woodner, New York; fig. 4: Photograph © The Walters Art Museum, Baltimore

IMPRESSIONIST DRAWINGS

fig. 1: Photography © The Art Institute of Chicago; figs. 2, 4, 6, 7: Images courtesy of the Board of Trustees, National Gallery of Art, Washington; figs. 2, 6: photographer Adam Davies; fig. 4: photographer Lea Ingold; fig. 3: Réunion des Musées Nationaux / Art Resource, NY; photographer Hervé Lewandowski

THE NABIS AND SYMBOLISTS

figs. 1, 4, 5:, Réunion des Musées Nationaux / Art Resource, NY; photographer Hervé Lewandowski; fig. 5: © 2012 Artists Rights Society (ARS), New York/ADAGP, Paris; figs. 2, 3, 6: Images courtesy of the Board of Trustees, National Gallery of Art, Washington; fig. 3: photographer Lea Ingold; fig. 6: photographer Adam Davies

NEO-IMPRESSIONIST DRAWINGS

fig. 1: Image copyright © The Metropolitan Museum of Art. Image source: Art Resource, NY; fig. 2, © All rights reserved, photographer: Patrice Schmidt; fig. 3, © All rights reserved, photographer: Jacques Faujour; © Paris, ADAGP, 2011

SECTION OPENINGS

pp. ii–iii: detail pl. 51
p. vi: detail pl. 50
p. viii: detail pl. 94
pp. xiv–1: detail pl. 84
p. 16: detail pl. 8
p. 46: detail pl. 27
p. 72: detail pl. 45
p. 94: detail pl. 69
p. 126: detail pl. 76
pp. 154–155: detail pl. 35